I Did My Damnedest

Chuck Custer on a Spokane Street, approximately 1938

Charles Joseph (Chuck) Custer

ISBN: 978-0-6151-6011-5
Charles Joseph Custer: August 21, 1911 – June 5, 2005

Front Cover Photo: Chuck Custer, Coeur d'Alene, Idaho, 1991
Back Cover Photo: Chuck and Agnes Custer, Coeur d'Alene, Idaho, 1991

Foreword

The following poem, written in honor of my Grandpa Custer's 80th birthday in 1991, captures my feelings for him and seems an appropriate introduction to a man I greatly admired and respected. It would probably surprise him to know that he had, and through this book and my many wonderful memories of him, continues to have, a profound influence on my life.

Grandpa
By Colleen Custer Neymeyer

There's a man that I know in Eastern Washington
I'll tell you about him and when I'm done
You'll agree with me that he is quite a guy,
So just continue reading and I'll tell you why.

We didn't get to meet until 1959
(I really don't remember the first several times)
Since then we've spent a lot of time together
Creating special memories that I will always treasure

He taught me how to jitterbug when I was just a toddler
He was Fred Astaire and I was Ginger Rogers!
On visits to his house, I liked to follow him around
I wanted to be just like him and become a rock hound.

A trip to his basement shop was the ultimate reward
We could stay down there for hours and I never would get bored.
During visits in the summer we'd spend evenings on the porch
Listening to his stories about Indians and such.

There were times when we went camping or out to the lake
Once we saw a tremendous storm – I thought that was really great.
We took boat rides and picked berries, were they huckle or blue?
I never can remember but I know he could tell you.

He's a mechanic, a blacksmith, a carpenter, a cobbler,
A woodsman, a fisherman, and also quite a hunter.
Electrician's work and plumbing, to him are nothing new
And if you need something invented, just give him a day or two!

He's lived his life in a way of which anyone would be proud
He has morals and standards with which more should be endowed
He's a man who's liked and respected everywhere he goes
Trusted and admired by everyone he knows.

By now, I think you've figured out
(And you will all agree no doubt)
That I think a lot of this man I've described
And I'm glad that he's been a part of my life.

I've learned so much from him that I can't remember all of it
But I think I'll do just fine in life if I can just retain a bit.
He's a man of so many talents that I cannot name them all
He's a man I'm lucky to have known, and proud to call Grandpa.

On May 29, 2005, during what was to be the last time I visited Grandpa in person, the subject of "The Book" came up. For years, most of the family had known that Grandpa was recording his life history and, from time to time, I had been allowed to read stories he had written as part of his effort.

Because of his unique experiences – the changes he'd lived through and the challenges he'd faced – Grandpa wanted to capture some of his personal history to share with his children, grandchildren and great-grandchildren. He'd been working on "The Book" for a number of years, but refused to allow anyone to read it until it was done, saying, "I don't want anyone to change one damn word." Having been enthralled with the tales he'd told of his life experiences over the years, I was eager for him to complete his work so we could continue to enjoy his stories, and I had often asked about his progress and encouraged him to keep writing.

During that final visit, Grandpa told me that he was tired and ready to die. He was concerned that he hadn't had a chance to finish the book, having lost enthusiasm for the project after Grandma's death seven years earlier. Grandpa then paid me the greatest compliment I've ever received from him, by asking me to take responsibility for getting the book finished. I humbly accepted this responsibility, knowing it was a great honor to be entrusted with such an important task. I know he considered this book one of his most valuable possessions and invested a huge amount of effort in writing it.

Here then, is the first (and probably the last) book I've ever edited and published. I've done my best to present Grandpa's work in a way that would make him proud – and I think I've accomplished that. To the extent possible, I've honored his request that nobody change "one damn word", making only the spelling and grammatical corrections necessary to ensure his message was clear.

Coming up with a fitting title for this book was one of my biggest dilemmas. That problem was finally solved when, during a recent conversation with my Uncle Jim Custer (Grandpa's youngest son), he mentioned a running joke Grandpa used to make about wanting his tombstone to read "I Did My Damnedest." Well, that may not have been appropriate for his tombstone, but it certainly captures Grandpa's personality and attitude better than anything else I've come up with, so thanks, Grandpa, for providing the title!

Although completing this project has required a considerable amount of effort, the personal reward I received was far greater. In reading and re-reading this book, I've come to know and love Grandpa on a completely different level. Not only has his book been educational, but he continues to inspire me to do my best, see obstacles as challenges to be overcome, and live my life with integrity. I know that I will enjoy reading Grandpa's memoirs over and over in the coming years, and I hope each of you will find that his message touches your heart in some way!

I want to thank my husband, Denny, for his constant support of my efforts on this book. Without complaint, he ran copies, helped scan documents and was always available when I needed a sounding board. Thanks also to my sister, Maureen Custer Benton and my cousin, Cheryl Custer Branz, both of whom shared their opinions and gave me valuable advice whenever I asked!

Special thanks to my dad, Chuck Custer, for sharing his journalistic expertise, providing ongoing encouragement and his continued confidence in my ability to get this done; Uncle Jack Custer for his written contributions and wonderful sense of humor, and Uncle Jim Custer for helping gather many of the facts, old photos and records that enhanced the final product. Most of all, I thank all three of you for sharing your treasured memories of Grandpa with all of us. He was proud of his boys and I know he'd be moved by your contributions.

The author and his editor in an early meeting

Colleen Custer Neymeyer
Granddaughter, Editor
April 2007

Dedicated to
Agnes, Charlie, Jack and Jim

Contents

List of Photographs

Chapter 1

This story actually begins before I was born; however, for reasons that will be obvious, I think the events I share with you here are some things that will be found to be interesting to the reader. They do have some historical value and also do have an impact on and are relevant to the story of the first eighty years of this one man's life in the world. I am going to recount them here, as best I can, after having done some research and from what I have been told or heard others tell about. The things set forth in this entire narrative are not deliberately exaggerated nor are they minimized. I think my memory is still quite good at this point in time and I have here recorded times, places, and events as accurately and as honestly as I remember and perceive them to be.

We don't know very much about my father's background but I gather his childhood was not an ideal situation as he left home at a very early age and he wasn't much to talk about his bringing up. He was born in the state of Maine in a village named Danforth, where his father – my grandfather – was a blacksmith. In those days (my dad was born June 13, 1871), a blacksmith was an important businessman in the community. Unfortunately, he died at an early age, the result, as I understood, of having been kicked in the side of his body by a horse that he was shoeing. This might have had some bearing on Dad leaving home so young, I really don't know.

About my grandmother on my dad's side, I know nothing. I heard my dad mention once that he had an older sister that had a bakery with a big brick oven. The kind they made a fire in and when they got the bricks hot enough to bake the bread, they pulled the fire out and swept the floor of the oven and then put the bread in and the hot bricks baked the bread. He also mentioned in connection with that, that he would go to the bakery on Sunday morning the first thing when he was little and get a pot of freshly baked beans for breakfast as this was tradition at the time. Beyond this, I don't know anything.

I will here relate a rather pitiful story that I heard him tell several times. It happened when he was young and after he had left home and was on his own. He was only twelve years old and was cooking in a small logging camp. There were not many men in the crew, about 6 or 8, I gathered. He was the cook and had no help. One day a boy about his age who lived on a homestead not too far away came over to visit him and they were both lonesome for company their own age. They got interested in visiting and playing in the rafters of the cook house and the first thing my poor father knew here came the crew in from the woods for their supper and he hadn't even started supper yet, he had lost all track of time, he had had such a good time. The poor boy really got chewed out for that one, he said. My dad only went through the third grade in school, but he could add a column of figures quicker than anyone I have ever seen and was extremely accurate. He was self-educated and was very well read; in fact, he read Shakespeare for entertainment and had a wonderful memory. He was often asked to recite poetry from memory at neighborhood parties when I was small.

My father worked his way across the United Stated doing various kinds of things from logging to working in coal mines, oil fields, cattle ranches and, at one time, was briefly a prison guard at the Oregon state prison at Salem, Oregon. He then worked in the woods in western Oregon and worked for the U. S. Forest Service there. He came to northern Idaho because that country was in a lumber boom at the time. Another attraction for northern Idaho was to be the opening of the northern part of the Coeur d'Alene Indian reservation for settlement, more of which I will get to a little later.

My mother was born in the state of Michigan in a village named Zilwaukee on the Saginaw Bay of Lake Michigan. She came from a family of thirteen children, being the tenth child born to the family, who were Irish immigrants. My grandfather's name was Joseph Maloney and my grandmother's name was Maria. They both came from Ireland, but at different times, and met in this country and were married here. My grandfather's name in Ireland was O'Maloney but he dropped the O' when he immigrated. He was a ditch digger and a grave digger by trade.

Both of them died in about 1883 in a flu epidemic. My mother and two younger sisters were young, as my mother was born June 11, 1876. They were taken by an older sister, an adult by the name of Maryann, and were raised by she and her husband whose name was Donald McCrimon, a full-blooded Scotsman. My mother was educated and graduated from college at Gailsburg, Illinois as valedictorian of her class.

She taught school in South Dakota and Michigan for several years and then moved to Washington, where she taught at the city of Davenport. Her teaching career covered a span of fifteen years all told. In about 1906, one of my mother's brothers who was in the clothing business in Spokane at the time and who, incidentally, was instrumental in getting her to move out west, built a hotel in Spokane. This was a residential hotel named the Justin, which was torn down at the time Interstate 90 was built through Spokane. At the time of building, it was on the edge of the main business district. When it was completed, he persuaded my mother to give up teaching to manage the new hotel for him. This she did and everything went fine for both of them for a couple of years — my mother making a success of the hotel business and with no thought of changing careers at this time.

Now my story changes dramatically, for the time being. I think the reader will find this bit of history interesting, especially since it has great bearing on the events to follow.

The Coeur d'Alene Indian reservation was established on November 8, 1873, by treaty. Before this time, the Coeur d'Alenes had claimed and defended some four million acres in western Montana, eastern Washington and northern Idaho. In subsequent agreements, the U.S. government and the Indians agreed to further reduce the size of the reservation by many thousands of acres. This was agreed to and ratified by numerous agreements made from March 26, 1887 to August 15, 1894. In this agreement the government allotted each and every Indian belonging to this tribe one hundred and sixty acres of tillable land and granted them some other concessions such as a flour mill and a blacksmith shop with trained men to operate each of them for a stipulated period of time.

There may have been more but if so, I am not aware of it. (This is comparatively recent history but I had a hard time digging it out probably because I don't know how very well.) It is important, I think, to point out that at this time, with only man and horsepower, that was quite a bit of land to take care of.

When this was done, it was found that there were many thousands of acres of land left over or, as it was called at the time, vacant land. The government chose or at least didn't do anything about it till June 21, 1906 when an Act of Congress was passed to open this vacant land to settlement.

On May 22, 1909, President Taft signed the proclamation opening to entry and settlement a million acres of farm and timber lands on the Coeur d'Alene Indian Reservation, located in Idaho; the Spokane Reservation in Washington; and the Flathead Reservation in Montana. In this proclamation, it was set forth that a lottery procedure would be used to determine settlement rights on the former Indian lands. Registration will take place at all three area places. The drawing for all those "lucky" winners of the three Reservations will take place in Coeur d'Alene on Monday, August 9, 1909 at 1:00 P. M.

The above notice then is as was officially published.

The opening of the Reservation lands created much excitement all over the United States. The railroads made more liberal rates available and gave stopover privileges, making it possible for more people to register and then visit other parts of the west, than ever before.

On the opening day of the registration, July 15, 1909, between 4,000 and 5,000 people registered with sixteen Notary offices, which were kept busy all day long. The electric trains from Spokane arriving in the city of Coeur d'Alene were loaded with prospective applicants. Trains ran from Spokane on an average of every twenty minutes during the height of the registration stampede. In two weeks time, 62,746 people had put in applications.

People were coming by way of Sandpoint and Rathdrum. They came in buggies, wagons, by stagecoach, (horse drawn) and on horseback. Many gold seekers dropped their tools and walked out of the mountains to register. Many came by boat on Coeur d'Alene Lake. Every profession or calling that could be imagined was represented. Schoolteachers, bankers, the rich and the poor, all were part of the excited throng. It was said that several people in the east sold their homes in hope of getting lucky and being able to settle in the west.

Two weeks after registration began 62,746 people had registered, and all told at the time of the drawing, there were 105,000 applicants. A side light I might mention at this time that I feel is worthy of note, is about the big train wreck. Many extra electric trains were running to Couer d'Alene and back and on Saturday July 31, 1909 there was a mix-up in train communication, resulting in a head on collision between two trains just outside Coeur d'Alene, killing 17 people and injuring somewhere between one and two hundred others.

The day of August 8, 1909 my mother went to my uncle's store to see him about something and, during their conversation, he asked if she was excited about the big land drawing the next day. Her reply was "No I am not a bit interested in it, when is it?" My uncle was furious and said, "You don't know? Have you registered?" My mother had to confess that she had not even bothered and didn't care anything about it. He said, "You must get on a train immediately and go to register – the drawing is tomorrow. Why, people are coming from all over the United States for this." My mother protested, raising the incident of the recent train wreck as an excuse; however my uncle would not hear of it and insisted she go straight from the store to the depot, get on a train to Coeur d'Alene and register, which she did – only because he was so insistent.

During the time of registration, a large platform was constructed on some vacant property near the land office for the purpose of holding the drawing. The applications had all been sealed in cast iron cans and the morning of the big event, the cans were brought out, opened and dumped on the platform floor. They were then stirred by two men with pitchforks and well mixed to everyone's satisfaction. The drawing was then started and was done by three little girls, promptly at 1:00 p.m.

There were four names drawn by men and then the first women's name was drawn. The name was Miss Ella T. Maloney of Spokane, Washington. The next day after registering my mother was walking down the street in Spokane and heard her name announced in a loud voice over a megaphone, "Ella T. Maloney." She saw a big crowd in front of one of the large department stores with a marquee out in front, on top of which had been installed a platform with a large blackboard on the front of the building right behind it. A man was up there with a megaphone announcing names as he wrote the names on the blackboard. (For those of you who don't know, a megaphone is a big horn, similar to a big funnel, which was held up to the mouth to amplify sound in those days. There were no electronic amplification devices then.)

She asked a man on the fringe of the crowd what was going on. He said, "They are just announcing the winners of the land drawings being held in Coeur d'Alene as they come over the wire." She got where she could see better and, lo and behold, there was her name just being written on the board as being the fifth name to be drawn and the first woman in the Coeur d'Alene land drawing.

My mother hurried over to the store and, rushing in, she yelled to everyone "I won! I won!" I don't think, by her accounts of it in later years, she was even sure what she had won, the fifth name to be drawn from 105,000, but she knew she had won a great prize, and indeed, she had: the right to the fifth choice of any one hundred and sixty acres of virgin timberland that was thrown open to settlement.

She had two brothers to advise her, as she had no idea what to do. I don't know the exact time sequence from here on, but I do know the story. Settlement could begin September 1, 1910, but first the choice of land had to be located and filed on.

My Uncle Tom Maloney, who was in hopes of getting a number but who didn't, took over for my mother as an adviser. The first thing to be done was to find a piece of land desirable to file on. This required the services of a locator, a person capable of going out in the field, locating desirable land, finding the section lines to establish the borders and then finding the land on a map. This was necessary because when filing on land a complete and detailed description had to be given, as to location by section line and parts of sections that were being filed on. My father, anticipating this land rush and having the required skills to be able to do this type of endeavor, went into a partnership with another man who possessed these skills by the name of Gus Wolk. They went onto the land to be opened up and ran preliminary lines for future use. They had cards printed and ran ads in the papers to let it be known that they were professional land locators.

My uncle contacted C. F. Custer of the firm Custer and Wolk Timber and Land Locators of Harrison, Idaho to locate four forty-acre plots, or one hundred and sixty acres of choice land for his sister.

This was done sometime after the drawing and before the settlement time – I have no way of knowing just when and I don't believe it is too important. There is no one alive that knows any more than I do about it as I am an old man at this writing and although there are older men than I am, none of them would be familiar with the details of this transaction.

When it was time to file on the land, it had to be done at the land office and my mother had to have the timber locator there to describe the land he had chosen for her.

The appointed day came for everyone to meet in Coeur d'Alene at the city dock. My Uncle Tom who had met one time with the locator, Mr. Custer, (who later turned out to be my dad) and my mother were there at the appointed time, but no locator showed up. There were many passenger and freight boats coming and going on the lake at that time and so if you missed one, another would come along sooner or later.

My dad was real busy locating would-be landowners at that time, as everyone had to have a locator and, too, the thing wasn't going to last long, it would soon be over; so he and his partner were going as hard as they could. My dad stayed in the woods till the last minute so as not to waste time in the land office and when he went to catch the boat it was just leaving the dock in Harrison. He ran for it, but they wouldn't put back in for him and he had to wait about an hour for another. The boat he did get on was supposed to make several stops on the way, so my dad tried to give the captain $ 20.00 to skip them, but the captain wouldn't do it even for this princely sum.

My mother and her brother waited at the dock and finally another boat came from up the lake and as it got near the dock, a man with corked boots and cut off pants and a days growth of whiskers and a lumber jack coat on jumped from the boat to the dock not waiting for the gang plank and explained that he had just missed the boat and the so and so captain wouldn't pull back so he could jump on, therefore he was late.

He also was not in a good humor and my mother said afterward that she took an immediate dislike to this rough looking character. They went to the land office and filed on the land that my dad had picked out, except one forty-acre piece had to be substituted for another because someone had squatter's rights on the first choice.

The land was chosen with several things in mind. First, there was a good stand of virgin timber on it. It was close to the wagon road, as the existing road ran right through it. It was nice land with no rocks and it was nearly flat and would make good farm land when cleared of trees and brush. It was close to town as it was only three miles by wagon road. These things were all considered in the choice.

This land was granted by the U.S. Government under the Homestead Act of 1862, which was amended from that time on as to requirements and restrictions. At the time my mother filed, I think the person had to live on the land for fourteen consecutive months and had to clear one acre to prove up, (a term used for meeting all the qualifications that were required by the government) and by a small payment of money, then they were issued a patent on the land. (A patent is similar to a deed but was used in those days.)

4—1023-R.

The United States of America,

To all to whom these presents shall come, Greeting:

WHEREAS, a Certificate of the Register of the Land Office at COEUR D'ALENE, IDAHO, has been deposited in the General Land Office, whereby it appears that full payment has been made by the claimant ELLA T. CUSTER, FORMERLY ELLA T. MALONEY, according to the provisions of the Act of Congress of April 24, 1820, entitled "An Act making further provision for the sale of the Public Lands" and the acts supplemental thereto, for the WEST HALF OF THE NORTHEAST QUAR-TER AND THE NORTHEAST QUARTER OF THE NORTHEAST QUARTER OF SECTION EIGHT AND THE LOT FOURTEEN OF SECTION FIVE IN TOWNSHIP FORTY-SEVEN NORTH OF RANGE THREE WEST OF THE BOISE MERIDIAN, IDAHO, CONTAINING ONE HUNDRED FIFTY-TWO AND EIGHTY-EIGHT-HUNDREDTHS ACRES,

according to the Official Plat of the Survey of the said Land, returned to the GENERAL LAND OFFICE by the Surveyor-General:

NOW KNOW YE, That the UNITED STATES OF AMERICA, in consideration of the premises, and in conformity with the several Acts of Congress in such case made and provided, HAS GIVEN AND GRANTED, and by these presents DOES GIVE AND GRANT, unto the said claimant and to the heirs of the said claimant the Tract above described; TO HAVE AND TO HOLD the same, together with all the rights, privileges, immunities, and appurtenances, of whatsoever nature, thereunto belonging, unto the said claimant and to the heirs and assigns of the said claimant forever; subject to any vested and accrued water rights for mining, agricultural, manufacturing, or other purposes, and rights to ditches and reservoirs used in connection with such water rights, as may be recognized and acknowledged by the local customs, laws, and decisions of courts; and there is reserved from the lands hereby granted, a right of way thereon for ditches or canals constructed by the authority of the United States. AND ALL THE COAL OR OIL DEPOSITS THEREIN OR THEREUNDER.

IN TESTIMONY WHEREOF, I, WILLIAM H. TAFT President of the United States of America, have caused these letters to be made Patent, and the Seal of the General Land Office to be hereunto affixed.

GIVEN under my hand, at the City of Washington, the THIRTIETH day of OCTOBER in the year of our Lord one thousand nine hundred and TWELVE and of the Independence of the United States the one hundred and THIRTY-SEVENTH.

By the President: Wm. H. Taft

by M. P. LeRoy Secretary,

John O'Connell Acting Recorder of the General Land Office.

(SEAL)

RECORD OF PATENTS: Patent Number 298426

Land Grant signed by President William H. Taft
October 30, 1912 after my mother, Ella Maloney Custer, met "proving up" requirements

Again, I am not sure of exact dates. My mother and two of her sisters were used to camping out for the summer vacation when they were teaching. They had a tent and the necessary equipment for camping and my mother thought it would be a lark to camp on her land. I don't know what she figured on doing when it got cold, but she would have done something I am confident, as she was a resourceful type of person. She got her younger sister, whose name was Agnes, to come with her.

She hired the locator to help them get set up, as she knew no one in Harrison to go to. He, in turn, hired a man with a team and wagon to haul their goods out to the land and they chose a nice, level place near the road and not far from an existing well on the property in among some big trees and set up camp.

The well had been dug by some old homesteaders by the name of McKinneys who lived just on the other side of the boundary line and on settling on their land some years before found they had a somewhat unreliable supply of water. They had gone down on the reservation land and dug a well for their own use. It turned out to be an asset for my mother as she had water on the place. The people were quite concerned when they found that my mother was settling there because of the water situation but Mother assured them they could always have water from her well. Now people think nothing about water and take it for granted, but it has not always been so – at that time or in my time.

Chapter 2

Well, Mr. Custer shortly overcame his first bad impression, and soon established himself as a gentleman and a man of many talents. He seemed to be knowledgeable about everything and was extremely capable. He knew how to do everything and was willing to do anything for the young ladies and, too, he seemed to be much more affable when he hadn't just missed the boat.

My father had been married when he first came to Harrison and had moved there with his wife, Ida. They had been married for several years but had never had any children. Ida finally became pregnant and they were looking forward to the birth of a child but, unfortunately, she and the baby both died at the time of childbirth. This had happened a couple of years before the land settlement business took place.

As mentioned before, the times of some of these events are not perfectly clear to me and therefore are not set forth here as firm, only in generality; nevertheless, they are of some importance and are relevant.

Before long, my dad was making frequent trips to the girl homesteaders' place of abode, to check on things, to see if every thing was all right, wood, food, water, and so forth. They were out in the wilderness and were completely surrounded by timber and strictly on their own, except for the McKinneys, whose place was about two hundred yards away through heavy timber. Dad would come on weekends, or as time permitted, as he still made Harrison his headquarters.

After his wife had died, he was very lonesome and soon sold his house and got a room in a rooming house as he was out of town on different jobs a good deal of the time. It was less trouble than looking after a house. It soon developed that the girls were as glad to see him as he was to see them, especially the one who had won the land, later to be my mother.

Well every thing went along fine, the girls living in the tent, the summer wore on and the trips out to the homestead became more frequent. My dad proposed to my mother sometime that summer, telling her she needed a husband as well as a full time man on her homestead, and she thought this a good idea so they became engaged.

Miss Ella T. Maloney.

My mother's marriage announcement made the news!

My parents were married in the old St. Aloysius Church (long since torn down), in Spokane, in September of 1910. Sadly, I have none of the family records, as they were all lost when our home came apart later on.

Winter was coming on and they needed something more substantial to live in than a tent. They had a good building site and my dad, being a woodsman and being surrounded by trees, it was a natural to build a home out of logs if one knew how.

Well my dad knew how all right and got started right away. He cut and peeled the logs and notched them where they fell and then hired a man with a team of horses to drag them in and help place them to build the walls. It was said by my mother he built the house in twenty-one days. It consisted of four rooms and a large pantry and clothes closet combined, with a full-length front porch, and a small back porch.

The inside was boarded up and then covered with cloth sheeting, then wallpapered over this, resulting in a very comfortable house – warm in winter and cool in summer. The outside of course was logs that had been peeled and were smooth and painted red. The chinks in between the logs were filled with mortar, which was painted white. The gable ends were lumber and were a dark green and there was a red brick chimney coming out of a shingled roof.

My family and some friends at our Harrison, Idaho home.
Pictured, from left: Mrs. Iverson, my mother Ella Custer, Ramona Iverson, me, and my dad Charles F. Custer – appx. 1914.

I never thought of it as anything but a house, but some who have seen pictures of it have called it a cabin. Whatever it was, it was home to us, and very comfortable. There were trees all around when he built it, as it was built right in the virgin forest. When the house was completed, he cleared off some more trees and brush to make room for more buildings. He then bought a team of horses and a wagon and hauled the logs that had been cut from the clearing venture to a sawmill about two miles away where they were cut into lumber which he hauled home and used to build a small barn and a chicken house and the homestead became a small farm. When he wasn't doing this, he was busy cutting the smaller trees into firewood and cutting the brush and piling it to be burned the next year when it got dry enough. Then there were the stumps to be removed, small ones could be pulled with the horses but the big ones had to be dug around by hand and the roots cut below the plow line with an ax or a mattock and then pulled with the horses if they could.

Work, work, work, not enough hours in the day, every thing had to be done by hand except what could be done with the team. The big stumps had to be blasted with dynamite and the roots pulled with the horses.

Sometime during that first year, my mother became pregnant and the next August 21, 1911 I was born. They have said that when my mother told my dad she thought it was time for the baby – it was about ten o'clock at night, and they were in bed – my dad jumped up, dressed and ran all the way to Harrison to get the doctor. This was three miles, but I guess he ran all the way, because after having lost his first wife, he was terrified that it might happen again.

Fortunately, the doctor was in and had a horse and buggy so poor Dad didn't have to run home. Every thing went smoothly and I arrived on the scene, being given the name of Charles after my dad and my Grandfather. I don't remember anything about it.

Some of my earliest recollections are of the trees being around the house and isolated bits that are not connected. I can remember some rather dimly. One of which I will relate here. That is of being very young and it was wintertime and we could not see out the front room window because of the snow being so deep. Dad went out and dug a big ditch through the drift so we could get light in the house. This I remember very clearly. I think that was the winter that the roads were snowed in so deep. In those days there were no snowplows, people just tramped it down or wallowed through it the best they could.

I am sure that was the winter that my dad and a neighbor, Clem McKinney, got together after no one had been to town even to get the mail for a couple of weeks because the roads were impassable; so full of snow. They took the front part of a horse drawn sleigh called the front bob, took the door off of the blacksmith shop for a platform to ride on, fastened it to the sleigh which now consisted of only two runners and a platform with a tongue, and hooked four horses to their contraption. The snow was so deep it took them all day long to go the three miles to town and back.

When the snow gets so deep, a horse just lunges ahead and kind of flounders through if they can. The men had to change the horses around and put the rear ones in the lead after while because the leaders got so tired breaking the way. This episode I can recall clearly, and is one of my early memories.

Another is that I can recall having a red knitted suit, pants, coat and cap and being outside with nice big trees and little trees and bushes, fascinating landscape all around, which I enjoyed very much, but being tied to a tree with a long piece of small rope, which I didn't enjoy a darn bit and protested vigorously at the top of my voice, all to no avail, every time I was subjected to this grave indignity.

I recall it was a very frustrating experience because I didn't know how to untie a knot, and I couldn't go where I wanted to. It seems that the reason for this cruel injustice being inflicted on me was that I was an adventurer and an explorer and I had taken off a couple of times and didn't bother to notify anyone that I was going to do a little exploring on my own, where I didn't know one direction from another. After having made several of these excursions, and some people like my mother getting very excited and upset when they couldn't find me right away thinking I might be lost or had been eaten by a coyote and having gotten unduly concerned, at least in my estimation, my mother had outfitted me in the red outfit so I could be spotted in the brush and timber but as that didn't work she resorted to the rope trick.

That worked for her but it didn't work very well for me, as it seems I wanted to range farther afield than just around the house as she had in mind. There were one hundred sixty acres of timber to be harvested and the logs sold to get money to clear the land to make a farm. Unfortunately, little did they know how little profit there would be in this venture. As it turned out those who got land in the drawing and proved up on it, then sold the timber and went on to other things were way ahead in the long term. Some stayed, some moved on.

Those who stayed had a life of hard work and many eventually went broke or just gave up and moved away. Sometimes it was heart breaking – so much put in and so little came out.

I know it was my mother's wish to have proved up, sold the timber, then sold the logged off land and with the money, gone into something else. This was not her kind of life. She had a good education, and had good business sense.

On the other hand my dad with his background, thought he could make a living farming, which he knew nothing about, and little realized what lay ahead, between a timber claim and a farm. He wasn't cut out to be a farmer; he needed more action and more of a challenge than a day-to-day routine type of life.

There was a vast amount of timber to be cut on the Harrison Flats as the area where my folks settled was to be called. The most expedient way to get the logs to the lake was to build a timber chute from the breaks of the flats to the lake. At that time all logs were taken to the water and then to the mills. The flats were high above the lake level, several hundred feet at least in elevation with a very steep mountainside to the lake, with only the railroad tracks near the lakeshore in between.

I don't know how permission was obtained or by whom for the chute to go under the tracks but it was constructed that way. There was a proviso in the agreement with the railroad that there would be no logs in the chute when trains were near. It was built from the top of the hill down under the railroad track into the water. (My dad undoubtedly had a part in it.)

A log chute is made from two logs laid side by side and end to end, the joints being made on a short length of log laid cross ways nearly buried in the ground like a railroad tie to hold every thing in place. The main logs are then spiked to these short cross logs with long square spikes we used to call drift bolts, which you drive with a maul. The long logs or main logs then are hewed with broad axes. (A broad ax is a unique tool that can be either a right hand or a left hand ax. It has a broad head and a flat surface on one side so it can be swung parallel to the surface of the wood being hewed. This then will leave a flat surface).

Chute logs are hewed flat on an angle of about 45 degrees sloping toward the center between the two main logs with the center between the logs being lower than the outside, this then forms kind of a trough for the logs to lay in when they are being slid along either by gravity or being pulled with horses. This was an economical way to transport logs if the conditions were right, in other words if it was a chute chance. (The term chance meant that it was a suitable method of operation for the prevailing conditions.) This chute was quite famous as there were many millions of board feet of logs sent down it over the period of its existence, which was several years. It was quite a spectacular sight to see the logs go down as it was steep and once the logs were started, they needed no encouragement to go. When they went under the railroad track, they hit the water with tremendous speed making a big splash and shooting spray high in the air.

My dad cut and skidded logs all summer and fall, decking them along the road to the chute. (Decking is stacking them in a neat pile so that they will be handy at a later date to load for hauling.)

He had a sleigh haul chance in mind. (A sleigh haul chance means that sleighs will be used to transport the logs.) The main advantage of this was that with a good sleigh haul chance, logging could be done much more economically as the teams could haul many more logs on a sleigh than they could on a wagon. He had a camp and a crew of men working, cutting and skidding and decking, and waiting for snow. No snow came that winter all through December and January and he faced severe financial losses if he had to wait till the next summer, till the road dried out enough to use wagons for the haul to the top of the chute.

Well about the first of February it started to snow and it snowed and they had plenty of snow. My dad went to the banker in our town and borrowed several thousand dollars, which was a lot of money in those times.

He hired all the men and logging sleighs and horses he could get hold of and hauled logs day and night. It must be remembered that there were no electric lights then, not even flashlights, only kerosene lanterns and the light reflecting from the snow, or when lucky, moonlight. I can remember my mother getting me up in the middle of the night when I was real small and taking me out into the front room of our house and there were men eating, of course by lamp light, which I thought was different. I didn't know till I got bigger and then realized it was when dad was logging nights.

The snow lasted into early March and he got all his logs in the lake. It was quite a feat and was talked about for several years afterward. The time Charlie Custer hauled logs on sleighs at night.

I can remember another incident of that time when my mother took me to the logging camp. We walked down there and the cook, whose name for some reason I still remember was Mr. Gates, gave me some jellyroll and I thought it the best thing I ever tasted.

My folks spent all the money they made on the sale of the timber clearing the land. The trees and brush had to be cut and burned and then the stumps had to be blown out of the ground with dynamite, which was expensive. Then the land had to be leveled and there were roots to contend with for several years afterward, there were no bulldozers then. It was a hard go, then if you managed to raise something it was so expensive to get it to market that it would not be competitive or profitable.

My dad tried raising horses one time, hogs another, cattle, another and hay. I think the hay was most profitable of all, probably. We always had horses, cows, chickens and sometimes hogs and sometimes some beef cattle and calves.

Chapter 3

After our place was logged off, the land had to be cleared as previously mentioned. This took a lot of work and considerable expense. My dad, of course, always had a job when he wanted to work out which was necessary to get money to put into the ranch trying to get the land ready to raise crops. There was, too, the problem of putting food on the table. After the timber had been sold, there was no income from the place.

My dad was gone a lot of the time running logging camps or scaling logs or cruising timber. (Editor's note: "Scaling logs" meant measuring them to determine the total number of 1" boards they would produce. "Cruising" was surveying forest land to locate timber and estimate its quantity by species.) And at one time in the early twenty's he had a job as timber superintendent for a large lumber company in Coeur d'Alene, which required him to be gone all the time. As a result of this, we (my mother, my brother Don and I) were alone on the ranch a good deal of the time.

An incident I remember happened when I was small and we were alone. I think Don was just a baby then, I don't distinctly recall that part, but I wasn't old enough to go to school yet anyway, and my mother told me about it the next morning after it took place. She woke up in the night sometime and someone was walking on the front porch, which was the full length of the house. It of course was made of lumber, and anyone walking on it could readily be heard in the house. We were all alone and there was no knocking, just this pacing back and forth.

She got up and didn't light a lamp but took a peek out the window and in the dark, she could see a strange man going back and forth. She called the McKinneys on the phone (we had a phone then) and asked if Mr. McKinney could come down to our place and do something. Mrs. McKinney said they didn't have a gun so there was nothing they could do for her.

Well my poor Mother pulled all the window blinds as tight as she could, lit a lamp (kerosene), armed herself with a claw hammer and a long butcher knife, and sat up the rest of the night. She thought these two items the best weapons she could find to defend herself with if he made any attempt to enter, which he didn't. He kept this walking up all night long but about daylight, she saw him disappear in the direction of a logging camp. That very next day, whoever was in charge at the camp where he went after having left our place called the authorities in Coeur d' Alene and a deputy sheriff came and got the man as he was insane.

Boy when Mother told me about that the next morning it was an attention getter, believe me. She was a brave and determined woman and was not easily deterred; once her mind was made up she would see something through. This she demonstrated on many occasions.

I mentioned the telephone; it was a party line and I think it had twelve parties on it. It must be remembered there was nothing, so if the people wanted it they mostly had to do for themselves. The people got together, elected a board of directors of which my dad was one, purchased their supplies such as phones, insulators, wire and etc. It was built by the people on the line. They all got together, cut and erected the poles, strung the wire and installed their own phones. They paid a nominal monthly fee to be connected to the switchboard in Harrison, which would then upon request connect the caller to another party line, or long distance or whatever was desired. (Each party had their own call rings, ours was two, either long or short but of the same length.) Some were of different combinations such as two long and one short, two short and one long.

The phone was a wooden box affair that hung on the wall with a small cup like arrangement sticking out from the front of the box on a metal arm that the caller directed their voice toward when speaking.

For listening there was an elongated tube-like device with a wire coming out of one end which was connected to the box and on the other end a ring with an indentation for putting to your ear for listening, called the receiver. The receiver hung on a hook sticking out the left hand side of the box and this also acted as a switch and shut the phone off when the receiver was hung on it.

When the phone was used to make a call on the local line, you took hold of a small crank sticking out from the right hand side of the box and gave it a twist for a short ring or two twists for a long ring. This little crank was hooked to a magneto and when turned rather briskly it generated enough current to ring the bells on the calling phone and all the other phones on the line. When the phone rang, you listened intently to see if it was your ring. If so, you answered; if not, you ignored it, or were supposed to anyway.

Eavesdropping was a great pastime for a lot of people in those days, and if too many people were listening, sometimes the principals couldn't hear each other and the hangers on would have to be told to get off the line. (When this happened you would hear a lot of clicking as people hung up.)

If you wanted to call someone other than on your line, you would ring one long ring and take up the receiver and wait for the operator (called central) to answer. When she did, you gave her the name of the party you were calling and she would connect you with them and ring them for you.

In case of an emergency, central could be called and she would try to help if she could. In those times, there were no emergency services out in the country, no ambulance, fire or police of any kind. If, as sometimes happened, the doctor was needed for an emergency, she usually knew where he was and she would try to get hold of him for the caller. In those days, doctors made house calls.

Another thing that may be of interest about the phone was the lightning arrestor. This was a device that opened the line so when there was a lightning storm, which we had many of, the lightning current that came in on the line would go to the ground rather than into the home. When there was a severe storm, it was advisable to pull the lightning arrestor and to stay away from the phone, as it was very dangerous.

Many times, I have seen lightning bolts jump from the phone to the kitchen stove, which was across the room, and it would scare the hell out of you, believe me. We tried to not go between the two if we could help it till things would cool off a little.

We seemed to have more thunderstorms then than we do now, and I don't think it is imagination. I recall one time I went with my dad over to see a neighbor about something after supper one summer evening and while we were there, a severe thunderstorm came up. We were just about to leave to go home and this man had borrowed my dad's rifle for some reason or other, probably to shoot a coyote as sometimes they would get brave and come up to the places that were close to the woods and steal chickens. In those times, people just let the chickens run where they wanted to go and they picked up most of their living in the barnyard or the nearby fields.

Well anyway, as we were leaving, the man, Mr. Farmer by name, got the gun for Dad to take home with us and we were standing on his front porch with Mrs. Farmer watching it rain. It had started to pour so as we expected it to let up in a short time, we just stayed there where it was dry and were enjoying the downpour.

My dad had the gun in his right hand and it was pointing toward the ground. I was standing next to him on the right-hand side and Mrs. Farmer was on the right of me. A bolt of lightening came from above and hit the gun Dad was holding which was actually between us because of the way we were standing and jumped off the end of the gun and went into the ground. At the same time, there was a terrific clap of thunder, a real roof raiser. Well I was scared enough as it was but Mrs. Farmer let out a bloodcurdling shriek and turning to me, dug her fingers into my little old arm above the elbow. (She was a little old lady and skinny and she had hands more like talons on an eagle than hands.) Anyway, afterward when I could stop shaking I stole a glance at them to see how any one could hurt so bad by just taking hold of you. She dug her fingernails into me to the bone, which wasn't far of course as I was probably nine or ten at the time. Well that was one to remember.

Chapter 4

I can't remember when my brother Donald was born which was just a little short of being three years after I came on the scene. I can remember my dad having a hired man by the name of Lew Sholts and him bringing the cow in toward evening to milk her and I would get excited when I saw him coming down the lane and being teased because I couldn't say the word cow and I would exclaim "Here comes Lew and the gow."

I can recall the men going to World War One and our neighbor had to go. My mother taught me how to make little things out of paper, like flags and so on, to send to him because she said he was lonesome. I don't think she ever sent them but she made me feel good because I was helping with the war effort.

I think it was about this time that I got afraid of the dark, maybe after the episode of the man walking back and forth on the porch all night. Well anyway, we didn't pull the window blinds at night and that didn't appeal to me. My mother got some new quite sheer panel window curtains and got them all installed and was very proud of them.

I had seen her sew buttons on things and make buttonholes so when she was preoccupied with something I got her button box and found a big old button that had been redeemed from an old coat or something. It was the biggest one I could find and I sewed it on one of the panels. I then cut a nice big buttonhole in the panel opposite the button and pulled them together and buttoned them.

It worked fine and I figured that would keep out some of the dark. After I had finished my handy work, I got my mother to show her what a nice invention I had created. I vividly recall she burst out in tears when she saw what I had done, exactly the opposite reaction I had expected. I was dumbfounded and had no idea what was wrong. I sure felt bad, I had made my mother cry and I didn't even know why. She didn't get after me; she realized my intentions were strictly honorable.

One time I got to go with my dad to town for something he had to get; we had a team of horses and the wagon. While we were there (it was before the fire that will be mentioned later) my dad took me into a funny kind of store and it was quite dark and sort of cool. There were no shelves and the men all stood up along a high counter that I couldn't see over to see what was going on. They were all talking and having a good time and seemed to be drinking something but didn't offer me any, which was unusual. I wasn't in on it and felt left out so I got my dad's attention and asked if I could have some of what he was having. He had a little glass like I had never seen before with some liquid in it and he held it to my lips and cautioned very strongly to take only a very small sip, just stick my tongue in it. I tried it and it was the hottest and worst tasting stuff I had ever encountered. Boy, it was awful. Years later, I figured out that that was a saloon, it was before prohibition, and what I had tasted was whiskey.

It might have been on this same trip, because I didn't get to go to town very often, that we went into the hardware store for something and when Dad got through with his business he turned to me and said. "Is there anything you need?" Well there sure was. I had had my eye on some little red wheelbarrows hanging on some hooks high up on the wall near the ceiling. I think my dad was surprised, but I said, "Yes there is, I need one of those wheelbarrows up there." Well much to my surprise and needless to say, delight, good old Dad said to the hardware man, "Get one of those for the boy." I sure got a lot of pleasure from it and had it for a long time.

Well things went along and I got big enough to do chores like keeping the wood box filled and the kindling box filled. The kindling was wood that was split real small and used to start fires, and was in our case usually pitchy and was helpful for quick action to get a fire going.

Perhaps I should explain. The stoves both burned wood. In those days, cooking was done on wood burning cook stoves. The wood for the cook stove was split small, about three or four inches at the most on a side and all wood was standard length sixteen inches long. The wood for the heating stove was the same length but wasn't split as small so it wouldn't burn as rapidly and would hold fire longer, sometimes nearly all night when it got real cold. The big pieces of wood for the heater I didn't carry into the house till I got bigger. I might add that every home had a woodshed in those days for storing the wood to keep it dry and my dad always had a good supply of wood ahead, all split and piled up neatly for carrying to the house.

I guess it was along about this time that I got into trouble for the nail driving episode. There were so many fascinating activities to engage a small boy it seemed.

My dad had bought several pounds of shingle nails. They were in the blacksmith shop and I was looking for some interesting project to engage in when I discovered the bag with the new nails. I got a claw hammer and looked for a good place to drive some. After hunting for a suitable place, I settled for the chopping block in the woodshed. The nails drove fine in the end grain of the block and in fact, they drove so good that I drove the whole bagful.

It took quite a while but I stayed with it diligently with a feeling of accomplishment that I indeed was a pretty good carpenter till I had every last one driven. The top of the splitting block was blue with small round nail heads and it was a big block, now covered from one edge to the other with nails.

When I stepped back to look at my handiwork I remember suddenly feeling that my dad wasn't going to like this very much. Well that was a very valid feeling, believe me. He was not only mad about the loss of the nails but he had to get the crosscut saw and cut a slice off the end of the chopping block before he could use it.

Another job I got when I was pretty young was churning butter. We had cows and we never had a cream separator. I guess they had been invented by then but we didn't have one.

The milk was strained through a clean cloth when it came from the barn to take out any foreign material and then poured into shallow pans to cool and for the cream to rise to the top. After about 24 to 36 hours, the cream was skimmed off the top with a special sort of shallow ladle with little holes in it that the milk would go through but the cream wouldn't and it was put into something to keep till time to make butter.

The butter making was a slow and tedious process. The cream was put into a stoneware jar called a churn, about twenty-four inches tall and about fourteen inches in diameter with a little taper toward the top, and then a little flair out with a ledge just below the top for a lid to rest on. The lid had a small hole in the center of it about the size of a broomstick. A wooden cross made from two boards about ten inches long and three inches wide and fastened to one end of a piece of broomstick about three feet long to go through the hole in the lid completed the churn.

The cream, sweet or sour, was put in the churn filling it about two thirds full if you had that much, and the plunger, if you will, was put into the cream. The lid was put over the top of the jar with the plunger handle sticking through the hole in the lid and small boys were attached to the broom handle and this evil device was pumped up and down forever, or till the small boy grew old or his arms fell off from sheer over-use or something else catastrophic overcame him. I knew it would happen sometime and I would tell my mother it was going to happen to me any minute, but she never seemed to get concerned. Sometimes she didn't appreciate the seriousness of the situation, or it appeared that way to me at least.

After about an hour of this irksome procedure, if you were lucky and your arms didn't fall off, the butter came – and freedom, freedom at last. There were always more important things for a boy to do such as throw sticks for the dog to chase or climb trees that were not supposed to be climbed except when the mother was going to be tied up for awhile and wouldn't see one. When I had to churn butter or pull weeds, I could think of a dozen fun things I hadn't had time to do for a long time, like since yesterday.

Mother took over the butter making process then and poured the whole thing through a fine wire sieve to strain the little chunks of butter out of the buttermilk and then put it, or part of it, in a large wooden bowl and with a wooden paddle and some clean water in the bowl, worked it back and forth across the bowl, kind of mashing it against the sides.

This went on for a long time, back and forth till the butter got all the milk out of it and the fresh water stayed clear. Then she added salt to it and put it into whatever she was going to do with it. If she was going to sell it she had a square wooden mold that would, when filled and packed in tight, hold just exactly a pound, then she had butter wrappers made of parchment paper with her name printed on them.

The butter then was taken from the mold and put in the wrappers and the ends folded and when this was finished, they looked very professional. If it was to be for our own use and to be kept for awhile, it went into a crock or stoneware jar that would hold about a gallon. This then was covered with a damp cloth placed right on the butter and packed down and then the cloth was covered with salt. Then a stoneware lid was put on top and the crock was put in some cool place. It could be kept in this manner for a very long time. This process must have been very boring too, but after all that was what mothers were supposed to do. It wasn't a thing for a busy boy to waste his time on.

When I was pretty small I was given the job of cleaning the lamp chimneys and the lantern chimneys. I was good at it because my hands were small and I could get my hands in them easily. This was done with old dry newspaper crumpled up and wiped around and around till you had all the soot off and they were bright. Sometimes if the lamp wick wasn't trimmed properly, the lamp would smoke and if it was real dirty, they had to be washed in warm soapy water, usually by the mother.

The lamp wicks had to be trimmed every so often as they would burn off unevenly and then the lamp or lantern would smoke and get the chimney sooty and then light wouldn't come out from that side of the lamp or lantern.

After I got a little older, I got the job too, of filling everything with kerosene when it was necessary. Hooray! I had more responsibility and I felt like I was getting to be a man. I liked the words and the praise, but other aspects of becoming a man soon lost some of the appeal and seemed like work and in fact it was work and it slowly dawned on me that there was no end to it and it appeared to me that it was going to go on for a long time and sure enough it did, in fact till I got to be an old man.

I don't know if it was then or not, but at an early age and about this time, I came to the conclusion that work had to be done and I might as well get with the program. I made myself work when I didn't feel like it and I soon didn't mind it and have never shirked work to this day. I don't know if this had anything to do with not being lazy or not, but I have always been grateful for the fact that I am not or never have been. I have seen people in my time that would go to great lengths to get out of work, thus in the end doing more to avoid it than doing it in the first place.

In the winter of 1916 and 1917, my dad was sick in a hospital in Spokane for quite some time. At that time, we had quite a few cattle on the ranch. Dad had hired a man to feed the cattle and take care of the horses and do whatever else had to be done while he was to be gone. I can't remember a lot about it because I wasn't very old at the time. Well I guess I was only five and that was a long time ago.

Dad was going to be in the hospital at Christmas time so my mother had the hired man take us to Harrison, where we took the steamboat across and down the lake a ways to a place called Amwaco where the boat had a landing and a dock.

A train met the boat there and all the passengers and freight transferred to the train to continue the trip to Spokane. The only thing I can remember about the trip to Spokane was that when a passenger boat left the dock, just after they pulled out they blew a steam whistle, which was on the roof of the upper deck, which was where the passengers rode. This is where they rode unless they had on corked shoes. This was very common in those times. The steamboats were the only means of transportation around the lake communities and towns at the time. A good many men would be going from one job to another and so forth, and all men who worked in the woods and those who worked on the water on the logs wore caulked boots. That is what they are called now, but to the lumberjacks and those who wore them they were corked boots. They were very standard equipment and very practical and necessary too, as nearly all work was done by hand or with a team of horses and many times it required being on the logs and because logs are round by nature and when moved or when floating they invariably rolled. Without the corks, it would have been virtually impossible to stay on top, which was rather important if you were to survive. (Editor's note: The corks were short steel spikes protruding from the sole of the boot, much like the spikes that protrude from studded winter tires today.)

Now back to the upper deck. The stairway to the upper deck had a big sign – no corked shoes on the upper deck – this was because the corks would tear up the wood and the upper decks or deck were finished floors and were nice.

Well back to the trip. As I said, when they pulled out from the dock with the steamboat they always blew the steam whistle and it was on the roof of the passenger deck. If you have never been close to a big steam whistle when they cut loose, you haven't heard anything yet. I always knew this was coming and would stand around with my fingers in my ears till that whistle blowing business was over with, then I could sit down next to my mother and enjoy the trip till we got almost to the dock of our destination and then they did it again. It used to scare me so bad that I would almost wet my pants.

We stayed at the Sillman hotel in Spokane where my Aunt Gee lived as she was teaching in Spokane at the time. I can remember some more things about that trip. I guess I wasn't very brave about then because I was terrified by the nuns at the Sacred Heart Hospital in the long black robes. I thought they were witches, at least they looked like it to me, and they always insisted in talking to me, and I wished they wouldn't. I was so scared that I could hardly talk, and they were pesky too. They always wanted to know how I was and other things that were none of their business. Some of the other things I can recall are that I sure was glad to see my dad but he looked mighty good to me even if they had him in a bed and he didn't look like he felt very good.

Another thing I can remember very vividly was one day we came back to the hotel from the hospital and the owner of the hotel, Mr. Sillman, came out of the office and said that Santa Claus had been there while we were gone and had left something for us. He had a horn for me and a drum for my brother, my poor mother hadn't had time to plan for Christmas, along with all her other troubles.

The other thing I can recall very clearly is that when we went home we took the train to Amwaco and when we got off the train it was dark and cold, probably about six in the evening. It was cold after getting out of the nice warm train, the snow was deep, and we had to stand around in the snow quite awhile waiting for the boat to get close enough to the dock so the men could get a gangplank over to the dock for unloading and loading passengers and freight.

The reason for the delay was that the ice was so thick and it was so cold that the channel they had open would freeze up between runs and they would have to break ice with the steamboat as they got close to shore. There was plenty of power but the boat was a big stern wheel paddle wheel job named the Steamer Harrison. If they gave it too much power it would turn the paddles too fast and they would break paddles in all the broken ice in the channel. The only way to break the ice was to back up slowly and then come forward slowly and keep doing this back and forth till they got up to the dock. The thing that stands out in my memory most was, I guess, the big headlight on the boat. We, of course, were standing in the glare of it and it seemed to me that it was as big as a washtub. Not being used to bright lights like that it was so bright I thought it should be warm like the sun but as I remember it, it was awfully cold. They finally got up close enough and they got a plank over and everyone got in where it was warm and then all I had to worry about was that whistle blowing business again.

This is all I can remember of this particular time in my life. My dad got well after awhile and came home but we had the hired man for quite a while as my dad couldn't do hard work, and for some reason the hired man's name still comes to me, it was Henry Breaman. I can also recall that he wasn't in too good a shape as he was recuperating from having suffered a severe sprained ankle when he fell off a load of logs.

The Great Fire

One day in July of the year 1917, my dad announced he was going to town to get some oil for the mowing machine as a neighbor was coming to our place to mow our hay. My dad had been seriously ill prior to this time and was not yet up to rough heavy work such as running a horse drawn mowing machine and maneuvering it around stumps.

In those days there was very little use for lubricating oil as most machinery, which was very little on the ranch, used heavy grease called axle grease.

Dad asked me if I would like to go along and told me to go in the house to tell my mother where we were going and that we would try to be back before dinner time, which was high noon. In those days dinner was at noon and the evening meal was called supper. (Lunches were something carried to work or on picnics.)

He hooked up a single horse to a light buggy we owned. This was before we owned a car. It was about 3 miles to town over a rough dirt road and in places rocky and rougher. This was a big deal for me as I seldom got to go to town which was exciting, and too, I also got to ride in the spring seat in the place where my mother generally rode, beside my dad. I sat up high in front where I could look all around and see everything that was going on which wasn't much, unless you could call looking at the back end of a horse interesting. I guess I thought it was because I enjoyed the privilege.

As I recall it was about nine in the morning when we left home on a beautiful sunny day, which gave every promise of being good and hot later on, which it was. Dad told the neighbor to go ahead and get started cutting hay and we would be back before he needed more oil for the gear box.

When we got to town, we drove to the hitching racks where dad tied the horse and didn't bother to unhitch from the buggy, as we wouldn't be gone long. We then went down the side street to the corner of Main Street where we saw smoke coming up from the waterfront across the railroad track, which was down a steep embankment and which was also a little above the shore of the lake. The lakeshore was lined with sawmills at the time.

Well, we hadn't gone much farther when we encountered the proprietor of the hardware store, Mr. Ribstein (the man who kept the oil in a barrel in the back room of the store). Mr. Ribstein was at a fire hydrant just standing there looking at the smoke and was not very much concerned. We stopped to talk with him. My dad told him we wanted to buy some oil and get back to the ranch. Mr. Ribstein said he would be tied up for a little while as that was his station when there was a fire. He went on to say that the fire didn't amount to anything and then he would be with us. We waited a little while and things were beginning to look worse all the time and indeed they were. My dad said to me, "Let's go on down the street." When we were out of earshot of the hardware man, he said, "I don't like the looks of this, I don't think that they are going to get the fire out."

Harrison, Idaho – 1910

We went into the hardware store and on into the back room. There was the oil barrel but nothing to put oil in. We didn't waste any time. I noticed my dad was getting in kind of a hurry. We went back to the street and down a couple of doors to a restaurant which was operated by a man by the name of Jim Jones (sometimes referred to as Greasy Spoon Jones).

There was no one there either, everything deserted. We went on through the dining room and out through the back door of the kitchen into a yard in the back. In the middle of the yard was a pile of empty tin cans that you couldn't see over, it was so high. They must have been accumulating there for years.

Dad hunted around until he was able to find a new empty gallon syrup can with a screw cap on it, which he took to the kitchen and washed out. When we got back to the street the flames were shooting up in the air from one of the sawmills. People were rushing about; there was a lot of commotion and hollering going on. I could tell then that it was mighty serious. We headed straight for the oil barrel and after filling the can went directly to the hitching rack and the horse and buggy. By this time Dad was walking so fast I could hardly keep up with him. The town of Harrison is built on a hillside and the source of the fire was at the bottom of the hill and, of course, as the fire got hotter it created a draft so the situation compounded itself in short order. By this time, the air temperature was higher; which didn't help the situation.

Dad drove the horse and buggy and me up on the hill (still in town but out of any danger from the fire) to some people's house who we knew. There he left us and went back down where he could see the fire better and see what was going on. I asked to go along but he said no, that was no place for a boy, which I sure didn't agree with but I didn't mention that because you didn't argue with my dad, at least not very much.

Well, it wasn't so bad after all as the people that I stayed with had two boys older than I and they didn't get to go either, which made me feel a little better. Soon we could see the flames high in the air and could hear loud banging as ammunition exploded. We could feel the heat even though we were several blocks away. I guess it took about two to three hours for the flames to die down and things began to cool off a little. The whole business part of the town of Harrison had burned to the ground.

Finally, my dad came back up the hill. He had a side of bacon in one hand and a big ham in the other hand. I don't remember if my mother had ordered any groceries or not, but anyway that is what we had to take home (a gallon of oil, a ham and a slab of bacon). Later when my dad went to town, he went to Mr. Ribstein's store, which was set up in a tent, and paid him for the oil. Mr. Ribstein thanked him for his honesty and said he never would have known the difference. It was the last sale he made before he was burned out. He did some business from a tent for a while, but gave it up as I remember. He had no insurance and could not afford to rebuild his store.

When my dad had gone back down to the fire, he could readily see that the town was going to go. He dashed into the butcher shop, grabbed a ham and a side of bacon, and took them up on the hill where he left them to be retrieved later, which he did. That was the last sale that the butcher shop made as it turned out also.

When Dad later paid them, they too thanked him for his honesty and said that they never would have known the difference. It was their last sale too as everything was gone. They did rebuild to the best of my recollection and the store building stands to this day with their name on it (Marler and Brass).

The main business district was rebuilt, after a fashion, but it never did recover fully to what it had been before the fire.

Several big sawmills burned at the same time and although there were a couple of mills left, things were never the same again. From then on, as I recall, it seems things just slowly went down hill. The fire burned right up to the bank in the south end of the business district before they finally got it under control. I don't think any homes were burned although I am not sure, however it was a major disaster for the community.

We, of course, had big news when we got home as we had first hand knowledge of the big fire. This is a true story of an exciting day in the life of a small country boy.

Our St. Joe Fishing Trip

In the fall of 1917, my dad wasn't in very good shape yet from having been in the hospital the winter before for so long. In late September, the weather was good and my folks decided to take a fishing trip. My dad and the hired man built a big wooden box and took a couple of big hay tarps and some bedding and the box filled with food and loaded it on the wagon. We all got in then and rode to Harrison where everything was loaded on a small passenger steamboat headed for St. Joe City on the St. Joe River and we were off. High adventure, believe me. When we got within about a mile of St. Joe City my dad stood on the foredeck of the boat and chose a place for us to camp. He told the captain to pull into the bank and as it was about level with the deck they did and left the steam engine turning over slowly to hold the boat against the bank. They got a gangplank over to the bank and off-loaded our supplies for us and there we were in the wilderness, or so I thought at least.

After Dad got the camp fixed up and one of the tarps over a pole to make us a fine lean-to for shelter, and a big fire log fixed for a cooking fire and heat when it got cold, he took off.

He soon came back with a wooden rowboat and a bucket of fresh milk. It seems he knew where we were going all the time and we were camped on a man's land by the name of Mr. Reed, who had cows. This land was part of his pasture. There is a canyon to this day named after him, called Reed's Gulch. Well, it was an ideal campsite, level and big trees with openings between and plenty of wood and with Mr. Reed's permission, we had it made.

We would go out in the morning after breakfast and the chores were done and my mother would row the boat down the middle of the river, or just drive with the current while my dad fly fished both sides of the river. The cutthroat trout were plentiful and I don't think there was a limit then. If so, no one paid any attention to it. We never heard of any enforcement. It seemed he always caught fish. Sometimes we went out again in the afternoon and did the same thing. After we had gone a mile or so, my dad would take the oars and row us back up to camp. Some of the fish we ate, and some Dad salted down in wooden candy buckets.

Hard candy came in wooden buckets in those times and candy bars had not yet been invented. These buckets would hold about three gallons and could be obtained from grocery stores after they had finished with them. The folks would put in a layer of clean fish and then salt, then more fish and then salt packing everything down tight and then put the lid on tight and the fish would keep for months.

The weather was delightful and we all had a good time, as neither Don or myself were in school yet. My folks decided to stay another week after the first week was up. We ended up staying there for three weeks, which was remarkable because it was October.

There was a road up to where we camped and I guess Dad had made previous arrangements with his good friend Mr. Russell because after we had been there for a while, Mr. Russell showed up and stayed with us for a few days. He took us in his car one day farther up the river road to a placed called Falls Creek where a man lived by the name of Honey Jones. This man lived alone and was an eccentric. He was a beekeeper and had honey for sale. It was a real treat to get to go for a ride in a car and of course the folks bought some comb honey and we had homemade biscuits quite often after that.

My dad was a good cook among other things and an expert at camping. He always helped my mother with the cooking when we were camping. I should say she helped him. He could make the best biscuits in a cast-iron frying pan (called a dutch oven frying pan) over an open fire that I have ever tasted.

When it was time to go home Dad stood on the riverbank that day and when the boat made the trip up the river, Dad called out to them to pick us up on the way back down. This they did and when we got to Harrison the hired man was there with the wagon to meet us.

What a trip and the remarkable thing was that it was in October. I still have pleasant memories of that trip and how much we all enjoyed it and what a good family time we all had. The only thing I didn't particularly care for was those salty fish afterward and I think they lasted forever. I was glad when they were gone.

Well it came time for me to go to school and there was no school. No public conveyance, such as a bus, as they had not yet been invented .My mother taught me the first grade at home but as I recall I wasn't much interested and I really didn't get as much out of it as I should have, mainly probably because I didn't put any more into it than I had to.

I think the year was 1917 or 1918. Anyway, I was glad when it was over and my mother said it was vacation time. It sure curtailed my other activities when I had to sit in the kitchen and practice reading and so on while my mother worked and listened to me recite. There were more important and much more interesting activities to be pursued than the Little Red Hen book, and the business called arithmetic, with numbers, which have always been hard for me. What the heck, I could count and that was good enough for me at the time.

During the summer vacation of the year of 1918, my Aunt Agnes, my mother's youngest sister who was a school teacher in Seattle, came to our place to spend the summer with my mother and our family, which she did for several years. They had always been close and came out west together and had both taught at Davenport, Washington, at the same time before my mother took over the hotel for my uncle. At the time there were some other kids that got to be of school age in the vicinity and after my folks talked to the school board in Harrison, the district where our school tax money went, they decided that a school would have to be started out in the country for us.

My aunt was persuaded to teach that year. I think she made quite a sacrifice in salary but she did it anyway, and boarded at our place. This was the fall of 1918. There was no school building, but an old shack covered with tarpaper was found not too far from where the school was to be built. My dad had agreed to donate one acre of ground for the school on the farthest corner of our property if the school board would agree to build the school there. This they readily agreed to because this saved the district a considerable amount of money for property.

As I mentioned, the building was a tarpaper shack, which had been constructed for a temporary bunkhouse for a small logging crew. It was built on a couple of logs and could be skidded with four horses. When we started school, the building was in the yard of a nearby farm where people lived, and all the men who had kids in school were too busy to move the building to the new location for us, so we went there for a month or so till someone got time and then one Monday morning we found that the school had been moved to the newly cleared corner of our property but out of sight of our house, which was about three quarters of a mile away through the woods.

As I recall we went there that year and the next before the new school was built. It was a poor excuse for a school – poor windows for light and no insulation.

The Harrison School class – 1918 or 1919

Chapter 5

I went to the little tarpaper shack school for that year and my aunt was our teacher. I think she was a good teacher but I think it was a handicap for me and maybe her also that she was my aunt. I don't think I got as much out of it as I should have. I recall that I understood she was the boss at school but she wasn't at home, at least as far as I was concerned she wasn't. We used to have a little trouble over that I recall.

One time in the early spring of the year, at home just before supper, we had some kind of disagreement and she and I got into it. I have no idea what about now. She was real bossy at times and this didn't appeal to me, at home anyway, after having had to listen to her all day. She made a dive for me and I ran out the kitchen door. It was just getting dark and I took a turn around the yard, but I wasn't doing so good and she was gaining on me. The situation was desperate. After I had time to evaluate this turn of events I made a hasty decision but a good one.

The field next to the house had been plowed late the fall before and was a sea of mud and mud puddles and it was deep. I had on boots and I didn't think it would go over the boots so I took a chance, as by now she was gaining fast. Well maybe because of the boots I couldn't run so fast but they sure worked better in that mud than what she had on and she soon lost both of her low cut shoes. Then she was really mad.

She made it back to the house in her stocking feet through about six inches of mud and water puddles, threatening me all the way at the top of her voice. I knew I was in big trouble, and of course she reported to my mother, the sergeant in charge, as my dad was away. And then the hollering started for me to come to the house

I had been doing some deep thinking while I was loping around in the mud and water enjoying being able to outrun her and also her misery in the mud. Supper was ready and I had her shoes so I figured I was in a pretty good bargaining position. So I hollered back that I wouldn't come in till I was granted amnesty. I made my case that I had her shoes and I would stay out there all night if necessary and I might just lose her shoes, never to be recovered, if the pressure on me got to be too heavy.

Well it worked and she never did chase me again as far as I recall. After that little episode if she couldn't grab me quick, she would give up.

Most of the time we got along fine and I did have deep respect for her. When I look back, she really made quite a sacrifice to teach there that year and it was hard, as I think she had nearly every grade, one through eight, and was used to teaching little kids only. Probably not used to little knot-headed country kids like me either.

I recall one day I was looking out the window at some birds in the trees near the school window and she said to me "Charles I think you would rather be out there with the birds than here in class." I thought Oh Boy! I am going to get to go out, so I said "yes", full of glee. But no such luck. That, unfortunately, wasn't what she had in mind at all. She apparently didn't expect such an honest answer nor did she appreciate it either as was evidenced by her abrupt change in manner, as she said in her best commanding voice full of authority: "Now you get busy and read your lesson in your reader as you are supposed to be doing." What a disappointment, what a let down. Well, there were to be many days like that I found, before I got to be an old man.

This was the year of 1918 and some of the things I recall of that era are of World War One. I can recall my dad coming home from town one evening rather late. He had been to the Hotel Harrison for some reason or other and the newspapers came in on a steamboat from Coeur d'Alene. They were brought to the hotel and a man who was the grandfather of our good friend Henry Kuehl, who we went to school with, was there.

He was from Germany and was what they referred to as a pro German during the world war (a German sympathizer, in other words). When the papers were unpacked, someone in the group of people there said, "What are the headlines?" The first one to get a paper called out "The Germans have just won a big battle." With this, this man threw his hat in the air and yelled "Hooray for Germany, hooray for the Kaiser." A crowd gathered around him and they started to shout and there was very nearly a riot. Someone got things cooled off a little and they told him to get out of town and never come back and as far as I know, he never did. Boy, my dad was worked up when he came home.

One of the things we kids did that we thought was kind of neat was to recite this little poem: "Kaiser Bill went up the hill to take a look at France. Kaiser Bill came down the hill with bullets in his pants." That was quite daring for us and showed our patriotism.

During this time two men came out from town one day and it so happened that my dad wasn't home; so they talked to my mother about our wheat crop that was nearly ready to be harvested. These men, both of whom my mother knew and who were on some kind of war resource board, were going around the local area making sure that all grain that was raised would be threshed, and not be used for feed. This was for the war effort so people would have grain for flour for bread.

32

They didn't have the foggiest idea what they were doing; however, they issued an order that the wheat Dad was raising for chicken feed had to be thrashed and the grain delivered to the dock in Harrison to be shipped to a mill to be ground for flour. (Probably the one I worked in many years later).

Well my brother didn't like the crust on the bread at this time and would not eat it when he could get out of it. Our mother would threaten him sometimes by saying that some little kids were going hungry because of the war and would love to have the crust if they could get it , and that if Kaiser ever came, all we would have to eat would be crusts as there wouldn't be enough food to go around.

Don related the conversation of the war efforts and the talk of war by these men to the threats and became frightened unbeknownst to Mother or me. When the men left, we couldn't find brother Don anywhere. We looked everywhere, in the house and outside, in the woodshed, the barn, the chicken house, everywhere – no Don.

We became very concerned and were almost to the stage of panic when my mother thought of looking under her bed. There was Don as far back in the corner as he could get and all curled up sound asleep. His explanation was that he thought the Kaiser was coming to get him because he wouldn't eat his crusts, so he had hid there and after they left, he had gone to sleep.

That was 1918 and along in the fall of the year, November 11 to be exact, the war was declared over. The armistice was signed on the eleventh hour of the eleventh day of the eleventh month; the great world war was over. I don't remember how we got word at the school, as there was no phone there. I guess the nearest neighbor with a phone, Mr. Farmer, must have come to tell us. My aunt let us out of school for the rest of the day. When we got home, we told my mother and she got on the phone and confirmed this by calling someone, probably central, as she always had the answers.

Mother said we had to celebrate so she took pans from the kitchen cupboard and we all went outside and pounded on them with sticks of kindling wood. This was pretty tame because the neighbors couldn't hear it, so we soon resorted to cowbells, which worked much better and made considerable racket.

This attracted the attention of the neighbors, the McKinneys, and after all, we had to share it with someone. I really didn't appreciate the full significance of it but I knew it was a real big deal. I do remember that our neighbor, Clem McKinney, the old folks' son, would be coming home in due time and that was cause for celebration. Some of the restrictions would be lifted, which was good news. We knew that Kaiser Bill had been licked and that the war was over and this I understood.

We lived quite a way out in the country but we could hear whistles from the sawmills and from the steamboats on the lake and sometimes the trains, very clearly most of the time. The owner of the export lumber company (which I later worked for one summer) ordered the big steam whistle on the sawmill tied down for twenty-four hours to celebrate. The mill was shut down for the day. Everyone got the day off with pay. They blew the whistle continuously all the rest of that day, all night and till eleven o'clock the next day, even keeping one man on to fire the boiler to supply steam for the whistle.

Shortly after this happened the great flu epidemic of 1918 took place. The whole country was afflicted with the disease and many of the troops returning from overseas were stricken with it. Many people died of it and in fact I lost an aunt and a cousin with the flu. It caused great sickness and was almost like a plague. People where we lived out in the country didn't go to town unless they had to, and when in town you were supposed to wear a handkerchief over your mouth and nose. There wasn't really any cure for it but people did the best they could and helped each other out if they could.

The doctor was on the go constantly and very much in demand. Our school was shut down for a long time. I can't say how long, but a long time during the winter. Fortunately, no one in our vicinity got it, and none of us got it. We lost a lot of school time and it was never made up.

It was along about this time that I went out to the outhouse one evening about bedtime. There was an apple tree near the path and up in this tree was a strange animal. It was as big as a small dog and kind of hissed or spit at me when I went by.

Well, it was pretty dark and about eight thirty but I could make out that it was something strange to me. We always left our chicken house door open at night as the chickens had the run of the place, and I reasoned with good cause that whatever it was it would probably feast on our chickens before morning. In the excitement of this turn of events, I forgot all about why I was out there in the first place and streaked for the house full tilt to report this frightening event. Mother lit a lantern and she, Don and I all went out to see it – Dad was away working.

There it was up in the tree and it hissed at us and kind of yowled too, pretty scary stuff for a first or second grader I'll tell you. After having seen it with her own eyes, Mother thought we should do something about it. She called the McKinneys and it happened their grandson was staying with them for a few days. He was about twelve or thirteen I guess, practically a man in my estimation, at that time at least.

He came down with a shotgun and after another consultation, all parties agreed that whatever it was, it should be dispatched before something really bad happened. Glen took careful aim and pulled the trigger and down came the wild animal.

When we were sure it was good and dead and we could get a good look at it with the aid of the lantern we could see that it was the biggest tomcat we had ever seen. It was huge and we surmised it was indeed a wild cat that had been in the wild for a long time. It wasn't far back of our place to the deep woods. Yes, it would have been in our chicken house before morning.

Incidentally, none of the neighbors knew anything about this cat, nor had any of them seen it. House cats will go wild if they are left in the wilderness or are abandoned sometimes. This cat must have been wild for a long time or it may have been the second generation of wild cats. We never knew but it sure was a big one. The biggest one I have ever seen.

Our First Car

Well, we got through that winter and the next spring my dad bought a car. This was 1919 and as I look back on it this sort of changed our lives. Before this, if we went any place it was horses. Now, because it was so much easier, we got to go more. When you take horses you always have to consider the horse or horses. If you went someplace with a team or one horse you had to harness the horses or horse as the case was and then hook them to whatever you were going to use, wagon, buggy or sleigh. Then you tied them up while you went in the house to get cleaned up for whatever it was you were going to do when you got to where you were going to go. If you put on your good clothes first, by the time the horses were all hooked up you smelled like a horse and that wasn't always good. When you got home, you had to take care of the horses first off. They had to be unhooked first. Then watered, if they were not too hot. If they were, they had to be left to cool down and watered later, and then stabled, unharnessed and fed.

After all this, you could look after other things such as yourself. Sometimes it was just too discouraging to go to the trouble. After Dad got the car, what a difference.

He bought it in Coeur d'Alene and it was shipped to Harrison on the deck of a passenger steamboat. My dad didn't know how to drive a car and after he bought it, he had to take driving lessons to learn how to drive the thing. It seems strange now, but at the time, very few people knew how to drive a car.

This was a Model T Ford and they were a little hard to drive. Dad mastered it in a few days and the dealer at the garage where he bought it in Coeur d'Alene loaded it on the deck of the boat for him and up the lake they came. Poor Dad said afterward he worried all the way to Harrison about driving it off the boat and up the incline of the dock to the street when he got there. When they did get there, no one else knew anything about driving the car so Dad had to drive his new car off the boat. He couldn't make a mistake because if he went backward he was in the lake, car and all. If he stalled the engine, he would have to back it down onto the deck, get out, crank it, and start over. Well he managed to get on solid ground, and to make it more difficult there was a good crowd on hand to see the boat come in and to watch him drive off.

He called my mother and said he was in town and would be home with the new machine soon. (That is what they were sometimes called in those times). They were very uncommon in our country then.

In fact there was only one other car out in the country at the time. My brother and I were really excited and ran down to the gate and had it open long before he came in sight. Boy what a thrill it was to see that black, shiny car come into sight with my dad sitting proudly at the wheel. Well, it was really something and we were awed by it. It was called a touring car and had a top which folded down when not in use. For a long time we went around with the top down – I guess it was because we were used to an open buggy or a wagon. I don't know why else. I guess I had at that time only had a ride in a car three or four times and if was fascinating to all of us, including our mother.

It had no self starter as they were called. When you wanted it to go, you first had to set the hand-operated accelerator, then adjust the spark control lever and turn on the key and make sure it was in neutral. After these arrangements were all taken care of, you went around in front and pulled the choke wire with left hand and pushed in the crank with the other hand, got it engaged and then cranked it, which wasn't easy. After one got the hang of it, it wasn't so bad. It was a lot easier when you got to be about sixteen years old too, and had more cranking power. (Editor's note: A person cranked the engine in a circle, like a propellor.)

To a new driver it was all somewhat overwhelming and rather confusing, and I can say with all honesty this is somewhat of an understatement.

Our new Model T
Mother, me, Don and Dad with our new car!

Killing the engine (stalling the engine) was a very vexing problem, and it would happen at the most inopportune times. A Model T was operated differently than other cars as they had what was called a planetary transmission and this device was operated with three-foot pedals. One of the problems was the fact that Henry Ford, when he invented the Model T, overlooked the fact that most of us come equipped with only two feet, which at times left you short about one, and sometimes a third foot was desperately needed, as the shifting was done with the feet.

They were tricky and to use the right amount of gas, which was done with the hand operated throttle, (not as you know it today with a foot operated gas pedal) and control the pedals with the right amount of pressure, letting some off on one pedal and at the same time applying more with the other foot on a different pedal did take some dexterity and skill. They were very hard to learn to drive.

For awhile if Dad got a little nervous, he would kill the engine and then he would have to get out, displacing the front seat passenger as there was no door on the driver's side, go around in front, crank the car and get back in to try it again. This usually happened in a tight place or where a good-sized crowd was watching a driver perform some almost impossible feat of driving skill, or when one wasn't very good at driving but you didn't want everyone to know it.

I started to drive when I was thirteen and was driving to town alone when I was fourteen. We had no garage for the car so Dad kept it in the yard covered with a big haystack tarp for a while. Then when he got around to it, he cut a big doorway in the end of the woodshed and that became the garage. For several years, no one drove cars during the winter or spring because of the snow in winter and mud in the spring. The car went up on jacks about the first of November and stayed there till about the first of April.

Chapter 6

Well, it got to be time to go to school again and this year we had a new teacher. She was a girl who had graduated that spring from high school and had gone to Cheney Normal School (college) for the summer, and then got the job of teaching our school for the coming year. We still had to go to the tarpaper shack school again.

Some of the ways of those times I might just relate here, for the benefit of those of you who take the trouble to read this far. Things were so different than they are today that some of you may find them interesting.

The school consisted of only one little room and everyone could hear everything that was said by anyone, so as a result it was hard to concentrate on your own business.

There was very little homework and one of the reasons being that the lights were poor at home, so when the days were short there was no homework. For someone like me, who wasn't interested in the first place, it was hard to get much out of it. We had no water at the school so the teacher would send two of the kids to the neighbor's house to get a pail of fresh water about every other day. The Farmer place was closest and they had a well with a pump; the reason for two kids was that we were not big enough at first to carry a pail of water all by ourselves. There was a shelf in the corner of the room and that is where the water pail was placed. In the pail was a dipper with a wooden handle and everyone drank from the dipper. It was bad manners not to drink all that you dipped up. In other words, you were supposed to drink all of what you dipped up and not put some back. Sometimes we would have to go farther for water because the Farmer's well would go dry and then we went to the Smith house which didn't have a pump and the water had to be pulled up over a pulley with a rope tied to a bucket. This required a couple of bigger kids and if the kids were small, Mrs. Smith had to be recruited from the house to pull the water up and fill the pail.

We had two little outhouses out in the back, one for girls and the other for boys. We had a woodshed for the wood and the district would hire someone to bring the wood for our stove. We had to split it ourselves and carry it in. The teacher got there a little early in the morning and started the fire and sometimes when it was bitterly cold she would let us stand around the heating stove and get warm before classes started, as we would be cold from the walk.

My Harrison School class
(I'm in the top center)

One time we ran out of wood. The teacher said she had been complaining to the principal in town, who was in charge of us, that we were getting low on wood. It was in the middle of the winter and quite cold. We kids were all watching the wood pile and finally came the day when sure enough there were only some odd scraps and some chips left. We didn't know what was going to happen but we were looking forward to some kind of excitement with ill-concealed enthusiasm. She had us gather up all the chips and odd sticks and we kept burning it till it was all gone much to our satisfaction. Along in the middle of the afternoon it started to get cold in the room and we had burned the last of everything that would burn.

We had all been watching with glee to see what would happen. I think maybe we thought we would all have to be martyrs, sitting around in the cold with our hats and coats and mittens on, suffering in the cold and feeling sorry for ourselves.

Well, it was even better than that. She announced that the school would be closed till we got some wood and that we could all go home. Boy what a joyous turn of events. She said there would be no more school till we had plenty of wood, that she wasn't going to put up with this any longer and if the parents didn't like it for them to call the principal in town and help her complain.

We emptied the water bucket so it wouldn't freeze and put the ink bottles in the box of sawdust that was kept for that purpose so they wouldn't freeze and break. She locked the door and marched bravely down the road to town, and we all went home with the good news. When I look back on it, it took courage for her to do this as her job was at stake and she was just a kid herself on her first job.

In a couple of days Mother got a call that school would be open the next day much to my disgust. We never did run out of wood again.

I might explain here that we had pens and ink bottles to write with. There were some fountain pens then but they were not very satisfactory and often leaked. However if we had had the money to buy one they wouldn't permit the use of them anyway.

We used pen points and wooden pen point holders and had to dip the pen point in the ink every once in awhile to get a little dab of ink and then write and the ink would always run out right in the middle of a word. What a pain they were and some one was always spilling ink or tipping a bottle over or something. The desks had a hole in the top near the front right hand corner to put the bottle in, and the cork top for the bottle could be removed so the pen could be inserted when writing.

About the only good thing I can say for the whole arrangement was that it was good for dipping the tip of the braids of hair in if you happened to have a girl with long braids sitting at the desk in front of you. The braids would hang down on one's desk and every time the girl turned her head, the braids would swish back and forth. A guy could only resist the temptation for about so long and then the tips just had to be dipped in the ink bottle and dyed. Sometimes you would start with just a tiny bit, but if they kept sitting up straight and the swishing went on for too long the process would be repeated and the dye had a way of creeping up a little farther and then there was trouble aplenty.

Sometimes the desk would have a crack in the top where wooden pieces came together. The crack would be just the right size to tuck the end of a braid of hair in, and wait for the unsuspecting victim to stand up, or I should say try to stand up. Wow, a guy could get in trouble so easy it seemed like.

This was the year for a general election to be held, the year of 1920. The Republican presidential nominee was a man by the name of Harding. The Democratic nominee was a man by the name of Cox. Our dad was a Democrat and Mother was a Republican. The Democrats were in favor of repealing the Volstead Act, which was the prohibition act, banning all alcoholic beverages in the United States. The Republicans were not in favor of this so the two parties were called the wets and the drys.

Our mother and dad used to have some rather heated discussions over this issue before the election. My dad was not a drinking man by any sense of the word, but on the other hand he didn't like not having the privilege of being able to have a nip once in a while if he so desired, which I think is reasonable. But this view was not shared by our mother.

For some reason she was dead set against any form of indulgence. When Election Day came, the folks had to drive about five miles to vote. It was very uncomfortable, a lot of tension in the air. Our mother sat up very straight and there wasn't a word spoken all the way over there. I know when they voted they canceled each other's vote, which must have made them happy because when they had voted, everything was fine and they were talking again.

It turned out that Harding was elected (Warren G. Harding) and if I am not mistaken, he died in office, after some big scandal called the Teapot Dome Oil Scandal

I might mention here some things that seem strange now but they were real at the time. When cars first got on the road, and the roads were very poor and narrow, it was sometimes necessary to shut the engine of the car off to get horses to pass when meeting them in the road. If they were extremely excitable, as was sometimes the case, the car driver had to get out and take the horse by the bit and lead it around to prevent a runaway, while the horse's driver stayed in the seat and held on to the lines. Some horses were a lot worse than others depending on their temperament. Runaways were common and sometimes people were hurt badly as a result of having been thrown out of a horse drawn conveyance.

There were some car accidents then because people didn't know how to drive very well and a car would get away from them and go over a bank or they would forget how to stop and run into a tree or big rock or something.

About this time, we got rural free delivery of mail. Three times a week it came and we thought we had it made. The mailman was the source of information and did a lot of things for people as favors.

I can recall one time my brother and I didn't think there was going to be any firecrackers for the Fourth of July because Dad was away working and we didn't think he would get back before the fourth. Mother contacted the mailman and gave him some money and he bought some firecrackers in St. Maries for us and left them the next trip.

Mother was thoughtful about things like that. She always made a fuss over Christmas and the other holidays and made them special for us if she could, even if we didn't have much. They were special because of her and I am grateful to her for her efforts and her values.

It is from her that I got some of my cultural values and appreciation for some of the finer things in life. It was from both my parents that I learned manners and honesty. They were both mannerly and orderly and I have deep respect for them because of it.

I recall one incident that took place at the supper table one night. I had heard the neighbor kid, Buster Jarrard, refer to another neighbor, Mr. Farmer, as old man Farmer. That seemed to me to be rather sophisticated sounding so I tried it at the supper table. Boy, was that ever a mistake. Dad straightened me out on that, much to my embarrassment, explaining to me in a manner that I never forgot, that boys didn't call men old, no matter how old they were. It was Mister or Mrs. This I never forgot and I am glad of it to this very day. To this very day, I can hardly stand to hear someone refer to their father as the old man or to their mother or their wife as the old lady.

We had good Christmases because of Mother. She would struggle around and order things from the catalog for us with strict orders to us, after we got mail service, to bring any packages that showed up in the mail to her. She got very little help from our dad, as he didn't seem to have any of those values. She would see to it that we would have a present and a Christmas tree and we would always have a stocking hanging behind the heating stove (that was the closest thing to a fireplace we had). We always used one of my dad's socks because they were bigger and would hold more goodies. We always got one main thing for a present and then maybe some little knick-knacks in our stockings; it was great.

I recall one time when I was pretty young, it was the day before Christmas, and Dad had been away working someplace all week. We didn't have a tree. Dad wasn't home yet when it was time for me to go to bed, (Don was already in bed). Christmas Eve and no Dad, no tree, no sign of Christmas. So I went to bed pretty glum. My brother wasn't big enough yet to know the difference, but believe me I was pretty despondent. Mother had some presents hidden for Santa Claus to bring, but of course, I didn't know about that.

The snow was deep and finally my poor dad got home after I was asleep, all worn out, having had to walk out from town in the snow. My mother made him go out in the woods (which wasn't far at the time) with the kerosene lantern, in the snow late at night, find a tree, fix a stand and then they both put it up. When I got up in the morning there was a tree in all its splendor with a present under it for everyone and two socks hanging there with exciting looking lumps sticking out and an orange sticking out the top of each. Boy what a turn of events.

It might be worth mentioning that at the time there were no lights for the Christmas tree. I don't know if they had been invented yet or not. It didn't matter because we had no electricity anyway. We used little candles that were placed in little candle holders that had a clip on the bottom that clipped to a limb of the tree. They were beautiful when lit but what a fire hazard; you never left them unattended. We had a few decorations, tinsel balls and little bells etc. We had popcorn and rose hips, that we would string as garlands to trim the tree; we thought they were great. (Rose hips are those little red balls that are left on rose bushes after the roses are through blooming.) We would get oranges, peanuts, walnuts, brazil, and hazel nuts, and hard candy in our stockings at Christmas but we seldom ever saw them any other time of the year.

I mentioned Buster Jarrard; he was a case, and dealt me a lot of misery through the years. He was about two years older than I was and he was a bully. He could lick me and he could run faster than I could. In fact, he could outdo me at everything. He got a goat someplace and I don't know why because it wasn't good for anything. When I would go to their place to play with Buster, which was seldom because my mother didn't like me to be around him and now I know why, I would have to contend with that blasted goat.

Buster had bullied the goat and teased it till it was mean. When I went there, it would chase me up on the porch and then I would have to get up on the banister where he couldn't butt me, and holler for someone to come to my rescue. The Jarrard kids had the fear in him and he would mind them but not so with me. When I wasn't looking that miserable creature would butt me in the back side every chance he got and sometimes it would knock me down if I didn't see him coming, which Buster thought was quite funny.

Well I didn't. In the first place, it would scare the heck out of me when it caught me by surprise. The second thing, it would sometimes hurt, and lastly it was hard on my dignity.

One time when I was going to their place I had had enough of that goat. Before I got there, and fairly close to their house, was a barbed wire fence that I had to crawl through. As I was negotiating the fence, I saw that blasted goat and he was making his way toward me. I could anticipate the greeting I was to get from him and didn't relish it too much.

However as I looked down, there on the ground was the answer to my problem I figured, if I just played my cards right. There on the ground, was a good sized tree root, just the right size and length, where Dad had thrown it when he had plowed the field, to get it out of the way when using the mowing machine. It was just right and this would be my opportunity to settle the score with mister goat.

I picked it up and held it close to my leg as I walked to meet the goat, hoping he wouldn't see it and he didn't. I also hoped no one would see me coming but the goat. It worked out just fine. The goat saw me before anyone in the house did. The goat took the bait and made for me on a dead run with his head down and already to give me the old goat treatment. I was watching carefully and when he got real close I stepped sideways and he couldn't stop in time so when he went by me I let him have it right across the nose with that club, I really scored a direct hit with a good show of force, and it knocked him down.

At first I was afraid I had killed him, but in about ten seconds he got up, shook his head a few times, took a look at me kind of cross-eyed (I don't think his eyes were focused yet) and apparently wanted no more to do with me.

You know that was one smart goat; he learned his lesson well and never did bother me after that. No one saw it and they never did know why the goat quit bothering me. That was a well kept secret between the goat and me. He couldn't talk and I didn't!

I think this is a good time for me to tell about my dad running a logging camp one time and as it was a small operation, he was the timekeeper as well as the boss. He hired a man who couldn't speak very good English, as he was a foreigner. He wrote his name down for my dad and when Dad got around to put it in the time book he couldn't make it out. He struggled with it for awhile and losing patience with trying to puzzle it out he just wrote down what it looked like to him.

That turned out to be Peter Radish. When it came time to give the man his check Dad told the fellow he wasn't able to figure out his foreign name and what he had done so the check was made out to Peter Radish. The man said it sounded good to him, as he had always had trouble with the spelling of his name in English.

Many years later in the 1920s Dad was in Spokane and was on a downtown street one day when he saw his old friend, Peter Radish. In those days, as cars became more plentiful and traffic increased and as there were no traffic lights, when traffic got heavy in the late afternoon, particularly, police would be stationed at the busy intersections. They would get in the center of an intersection with a light pipe post that fit in a hole in the pavement.

This pipe had a two way cross sign on top of it saying stop when turned one way and go when turned at a right angle. This pipe then had a handle on it and the officer would blow his whistle and turn the sign with the handle to regulate traffic so the sign would read go one way and stop the other direction. After a short while then the officer would blow his whistle, turn the sign and then traffic would go the other way.

My dad looked out in the middle of an intersection and there was his old friend, Peter Radish, directing traffic. When Dad could get out to him, he did and they were glad to see each other after all the years. Peter Radish had become a Spokane police officer and he said his name was still Peter Radish, thanks to Dad.

Chapter 7

Along about this time I learned to take on more responsibilities and take over more of the work at home. Dad was gone much of the time and Mother wasn't too well and there were things she never did know how to do, so I learned to do them.

Killing chickens was one of the things. We always had chickens and sometimes we would want to butcher them but Mother wouldn't cut the heads off. We only had axes with double bits and they were too heavy for me to hold in one hand, while I held the chicken in the other. I came up with a way, not a good way, but a way that worked.

Don and I would catch the chicken that was to be killed and tie a string around its feet. Then we would tie one around its neck rather loosely. We would place the chopping block where we could tie the feet to a post and put the chicken on the block and Don then would pull its neck out straight but still on the block and I would use both hands on the ax. I wasn't a very good marksman with the ax so we had to resort to the string on the neck for safety purposes, not for the poor chicken but for Don's hand. It wasn't the best, but it was a way, and it worked.

We had a well for our water supply, with a pump. We had to carry the water to the house in a pail. All water had to be pumped for the animals and the house. The water for the animals went into a wooden spout that took it to the big watering trough in the barnyard that the cattle and horses drank from. This was to be kept full all the time so that if the stock was loose in the corral they could drink any time they wanted. When Dad would come in from somewhere with the team of horses they would have to be watered. The rule was that I was to leave the watering trough full after the team had had their fill.

Sometimes the horses would horse around and splash the water out with their noses and they would drink and then look up and dribble and slobber, not caring if they wasted my hard-pumped water on the ground. I sometimes would throw clods of dirt at them to chase them toward the barn as they were wasting my time waiting for them to quit fooling around so I could leave the trough full. Sometimes life has its problems.

Sometimes the neighborhood would have a community picnic on the Fourth of July, a much looked forward to event by us kids. There would be ice cream and that was a rare treat in those times for us country kids believe me.

Some people by the name of Lamb lived about two miles away and they had a small sawmill and consequently sawdust. This was the key to the ice cream. They would put up ice in the wintertime, which entailed a lot of work. They would go down to Anderson Lake, which was about another two miles down a canyon, with a team of horses and a sleigh, cut ice with a crosscut saw, pull it out of the water with ice tongs by hand, slide it to the bank, load it in a sleigh, haul it up to the ice house, dig a place in the sawdust left over from the year before, manhandle the big chunks of ice into the ice house and finally cover it with sawdust. This task always had to be accomplished when the weather was cold, naturally. What a job that must have been.

Well, when a picnic was held the Lambs had two big ice-cream freezers and they furnished the ice. That was their contribution. The rest of the people brought the cream and all the food, etc. The men would gather around and take turns turning the freezers to make the ice cream and we kids would look on with great anticipation. Sometimes on a super lucky day we would get a bonus, we would get two dishes. This then was an event to be remembered and talked about for some time, the time we got two dishes at the picnic. Such was the life of a country kid in those times.

The first time I ever had a job that I recall, that had any importance connected with it that I felt was recognized by anyone, was when the first threshing crew came to our place. It was almost beyond comprehension it was so exciting. The big steam engine came up the road puffing and belching black smoke, pulling the threshing machine behind it. This was followed by a team of horses pulling a water wagon.

When my brother and I opened the gate for the procession, the engineer even blew the whistle at us and waved. What excitement! What an honor! I was ecstatic and that is an understatement. The steam engine had a special smell that to this day excites me. I can't describe it; it is a hot grease, hot steam odor that I relish for some unknown reason. It gives me goose bumps up and down my spine even yet.

This reminds me I must tell you of my first encounter with a goose. This I shall do a little later, but now back to the threshing story.

Well, I was fascinated by the activity as the men went about the business of setting up to get ready to thresh for us. First, they got the thresher machine itself, (called a separator) in position.

Then they dug shallow holes for the wheels to drop into so the belt from the steam engine wouldn't pull it out of position. The engineer then backed the engine into place or nearly so, then they got out the big drive belt and put it on the belt drive wheel of the engine and on the wheel to be driven on the separator. After this was done, he backed the engine into the belt till it was tight. I was hanging around at a little distance watching every move with bug-eyed, rapt attention, especially the steam engine. And every time the engineer opened the fire box door to put in some more wood I am sure I watched as though I had never seen a fire before.

About the time they were ready to go, the engineer came over to me and said, "Kid do you want a job?" I could hardly believe my ears. This important man was condescending enough to talk to me, a mere little boy. I of course said "yes."

He got a bucket about half full of water, got a gunny sack, wet it in the bucket, and said, "You go around and look for sparks from the engine." He then took me into his confidence and said, "You know when the engine pulls real hard it sometimes throws sparks and if we don't get those little fires put out right away we will have a big fire and burn everything."

Well I was almost overcome that he would impart such important information to me, just a little kid. He went on to tell me how important it was and then came the clincher. He said, "If you will do this for me I will let you blow the whistle when it is time to stop for dinner and again when we start up."

Boy what an honor! I was gung-ho and ran my little butt off the rest of the morning looking for sparks and little fires. When I figured it was about noon time I got around where I was good and visible to do most of my spark chasing and made sure I would be seen when the important task of whistle blowing was to be taken care of. Finally after I figured it must be way past noon time I saw the man look at his watch and he motioned for me come up to the platform on the back of the engine. I got up there with him and the whole thing was jiggling back and forth, and it was hot, and steam was leaking from several places, making the most intriguing sounds, and it had that good smell, and the piston was going back and forth making the drive wheel go around. Boy, talk about important!

He showed me the cord to pull and said to pull it one long blast. I got a good hold of the cord and gave it a good pull, but it was so loud it scared me so bad I let go. I quickly recovered, however, and gave it another tug and this time I stayed with it.

I looked at Mr. Swindig (the engineer) but he was very reassuring and said I had done a good job. Boy, I sure was glad to hear that. To have so much responsibility and to "blow it" the first thing was kind of disheartening, especially after having worked so hard. After dinner, I was Johnnie on the spot, and now that I was experienced I blew that ol' whistle like a real pro.

Now to the story of the goose. One Sunday our family went to visit some people by the name of Jensen who lived quite a distance from our place, about ten miles, and they also lived on a farm.

When we got there the kids were gone somewhere with an older brother so Mrs. Jensen told my brother and me to go out and look around, that the kids would be back soon. Don and I were looking things over when we came to the barnyard. There were a couple of great big geese there and as we had never seen geese before we were curious. We climbed the rail fence, got down the other side, and approached the geese. They were big old things and we thought we would just pet them a little, as they looked friendly enough and didn't make any effort to avoid us.

When we got close, I kind of sensed that all was not well. I told Don to get out of there and I kind of held back a little to see what was going to happen. Well, I wasn't prepared for the next turn of events. One of those geese stuck his old, long neck out, made a hissing sound, and started for me. It was immediately obvious to me that he was not on a mission of good will. To the contrary he meant to do me harm, in what way I was soon to find out. Well, I made a run for the fence and that goose was right behind me, hissing all the way. It was a sound like I had never heard before, which offered me great encouragement to get to my goal – the fence – in the shortest possible time, and more importantly, ahead of the goose.

I thought I had it made and I started up the fence but the goose had gained on me and he jumped up and nailed me. I felt the pain of a big old goose locked onto me like someone had taken a fold of skin in a pair of pliers and squeezed real hard, right on one side of the seat of my pants where I usually sat and where he had had a good target as it was worn kind of white there from frequent washings.

I was well up on the fence when he latched on to me. That was one extremely unfriendly, mean, miserable, goose I'll tell you and he wouldn't let go. I hung onto the fence for dear life and he hung onto me just as hard. I had a heck of a time trying to shake him loose. He had a long neck, like a rubber band, and the more I pulled the more his old neck stretched. He had an advantage in that he had a nice tough bill and he had me by a nice tender place and it was getting more painful all the time.

I finally shook him off after he decided that he wasn't going to get some of my nice, tender flesh but for awhile I wasn't so sure that he wasn't going to be successful. There was a sore spot at the target zone for a long time afterward.

Here are some things I might mention that happened in this time frame, not necessarily in the time sequence that they are mentioned but they may be of enough interest to merit comment. I have often read accounts of the past and was left wondering about details. I hope I haven't been boring with them. Only the reader will be able to make this judgment I guess.

Sometimes the coyotes would howl at night and get quite close to the house. Our dog, old Bounce, would bark back at them and sometimes he would go out in the field toward them and keep getting braver and braver till he got quite a way from the house then the coyotes would gang up and advance on him.

He then would come to the house in a high lope expressing his resentment at the top of his voice. This would go for quite a while and it was very annoying when trying to sleep. On occasion Dad would get up and fire a shot from his rifle in the air and this would usually end the serenade.

When the men were clearing land and the stumps were being blown with dynamite it was always fun to see the charges go off and the resulting debris thrown high in the air. Depending on the circumstances, sometimes they would set off a whole bunch at once and then again, there would be only one or two. It took quite a while to poke or bore a hole under a big stump and then load it with several sticks of dynamite (commonly called powder) and a cap with fuse.

The cap was a small, copper, thin-walled, partly-hollow device about an inch and a half long and about a quarter of an inch in diameter, containing a small amount of nitroglycerine. A fuse of the proper length (determined by the span of time needed from lighting to detonation) was attached to this cap.

When there were a lot of stumps to be blown, they would usually use long fuses on the first ones to be lit and shorter ones on the last. They would load for sometime and then set them off by running from one place to another. When a man got a fuse lit it was customary to call out in a loud voice "Fire in the hole."

The thing was to get them all lit before they started to go, and get well away from the first lit before the action started. The dirt, mud, and pieces of wood would go flying in the air and it was very interesting to observe. Our dog, old Bounce, liked to be where anything was going on. He also enjoyed going to the holes as soon as he could after an explosion and sniffing around. I guess he was looking for mice or the remnants of them.

He insisted on doing this and he would get in the hole made by the blast where there would be little wisps of smoke lingering, and smell of it. This was strong with the odor of nitroglycerine, which is what dynamite contains, and which smells like gun powder after it has been discharged. It will give a person a severe headache. (The same kind I get when I take a nitroglycerine tablet for my heart.)

The men avoided this if at all possible because of this effect, (it was called a powder headache) but the dog never seemed to learn. After sniffing around for a short while old Bounce would be seen heading for the house with his head hanging down and he would lay around all evening, and wouldn't even eat his supper. We would feel sorry for him but he would not stay away, he never seemed to learn.

We had many quaint ways in those times. There was no refrigeration, which posed problems particularly in warm weather. We had a hole in the ground on the northeast side of the house under a big elderberry bush that grew there making a lot of shade. This had a wooden box in it and we could keep butter and milk there reasonably well.

Fresh meat was something else. My mother used to put meat in a lard pail and then in a clean flour sack and suspend it in the well on a rope. It was cool there and fresh meat could be kept in this manner for a couple of days.

I should explain that lard was the shortening of the time, as no one had ever heard of cholesterol. It is the fat of hogs and is rendered (heated in a cauldron or in big pans in the ovens at home and then strained through a fine sieve or cloth into some type of container) where it will set up and can be kept for a long time. It was put up in tin pails which held either five pounds or ten pounds when put up by the butchers. Everyone used these pails. They were handy for many things and the small ones were often used to carry school lunches in if tobacco tins were not available. They were used by men going to work as well as kids, as there were no lunch buckets as we know them today.

Thermos bottles were just invented then, and a few men carried them to work but they were hard to handle as there was no compartment in a lard bucket for them, and therefore they were easily broken. They were very expensive and consequently there were few in use. Tobacco tins were in general use as lunch boxes and were convenient, as the lid opened fully and they had two handles on them and were of rectangular shape, making it easy to pack sandwiches in.

There were few cigarettes smoked then, and those who did smoke them usually rolled their own. Pipes were in common use, so tobacco was sold in bulk in these boxes, which were decorated with fancy printing and pictures, and were to be prized.

In the wintertime, of course as the weather was cold, we had no problem keeping meat. When the weather got cold, along about Thanksgiving time, is when the butchering was done and then we would hang some of the meat in the woodshed to be consumed fresh.

People would preserve meat by putting it down in brine. Brine was made from salt and water. This was done in wooden vinegar barrels and I can still remember how the brine was tested for the right proportion of salt to water.

The amount of water to be used was put in the barrel and then salt was added as the mixture was stirred 'til it would float a fresh egg. The meat then was packed in this solution, not too tight so the brine could get to the meat freely but close enough to save room. It was surprising how much would go in a barrel. The cover was then placed on it loosely and this all took place in the woodshed, and there is where it stayed.

When meat was to be retrieved from the barrel, we had a long rod with a hook on the end of it and we would reach down in the barrel and hook a piece of meat, pull it out and take it to the house for cooking. This meat was what now is known as corned beef.

I don't know how long it would keep this way, but I remember how tired of this corned beef we would get along in the spring of the year and how glad I would be to come in the house and report to my mother that I had fished diligently with the long rod and I couldn't find any more meat in the barrel, after she had sent me to the woodshed to get meat for supper.

Sometimes my dad would smoke some of the fresh pork, like the hams and some of the bacon after it had been brined, in a different brine.

My mother would make butter, put it down in stone crocks with a cloth and salt on top of it, and store it in a cool place in the house and it would keep for a long time.

Eggs were another problem as it was necessary to store them sometimes to have them on hand when the chickens would quit laying, along in the fall of the year. They would molt (molting is when they shed most of the feathers and grow new ones for the cold weather to come).

To preserve eggs they were put in a stone crock and covered with a solution of water and sodium silicate called water glass, and put in a cool place where they wouldn't freeze and would keep indefinitely. Mother would have several stone two-gallon crocks filled with eggs to tide us over the time when the chickens laid few eggs, if any. Eggs kept in water glass are fine but they don't fry well. Our chickens never got much care in those days except in the wintertime, when they were kept in the chicken house all the time and were then fed on a regular basis. In the summertime, they ran loose, and the chicken house door was open all the time, day and night, leaving the chickens free to roam where they wished. A chicken will dig and scratch in the dirt and chase grasshoppers and find worms and can get by with very little care during the warm weather on a farm where they have lots of room. We would always give them a little wheat a couple of times a day and that would be it. Of course, they have to have water all the time.

As Dad was away or didn't have time because he would be working in the woods near home and wouldn't have time to go to town frequently for supplies we always had plenty of food on hand. My folks would go to town in the fall of the year and get about three or four 49 Lb. sacks of flour. A sack of sugar or sometimes two and that was 100 Lb. sacks, cases of canned vegetables, several cases of canned milk, 25 Lb. box of spaghetti, beans, rice, split peas, a case of soda crackers etc. I can't remember all the supplies that would be laid in. They bought syrup in two-gallon cans. We always had ham and bacon on hand. Mother made all of our bread, when we would get bakery bread we thought it was a treat. She always had dessert on hand and if someone came, anywhere near meal time, it was taken for granted that they would stay for whatever meal that was to be served.

That was the custom of the country in those times. If the cook didn't have enough prepared they always fell back on some ham or bacon and eggs, if more was needed baking powder biscuits was a good fall back and, if need be, milk gravy to go with them.

My mother could whip out a batch of biscuits in nothing flat and they were good too. The housewives of those early days were very resourceful; they had to be because the store was a long way away in terms of time. And too, when men got through working the stores closed also, so there was no going to the store after work, or on Sunday. Also, when a team had to be used for transportation it took time from whatever you were doing to get them ready, hooked up, make the trip and then put every thing away again. Sometimes the team or a single horse and buggy would be at the ranch even when Dad was gone or too busy but Mother couldn't harness a horse or hook one up. Neither could she drive, so that was out. The women of the time worked hard believe me, everyone did.

When we got the car things changed somewhat; however, for the first few winters the roads were still so poor that no one tried to drive a car during the winter or early spring because of the snow or mud, but things gradually improved to some extent

I was too small to hook up a horse yet but I knew how, just wasn't big enough to handle the horse collar and I couldn't have held a horse if it had decided to bolt, probably while driving.

Chapter 8

One of the big deals of that era for my brother and me was to get to go to Spokane. We would get to come once a year if we were lucky, and what an event that was. Sometimes we would come by way of Coeur d'Alene, on a steamboat from Harrison and then on the electric train from Coeur d'Alene to Spokane.

When we came this way the electric train usually consisted of two self propelled cars hooked together. The train backed out onto the dock in Coeur d'Alene so all you had to do was get off the boat and get right onto the train, no fanfare so to speak. When we got to Spokane, the train had a small depot where the McCain Public Library is now located and when you got out of the train you were practically on the street, known then as Trent Avenue. That was before they changed the name of the street, for the 1974 Spokane World's Fair, to Spokane Falls Boulevard. (It's a shame that the depot had to be torn down for the fair as it was a fine building, a piece of classic architecture.) Coming from the country as we did Spokane seemed even bigger. Don and I would be scared we would get lost from Mother as it was overwhelming. When we got into the station, with its many tracks, and the train stopped, we would get out of the train itself. There was always the conductor standing at the foot of the steps, with his portable step and a willing hand, to help ladies and little boys so that they didn't fall, which was impressive in itself considering that he was all dressed up in a nice, dark, blue suit with shiny brass buttons and a cap that said Conductor in gold letters right on the front of it. This gave him the look of real authority and confirmed that he would direct us toward the proper exit stairway.

We would go along the platform between the tracks and across several, always on the lookout for a stray train that might just happen to be using the track that we were crossing. Then down a covered stairway and through a short tunnel and then up a short flight of stairs and into the huge waiting room.

It was huge by any standards and had a high domed ceiling. There were all kinds of fascinating noises to be heard and sights to try to keep track of. First, there were the echoes of the activity going on in the huge room.

Sometimes there would be the station master calling out a departing train (at that time there were four different railroads using that same station with each having several different trains with many departure times, and different destinations). It was customary for the station master to call out the departing trains and their final destinations, as well as the stations where they would stop on the way there, in a very loud voice. His voice would echo from the high vaulted ceiling with (to me, at least) a sound of grandeur, and he would have to wait sometimes for the echo to die out before he could continue with his announcement as the sound went back and forth several times before it faded out.

I would be fascinated by the performance. To a small country kid this was highly entertaining and heavy stuff. There were many trains leaving for different places and this then was a ceremony to be looked forward to, for starters. Some of those train announcers were masters of the art and were showmen as well.

There would be people rushing about and men with little red caps carrying suitcases under their arms, as well as in their hands, for other people. Sometimes they had little carts with trunks on them, with pretty pictures on stickers on the trunks, that looked like they were stuck on and might fall off (which they never did) and that if one walked sort of backward and still kept track of the mother he might be able to salvage one for a souvenir.

Then there were the restrooms, which it seemed were always high on our mother's priority list. I don't think she ever missed a chance when there were facilities available, to take advantage of them. With all the distractions, noises coming from the street, and the strange plumbing and everything so spick and span, and all that clean water, about a whole bucket full in the vessel, which looked like you should be dipping a drink from it rather than making a deposit in it, it was hard to remember what you came in there for in the first place.

Then too there was always the fear that the mother would mysteriously disappear while you were absent, so that stop was cut short most times, sometimes to be regretted later but to be suffered in silence so as not to be the object of a scolding.

The next thing would be to claim our baggage. We would go down some more stairs to the street level and Mother would go to a sort of a low cut window that opened into another room with a low counter in it that was covered with some kind of shiny metal, and give a man our train ticket, and soon he would appear with our suitcase and, puzzling to me, he always had the right one. How he could get the right one, I didn't understand.

We then hit the street, where the sidewalk was as wide as our roads, and more noises, which were fascinating as well as distracting because a guy wanted to stop and see what all was going on. It was too much to take in and keep walking at the same time. However Mother didn't seem to appreciate the value of all this and would keep on going. So if one didn't want to get lost and abandoned forever, and maybe starve to death before one had time to grow up, he had to try to walk and keep up while looking backwards, which was hard.

Streetcars for example had noises all their own. They had a bell that the motorman stepped on, always twice, when he started up to warn people to get out of the way. They always went sort of clang-clang. The wheels had a squeal when they went around a corner that was made as they resisted the curve in the track. They made a lot of noise when they crossed another track going at a ninety-degree angle – bang-bang.

There were the sounds of the automobiles blowing their horns – auga, auga, auuuuuga (cars were quite new and few and there was a lot of horn blowing then). Then there was the sound of horses as they walked on the pavement – clip-clop, clip-clop, or when they trotted – clippety-clop, clippety-clop. On the street corners were newsboys or men selling papers. They would yell out in as loud a voice as they could muster "READ ALL ABOUT Ittttttt! READ ALL ABOUT Ittttttt!" and then recite the headline of the day. Then as you walked by, they would hold out a paper and say to the passer-by "Buy a paper Ma'am?" or "Buy a paper Mister?" Really exciting stuff when about the most exciting thing a small country boy saw or heard in the course of an average day was a team of horses and a wagon go by out on the county road, or on a rare day a car going by.

We would go to a certain street corner and stand around 'til a certain street car came along and Mother would get us in and away we would go. She sure was particular what streetcar we got on and would let some go by before she got one that would suit her. She wouldn't settle for the first one or sometimes not even the second or third one. I finally caught on that only one particular one went where we wanted to go, which was to our Uncle Johnnie's and Aunt May's house where we always stayed.

There were interesting things then that are no more. One of the sights was the Western Union boys darting around town on bicycles, delivering telegrams to people. They didn't call the messages on the phone as they later did, but hand delivered them. These riders were very expert and would dart in and out among the horses and the cars and street cars; they were real pros. There were also men who would deliver hot food on trays covered with a white cloth from certain restaurants. They always wore coolie type hats, black pants, and black shirts that hung out over their pants. They appeared to be Asians as they had long hair tied in a long pigtail that hung down their backs. They delivered to offices downtown at noontime, and they balanced those trays on their heads while they rode on bicycles. How they ever did it, I will never know. They didn't dart around like the Western Union boys but rode serenely along. I never did see one lose a tray but I always kept them in sight as long as I could, I guess hoping that they would. I never did see one when the weather was inclement either. I don't know what they did then.

One of the highlights of our trip was when we got to go to the ten-cent store and buy something. We would get to buy whatever we wanted if it didn't cost over twenty-five cents. This was always a big deal and we looked forward to it.

It was unbelievable all the things that were for sale, and we were careful to choose our selections wisely. I remember one time we each bought little horseshoe magnets with a little iron bar, fascinating little objects. Another time we each got little wrecking bars, another time hacksaws. That was it, we never got frivolous things nor did we ask for more, we knew where our limits were and were satisfied.

On one of our trips to Spokane when we got a little bigger, Mother took us to Natatorium Park, a big amusement park down near the river that no longer exists (regretfully). That was the optimum; boy that was something – Merry-go-round, rollercoaster (which Mother wouldn't let us ride on – too dangerous), a giant slide where you paid your nickel and they gave you a burlap sack. You climbed a mysterious set of stairs that were partly covered, with just enough light admitted to make them good and spooky, and then when you got to the top you put your sack in the top of the slide, sat on it and away you went down and around, in and out of the dark and over a big hump near the bottom. And out you came at the finish, all nice and scared but safe.

And there were little machines to look into to see little movies, and bumper cars you could drive around in an enclosure. These had spring bumpers all the way around them so that nothing would get hurt when you bumped into it, which happened all the time because they didn't steer in a conventional fashion so you were never quite sure where you were going. There were other things too, to see, such as a monkey in a cage, and a couple of peacocks, all interesting to us.

Once Mother took us to the zoo at Manito Park. That was a highlight, as we had never seen a real live bear or an ostrich or an elk, and many more eye popping sights to be talked about afterward. Incidentally, there was a huge polar bear there in a big cage with iron bars, and several years later a little girl got too close to the cage and the bear reached out and got her by the arm and pulled it off. The bear was destroyed after that episode.

On our trip home, if we had come by train, we would wait in the depot for the train master to make his announcement and then go up to the train and get in. Mother would find a place for us and soon the conductor would call out in a loud voice that could be heard even in the coaches "All aboardaaaaaa", and you could hear the steam engine puff and you could feel the train respond to the first few strokes of the steam pistons as the engine picked up speed. The train came out through Dishman and all the stations along the line would be called out by the conductor as he came through the cars and announced them before we got to them so people could prepare to get off. Some of the stations were just whistle stops.

I guess I had better explain what a whistle stop is. That was a stop that would be made if there was a passenger to get on or off the train there, otherwise the train didn't bother to stop. If you wanted to get the train at one of these stops, you waited 'til the train came into sight and then got in the middle of the track and waved to the engineer. And when he blew the whistle you knew he saw you and would stop. You then got off the track on the left hand side of the track facing the way the train was coming and they would stop for you, but not for long. When you boarded you paid the conductor your fare, which was of course based on your destination.

On one of our trips, we had come by way of Coeur d'Alene, and when we boarded the boat in Coeur d'Alene to go to Harrison, it happened to be summer time and the middle of the day and was warm. There were boys hanging around the dock beside the boat. They were in swimsuits and would call out to the men on the boat "Throw a nickel mister" and when someone did, they would dive in the lake and get it before it hit the bottom. Sometimes they would put the money in their mouth to keep it 'til they got to the dock again. We stood on the boat where we could look over the railing and, needless to say, were quite impressed with all this.

Once when Mother, Don and I were returning to our uncle and aunt's place about five in the evening we walked by the Heath House on Mission Avenue. The Heaths had homesteaded their property in the early days and had made a lot of money selling land for home sites, but had kept a whole square block for their home, which was a mansion. The back part of this property was fenced in with a high board fence. When we came walking by we could hear some blood-curdling, high-pitched yelling and yelping and howling coming from within this sort of a compound. It was scary to say the least. When we got almost past, there was a big knothole in the fence and I stole over and took a look in, and there was a big Indian man all decked out in Indian garb with headdress of feathers and all. Mother said he must have been practicing for some ritual or something. Well we couldn't leave the area fast enough for me. I thought for sure he would scalp me if he caught me looking at him. We found out later that Mr. Heath had many Indian friends and that sometimes they would pitch a tepee in the fenced-in area and stay for a time at the Heath place, and no doubt he was a welcome guest.

Speaking of Indians, in those days they would come to Spokane in the spring of the year and have an encampment out in Indian Canyon where the golf course is now located and have sort of a spring festival. They would pitch teepees and camp in them staying for several weeks, enjoying themselves and holding Indian ceremonies. This continued into the twenties after I had come to Spokane to live.

Chapter 9

A thing we used to enjoy for amusement was rolling hoops. The best hoops were obtained from an old wagon wheel that had been discarded. It was an iron band that went around the hub part of the wheel and was about a foot in diameter the large way of the rim and about an inch across the face of the rim. The metal was about three eights of an inch thick so it had just the right weight to be kind of stable. The stick was about three feet long or a little longer, with a short cross stick about six inches long nailed on the bottom end.

To roll the hoop you stood the hoop on its rim, put the stick behind it, and pushed. When you got a little better at roiling them you could just hook the hoop on the end of the cross piece and give it sort of a flip and away it would go. By turning the stick, you could maneuver the hoop wherever you wanted it to go. The idea was, I guess, to see how far it could be rolled without it falling over. When one became accomplished at this business the hoop could be jumped over obstacles such as sticks and limbs in the trail, you could run with it or walk, go in circles… many things to break the monotony. Many days I had rolled one to school and, of course, back again.

The Stilts

Another thing we used to do was walk on stilts. First, we had to build them. We would get two pieces of lumber about four feet long or a little longer and about an inch and a half on each side for the uprights. Then we would nail a block on each one about a foot or more, depending on how brave we felt, from one end to stand on. Then we would nail a leather strap from the top of the block to the upright main stem leaving just enough room for your foot to fit in under the strap and on top of the block.

This was for the purpose of holding the foot in place when you walked, which worked fine for holding but could be a real problem sometimes when one was in an emergency situation. Sometimes there was a great urgency to dismount with extreme haste, which happened rather frequently, it seemed, 'til one got the hang of things.

Sometimes a guy would trip or get off balance for some reason and then you would need one foot out of the strap almost immediately if not sooner to get on the ground and kind of sort things out. Well if you couldn't get your foot loose, you did sort of a one-legged hop dance on one stilt for a while, usually not long, and it was anything but graceful. Because of the inevitable certainty of the usually unpleasant ending, a guy put forth his best effort to forestall it as long as possible. Then came the grand crash and assessing the damages.

First off, you checked to see if all arms and legs were still attached, along with the head, and then to see how much skin was gone, then checked to see if everything worked. After this, one usually gave up stilting or whatever it's called, for awhile at least, 'til the scabs healed, or 'til one forgot how painful the last moments of the last attempt had been.

Rainy Days

Sometimes when we were real small Mother would be hard put to find amusement for us when the weather was real bad outside. One of the things she did was to soak dried peas in water and when they were soft she would give us some, and a supply of toothpicks, and we would make things like figures and animals, etc., using them as one would tinker toys. I don't think there were tinker toys then; if there were we never had seen them. We later got some, however, not a big assortment such as was shown on the box that you could make all sort of interesting things from but some simple things could be made.

Another thing she used to do under similar circumstances was to give us several pieces of thin paper that she kept hidden somewhere, that came on a roll and which had perforations about every eight inches for tearing it off if need be. This was quite thin and smooth; we would put it over a picture or a drawing or something and hold it on the windowpane and could trace an image on it with a pencil, if we were careful. Then again, if we were careful we could color on it with crayons. It was something for a rainy day.

It was sometime later in life that I discovered the real function of this nice thin paper was for personal sanitary purposes. Bless my mother's heart; I wish she were here today as I write this so I could thank her and express my appreciation for the things she did for us.

The New School

I think it was the summer of 1920 or it could have been '21 that the new school was built, and the old tarpaper shack was relegated to the use of a woodshed.

Boy, that was fancy when we got into the new building. We had a closet for our coats and boots, when they were worn, and a shelf for our lunches, a shelf for the water bucket and a wood box, to keep the firewood in, and an open-faced bookcase to keep the meager supply of books that belonged to the school in, and a shelf with a dictionary on it.

The New Harrison School — 1926

All the windows were on the north side, because north light was supposed to be the proper light for studying. It had a wood floor that was oiled once in a while to keep the dust down. The floor was nice and solid and had no holes in it so one didn't have to worry about dropping something small for fear it would go down a knothole never to be retrieved again. Too, the building was nice and tight so no mice could get in and eat your stuff.

We had a nice big blackboard, big to us anyway, about three by four feet and one little one, and a map of the U.S. hanging on the wall. We considered ourselves quite modern and up to date.

The Cowboy Story

I have to tell about the story that we used to tell each other every so often when we had a listening audience. This was told several times during the course of the eight grades that I went to school there but whoever elected to tell it was always listened to politely and was never interrupted or corrected by any one of the listeners even though they had heard it before.

It seems that a cowboy was caught out on the range overnight and, not being prepared, he did what all tough old cowboys do, he unsaddled his horse, tied one end of his lariat around the horse's neck and the other end around his ankle so that his horse could graze without wandering away, took off his boots, laid his head on his saddle and went to sleep. In the morning he woke up all stiff and sore, it was daylight and when he looked down at his feet, he discovered he had a large hole in one of his socks and his big toe was sticking out. That was bad, but the worst of it was that a big tarantula was sitting squarely on that toe.

He was terror stricken because he thought the bite of the beast would poison him and it would be almost instant death, and if he moved he was sure to be bitten. (I much later in life found this is a myth and not true, and if they are treated gently, they won't hurt you).

Well he didn't know what to do. He was afraid if he moved even a little bit he would receive a deadly bite and that would be the end of him; what a dilemma. Being used to hardship and being very tough, after careful deliberation he cautiously removed his trusty 44 pistol from its holster and, taking careful aim, shot his big toe off and that, of course, took care of the spider, solving one problem but creating another.

We never knew any more so that, of course, was the end of the story. We would listen attentively, even when we knew the outcome. We would end up being all scared and big-eyed, with chills running up and down our backs, and sober-like, and we'd check, in as casual a manner as one could without being observed by any of the others, to be sure that we were not sitting next to a tarantula, or that there wasn't one on your own foot that you hadn't noticed yet.

We would discuss it and admire the hero and how brave he must have been, secretly feeling grateful that we didn't have to live like that but expressing outward confidence that that is just what we would have done if we had been faced with similar circumstances. Funny what little country boys will do for amusement.

The Sled with the Headlight

The winters were long and the days were short and by the time my brother and I got home from school and did a few chores it would be dark, and so this didn't leave much time to play in the daylight. One of our favorite leisures of the wintertime when we had a lot of snow and it stayed on the ground for some time, was sledding, which was called coasting in those times. It was a form of recreation that we used to enjoy, but the short daylight was somewhat of a problem. The only place that we had a hill was out on the county road, which was about a quarter of a mile from our house. When it had snowed a lot and stayed on the ground a while without any new snow the road would get packed down real hard and would get nice and slick from the horses and big sleighs that would use the road and it made a good place to coast.

We could go out to the county road and coast in the dark, but you couldn't see too good at times and one of the hazards of this was the chunks of snow that would come off the horses' hooves. They were big lumps of snow and ice that would build up and pack inside the horse shoes and the poor horse would be walking on these big lumps which would be very uncomfortable for them as they would get kind of round on the bottom. Every team driver carried a chunk knocker in the sleigh (a big heavy stick or club) to knock the chunks of snow and ice off the bottom of the horses' feet if they didn't fall off by themselves when they got to be too high, and the horse was having trouble keeping his balance on that particular foot.

The driver would stop, get the club and hit the hoof of the horse and they would usually come loose. Well anyway, when one was coasting in the dark and hit one of these big chunks it wasn't usually too much fun because one of two things usually happened. If the sled ran up on one of them it stopped but you didn't and then you got off in a very unconventional manner, becoming sort of airborne, as you were usually laying on your stomach on the sled. And when dismounting (if it could be called that) you sort of became airborne in a spread eagle fashion and soared briefly like a crippled airplane coming in for a belly landing and sailed through the air briefly, not having time to get your nose gear up, resulting in a nose first crash in the hard packed snow and ice.

The other consequence was that you tipped over and that could result in the same unpleasant experience of having your nose plowed rather vigorously in the hard packed snow in a somewhat harsh fashion. If you have never had this experience when your nose was good and cold you wouldn't believe how quickly this can change your mind about what is fun and what isn't. In other words, it took some of the joy out of things for a while and it was an experience to be avoided if possible.

We had no flashlights and no way to come up with a light. After giving this problem due thought and some consideration, my engineering instincts took over and I figured that I could make a headlight. I took a gallon fruit can and cut a hole in the front of it for the light to come out of, and nailed it to a short board, then wired the board to the front of the sled. The top of the can had already been cut out so the fire could have a vent. We had pitchy wood for kindling to start fires in the stoves, so this was ideal for a good, quick little fire and would burn hot and the wind was not apt to blow it out. I also made one of these devices for my brother and his sled. I was so enamored with my invention I wanted to share its benefits with him also.

Well, one night after supper when the chores were done and we had all the preparations made ahead of time, we took off for the hill. We had a good supply of pitchy wood for our little headlight fires and all systems were go. We didn't light them up till we got out of sight of the house because it would have entailed answering a lot of questions and would have wasted a lot of time. And besides, sometimes you were better off not to discuss events before the fact because things could get out of hand and rather complicated, and if the plan, whatever it might be, didn't meet with approval, after censorship it could result in complete shut-down, which could be very disappointing after having put a lot of serious thought and time into a project. Sometimes my folks didn't quite understand my feats of ingenuity, and on occasion didn't seem to fully appreciate the obvious talent and ingenious ability I seemed to be gifted with. Their intentions were good, of course, but on occasion they had some rather narrow views of some of my experiments (at least I thought so anyway) so sometimes it was just simpler to go ahead without consultation.

We could hardly wait to try out the new invention and see how it was going to work. We soon had good little fires going and we were ready for kickoff, so to speak, which we did in a high state of glee, which was short lived. I lost track of my brother, Don, shortly and at this time I can't remember what happened to him. The reason I did was that pretty soon I got real busy. When I got up speed, and that wasn't long, things kind of got out of hand rather quickly. The first thing was that the light was kind of feeble and I couldn't see where I was going too good. Another reason was that I had fire in the face and I determined why. The fire was coming up out the top of the can where only smoke and a draft was supposed to come. Because the wind was coming in the front, the fire was getting a mighty good draft. The fire was hitting me right in the face. I determined that different arrangements had to be made with great haste if I was to have any eyebrows left, or eyelashes either. I didn't worry about whiskers because I wasn't old enough to have any yet, but if I had had any they would have been well scorched.

Before I had time to come up with something – and believe me I was working on it – a turn of events solved the decision making problem for me in rapid fashion. Not in a manner that I would have chosen, exactly, if I had had a choice, but the truth of the matter was that I was in the driver's seat but I suddenly realized I wasn't driving and I sort of wished that I was somewhere else doing something else about then. Well, I hit one of those road hazards and it was a big one. It wasn't that I was a poor driver; it was because I was preoccupied with a little fire in my face which was somewhat disconcerting, to say the least.

Occasionally a guy has a better after-thought than forethought and this was one of those times. This seems to happen more when one is young for some reason. When the sled hit that big chunk of snow and ice, it went up in the air and there was fire and burning wood and sled and hot tin can and kid all over the road at the same time. As soon as I was able to get my face out of the hard packed snow and scrape the snow out of my eyes so I could see, I promptly got myself interested in where the fire was in relation to me. It turned out there were bits and pieces of burning wood all around. There were some hot nails steaming in the snow too, that I hadn't counted on. I was able to distance myself from anything that was glowing in the dark in short order and kind of take stock of everything else. All legs were still there and two arms. I could still see and hear the hot items sizzling in the snow, so I knew my head was still attached. Things weren't too bad after all. One other little detail I had overlooked in my calculations was the fact that the nails would get hot and burn themselves loose in the wood and then I wouldn't have any way to hold my headlight in place.

I slowly began to realize that I had made a few miscalculations in my design engineering. That was one of those times when I sort of wished I had consulted with my dad first as he seemed to have a knack of seeing what might happen ahead of time, maybe it was because he had lived so long.

Well, I never did bother to take it up with him because I knew he would have said that I should have had those things figured out in the first place, and in looking back, I guess he would have been right.

I can't, after all these years, remember how my brother came out, but I guess OK or I would remember. He probably lost some of his faith in my inventions, for the time being, at least.

The Smoking Experiment

I think it was in this time frame some time that my brother Don and I decided to have a smoke. We didn't have very good equipment or material but that didn't matter, at least to start with it didn't; we thought we could improvise. Our dad rolled his own cigarettes all the time so we had a good idea how to go about it or so we thought at least. He had tobacco and nice thin cigarette paper. When he got the tobacco rolled up nice and neat in the paper he would lick the side of the paper and press it down against the other side and then pinch one end, stick the other end in his mouth, light the other end and he was in business. We had neither cigarette paper nor tobacco, but figured we could make do.

We got some string from the string ball in the house to hold the paper together and stole some matches from the kitchen when no one was looking. We were not allowed to have matches but we got some, and hid them and the string for the experiment. We had sunflowers as seed to feed the chickens in the wintertime so we got some dried sunflower leaves to serve as tobacco and we were all set.

Came Saturday morning and as there was no school we figured it would be a good time to try out this experience that seemed to be so enjoyable to our dad. The outhouse seemed to be a logical place for this, as we would be more or less assured of privacy, and probably be able to avoid detection there.

It was our custom to make a visit to this little establishment every morning right after breakfast, and we usually went together. Sometimes it was mostly a social venture as we would sit and look at the pictures in the catalogues and do a lot of wishful thinking and forget what the purpose of the visit was in the first place. My mother was very determined that this chore be carried out without fail and with great punctuality, whether you were in the mood or not.

I should explain that we had a reasonably comfortable seat, with two holes, and as the door faced south onto a big open field no one could observe the occupants. So when the sun was shining the door could be left open and it could be turned into a somewhat pleasant chore if one could ignore the sometimes odiferous atmosphere and you didn't stay too long. If you did, your backside got grooves in it the shape of big horseshoes because the holes had been cut with a keyhole saw and were rough on the edges. If this became the case, it got painful enough to motivate one to accomplish the original goal and get off your paralyzed butt.

This then was a place for two small boys to contemplate worldly affairs and other important matters. Well, back to my story. As I said, it was real cold and clear. We went to the place and got our material all ready, and when we rolled the cigarettes, they looked like cigars because the paper was stiff and they were so big. When we licked the paper it wouldn't stick, but we had expected this so we bound them up with the string and pinched one end just as we had seen our dad do.

The sunflower leaves were very dry and brittle and were not good for this sort of thing, and kept falling out, but that was the best we had. When we finally got them done, they looked like they were in good enough shape to set on fire.

We hadn't done our homework very well though because we forgot to factor in the fact that the material we were using was very porous. When we lit them and had puffed a couple of times we got not only smoke but fire as well, and this was not good, believe me. It wasn't in the plan of things – fire in your mouth – not a bit good, not one bit enjoyable. I quickly came to the realization that I would never have to do that one over again. I also realized I had just made another mistake. The leaves and the paper were full of air passages and there was nothing to prevent the fire from coming into your mouth when it got a little draft, which was furnished when one puffed.

We both got a dose of fire about the same time and without even stopping to think we threw them both down one of the holes. They were burning pretty good about this time and as there was lots of loose paper sticking up, it immediately caught fire down in the pit. Boy, we not only had felt like we had just eaten something hotter than we had ever tasted before but we had a full-blown fire on our hands. I told Don to go to the house and get some water and I made a dash for the snow outside.

The trouble with that was that there was a hard crust on it. Nevertheless, I tore into it with everything I had and managed to scrape up some and carried it in, throwing it down one of the holes, never taking time to see what effect it had, and went back for more. I was frantic; it was tough getting snow with that hard crust on it. When I made the next trip, as I came out the door I met Don with the water. He had taken the dipper from the water pail in the kitchen and ran all the way with it, but when he got there, he must have had all of a tablespoon full left. We threw what he had down one of the holes and then looked in to see how things were coming along down there.

Lo and behold, and much to our surprise and relief, the fire had just about burned itself out as it just burned the paper that was sticking out and that which was loose. The pit was deep and the flames were not very high, not high enough to get the wood of the outhouse on fire. This we should have been able to figure out for ourselves but we were too excited to use common sense when we found out what a predicament we were in.

We were lucky on that one. Don got the dipper back without Mother even missing it and Dad was in the barn and didn't see the smoke. Don and I got busy and tore up a bunch of paper and threw it down the hole, and as no one was particularly interested in checking the contents of this depository very often as it wasn't something people gazed on for enjoyment, such as a beautiful landscape, no one ever knew the difference.

I was careful not to expose my knuckles for a few days, so as not to have to explain how they got scratched up so bad when I was digging that crusted snow. Needless to say, we had enough of smoking for a while.

My Brother Don and I in front of our Harrison, Idaho home (I'm on the left)

The Cat and the Kite

We didn't have many things that were bought in a store to keep us entertained, therefore we were left to improvise our own amusement a good deal of the time. Sometimes our efforts were rather crude but occasionally we would come up with something rather interesting and at times rather ingenious.

Well so it is with this story. A neighbor man who my brother and I thought of lot of and who was always good to us, taught us how to make a kite. Well, this was a real revelation to us as we had never seen one before. We had heard of them but lacked the engineering ingenuity to design one on our own without a pattern to go by. Needless to say, we got quite interested in it and soon devoted all of our spare time to making them and flying them. Or at least I did anyway. As I had more chores to do I didn't have as much spare time as my brother did. We got into this and were dedicated to our task, and as a result did quite well at it considering the handicaps we had to contend with. To begin with, we didn't have very good paper to use, only store paper and old newspaper which wasn't much good; it was weak and tore easily.

Sometimes we could con my mother out of a paper bag. We couldn't do this very often because they were scarce and hard to come by, but when we could we would take them apart and carefully flatten them out, for they were stronger and would stand the ravages of winter better than anything else we could get our hands on.

Another problem was with string. The only thing available to us – or so we thought to start with anyway – was store string. In those days when you bought something in a store it had to be wrapped in paper and tied with a string as nothing came wrapped as it does today. Our mother kept a ball of string, as everyone did then, and when anything came from the store, the string was carefully saved and wound onto the string ball, which everyone did in those times. If you needed string for any occasion this is where it came from. This was an important part of every household at the time. String was used for a good many purposes, for instance when you cut a finger, which was a common occurrence when whittling, an endeavor engaged in very often as a great part of a farm boy's life, and could be quite a hazardous pastime before one learned not to whittle toward a part of your anatomy such as a finger. When this happened – and it seemed to be quite often, to me at least (I guess I was a slow learner) – the finger had to be wrapped with a clean rag and tied with a piece of string, usually accomplished by one's mother.

In those days, there were no band aids or adhesive tape as we know it today and which we all take for granted. Well, the string wasn't up for grabs either, so to speak, and when a guy needed some you usually had to make a pretty good case in order to get it, which on occasion was hard to do because the mother was the protector of the string ball. The string was poor stuff at best and was full of knots, not too strong either.

Another problem was the wood to make the frame. All we had that was thin enough and light enough was box wood, as everything that came by the case came in wooden boxes at that time. And as we lived quite a way from town, considering that everything was walking or team and wagon, my folks bought a good part of our canned goods by the case.

We had plenty of box wood but it was too short after we got into this kite-making thing in earnest. We had a great time with kites – it was springtime, with lots of wind, but we did have a couple of problems as I mentioned before, the greatest of which was the string. The paper we could overcome by pasting two pieces together with flour and water and making two ply of it, staggering the seams. We could get by with this but the string would give us no end of trouble. However, in spite of all the obstacles we got quite proficient at the art of kite-making and had a lot of fun.

It was, as I mentioned before, the spring of the year and there was plenty of wind; however, when we would get the kite flying nicely an extra strong gust of wind would come along and the darn string would break and down would come the kite. Then we would have to start all over again. Well, our dad had a binder for harvesting wheat and oats and it used real heavy coarse twine. We liberated some of this from the binder while my dad was away (some things were more easily accomplished without asking). There was always the hope that it would never be detected, which sometimes was a pretty good risk we would be willing to take after grave consideration. To us, the action could be justified by telling oneself the consequences were worth that risk by achieving the goal. At least as I look back I think that was the thinking.

The binder twine didn't break but it was so heavy that the kites couldn't get up in the air. We needed bigger ones to take care of the string problem. That was going to require bigger wood for frames. There was an abandoned homestead about a mile from our place down in a canyon that had just the thing we needed. They, in earlier times, had put up high picket fences to keep deer from eating the garden and the apple trees. These pickets were made of nice straight cedar trees and they were nice and dry and light, and being straight, they split very well. We went back there and acquired some of them the first chance we had and that took care of the wooden frame problem.

The wood was ideal so we made some big kites with this, as it was nice to work with. They were at least five feet high and about three feet wide, surely that would pull the twine.

We worked on this project during the week and Saturday we were ready to go, and so was the wind. Well, it worked out well and was a great success. In fact, it worked so well that we had to get some gloves to hold the twine as it cut into your hands. This was fine for awhile but we tired of this and wanted to figure out some way that we could get a ride out of it. This was impossible we knew, but yet we wanted something more (success went to our heads, I guess).

My brother and I each had a cat and they were about half grown. The name of mine was Tippie and he had the misfortune of going by when we were casting about for someone small enough to send up for a ride. He was a nice gentle pet up till that time. We got busy and rigged up a harness with leather strips and secured Tippie in it real good as we rather thought that he wasn't going to cooperate too much in this type of endeavor.

We hooked him up so that he would dangle down from the kite about eighteen or twenty inches, as it appeared he was becoming tangled up in the rigging and we thought that would complicate things further as we were already having trouble convincing the cat that this little experience was going to be fun (some cats are dumb).

When we got everything in place, we waited for a big gust of wind and we launched him. Everything worked just as we had planned – our engineering skills were right on. The only hitch in the whole operation was that the cat didn't seem to be enjoying it too much, which was rather disappointing to us as we thought it was great, the first astronaut, at least in our experience. Well, maybe not the first aviator, but I'll bet it was the first cat aviator.

Well, we got him up pretty high, like about three hundred feet I would estimate, and flew him around for quite a while till we got tired of it. I think the cat got tired of it before we did. In fact, I think the cat was tired of it before he ever got off the ground by his attitude, as he became less cooperative all the time. But he wasn't exactly in the driver's seat, so to speak, or if he had been I am sure the flight would never have gotten off the ground and if it had, it would have been much shorter than it was. In fact, if he had been, it probably never would have occurred in the first place and then this experiment would have been forever lost to mankind (that is, that cats do not like to go up in kites).

It appeared to us that there was going to be somewhat of a problem with the astronaut when he came down. The way he was acting we didn't think he was going to stick around long enough for us to congratulate him on his pioneering achievement, so we got ready with big leather gloves from the blacksmith shop and reeled him in. We had a good sharp knife ready to cut him loose when he landed, as he seemed to be in a rather impatient mood if yowling, writhing and hissing were an indication of impatience (we thought it was). We finally got hold of him, which wasn't easy, long enough to cut him out of the harness and away he went, which is a gross understatement.

The dirt wasn't firm enough for him to get a good toehold and he dug it up for the first few leaps as he tried to set another record, this time for drag racing or whatever you would call a fast getaway from a standing start. At that time I don't know who was in the most disfavor, my brother and I or the kite. His tail was sticking straight up like a small flag pole and he was really talking to himself. Boy, if ever there was a wild cat, that was one wild cat.

We didn't see him for a few days after that. We got the impression that our friendship had been put on hold, for a while at least. In the evening and again in the morning when I milked the cows, I always milked some milk into a coffee can for the cats, but Tippie didn't show up. After three or four days, I saw him just barely peeking around the barn door, but when I made a move, he was gone in a flash. Eventually, we got to be friends again, but it took a long time before he had confidence in me after that episode and I think he never did trust me to the same degree he did before our great experiment.

Chapter 10

One winter we had a lot of snow and it got deep. We kids had heard of ski jumps but none of us had ever even seen pictures of them. We had no concept of what they were like – but they sounded great. It has to be remembered that this was a long time ago, and there was no radio, no television, and there were not many sports then, for average people to partake in, especially if you lived in the country as we did. I guess they ski jumped in Switzerland or somewhere, but they didn't where we were.

Our neighbor kid, Buster Jarrard, got hold of some old weather-beaten wooden skis that someone had made out of boards. They were a far cry from skis as they are known today. They were just boards with the ends turned up a little bit and a strap over the top about the middle for your feet. They were heavy and very hard to manage, but that was what we had. We thought that was the way all skis were made.

My dad had a haystack that he had been feeding the cattle from. It was lower on one end than the other, sloping down from the high end, which was about twelve to fourteen feet high, to the low end, which was about five feet high. The length between the ends must have been at least fifty feet.

The snow was deep – two feet at least, maybe three – and of course the stack was covered to the same depth. There was a heavy crust on it – thick enough for us kids to walk on without breaking through. Buster had the skis at our place one day when there was no school, and we were looking for some place to try a ski jump. When we saw the haystack, we thought, this is it! We were not permitted to play on the haystacks, as when you walk on hay that has been stacked for a while, it packs down where you walk. Then when it rains, the water runs down into the hay causing it to spoil. We figured because of the snow this wouldn't count, and so to the stack we went.

Buster, being a manipulator, talked me into trying the first jump. He was very willing to help me get situated on the high end of the stack and held the skis for me while I got my feet into the straps. When I was ready, he turned me loose. I thought I was ready, at least, but as soon as I was on my way I thought that over pretty quick and said to myself, "Custer, you have made a mistake", but there was no turning back.

The crust was firm and I gained speed rapidly, covering the distance to the jump in an incredibly short time, but when I got there, I wasn't ready for this jumping business. No turning back, no stopping – I was committed. Soon I was airborne, briefly, as the skis turned down over the end of the stack and stood on end, then stuck straight down into that hard-crusted snow at the end of the stack. That wasn't all that took place. My feet stayed in the straps and my head and shoulders made a big arc and when I came down, my head went through that hard crust and into the snow and there I hung. I was standing on my head, so to speak, feet in the straps, head in the snow under that crust. There I was with the hard crust of that snow around my neck. I couldn't get out and I couldn't get any air – not enough anyway. I thought for sure I was going to smother before Buster could tramp down that crust around my neck and help me get out. Needless to say, that was the only ski jump run made.

School Lunches

During the winters when the weather was cold, the teacher would sometimes assign one family to bring soup for the whole school (anywhere from five to eight or nine kids) for the day. We had a big heating stove and about half an hour before lunchtime, she would put the kettle on the stove. When it was time to eat, we would all enjoy hot soup.

There were never many kids so it wasn't hard to take care of. This was something to be looked forward to, as every mother had some different kind of soup. Even if it was the same kind, it had a different taste to it, and we enjoyed it. Our mother always made good, thick kinds with lots of meat and vegetables or other goodies in it. Some of the kids would bring soup that was kind of watery, and one family who were kind of poor always brought potato soup. It was the same kind every time – and it wasn't very good at that. We didn't look forward to their turn with too much anticipation. In fact, I never have liked potato soup much since then. Nevertheless, it was a break in the monotony

(Many years later, I had the pleasure of meeting one of the girls we went to school with, Myrna Jarrard, one of Buster's two sisters. In our conversation during our visit, she mentioned how much she and her brother and sister, Babe, used to look forward to the times when it was Don and my turn to bring the soup, as it was always so good. I wished our mother had been there to hear the compliment – I'm afraid she got many fewer than she deserved.)

The Tomahawk

I recall an incident that is somewhat humorous, depending on how you look at it. One day, the teacher was going to keep one of the girls after school for some infraction of her commands or rules. I can't after all this time recall what the trouble was over, but Babe (the girl's nickname) wasn't about to stay when the rest of us were going home. The teacher went to Babe's desk to push her down on her seat, but Babe stood up, refused to stay in her desk as she'd been told. Babe reached into her desk and drew out her wooden tomahawk. (We were into an Indian war phase at the time and we all had homemade wooden weapons). Babe threatened the teacher with her tomahawk. The teacher (I can't recall which one it was at the time) gave up on that pretty fast and that would be the end of it. We all kind of figured the teacher would retaliate in some form, but she never did.

I guess by modern standards, this would be nothing, but at that time, it was unheard of, and we were all scared.

The Smith House Fire

This event took place after the Jarrard family moved away so there were not as many pupils in the school as there had been. One time the teacher sent two of the little kids to the Smith house to get a pail of water. It was, as I remember, early afternoon and they hadn't been gone very long when they were back, all out of breath and big-eyed. They came into the schoolroom without the water bucket and waited politely near the door for the teacher to finish explaining whatever it was she was talking about. When she got around to it, she turned to them and asked, "Where is the water bucket?" The reply was, "Smith's house is on fire. Mrs. Smith didn't give us any water."

This news took everyone by surprise, of course, and a little while to sink in – longer for the teacher than for the two Smith sisters, Josephine and Dorothy. They immediately jumped up and started out the door. Henry Kuehl and I looked at each other and at the teacher for directions. She didn't say anything and seemed kind of stunned. We were the two biggest in the school at the time, but when we looked to her for directions like, "You can be excused to go help with the fire". But she was too overwhelmed to say anything.

Well, it was unthinkable to get up from your desk without permission, must less leave the room or the school. Without waiting for permission, Henry and I rose together and bolted for the door, half expecting to be called back. We heard nothing, and wouldn't have stopped if we had.

There was no form of fire protection whatsoever, and only the well for a water supply. The water had to be pulled up from a depth of forty feet, so it was not what you would call readily accessible. Well, we soon passed up the two Smith sisters and believe me, they were giving it all they had. When we got to the Smith place about an eighth of a mile away, Mrs. Smith was at the well pulling up some water with her two little kids gathered around her. The fire was on the roof of the house near the chimney, but there was no way to get up there. Henry or I asked for the ladder and she said, "It is leaning against the woodshed."

We told her to keep on pulling up water and pouring it on the roof. We got the ladder, and what a ladder it was. The rungs were breaking loose from the rails and it probably wouldn't have supported a full-grown man. Henry and I managed to clamber up there with a little water, and a good thing for us the roof was low pitch (meaning it wasn't steep). About this time, the girls arrived.

I might add here that Henry and I were about the same age – twelve at the time – and the girls were about ten and eleven. We hollered at them to start carrying water to us from the washtub and handing it to us on the roof as fast as they could, which they did. They couldn't carry a full bucket and hand it up to Henry or me, so when we got it, it would only be about half full. We used it to pour on the hottest places, but it wasn't coming fast enough. We were losing ground, so I started tearing shingles off with my bare hands. I would try to get hold of them where they were not burning, tear them loose and throw them to the ground. Some I couldn't get loose because they were too tight or too hot. After while, someone found time enough to get me a claw hammer, and then I was in business.

We had a good crew, but soon Mrs. Smith couldn't pull water up fast enough. However, it wasn't too long till we were gaining on the fire and then soon had it under control. Then we were able to conserve the water and use it to good advantage and get the fire completely out. I had peeled off quite a few shingled, and suffered a few minor burns on my hands, but if I hadn't pulled them off, we would never have been able to save the house.

After we got the fire out, we all stood around talking about it, trying to get our wind. Of course, we were all very excited. Mr. Smith drove up with his team of horses, having been away somewhere. His wife and the children all gathered around him, all trying to talk at once. If it hadn't been for Henry and me, they would have lost their house. Mrs. Smith was high in her praise for us, saying that if we hadn't taken the lead, it would have been a disaster, as she didn't know what she would have done. She was glad to have someone take over and tell everyone what to do. Of course, this made Henry and me feel like little heroes. When we had time to look around, there was the teacher. Maybe she got the hammer; I don't know, I was too busy to look. It sure helped, whoever got it.

Well, we had the teacher with us, so we all went back to school when things quieted down, with the exception of the Smith sisters, who stayed to help their mother clean up. The water came down inside the house and through the ceiling and it was a mess. Needless to say, there wasn't much studying the rest of that afternoon.

The Soldering Irons

Burgan's store in Spokane used to be a general store and had a catalog department carrying nearly everything, including groceries, clothing, furniture, hardware and tools, nearly as much merchandise as the Sears or Montgomery Ward stores that were the big catalog stores of the day. Buying from a catalog was very common for people in the country then as the small town stores couldn't carry a very big inventory. People could order from the catalog and it was quite satisfactory and a common way of life.

A neighbor (the one who taught us how to make kites) was a great fellow with kids, and since he and his wife had no children, he took a fond interest in Don and me. Their name was Alman, Roy being his first name. My brother and I were allowed to call him Roy instead of Mr., which was unusual, but we always called his wife Mrs. Alman.

Roy had a blowtorch which burned gasoline (fascinating), as our dad did not have one. Roy was a great one to make things out of tin and then solder them with his torch and soldering iron. One time he took an empty five gallon coal oil can (called kerosene nowadays), and made a toy boat out of the tin with his blowtorch and a soldering iron. It was a cute little boat and he gave it to Don and me. We didn't have any water to play in except the watering trough but we had a lot of fun with it nevertheless. This gave us the idea to get a soldering iron each so that we could make things from tin cans.

Burgan's department store in Spokane had them listed in their catalog, little ones and big ones. We had a little money, enough to order an iron each, and some solder from the wish book (as they were commonly referred to then), and a little bar of salammoniac (a flux to be used to make the solder adhere to whatever it was that was being soldered).

Mother helped us make out the order, getting the right numbers and all the technical stuff like the address etc. She wrote out a check, we gave her our money, then we put the letter in the mailbox, and sure enough, that same day it was gone. Then came the really hard part, waiting for the merchandise to show up.

Well, in due course the irons came and they were just dandy; we were all fixed. We didn't have a torch but we would use the kitchen stove when Mother wasn't busy cooking something and had a fire going. We would leave the door of the firebox open and could lay the irons in the fire and leave the handles sticking out on the firebox door and it worked pretty well.

Sometimes there would be a conflict of interest and Mother would want to use her stove, and then after a protest, which we always lost, we would have to postpone our project (and of course always at a critical time), which could be a great inconvenience, especially when a guy had some important project going, which was usually the case.

Little Steam Engines

We got an idea of how to make a toy paddle wheel steam engine, and I will explain it here as briefly as I can; however, if I don't explain in some detail the story will be somewhat meaningless.

First, we had to get a small flat-sided tin can that had held some sort of liquid and that had a small spout with a screw top. This was so that we could put water in it and seal it up again to hold the water and steam. Then we would make a little paddle wheel out of tin can tin and get a piece of nice straight wire for the shaft and solder this to the wheel. Then we would make two little stands out of some of the same material, to hold the shaft of the paddle wheel so that the shaft and wheel could turn freely. We then poked a small hole in one side of the can and this then became the top of the engine. We then mounted the stands with the shaft and wheel over the hole in the can so that when steam came out it would hit the paddles and turn the wheel. All these junctures were then soldered in place and we were ready to go.

We each had one and we would fill the little water tank about half full of water and screw the lid on tightly and set them on the kitchen stove. As the stove top was big and flat, and hotter in some areas than others, we would pull or push them around with the stove poker so that they would heat up and then they would start to sizzle and the paddle wheel sure would go.

We had to be careful so that they didn't get too hot or we knew that they would blow up. Our only safety feature was to watch the can and when it started to bulge, pull it to a cooler spot on the stovetop very quickly before it did blow up. We realized the danger but didn't appreciate the folly of our ways. Mother didn't seem to appreciate the hazard we were exposed to, as she never commented to us or made us quit. We didn't bother to inform her, as we were afraid that would have been the end of our experimental engines and the fun. We did know if Dad were around when we ran our little engines, he would have shut us down in a hurry. We got away with it and never did have any trouble. Strange what poor judgment some kids have with regard to hazards. I guess I must have been one of them.

The Hats

One time when our dad was working away from home and only got home on Saturday nights he came home bringing Don and me each a hat. Not just ordinary hats, but campaign hats! A campaign hat is what the soldiers wore during World War One. This time frame was shortly after World War One and we were very proud of these hats. (They are the kind that Smoky the Bear wears.) We wore them everywhere and would have worn them to bed if Mother had permitted it.

One day Mother and we kids, my brother and I, got a ride to town with one of the neighbors and of course, we wore the hats with great pride. While our mother was in one of the stores Don and I were walking down the main street minding our own business, when across the street a kid by the name of Bridgeman, (a town smart aleck, the hardware man's son) saw us and hollered out in a loud voice for everyone to hear in a very sarcastic manner, "Look at the country rubes with the hats."

Boy, that was fighting language to me and so I made a run for him. He was a tall skinny kid and he took off like he had the fear in him, and rightly so. I was insulted, humiliated and mad all at the same time. He had quite a lead on me as I had to cross the street to get to him, but I didn't hesitate. I was making good time and gaining on him but we came to his house before I could catch him. (They lived right on the end of Main Street.) He made the porch and ran in the door, closing it just as I got to the foot of the steps. I was afraid to go up on the porch, and besides he was in the house and I could hear him hollering for his mother and I knew he would get her in it and then she would get my mother and it would get completely out of hand so I had to give up on that one, but I had visions of how he was going to look with blood running down from his nose. It was a good thing for him that he made it home first because I was going to give him a darn good lesson in having more respect for country kids. I never did like that kid before that and less after but I never had any more trouble with him; he sort of shied away from me from then on.

It was a funny thing, but the town kids thought they were superior to we country kids and made fun of us when they had a chance, that is when we were not with our folks. We didn't have it as good as they did and we were country bumpkins to be sure but we were not smart alecks looking for trouble; however some of us didn't run from it either, when it came to a showdown. I always felt and resented this attitude but did not let it intimidate me one darn bit.

It was common for all farms to have dogs, cattle type dogs usually, and they seemed to have an affinity with the horses. They seemed to enjoy each other's company and when the team went somewhere very frequently the dogs just went along unless they were made to stay home. Well, if a country dog went to town with a team, you could just bet he would get in at least one fight while there or sometimes several. I guess those town dogs were kind of troublesome too.

Halloween

One Halloween Buster Jarrard came up to our place and Mother let us go out with him. He was good at doing things that we would not have thought about on our own. He suggested we go to Mr. Farmers place and pull some kind of caper on him.

When we got there we didn't know what to do, but after scouting around a little, we hit on something. Mr. Farmer was in the process of building a new root cellar. This was a building for storing vegetables, apples, etc., during the winter and for that matter, the year around, as it was well insulated and was warm in the cold weather and cool during the warm weather. They were built with a double wall with about eighteen inches between the walls and then this space was filled with sawdust for insulation.

He had the walls up but didn't have the roof on yet so that the walls stood there open at the top. There were a lot of board trimmings, ends, etc., scattered around, so we gathered up a lot of this stuff and dropped it down between the walls where he couldn't get it out without getting down in there and it had to be removed before he put the sawdust in. Well, we were congratulating ourselves all the way home on the neat trick we had pulled on Mr. Farmer because he would have so much trouble cleaning this area out. He wasn't one of our favorite characters anyway (kind of an old busybody) or we wouldn't have done it in the first place, and I will define that observation a little bit in the next story. Well, the old boy was smarter than we gave him credit for and the next day we were to find that out.

About noontime at school the next day, Mr. Farmer came to the school and knocked on the schoolhouse door. The door had a glass in it and when I looked up and saw who it was knocking I thought OH! OH! The teacher invited him in very politely and after greeting her and the students, he asked in a very courteous manner if he could talk to the students. I was beginning to sweat a little by then; everything was too polite and I knew it wasn't going to last.

He said that he was building a new root cellar, which we all knew, and we knew that he knew. He went on to say that somehow he had gotten careless and put the scraps of lumber that was trimmed from the boards as he worked, up on top of the walls and that during the night the wind must have come up and blew them off and they had all fallen down inside the walls. He said, "I wonder if you boys would be good enough to come down to my place during your noon hour and get down inside those walls and hand the pieces up to me as I am getting kind of up in years and it is hard for me to do something like that."

Whew! What a relief! As soon as we could we ate, then we went down there and cleaned up all the spaces inside the walls and everything else we could find to do and assured him that we were only too glad to be of help to him, all the while afraid to look him in the eye. The worst of it was that we thought he knew how the board ends got down there and we kept hoping that he wouldn't bring it up. But we couldn't be sure and we couldn't ask so all we could do was be as nice as we could and hope that would be the end of it, which it was.

Mr. Farmer and the Grind Stone

We had no power on the ranch so if any wheels were turned it was done with muscle power, either man or horse. My dad had a sickle-sharpening machine that was just for grinding sickle blades (called sections) and would do a good job getting just the right taper on them and would sharpen two sides at the same time. These sickle sections are riveted to a long bar that moves back and forth to cut the hay. If the sections get dull, which they do, not all of the stalks of hay get cut and some of the hay is wasted; also sometimes the bar will plug up and then every thing has to be stopped and it is a hard job to clean it out and get going again. For this reason, the sections have to be kept sharp.

Dad had a special machine to do just that. Not many of the neighbors had one and had to do theirs on a grindstone, which doesn't do a good job. Ours was a good machine as it would sharpen two sides at the same time and did a much better job also. The only drawback to it was that it took two people to operate it. One to turn the crank to make the sharpening wheel go around and the other to hold the sickle bar and move it along when it was time.

If our dad was not there, which he usually wasn't, and a neighbor came to use the machine I usually got the job of turning the crank as soon as I got big enough to do it. Most of the neighbor guys who would come would humor me a little and joke with me and talk to me as though I was an equal and this made me feel good of course and I would turn my little butt off trying to please them. If they saw that I was getting tired they would let up a little on the pressure and it would turn a little easier and they would say something like, "The next time you are over remind me and we will throw a saddle on that new roan horse that I traded for the other day and you can take him for a ride, see what you think of him, see if you think I made a good deal or not." Boy, this would boost my ego and I would turn with renewed vigor. I would turn 'til my arm would just about come unhooked at the shoulder, but I would feel good about it. In other words the old cliché would apply (the spirit would be willing but the flesh would be weak.)

Well, Mr. Farmer would come and after he had been there the first time with his sickle bar, I knew what to expect and sure dreaded to see him coming. If I saw him coming before he got to the house I would duck out and Mother wouldn't be able to find me for awhile, like about five minutes. She would then start hollering and I knew the jig was up, never worked but it always seemed worth a try. That old bugger would press down harder than anyone else, and then would complain because you didn't turn fast enough. Boy, he could wear me out in no time and we wouldn't be halfway done. He would never give me any encouragement or a kind word but would say something like, "When I was a kid I never knew what it was to be tired."

Baloney! He would never make any false promises as the others did even though you had serious doubts at the time that they were very sincere, it made you feel good then and gave you something to look forward to. He would complain and be kind of miserable and sarcastic. Believe me I didn't relish seeing him come I can tell you that and I would have put a burr under his saddle if I had had the chance.

Maybe I had better explain that old expression for the reader. (Putting a burr under a saddle.) When the saddle is on the horse you can pull a prank or a dirty trick on someone, kind of depends on how the horse takes it and how the rider takes it. I might add how good a buckaroo the rider is sometimes enters in to it. You lift the saddle up and carefully place a cockle bur under the saddle on the horse's back so that when the rider gets in the saddle and his weight comes down in the saddle on the horse's back it sticks the poor horse and hurts which he takes a dim view of naturally, and immediately takes measures to get rid of something on his back that is extremely uncomfortable. The horse usually isn't too particular what it is as long as it quits hurting soon, sometimes with dire consequences for the unsuspecting rider.

I am tempted to tell a couple of stories here. Mr. Farmer was from the state of Kansas and was always bragging about Kansas. They too were winners in the great land drawing as was my mother, and had settled near our place. My dad was quite talented in many different ways, one of which was his ability to come up with poems. He could make up poems sometimes on the spur of the moment, and he used to humor the family with them.

One time when he was sort of disgusted with Mr. Farmer after having listened to him brag about Kansas, he came home and made up a little ditty about him. I should say first that Mr. Farmer was a great tobacco chewing man, and sometimes when it got cold, I guess he couldn't feel his face very good because the juice would run out the corner of his mouth and down his chin.

My dad said, "In Kansas they chew tobacco thin they spit it on their chin and then lick it off agin." Needless to say, Don and I thought this hilarious.

The Lost Man

My dad told a story about a happening that took place one time when he was working in the woods in Minnesota. He said he was running a logging camp and the work was quite a ways from the camp so they didn't go in for lunch, (at the time called dinner), but had the cook's helper (called a flunky) bring the food out to them. The land was flat and there were no landmarks so it was easy to get lost.

This flunky was a young man from town and not familiar with being alone in the woods and got lost on the way to the crew. When it came time for lunch, he didn't show up and after waiting awhile, the crew went back to work. Well, they worked all afternoon without anything to eat and without the flunky showing up.

When they got back to camp in the evening and after checking with the cook as to why there was no dinner sent out to them, they came to the conclusion he was lost, as he had left camp with the box of grub strapped on his back in plenty of time to be there by noon.

Well, it was late, the weather wasn't cold and they had no lights so they waited 'til the next morning to look for him. They knew he wouldn't suffer from exposure and he had plenty of food so he would be all right 'til morning. The crew spread out and looked all morning for him in every direction. Just before noon, my dad found him. Dad was glad to find him and the flunky was glad. The poor fellow had walked all night and didn't know he was going in a circle. The first thing he said to my dad after he settled down a little and realized he was safe was, "Did you bring me anything to eat?" Dad said, "What is that on your back in the box?" The poor fellow had been so scared that he hadn't stopped walking nor had he thought about the food in the box. He never even took it off his back, carrying it all night not realizing that it was full of food. Interesting.

The Hunters

One time my brother and I went out to our pasture to look around and check everything out, which we often did during the good weather and when we didn't have something more important to do. Our pasture was about a quarter of a mile from the house and across the main road or county road. It consisted of about twenty five or thirty acres of logged off land but it was not cleared. In other words, it was still in tree and brush but the big timber had been removed. It was quite wild and what it lacked in wilderness we could invent in our imagination so it was pretty wild one way or the other.

In the particular incident I am going to relate here, I was about eleven years old I guess and my brother, Don, was about eight. Well anyway, we were prowling around in the woods and we came across a strange animal. It was about two feet high and probably three feet long with small beady eyes and was heavy bodied. We were excited and didn't know what it was but hunters that we were, or at least we thought we were, we didn't want it to get away. It didn't try to run but it did try to get away but we each got a long stick and every time it tried to get away, we would hit it with a stick or poke it and this way we kept it from getting away from us. It didn't do much of anything but hump up when we poked it.

We studied this predicament quite earnestly and came to the conclusion that this animal had to be a porcupine, although we had never seen one but we had heard our dad speak of them and he had said they were a nuisance to have around. They would get quills in horse's legs and dogs would try to fight them and get quills in their faces. We had also heard that they could throw quills anytime that they wanted to at humans if you happened to get near them and all kinds of weird things, so we came to a decision that something had to be done about it without fail and right away.

We talked it over and decided that a good killing was in order and we needed a gun to accomplish this deed. Don was to go to the house and see if he could talk our mother into letting him bring back a shotgun and some shells then we could get the situation under control. I didn't have much faith in this happening as our mother was not what, as I would describe her in these times, you'd call a liberal thinker as far as boy ideas went, but we thought it was worth a try. In the meantime, I would stay there and keep the animal rounded up with a long stick. Don took off and it wasn't too long until he was back, and lo and behold he had the gun and three shells. He must have put up a good story and did a good selling job that worked.

Our dad was away from home working; however, he had given us instructions on guns and we had shot some under his supervision, so I was very confident. I loaded the gun and took careful aim and blazed away. It downed the wild beast but it didn't completely kill it, as it was still kicking, so I loaded up again and gave it another round. That did the job.

We went to the fence and hunted around till we found a piece of extra wire, tied it around his neck and dragged him home. We could hardly wait to show it to Mother, who agreed with us that indeed it must be a porcupine although she had never seen one before either.

We pulled a lot of quills out of it and examined it thoroughly but my dad was away working so that dampened our glory somewhat as we didn't get to show it to him.

In a couple of days, a neighbor kid by the name of Bill Lamb came along on a saddle horse. He had never seen a porcupine either, but he liked the looks of it so we gave it to him. We would have liked to have kept it till our dad came home on the weekend but it was summertime and we were getting the strong impression that he wasn't going to keep much longer. In fact, every time one approached it, it was a little stronger and a little more difficult to tolerate the odor. Bill had a rope on his saddle so he tied it to the porcupine and took a hitch around the saddle horn and the last we saw of it, he was dragging it down the road toward home.

Dad Working in Coeur D'Alene

Dad got a job in Coeur d'Alene working for the Atlas Tie Co. as timber Superintendent, being in charge of buying logs and getting them to the mill. He was gone all the time, and sometimes didn't even get home on weekends.

I gradually had gotten bigger, of course, and was able to take on more of the work around the ranch. It wasn't really a matter of choice. That was the way it was so I was given quite a lot of responsibility. Sometimes our well would go dry on a dry year and when it did, we had to haul water from the lower field. This was accomplished with a horse and a stone boat.

A stone boat is a sled with two runners that are made of poles or small logs beveled up on the front ends with planks nailed across them to make a sled. There would be a chain fastened to the front end of the two runners to hook a horse or team to for pulling it. We would put a vinegar barrel that had had the top removed from it on the stone boat and hook up a horse to haul one barrel or a team for two barrels. Then we'd drag it out to the county road, down the road to a short road to the well in the field.

The well was covered with planks with a hole in the top, with a cover on it that could be removed to pull the water bucket through. The water had to be pulled up with a bucket on the end of a rope and dumped into the barrel, which took a lot of buckets to fill, taking forever. Many more than it took to empty it when we were using it on the other end, it seemed.

Chapter 11

I wasn't big enough at first to pull water up without danger of falling in the well, which was about six or seven feet in diameter and ten feet to the water. There was no guard rail around the hole in the well top itself. When water was pulled up some water would always dribble from the bucket when it was lifted out of the hole or some would be spilled on the way to the barrel and then things would get slick.

Mother was afraid that I would fall in and that would be the end of me. We made a great team. She couldn't harness the horse, or drive it for that matter, and I couldn't fill the barrel, so she filled the barrel and I was the teamster. We had to cross a ditch coming from the field where the well was to get on the main road and if the road had been worked on, the first few trips afterward were rather precarious 'til the stone boat kind of got the edges of the ditch caved in so they were not so abrupt. The barrel wasn't fastened down and I was usually able to hit the ditch so as not to upset the water barrel, but one evening after school we were crossing the ditch. It was a dark, cloudy, cold, late afternoon in the fall of the year and not too long before dark. I was trying to go slow and the horse knew what was up and didn't want to go slow as it made it harder to pull the stone boat. Poor Mother was trying to steady the barrel to keep it from tipping over, and lost the battle. The barrel got rocking around and finally tipped and when it did, Mother was on the downhill side, it got Mother down and they both went in the ditch, which was about eighteen inches deep. She landed on her back in the ditch and the whole barrel full of water poured over her. She wasn't hurt, but she didn't have a dry stitch on when she got up. She sure got a quick bath, but not at a time or place of her choosing, believe me.

I felt so bad. She was drenched and it was quite cool. It was getting dark and she was tired but we had to turn around and go back to the well and start over again. I don't know why my dad didn't make better provisions for holding the barrel. Sometimes life was hard.

There were times when it was real cold and we had to haul water and by the time we got to the house with the water everything would be all ice where the water had slopped out of the barrel. Then too after a cold night when one went to the barrel it would be frozen almost solid, down from the top, up from the bottom and in from the sides and the ice had to be chopped with a hatchet. Believe me, you sure saved the ice and all the chips to melt on the stove, as water was a precious commodity.

There were times when we gathered snow and melted it for water on the kitchen range. It is pitiful how much snow it takes to make a little bit of water, like a gallon.

Dad and His Teeth

When our dad was working in Coeur d'Alene, he had his teeth pulled and soon got some dentures made. Dentures in those days were not as satisfactory as they are today and gave some people like Dad no end of trouble. He wouldn't leave them alone and consistently wear them and sometimes when they annoyed him he would take them out, wrap them in his handkerchief, and place them in his pocket.

He was staying in a boarding house at this particular time and one evening some of the boarders were sitting around in the parlor visiting, Dad among them, when suddenly he had to sneeze and without thinking, he pulled his handkerchief from his pocket without thought of his teeth being wrapped in it.

The teeth went flying across the hardwood floor and slid to a stop right in front of one of the boarders, a rather dignified middle-aged school teacher sitting directly across the room.

Poor Dad, he was of course mortified, but he had a great ability to rise to an occasion. He said in a very serious tone of voice, "Don't anyone move" as he got up from his chair in a very cautious manner and sort of crept up on the teeth as though they were going to jump and when within striking distance he quickly reached out and grabbed them and said, "I was so afraid someone would be bitten." Well, that of course relieved the tension and accordingly some of his embarrassment.

The Snake Experiment

Don and I usually were watching when anything was going on around the ranch and learned how to do a lot of things, but some we were not allowed to do. We knew how to use dynamite or at least we thought we did but that was of course a no-no.

Dad was gone and one day on the way home from school in the spring of the year we found a garter snake about eighteen or twenty inches long, but we couldn't think what we should do with it. After pondering this problem and discussing the situation, we decided that we would fasten a stick of dynamite to him and see what would happen. We were quite sure what the outcome would be but we wanted to experiment with some dynamite (commonly called powder) anyway, and this seemed to be a good excuse. We took the snake home and put him in a box for safekeeping and went to the house to change clothes and to say hello to Mother and then when she wasn't looking I grabbed a couple of matches and we went outside.

We got a stick of dynamite from where it was stored, along with a short piece of fuse and a cap to detonate the charge with and some string, and the snake in the box and went out back of the barn on the other side from the house.

We put the cap on the fuse, crimped it to the fuse with a pair of special crimping pliers, and poked the cap into a hole we had punched in the stick of powder and split the other end of the fuse just as we had seen our dad do.

We got the snake but he wasn't very cooperative. I imagine if he had known what his destiny was to be the job would have been even more difficult, but we finally managed to tie the round snake to the round stick of powder, which took some doing, but we finally managed and we were set.

There was a big old stump handy and we placed our experiment on top of the stump, checked the house to be sure Mother wasn't coming, and lit the fuse, then ran in the barn where we could look out through a crack to see the results. Everything was fine except the snake didn't seem too comfortable and was doing a lot of squirming around but we had tied him well and then, boom! No snake, no nothing, except some blue smoke and an echo. Boy that was loud going off in the open air like that; fortunately, the house door was closed.

We had taken care of the snake problem but we hadn't dealt with the mother problem yet, and hadn't even stopped to give it much consideration in fact. Well, it now became a serious issue and something had to be invented rather quickly as a quick explanation was going to be required, we knew that. After a brief conference, we decided the best approach would be to take matters into our own hands.

We ran for the house and went charging in all out of breath and wild eyed and asked Mother before she had a chance to ask us anything, if she had heard a big loud noise just a little while before, that had sounded for all the world like an explosion. Indeed she had and was just coming out to see what in the world had happened. We were quick to assure her that it had scared the heck out of us (and indeed it had for that matter) but we had no idea what had taken place. It must have been a big blast over at the neighbor's place, and after talking about it for a while, we all came to that agreement.

We knew how to take care of the dynamite but the real problem could have been Mother and she would have involved Dad in it when he came home and things would have really gotten out of hand. Boy, that was a close one for us boys, and kind of final for the snake, I guess.

Cars of the Times

One of our neighbors by the name of Joe Lamb who was the town blacksmith and who had an old Reo car and whose mother and two single brothers lived a couple of miles beyond our place would frequently drive by our place on a summer evening to visit his mother. He had what was called an exhaust whistle on his car and that rated rather highly with a couple of country kids. If Joe saw us as he went by, he always gave us a good blast with his fancy horn, so was held in high esteem by my brother and me.

I remember a man by the name of Harry Dudley who acquired a car and at the time was past middle age, and had never driven one before. Someone got him started driving really before he should have been. Well one evening Shorty, as he was popularly known, came to town in his new car (new to him at least) and drove around the one block in town that could be driven around. Then he went around again and again. Someone who knew him saw him and wondered what was going on, so waited for him and called out to him as he passed by on one of his rounds to see if everything was ok.

It wasn't. Shorty forgot how to stop and just kept going and then got panicky. Finally whoever it was who found out his plight yelled instructions to Shorty as he ran alongside, and got him stopped and calmed down, at least to the extent that he was in control again. I don't think he ever was much of a driver though, as he later drove over a bank and ended up down in some trees on the shore of Anderson Lake and spent some time in the hospital recovering.

The First Radio

The first radio I ever saw was a fascinating device if ever I saw one. Our nearest neighbors, McKinneys, had a grandson who had one and one time he came to visit them and brought along his radio with all the attendant paraphernalia such as the batteries, the radio itself about three feet long, and about twenty inches square the other way, about sixty feet of antennae wire and a couple of poles to mount the antennae on as well as some insulators, headphones and other equipment.

I heard he was going to come and what he was going to do and later when I saw him and his grandpa erecting the antennae, I could hardly contain myself. My mother saw to it that I did, however, and I didn't get to see what was going on 'til the next evening when Mother, Don and I were invited to McKinney's house for a demonstration; Dad was away.

It was a far cry from radios as we know them today. They had this contraption on a table and a storage battery and assorted other batteries called "A's" and "B's" on the floor underneath and wires all over the place. The grandson, Clarence by name, a young man about twenty years old, was the operator, of course, and he explained to us that reception was not good 'til after dark for some reason or another. It was winter time so we didn't have to wait.

He had three sets of earphones and no speaker, so only those who had earphones could listen and we took turns listening to mostly squeals, squawks and whistles. Sometimes we would hear someone talking and once in a while, you could make out what he would be saying, sometimes music could be heard and then it would fade out.

The operator sat in front of the radio, which I think I mentioned previously was about three feet long and had numerous dials and buttons and switches on the front of it that required constant attention. He of course had to have one pair of the earphones so that he could monitor the performance and it required his full attention turning and twisting the numerous dials and making minor adjustments on the different gadgets.

This was very interesting to me and I was hooked so to speak. Boy what an intriguing device it was and how little did I realize at the time what changes I would live to see in its development. I was fascinated with the mysteries of this thing and immediately started planning how to acquire one.

I didn't have a very good way to make money but every penny that came my way I saved. We didn't have any pay or allowance for the work on the ranch.

Well a year or so later, Montgomery Ward had in their catalogue a one tube radio for twenty-one dollars, and it became my ambition and almost an obsession to acquire one. I worked every chance I had, I always did for that matter, but once in awhile I would get a chance to work for pay for one of the neighbors.

I pulled nails from lumber out in the hot sun for one man who had bought used lumber from an old camp. Another time helping a neighbor plant potatoes and things like that which was not often but I saved very diligently for well over a year to get twenty-one dollars together to buy that radio.

Well I got the money finally and was all set to fulfill my dream of ordering my radio but my mother insisted that I buy a suit of clothes with my hard won savings and it so happened that the new suit cost the exact same amount of money – twenty-one dollars. There went my little life savings and for something that I wasn't the least bit interested in. It was quite disappointing to me and it was much later in life that I was able to realize my dream of a radio of my own.

Chapter 12

L ife went on and things got kind of not so good. Dad had to work out, it seemed, to make a living, and was gone almost all the time except on weekends.

Mother started to have health problems and I had more responsibility as we had horses to be cared for, cows to be milked, chickens to be fed, and attendant chores to be done such as cleaning the horse part of the barn and the cow part and once in awhile the chicken house.

There was hay to be pitched to feed the stock and I had to see that they had water. It seemed that there was always something to do besides fun things but we did have some fun once in awhile.

The Home Made Sleigh

One time along in this time frame during the winter when there was quite a lot of snow, I got the idea of making a little sleigh (sometimes called a go-devil or a stone boat) to be pulled with our old horse, Queen. She was a gentle mare and very dependable.

Queen and I

Don helped me and we made a sort of stone boat sled with two small poles for runners and boards nailed across the top of them. When we got it done, we had to try it out of course.

It was a Saturday forenoon and I had time so I put the harness on old Queen and hooked her up and we drove around the place for a while, but that wasn't good enough, we had to show off our handiwork to someone.

We took a chance and opened the gate and away we went, old Queen liked the idea and trotted right along as we drove down the county road to Buster Jarrard's place, and after he had admired our little creation and given his approval we decided to go a little farther and give him a little ride.

We took Buster along with us as there was just about room enough for three, and went to the next place. This happened to be a place where the people lived in an old logging camp building. We paid our respects to the lady who lived there and her two little girls who went to school with us. After a brief visit, we thought we had better get home, as we hadn't bothered to check out with Mother before we left and we knew we were on rather thin ice in that respect because if she missed us she would be very worried, as we never left the place without informing her or getting permission first.

I was the driver and was going to leave with a grand flourish and in style so I reached up and tapped old Queen with the end of one driving reign (called a line) on the butt and she came to life real quick, probably wanted to go home anyway. She responded with a big jump and we were off.

Well we were off all right. This old camp building was situated in a small clearing in the woods and when it had been cleared of brush and small trees some of them had not been cut off very close to the ground, therefore there were little stumps sticking up here and there but because of the snow, they could not be seen.

Well the little sleigh didn't have much clearance for such eventualities, and when we started I was also making a turn at the same time and turned over a little stump, which ripped the bottom of our conveyance apart, and we were off for sure in the snow. I hung onto the lines and hollered whoa, which means stop in horse language.

Old Queen stopped and we assessed the amount of damage – which wasn't serious if you didn't count the humiliation of three boys, one of them with a mighty red face because he was the driver – scattered around in the snow and some loose boards that didn't seem to be attached to anything in particular.

The worst part was that I had to borrow a hammer and a few nails from our friend, much to my embarrassment, to make some minor repairs before we could continue our journey home.

We had quite a bit of fun with that little contrivance and I even built a little box with a seat in it and we inveigled our mother into going for a ride in it to another neighbor's one Sunday afternoon in the snow. She thought it was fun.

Doctoring Horses

Sometimes a horse would get cut on barbed wire, and would require doctoring. A horse will, when caught in wire, usually panic and start to lunge, further injuring themselves if not rescued, calmed down or cut loose. Sometimes it was quite a job to treat them, as the horse didn't understand that in order to help it you had to hurt it in the process.

The horse would have to be tied to a good strong post and sometimes ropes had to be used to tie them by the legs too. There was another method that was used that was quite effective most of the time also for making them behave. I got in on this when I was pretty young, sometimes standing on a box to reach. The horse would be tied by the head up short to a good strong post. If I helped, I would hold the twitch after Dad got it tightened. The twitch consisted of a good strong stick about thirty inches long with three holes drilled in it and a short piece of rope run through those holes.

This was an instrument of torture. A loop of the rope was put over the horse's upper lip and tightened by pulling the rope tight through the holes. (A horse has a long upper lip that can be pulled out quite a way) then the stick was twisted lip and all.

The idea was to get the horse's attention while the necessary doctoring was done. It worked quite well. If the horse got antsy about the foot or whatever was being worked on, the twitch was tightened more 'til the lip hurt worse than the treatment. They usually could be controlled in this manner.

I recall several times when we had a horse that needed to be given treatments with medicine for a cut that was in the process of healing and Dad was gone. I had to use a long syringe, get the horse tied to a post, then get out of kicking range and squirt the medicine on the wound with the syringe. It must have hurt because they would kick and jump around for little while. Life was hard for the animals even when we treated them as well as we could.

Dad and the Palouser

One winter about this time our dad was working for the Russell and Pugh Lumber Co., scaling logs and cruising timber, and looking after procuring logs for the sawmill at Springston, which was located on the Coeur d'Alene river about three miles from the town of Harrison. I will explain what cruising means later in some detail but at this time I will deal with it only to explain what the purpose of his forays into the woods in the middle of the winter all alone were for.

It was to ascertain how much timber would be on a given piece of land. Many a Monday morning he would take off in the dark to walk to Springston across a neighbor's field, then cut through the woods where there was no trail and cross Bell creek and down Bell canyon road and around Anderson Lake to Springston where he would get his orders as to where he would be needed or where he was to go.

It would be pitch dark when he had to go and as there were no flashlights then you had one choice for a light. That was a kerosene lantern, which was heavy, and after it got light was not needed but had to be carried anyway.

Well, Dad came up with what he called a palouser. It consisted of a gallon fruit can with the top cut out and of course emptied of fruit first and a hole punched in the side about half way down, big enough to put a candle through it. A piece of haywire was fastened on the opposite side from the top to the bottom of the can in a loose loop, and this then became the handle. You could carry this can-light horizontally by this wire bail.

The candle was pushed in from the outside, which was now the bottom. The sides of the hole for the candle were left jagged, thus gripping the candle so it wouldn't slip out, and as it burned down it could be pushed in from the outside. The flame set back far enough in the can so that it was protected from the wind most of the time. It didn't make a very bright light but it was a light. I have often said during my long life, "Maybe not a good way but a way," and that is better than no way.

Well, sometimes Dad would take his pack-sack with him and would catch the passenger train at Springston and ride up the river some place where they would stop for him to get off with his pack-sack with food and blankets in it and his snow shoes tied on top and would walk to the place where he was to cruise the timber.

He would first locate an abandoned cabin, if he could, and leave his provisions there. He would work out of there sometimes for several days at a time. He would go out through the timber on his snowshoes counting trees all day long, come back before dark, and sit around all evening with no light except a candle. He would usually come home on Saturday night walking out home from Harrison, which was about three miles through the snow, all in (meaning tired) from his week.

We would be so glad to see him as we all worried about him out there all alone, and if something had happened to him it could have been very likely that he would never have been found.

Sometimes they cruised timber in the deep snow because they could go over brush and too, the cruiser would be several feet off the ground and could get a much better view; however, it should be mentioned here that the accuracy was not as great as other more conventional methods.

Boy, some of those men of the time were tough and our dad was one of the toughest.

Chapter 13

This is a good time to tell you a story our dad told about when he was in Wisconsin before he had come out west. He and another man hired out to hunt deer for a logging camp for the camp meat supply. The weather was cold so fresh meat would keep and as it was a long way to town by wagon road, the camp boss figured it would be cheaper to have venison than beef. I don't know if there were any game laws at that time or not. If there were, they didn't pay any attention to them. This was probably about 1895.

Dad and his partner would hunt in a given area and when they had pretty well hunted it out and they had several deer hanging they would notify the camp and the boss would send a man with several packhorses over to get the meat.

They had pretty well hunted out an area and decided to move their headquarters. They were also low on food and agreed that one man would walk to town and backpack some food back, which would take a full day, and the partner would take their blankets and cooking utensils on his back and hunt for an abandoned cabin where they would make their new headquarters. They would meet at the new location that evening. They drew straws to see who was to do what and our dad drew the job of going to town.

He left at daylight and walked all day but it got dark before he could make it to the cabin that evening. There was a good trail and there was a little starlight so he had little trouble finding his way, but much to his disappointment when he got within sight of the cabin there was no light, no smell of smoke and no sign of life. Dad called out when he got close but no answer so he knew his partner had not yet arrived. He was real tired as he had walked all day but there was nothing to do but go in and get something going like a light and a fire

When he got to the cabin he pushed the door open and it so happened it swung in; as he started to take his pack-sack off something rushed by him bumping him on the leg. It was dark and he couldn't see but whatever it was it was pretty good sized by the feel of it; it reached almost to his belt and by the sound it made scrambling and rushing about he didn't like its company. To say he felt uneasy would be an understatement.

He got rid of the pack in a hurry and made for the door but unfortunately the door had swung shut and in the pitch dark, he couldn't see a thing and couldn't find it. He said he ran around a little but more than anything, he wanted to get out of there in the worst way, and quickly.

Whatever it was in there with him apparently had the same idea, by the way it was scrambling about and sort of snorting and grunting. Every once in awhile it would bump into Dad which offered our dad great encouragement to take desperate measures if necessary to exit as rapidly as possible.

When his eyes became a little more adjusted to what scant light there was he saw a small window-like opening about chest high that didn't appear to have any glass or frame in it; just an opening in the log wall, so he made for it in utmost haste but in doing so he collided with a table, which tipped over spilling Dad on the floor and making quite a clatter.

When he got untangled from that, he jumped up and tried to dive out the little hole. The animal apparently had the same intention and after the table collision and the commotion it created had more incentive than ever to distance itself from this place at all cost.

They both jumped for the hole at the same time, and became wedged in the opening together. Fortunately for Dad, whatever it was had its feet and claws turned away from him. He said he couldn't get in or out but he could get to his hunting knife in a sheath on his belt, which he did in short order, and began trying to cut, jab, stab and slash the furious object next to him, whatever it was in the opening with him. The animal, after what seemed like a long time, seemed to be gaining on getting out and of course, Dad was giving it great incentive to do so, with his hunting knife.

They both kept struggling but the animal was finally able to get free and dropped to the ground where my dad could hear it scrambling off in the dark.

Dad dropped back inside the building, felt around till he found his pack, got a candle from it which he lit to see what else was about to happen. Every thing seemed to be pretty much in place except for the table, which was lying on its side.

About that time, his partner came and Dad told him of his experience. They took a candle outside but could find nothing, so the partner kidded him all evening about imagining the whole episode.

Well, it was quite real to Dad; so in the morning after it got daylight he went looking around outside the cabin and sure enough under the little window he soon found a thin trail of blood which as he followed it became bigger, leading toward the creek. Sure enough after following it a short distance down the trail he had come in on the night before, he found a bear about half grown which had bled to death during the night.

He said he was glad to find the bear, as he took so much kidding from his companion that he was beginning to think the fellow doubted his credibility.

The Preacher

This is a story my father told as having happened to him when he was a boy. It took place in the village where he lived.

There was an evangelist came to the town and set up under a large tree in the village square. It was summertime and he held outdoor evening services there, and as there was little to do in town for entertainment, he got a big crowd every night, not all of who came for the redemption benefits but as a form of amusement. At a certain time during the services, when he got the ones who were vulnerable to fire and brimstone preaching and instantaneous salvation worked up to a frenzied pitch and in a semi hypnotic state, he would cry out in a high pitched shrill voice "Hark, I hear Gabriel's horn. All who wish to be saved come forward." And with this, there would be a big rush to the front where people fell all over themselves, weeping, wailing, moaning and groaning and all kinds of weird things took place on the promise of redemption and salvation.

My dad, who was a boy at the time, had gotten hold of an old beat up bugle someplace and had been going around town blowing on it from time to time. Some of the young men in town hired my dad to get up in the tree early, before anyone came to the gathering, with his bugle, and at the time Gabriel was to be heard, Dad was to furnish the music with his instrument if indeed it could be called that.

He got there early and concealed himself in the tree where he wouldn't be seen and waited for the proper time. When the preacher let out his rallying cry, my dad gave a mighty blast on his bugle. He gave it all he had and as he had been practicing for quite some time, I guess it was a mighty healthy blast. Well pandemonium broke loose down below. Some of the women fainted and others shrieked, and there was a general state of confusion to say the least. And in the middle of it all was the preacher, waving his arms high in the air and yelling at the top of his high-pitched, squeaky voice some very unpreacher-like comments toward the heavens about who had committed such a dastardly deed and what he was going to do to the culprit when and if he caught him, before he turned him over to the devil for final disposition and everlasting punishment.

My dad quickly figured out that it would be in his best interests to leave as rapidly as possible, all things considered, especially since the preacher seemed to be in a somewhat uncooperative frame of mind, and so, without further attention to all the amusement going on down below he hung his bugle on a limb of the tree, to be retrieved at a later time when there was less interest in the tree and less activity in the area. He slid down the trunk of the tree with the best tree descending skill he possessed and the speed of a somewhat terror stricken youth who has just been threatened by never having a chance to go to heaven and being committed to everlasting and eternal punishment wished on him by the preacher who was supposedly endowed with the powers of heaven. Once he hit the ground, however, the preacher didn't have a chance. This is a story that I have heard my father tell several times.

Another Story Told by Dad

Dad told a story about working on a survey crew for the Forest Service in Oregon sometime after the above episode. He said the crew was running survey lines on the upper reaches of the Smith River in southern Oregon and the man in charge had made arrangements with a homesteader and his wife to board the small crew for a few days. He said the wife was quite a good cook but was extremely frugal.

The lady made her own butter and served it every morning with breakfast for the pancakes. It seems she would mold it in a round ball and would keep it as cool as she could, then when she put it on the table she would warm a bowl and place the cold butter ball in the warm round bowl, it was almost impossible to cut any free; as a result after struggling with it for awhile the men would give up and therefore she saved butter.

Dad said one morning one of the men lost patience and just reached in, took the butterball in his hand and whittled off a chunk with a knife in his other hand, handed it to the next man and so it went around the table. Well, that ended that stunt; she never did it again.

This woman served chicken almost every night, in one form or another, and the crew got wondering about it. It wasn't a very big place and they speculated that she must be reducing her flock considerably. One of the men asked her how she could afford to feed them so much chicken, chicken almost every night. Her reply was that she hated to do it, but that the chickens just kept dying off, she really didn't know what was the matter with them. Dad said it was a good thing they were leaving.

My Camera

It was about this point in time I guess that Mother's health began to fail somewhat, and as Dad was gone all the time I had to help with the cooking and the washing and other chores, as she wasn't able to keep up. Mother promised me if I would help her when she didn't feel good she would get me a camera. She was good to her word and sent to Spokane for a Brownie box camera. I enjoyed it for many many years and have taken countless pictures with it, and in fact have it to this very day, with many of the snapshots I took.

Busy Boy

Our nearest neighbors, the McKinneys, were well up in years and one winter Mrs. McKinney got sick, and after a short time died, which was a great shock to all of us as it was assumed she just had the flu and would be well again soon. This left Mr. McKinney alone so a married daughter whose children were all grown came to stay with him and keep house for him till he was able to get adjusted. It wasn't long till she called early one morning to see if I could come up and milk their two cows as Paw (as she called her dad) didn't feel well.

I raced up there on short time, as I hadn't allowed time for this before school. I got the milking done and the other chores, as well as my own, and managed to get to school on time. That evening Paw didn't feel any better so I took care of things again and the next morning I got up early enough to allow for it.

I repeated the process but had more time. Well, this went on for some time and as I allowed time for it, I managed all right but I was quite busy. We had another neighbor by the name of Alman who lived about three quarters of a mile away in the other direction (the man who taught us to make kites and little boats). Mrs. Alman could not milk a cow and Mr. Alman had to go away on a short logging job, too far away to come home at night, so they asked me if I could milk their cow for them every night and morning for awhile till he would be back home.

Well, I would get up real early, do my own chores – milking, feeding the horses, cleaning the barn, pumping water for all the stock, feeding the chickens – eat breakfast, run up to McKinneys, do the milking, clean the barn, feed the chickens, stop by home, grab my lunch, run over to the Alman place, milk the cow, clean the barn and go to school. Then in the evening, I had to repeat the process. I kept this up for quite awhile.

Mr. McKinney didn't get any better; in fact, he got slowly worse and then the old fellow died. An interesting sidelight is that he always wore a long white beard and when he was being prepared for burial they combed his beard and found the pills that the Doctor had prescribed for him and that they had been giving him to take, in his whiskers. He had slipped them into his beard when they gave them to him to take instead of swallowing them.

It appeared he had no interest in living after his wife had died. This was an interesting time for me. It seemed there was always something to do – fix fence, haul water, clean the chicken coop or something, besides the regular routine, but we got by.

Passing the Seventh Grade

When it came time to pass the seventh grade all pupils in the State of Idaho had to take a state examination which was held in town at the schoolhouse and was administered by one of the teachers there. I was the only one in the seventh grade so I went alone. Boy, this was something new to me and I was scared, as I didn't know anyone and everything was strange.

I walked to town on the appointed day and I knew where the school was and that was all I did know. I asked someone when I got there and they directed me to the right room where I told the teacher who I was and she assigned me to a seat.

There were a whole bunch of kids there and one country bumpkin, and believe me I sure felt like one too. I managed to get through the morning and ate my lunch out under a tree in the yard. They were the most unfriendly kids I had ever come in contact with but I wasn't too surprised because the previous experiences I had had with those town kids hadn't impressed me too much.

It kind of made me feel like the country dogs that would accompany the horses and wagon to town when they went. The first thing that happened to the dogs was that they would immediately get engaged in a dog fight. I guess the town dogs had their territory staked out and resented any intrusion. I felt the same way.

There was a drinking fountain in the main hall of the schoolhouse, which was just fascinating to me, as I had never seen anything like it before. It had a white porcelain knob sticking up in the center of a big brass bowl and when you turned a knob under the bowl water spurted up and you could put your mouth over the stream and just sort of bite off all you wanted to drink.

What a device, and you didn't have to pump or anything. I made it a point to get by that thing several times just for the fun of it and then one time when I was getting a drink someone pushed me on the back of my head and I bumped my mouth on the porcelain knob which hurt and wasn't too funny, to me at least.

Well, I let that go and just before time to go back to class after lunch I swung by the fountain to get another drink which I didn't need but was so much fun I couldn't resist, when someone pushed my head down real hard and it resulted in splitting my lip inside my mouth.

This was enough of smart-aleck town kids for me. I looked up quickly, and seeing who it had been, I made a run for him and was able to catch him right as he was going out the front door of the school. I grabbed him by the shirt collar with one hand and the belt with the other and propelled him right on out the door with great enthusiasm. There was a wooden porch about twelve feet wide and then there were about twelve wooden steps down to the wooden sidewalk near the street.

I had a good start and kept him going and when we came to the edge of the porch where the steps were I gave him an added push and let go, sending him down those wooden steps. I went back inside and soon heard him howling and bawling. It wasn't long before some teacher grabbed me and there was trouble aplenty. I was mad and so was she. I was finally able to get her to calm down enough to listen to my side of the story and to show her my bleeding lip and then she cooled down a little more and became almost rational. She threatened to prohibit me from taking the rest of the exam but finally relented after warning me that if I ever did such a thing again I would be in big trouble. I assured her that if those town kids would just leave me alone there would be no more trouble; however if they didn't there would be more trouble and she could count on it. That was the end of the trouble.

The next year I had to take the state exam again to pass the eighth grade and the word must have gotten around because I had no trouble. Needless to say, I had gotten some smarts by that time and kept a wary eye out when taking a drink from the fountain. In fact, I never did have any more trouble in town after that.

The last two years of grade school, we had a man teacher by the name of Mr. Howe. He was a fine, old gentleman and we had great respect for him. The last year there were only five kids in the school and quite often, I missed class as Mother needed more help and I just couldn't keep up with everything. I finally graduated from the eighth grade but just barely.

Chapter 14

Mother was not well by this time at all and Dad spent more time at home. Mother was going through the menopause at this time of her life and as there was no doctor in Harrison then there was no way for her to get any medical attention. I don't think Dad knew what the trouble was and so things got sort of confusing, to say the least. Mother was in a state of mental depression and wasn't able to cope with things at times, didn't know the difference between reality and her imagination.

Dad stayed pretty close to home and I did most of the work as he looked after Mother because sometimes she couldn't be left alone, or so it seemed at any rate. I mowed and raked all the hay that summer with our team and Dad would help when he could. He hired a man with a modern hay baler to come to bale the hay for us and later then also hired another man who could drive truck, to use one of two logging trucks that were not being used by the lumber company and were stored at our place to haul the hay in.

I worked with the man, Mr. Porter, and Dad helped us when he could, and we were able to get all the hay in our barn and a neighbor's barn that wasn't being used. I don't know how much we put up but it was many tons, which was later sold. This truck we used was a Mack truck (called a bulldog model}, with a chain drive and hard rubber tires, no windshield, no doors but a roof over the seats. It was slow, but powerful, and took a pretty good man to drive, as it was direct steering and was extremely hard to turn.

The End of Our Home

Mother didn't get any better and Dad didn't quite know what to do so he finally called my Uncle John in Spokane who Mother had run the hotel for at one time, and he came up in his car. After he and Dad talked things over it was decided that our uncle would take Mother back to Spokane where she could get some medical help.

Dad couldn't go, as he had to stay there to sell hay and so forth, so it was decided that I would go to look after Mother, as she needed supervision. Don came along too and we stayed at Uncle John's house a few days. He got Mother to a doctor who put her on medication and she settled down quite a bit.

It was decided that she would stay in Spokane. Uncle John found a widow lady by the name of Mrs. Stimpson who took in boarders and who had room just a block from his house, and after conferring with Dad on the phone it was decided that Mother would be placed there where my uncle could keep an eye on things. Don could stay there with her and attend school and I would go back to the ranch with Dad.

We got Mother and Don settled at Mrs. Stimpson's and everything seemed to be going well, so I took the train to Harrison and then it was just Dad and me.

We had work to do digging potatoes and some of the neighbors had wheat to thrash and they needed help. We took our team of horses and I drove them hauling bundled grain to the thrashing machine and Dad pitched bundles out in the field on to the wagons. We worked at this for several weeks, going home each night.

Sometimes we would get our supper where we worked, sometimes we went home and while I took care of the horses, Dad would get supper. We usually got our dinner where we worked.

One evening we worked late to get through with this particular farm so we could move the first thing in the morning. It got almost dark and I was tired. We were thrashing oats and the bundles were long and heavy. When I got to the machine I had a big load and I was just about all in, but I had a whole load to pitch off yet. There would be a wagon on either side and the drivers alternated throwing bundles of grain in to the thrashing machine. I had been doing it since early morning and I can remember so vividly I would lift a bundle and I would think this is the last one I can handle and then I would think those guys will laugh at me if I don't keep up and I would do it again. Boy, was I ever glad when I got my last bundle off the last load of that day.

This particular place was going to give us our supper, as we knew that we would be late finishing. I unhooked the team, took the horses to water and then tied them to the wagon with plenty of oat hay to eat and went to the house. In those times, the people would put the wash water and a couple of washbasins along with towels outside when they had extra help as no one had bathrooms.

Well, we all washed up and went in to eat. Much to our disappointment all that was on the table besides the kerosene lamps were several boxes of corn flakes, and of course cream, milk and sugar.

Well, this was kind of a let down after a long hard day's work, but there seemed to be no choice so everyone pitched in and took a bowl of cornflakes. When every one had done so, the mother and the two girls took the cereal boxes away, and here came the real food.

Boy, oh boy, did they ever have a feed for us. They were Italian folks and this was sort of a treat before the main course. I shall never forget that meal; they had about everything you could imagine on the table. Dad and I had been batching and sometimes after working in the fields all day it was too much trouble to cook much. You can believe me I took full advantage of the situation.

It was a new experience for me to handle the team when the wagon was pulled up to the machine. The horses had to go right up real close to the steam engine and it would be puffing and sort of snorting and the big drive belt would be flapping which scared the horses as they were not used to machinery and they didn't like it at all. If one didn't get the wagon nice and close though, you had farther to throw the bundles so it made it well worthwhile to get in close.

My logging team and I
about 1926

It would have been a disgrace to have had to pull out and come around again because you didn't get close enough, I never would have heard the last of that from the crew. I had never had any experience driving a team of horses with a fully loaded wagon on hillsides before either so it was a challenge I accepted, and I learned.

It seemed to me that fall and winter, when I worked all day long with those older men, that they could go on working forever without rest. The same way walking. They could walk up a steep mountain trail and just keep on going, without pause, hour after hour. Sometimes I guess I would say I was getting tired and they would say that when they were my age, they never knew what it was to be tired.

This was rather discouraging to a young fellow who was just starting out. Dad wasn't the type of man who you talked this sort of thing over with and I learned to keep my troubles to myself pretty well. I heard that so much I believed it and used to feel bad because I would be getting tired and I thought the rest of the crew wasn't, and I would try even harder. I found out later in life that this was all a put on, a bunch of baloney, imagination on their part; they were tired and didn't want to admit it.

Everyone got tired. They were men and I was still just a boy, trying to learn how to work and be a man – how to use tools to advantage, such as axes, shovels, cant-hooks, peaveys, logging equipment, such as tongs, trail dogs – how to saw logs with a cross-cut saw, how to fall a tree, and so forth.

I had just turned fifteen in August and was still not hard like a full grown man but I sure was trying to be a man and I did a man's work; furthermore, it was expected of me.

We got everything on the ranch done that needed to be done that fall, dug the potatoes and hauled them to town in the old Ford and sold them to one of the stores.

Russell & Pugh was thinking of starting a big logging job up on a creek called Fitzgerald Creek, a tributary of the St. Joe River. It was about five miles up the river from the little town of St. Joe, and then up this creek about three miles by pack trail. No road, and believe me, the trail was steep in most places. Because of no road, everything had to be packed in on horses or mules.

There was a set of buildings there already, as there had been considerable logging done in the area before, but they had run out of timber that they owned and had shut the camp down the year before. The lumber company was thinking of buying more timber farther up the creek above the previously logged off area and would use the existing buildings for the headquarters camp.

Mr. Walt Russell, who was a good friend of Dad's and who Dad had worked for off and on for years, asked Dad if he would come up there and look over the job (called a chance) with him. Walt picked Dad and me up and we went up to the camp and spent a couple of days looking over the timber and the site for a dam to be built, a new log flume and some log chutes – everything that would need to be done to get into operation.

Well, they decided it was a feasible enterprise and that the company would buy the timber and take the job, and Walt offered Dad a job as a foreman and said I could go to work too.

We went home and Dad decided we should go to Spokane to see how Mother and Don were doing. Walt Russell had to go to Spokane on business so he invited us to ride down with him. Mother and Don were staying at Stimpson's place and Mother was much improved. We stayed a couple of days and took the train home. That was long enough for me. I wasn't comfortable in town and was ready to get back to the ranch or the woods or whatever.

Fitzgerald Creek

We turned our old horse, Queen, loose so she could go to the pasture where she could rustle enough to eat, get water at the lower well in the field, and could come up to the barn when she wanted to get out of the weather. We had a few chickens left and we just turned them loose to make it on their own. They could go in the chicken house at night, and during the day, they would just have to do the best they could for food. There was the barn and a big manure pile and the field to scrounge in.

We packed some work clothes in a couple of pack-sacks, greased our caulked shoes and were ready for the woods. Walt picked us up one morning in his Model-T Ford and we drove up to the trailhead at the mouth of Fitzgerald Creek, then walked up the trail to the camp.

The camp consisted of a small office building big enough for four double bunks, a few benches, a desk, a cupboard, a wash stand containing a water bucket, a wash basin and a heating stove. The rest of the camp consisted of a cookhouse and dining room combined, big enough to seat about thirty men at one time.

A bunkhouse that would hold about thirty men, a barn to hold about twelve horses, a blacksmith shop and a small sawmill. The buildings were built of rough-sawn lumber that had been cut with the small sawmill. They were one board thick and were covered with tarpaper (as it was called in those times), held on with thin strips of lumber nailed over it, or round, thin metal disks with a shingle nail driven through them to keep the wind from blowing the paper off.

The roofs were covered with heavy tarpaper which was nailed down with roofing nails. The floors were made of two thicknesses and were soon chewed up from the trod of caulked shoes, as everyone wore them; it was necessary.

I will explain at this time how the sawmill machinery was brought into camp. The only access to the road, which was down on the river next to the railroad track, was this pack trail, so everything was brought up this trail which was, as I may have said, very steep in some places. The trail itself stayed up on the bank or on the hillside above the creek in most places, but in a few spots it ran along the creek bottom beside the flume. (Editor's note: A flume was like a kid's slide, used to slide logs down out of the hills. Loggers would divert water from a creek into the flume so the logs had a water ride.) All of the supplies for the camp were packed in on mules and horses, even the grain and the hay for the logging horses.

A very ingenious method was used to get the heavy sawmill machinery up where they wanted to build the camp and the water dam and the flume. A big sort of sled was constructed using long logs for the runners, which were well braced with cross timbers. A heavy deck was then fastened to this and then cable was used to make a hitch to the front of it. This was then pulled into place for the trip; the equipment was loaded and secured with heavy chains so that it could not fall off if the sled was not kept on an even keel while in transit.

When everything was ready horses were hooked one behind the other, in single file, to a long chain and this in turn was then hooked to a long cable. The horses were kept on the trail where they could get footing and could pull.

This long cable then was passed through pulleys (at the time called snatch blocks) anchored to trees or rock outcroppings in such a manner as to draw the load in the direction they wished it to go. The creek was very narrow in places and full of debris, such as fallen logs and rocks. Most of these obstacles could be bridged over or spanned because of the length of the sled. In some places there were standing trees; they were felled (cut down) crosswise of the creek and were used to slide on.

I wasn't there to see the operation but I can imagine how many times the cable had to be realigned with the snatch blocks to get the proper lead, when you consider that the horses were in some instances going in a different direction from the load. It had to be an incredible task and a grueling job, to say the least, even for those times of having to do things the hard way. Can you picture three miles of this?

There was a dam pond there and an old log chute that ended at the dam pond. This was all built on a small flat in a fork of the main creek. We were to be logging on up the main creek, starting about a mile above camp.

When we got there a man by the name of Len McRey was staying there, watching the camp and the equipment. Another man by the name of Lew Howard was to be the boss. Both of these men, as well as Dad, had run logging camps for the company before.

Since Dad was one of the officials, he got to stay in the office and since I belonged to Dad, I got to stay there too, along with Lew and Len. Later we got another man, Len's brother Bob, who had also run camp for the company and who shared quarters with us.

It was a privilege to be able to stay there instead of in the bunkhouse, as the atmosphere was different. These men were more refined and the talk and conversations were more intelligent. Sometimes the talk in the bunkhouse was of a nature that would curl your hair, especially the hair of a young farm boy who had never been exposed to this sort of environment before.

Lew and Dad soon had things organized and the men started to come in to camp – a cook and men to fall timber and cut it into log lengths, called sawyers, and then a little later men with teams of horses to skid the logs and other men to be swampers (men who cleaned out brush and other debris) so the horses could get through. Later there were some men to build a logging chute and the flume.

This was of course fascinating to me. I was put to work sawing wood for the camp and when the company team wasn't busy, I skidded some of the wood logs into camp from a hillside above camp that had been already cut for that purpose.

Chapter 15

There were no chain saws in those times – they had not yet been invented – so we sawed every thing with a crosscut saw. A crosscut is a long saw about eight or ten inches deep in the widest place and then it tapers toward the ends on the teeth side to about six inches at the ends where the handles are fastened to the blade. The blade itself is about three sixteenths of an inch thick and six feet long or longer. The blade has teeth cut in the bottom of it that can be filed to keep the blade sharp. There are holes in the ends of the blade where the removable handles are fastened. If one man is using one, he only has one handle, if two men are using it there are, of course, two handles used, one on each end.

In use, they are pulled back and forth and when pulled to you the sawdust comes out on your side and then on the backstroke, the sawdust goes the other way. The slang terms for them in those days were a Swedish Fiddle or a Misery whip.

My first job was making camp wood – wood for the cookhouse, the bunkhouse and the office. It was a monotonous job; you just rubbed that wood to death it seemed. Push, then pull, back and forth all day long. If anyone ever tells you that isn't hard work they have never done any of it, I can tell you that. It is great for reducing the waistline and you never saw a fat sawyer, for two reasons: one was that a fat man wouldn't work that hard or two, if he did he wouldn't be fat for very long.

Some of the wood was very dry and hard and this was the best wood for fuel and heat, but it was slow to saw. There was one redeeming factor about this job, however, that I caught on to soon. I would hunt through the wood and save out the pitchy stuff and along about ten in the morning I would take an armful into the cookhouse and tell the cook I thought he might be in need of some pitchy wood for kindling and/or a quick fire.

He was a good guy and would tell me to help myself to a hot piece of pie right out of the oven and have some coffee, which was always on the back of the stove. I always tried to act surprised and would thank him profusely and accept as gracefully as I could. We would go through this little charade every morning and I think he kind of enjoyed it. I, of course, enjoyed it and got a piece of nice, fresh, hot pie. Coffee breaks were unheard of at the time; they were not to come till after World War Two.

After working at this for a time it was decided that the sawmill would be started to cut the lumber for the log flume that was to be built and for the dam that would store the water for the flume to float the logs to the lower dam and pond where the camp was. Then they would be floated in the lower flume to the river.

The Sawmill

They needed someone to run the steam engine in the sawmill, so I was chosen. Boy, what a revelation that job turned out to be for me. To begin with, I didn't know anything about steam and I didn't know anything about firing a boiler. The man in charge of the sawmill was a cranky old guy about fifty-five, by the name of Billy Deal. I don't know if he didn't like me or not, but he was sure miserable to work for.

The sawmill consisted of a main floor or deck where the main saw was, the edger saws, and the cut off saws. There was a rollway where they skidded the logs in with teams of horses, to be rolled onto the deck, and from there they were rolled onto the machine, called a carriage, that traveled back and forth past the saw with the log laying on it in such a way that the log was exposed to the saw and every time it made a trip past the saw a new board was cut off. The carriage then moved the part holding the log out sideways, the thickness of a board, and the process was repeated.

The saw was a big circle saw and was powered by the steam engine, which I was to run. This was down under the deck with a big belt running up to the saw. The mill was built on the edge of a bank and the steam engine was down under the deck but the area was open on the one side so it was not in a hole and amounted to being level with the ground.

The logs were green timber and the men would throw the green cut slabs down for me to burn. They didn't burn very well and I would have a hard time to get a hot fire and to keep it hot to keep up steam.

The boiler took water to make steam, and it used a lot of water, which was no problem as they had run a small part of the creek right underneath the boiler, except the water is added to a boiler with steam from the boiler and when there is pressure in the boiler. It is accomplished with a device called an injector.

This thing is a series of pipes and valves so designed that it will force water into the boiler against the steam pressure when there is high-pressure steam in the boiler if you can get the injector to work and work the valves in the proper sequence, and if the injector doesn't get too hot. Sometimes they are sort of temperamental and refuse to work.

There is another device, called a lubricator, used to put oil in the steam so that when it goes into the engine it will oil the cylinder walls and the piston.

There was the problem of the steam pressure in the boiler. If the fire wasn't hot enough there wouldn't be enough steam pressure and the engine wouldn't pull the saw, particularly if they were sawing a big log. If the fire was too hot, the safety valve on the boiler would open and blow off steam and that then would soon require the adding of cold water to the boiler, which cooled the boiler down, and then there wasn't enough steam for power.

I was told the boiler would blow up if I let the water get too low, which was the truth. I was told if I didn't get the lubricator going when I started the engine I would burn up the engine, which was true.

After getting all these instructions about how to operate these various strange devices, and a very stern warning that there would be trouble aplenty if I made any mistakes, I was on my own. I was terrified; the only previous experience I had ever had with a steam engine was blowing the whistle on one after chasing sparks to get that privilege.

There were a few other things, like the relief valve would open at 97 lbs. of pressure, and it required about 90 lbs. to run the saw in a big log, so there wasn't much leeway. There was the throttle to operate too. When they were ready to start sawing, they would holler at me and I would open the valves on each end of the cylinder part way, and then open the throttle a little bit and the engine would start to turn over, forcing water from condensate to squirt out with steam from each end of the cylinder. This was very important to remember. If the water wasn't expelled properly the steam pressure in the cylinder would push the cylinder head off and that would be the end of the engine.

Well, this was a lot for a country kid to remember, at least this particular kid. I would get down there the first thing in the morning, start a fire, and wait till it got going pretty good, fill the fire box full of green slabs, run by the office to wash my face, then make a run for the cookhouse as by then the rest of the crew was eating.

By the time Billy wanted to start the saw, I would have steam up. They would holler at me and I would go through my routine, hoping I wouldn't forget anything. The first time when I started up the engine, I didn't blow the water out of the cylinder heads good enough for Billy. He came down where I was and bawled me out, good enough so that I didn't forget that any more. Then I would look at the fire and see that the fire was getting low and would shove some green wood in and soon the steam would go down so the saw wouldn't run fast enough and he would holler at me. Then I would get a good fire going, look at the water gauge on the boiler and see that the water was getting low and I would get the injector going if I could. If I couldn't I would get frantic as they had told me if I let the water get off of the crown sheet it would blow up the boiler which I didn't want to happen, particularly if I was going to be around there.

Sometimes I would have to pour cold water on the injector to get it to take on water and by this time if the engine was working hard the water would be quite low, so it would take a lot of cold water and this would cool off the boiler and the steam would go down. Trouble again, and I would get bawled out again.

This was my first experience with having real pressure on me. Boy, did I have my troubles, and down there all by myself, and when I wasn't doing something else I had to cut some of those long slabs off with an ax, as they were too long to go in the fire box the way they were.

I hate to admit it but I shed a few tears and I sure didn't feel like I was measuring up to being a man very fast. So many things that I didn't know about, and I was trying as hard as I could, but in spite of this I would run out of steam every once in a while. I was miserable. If I could have, I would have left that miserable place but I couldn't. I had no choice, besides I was home sick I guess.

Dad was up in the woods all day and didn't pay any attention as to what was going on in my life. After a few days like this, a man who I didn't know that was working up there someplace, came down where I was with my engine and said to me, "Kid, did anyone show you how to fire a boiler?" I said, "No, they showed me how to put water in and about the oil and about blowing out the cylinder heads and that is about all." I was about in tears again; I was having so much trouble. He said, "Let me show you how to run an engine properly. I can tell that you don't know how by the way you are running this outfit." He said, "It's a shame that no one showed you how to fire the boiler before."

Well, this was fine with me as my spirits were pretty low about this time, and if the rig had been mine I would gladly have given it to him, free gratis.

He explained to me to have my wood already stacked by the fire box door ready to shove in before I opened the door as the longer the door was open the more cold air went in the fire box and up the flues, cooling the boiler with outside cool air. As I had the exhaust from the engine turned into the smoke stack most of the time, to give the fire more draft, it really sucked cold air. He said to fill the fire box as full of wood as I could get it when the engine wasn't working hard, and by the time it got down to where it was to burn it would be somewhat dry. He also instructed me to watch, and when the men were going to place a new log on the carriage, which took a little time as they had to do this by hand with peaveys, to take on all the water I could, then it would be hot again when they were ready to go.

Boy, was this news to me and I was very grateful to him. This made all the difference in the world in my ability to give the sawyer power when he wanted it. I struggled along and got to be quite proficient at that job. I never did see the man after that, I guess he was in camp somewhere but he sure was a nice fellow and he knew what he was doing.

After he helped me out, I got over being scared. I got so I enjoyed that job and was fond of that old steam engine, and was sorry when we got all the lumber cut that was needed.

The Honey Bee Tree

Len McCrey said he knew where there was a wild bee tree. He told about it several times and one Sunday, it was late in the fall and raining lightly, one of the men in camp asked him if he cared to tell where it was and if he would, if it would be all right with him if he cut it. Len said it would and told where it was. He said it was down the main creek about a mile and then up a little side creek about a quarter of a mile. He said it would be easy to find and told him it was right beside the creek in a dead cedar tree that appeared to be hollow, about three feet in diameter.

This fellow had a brother in camp and they talked it over and decided they would cut it. They asked me if I wanted to be in on it. That sounded interesting to me and I went too.

We got some empty kerosene cans and washed them out real good and put haywire bails on them to put the honey in if we got some, took a couple of sharp axes and went down there in the cold drizzle.

We found the tree right where Len said it would be. None of us had ever robbed a bee tree before but we had heard about it. The hole in the tree where the bees went in and out was about four feet above the ground and, as it was cold, there were no bees flying. One of the guys took an ax and hit the tree and sure enough, it was hollow, and sure enough out, came a few bees but it was too cold for them to fly very well, they just kind of buzzed around in a listless manner.

He cut a notch in the tree above the hole and one below so he could take out a big slab of the tree trunk. When the notches were made, he split one side and then the other up and down, then his brother and I got hold of the slab and he pried it out with the ax.

We hit it just right, there in front of us were five combs of honey just as pretty as a picture and of course, bees all over the place. These combs were about thirty inches long in the center and the two on the outside were a little shorter. They were about ten inches deep and three inches thick. We brushed the bees away the best we could, trying not to get stung, as we soon found that although it was cold they could still sting.

There was some rotten wood too that we had to contend with. We had on canvas gloves and had to use an ax to cut the combs up to get them in our cans. Boy what a mess – but what a mess of beautiful honey we had, probably well over a hundred pounds. There had been a forest fire through the area several years before and the ground was covered with fireweed so the honey was fireweed honey, reputed to be some of the best that is produced. We each got stung once but it was well worth that small price as we had some of the finest honey in the land for our hot cakes for quite a while after that.

The Big Horse

The next job was driving a big horse whose mate had been killed in a logging accident previously. It was a mare and she was big enough that she could do the work of two small horses. This horse was huge, weighing 2200 lbs. The blacksmith made what was called a go-devil to haul lumber on, up the creek, to build the flume and the dam to be built above camp. There was no road, just a trail along the creek bottom. This device was just a couple of runners sloping up on the front ends, set about four feet apart with supports between them and a round pole about six inches through fastened crossways on the top side of the runners with pieces of iron for reinforcement and was called a bunk.

One end of the lumber could be laid on this bunk and fastened down with a chain. The horse then was hooked to this and the lumber could be dragged up the creek bottom to where it would be needed. This was a good job until it got cold. It took me quite awhile to haul all the lumber and position it along the route where the flume was to be built. The dam lumber had to be hauled at least a mile or more. Sometimes in the morning I was able to time it right and would just happen to go by the cook house at the right time and would be invited in for a piece of hot berry pie, I don't think I have ever tasted any pie since that was as good.

That was about the only bright spot in the day. The weather was beginning to get bad, rain and snow and it was getting cold. My hands were wet all the time as I had to hook and unhook the rigging and it was constantly getting wet from the creek, or the rain. The only time my hands were warm was when I was in camp. Boy I suffered, they chapped and split and would bleed. After this job was done, I was put in the cookhouse as a flunky, a job I didn't particularly care for but the weather was better in there.

A flunky was a man cook helper and a female helper was called a cookee. I would peel potatoes, onions, carrots, and turnips, open canned food, carry water and wood, set tables, wait on them, clear tables, wash dishes and do anything else the cook wanted me to do. Our day started at four thirty in the morning and was over about seven at night. I had a chance to get a piece of hot pie every day though so it was not entirely without some reward.

The Mustard Plaster

One morning when the crew came in to eat one of the men told me that one of the crew was too sick to come to the cookhouse for breakfast and that when I got around to it I should go down and have a look at him and keep the fire going. When the dishes were done, I told the cook where I was going.

When I opened the bunkhouse door, I could hear him breathing. He was gasping for air so hard and after looking at him, I thought he was going to die. I beat it back up to the cookhouse and said to the cook, "You had better come look at that guy who is sick; I think he is going to die."

He came back with me and said, "I think you are right, do you know how to make a mustard plaster"? "No," I replied, "my mother never used them."

We went back to the cookhouse and he got a clean flour sack and we put some wet mustard out of a gallon can on the rag, and spread it around real nice. Well, we talked that over and it was cold and wet so we didn't think that looked very good so he put some dry mustard on top of that, quite a bit in fact as we had plenty of it, probably about a half a teacup full.

We went back to the patient with our poultice and told him what we were going to do. He couldn't talk he was so choked up. He had on long underwear; so we pulled this back from his chest but when we got ready to apply the plaster our mustard mess looked so cold and wet we decided to warm it up a little.

One of us got on each side of the stove and held it till it was real hot then we slapped it on his chest. We patted it down real good and the cook said, "You stay here and don't let him take it off, I have to get back to the kitchen as my bread is about ready for the oven." He said, "You stay right here and watch him and if he tries to take it off you put it back on and push it down real good."

Well, about this time the poor guy started to squirm pretty good and started to paw at the mustard plaster but I wouldn't let him pull it off. I stayed there for about an hour and figured that was good enough and this poor fellow was struggling and making noises all the time. I took it off finally and tucked him in real nice like a mother would and left a good fire in the stove and went back to the cookhouse.

At noon, the cook sent me down with some soup and I propped the man up and helped him eat. He was breathing much easier but was still in bad shape. I kept a good fire going for him all afternoon and that evening he was much improved. Some of the crew took him some hot soup for supper. The next day he was able to come up for his meals and in a day or so he was up and around.

He showed us his chest and we had blistered him from his Adams apple to his navel but we cured him. He said that if we hadn't done what we did he would not have made it. He said, "If I hadn't been so sick I would have poked you for holding that plaster on me for so long." After a couple of days he took off for town all alone, it was three miles by pack trail to the river and then six miles down the railroad track to St. Joe city where he could catch a train for town and a doctor if he still needed one. I guess he made it, we never heard from him again. Things were tough in those times and so were the men; you had to be to survive.

The Whipsaw

It started to snow along in November and the biggest part of the crew was laid off, so the cook didn't need a helper and I was sent to work back outside with my dad and a small crew. Dad was building the upper dam then and I got to work up there with him. They were just finishing the face of the dam and ran a little short of lumber to complete the job.

Len was working up there so he and I whipsawed some lumber. That is the way lumber was made when there was no power. Boy what a job. We rigged up some logs on the edge of a dirt bank with some log posts under them so they would stick out in the air and then put the log that we were going to cut boards from cross ways on them so one guy could get underneath and one could get on top. Then you take a crosscut saw and start sawing lengthwise of a log and saw forever.

The man on top has the hardest job as he is pulling up when he pulls the saw on his stroke and the one below of course gets to pull down. The guy on top watches the line too that you have marked on the log where you have peeled the bark off and snapped a line for a guide so the board is straight when finished. We had no chalk for a chalk line so we used charcoal from burnt sticks that we toasted in a fire.

This was hard work but by this time, I was in pretty good shape physically and could pretty well hold up my end. Sure made me appreciate that old steam engine though, after that. The snow got to be a couple of feet deep and one night after supper I wanted to have a little fun so there were a couple of big scoop shovels in the barn and I talked one of the lumber jacks, who was a young fellow, into going out to slide on the scoop shovels with me for a little entertainment.

The only place we had that was open and down hill was very steep but we had a good time when we could stay on them. I think he felt sorry for me, as it was pretty dull around there. About all we did was work.

The Ski Ride In the Flume

I made myself a little excitement one day after work. There was a pair of homemade skis up in the top of the blacksmith shop that someone had made that I had spied earlier. There was no binding just a strap fastened to them for your feet, which wasn't very satisfactory as it was hard to keep your feet in them. We were working up at the dam and walking back and forth in the flume, as it was nice and smooth and there were no rocks to stumble over and no puddles to step in as when walking in the creek bottom.

A flume for logs is made from two thicknesses of lumber with the joints staggered both end ways and sideways so it will hold water, and too for strength. The bottom of this one was about fourteen inches wide and the top was about four feet across, with a depth of about four feet. This made a good place to walk and we were using it for that purpose. It kept snowing and we would tramp it down and it got slick and icy, but as we all wore caulked shoes, that was no trouble.

I got the idea that I could take one of those skis and slide down to camp on it but I didn't know just how well it would work. After dinner (lunch was what they called dinner those days) one day, I took one of them back to the job and when everyone else had left for camp I got myself ready for my experiment. It was cold – I suppose about ten above zero – and the sun was just going down.

I cut a nice piece of a cedar limb about three feet long and about an inch in diameter to push on the side of the flume to keep my balance and for a brake if I happened to need one, or to push with if need be to keep going. I had a horsehide leather coat and I buttoned it to the very top and pulled my felt hat down real tight, put on two pairs of canvas gloves, got the ski in the flume, and much to my surprise it wanted to run away from me.

Steeper than I thought. Well anyway, I got all situated, squatting down with one foot ahead of the other on the ski and let up on my stick, and we took off.

I picked up speed in no time at all and I was really zipping along in great style. I would balance myself with my stick by pushing on one side or the other of the flume and it was working according to plan, just great. I was really enjoying myself and went about a half a mile I guess when I came around a bend and saw trouble ahead that I had forgotten about.

There was a big, old, red fir tree that had grown out of the creek bank and turned up so it kind of hung over the flume but high enough to be out of the way. It had been fire killed and had a thick coat of bark on it but the bark was loose and some one had hit it with an ax when walking by one day. A big chunk of this bark had fallen in the flume and rather than pick it up and throw it out we just walked on it.

Everyone wore caulked shoes and as a result this bark had gotten chewed up and scattered out for some distance and as it had not snowed for several days, it was laying there. I could see it coming but too late. I knew what was going to happen but my braking system was inadequate for an emergency stop.

When the ski hit the bark it was just like running up on some dry cork and the ski didn't slide any better than if it had been cork. The ski stopped extremely abruptly, but as I had nothing to hang onto, I didn't. I flipped up in the air and when I came down, I landed on my back with a crash, going down the flume headfirst on that horsehide coat. With my felt hat jammed on my head right down to my ears I must have looked like a big bullet and I felt like one too and was going about that fast, I think.

I was lucky the hat protected my head and the coat kept me from getting slivers in my body. I didn't get hurt but I thought I would never stop sliding and was beginning to wonder if I would slide clear into the lower darn pond before I stopped, which was pretty frightening. Boy, what a ride! I couldn't get hold of anything to stop, I was helpless.

I don't know where my braking stick went; it probably did end up in the pond. Finally I stopped, got up, assessed myself for damages of which there didn't appear to be any, and limped back up to retrieve the ski and sneaked into camp, hoping no one would see me and too, hoping no one wanted to discuss this little episode with me.

I was kind of stiff and sore for a day or two after that little caper. That was a memorable ride and I immediately took a solemn vow never to try that one again.

Chapter 16

We got the dam finished and started hewing the chute leading to the dam pond. The snow was deep by now; it was cold and Christmas came. There was only a small crew there by this time and several of the men went out for the holiday. There were no signs of the season in camp. Christmas morning came and, as was customary for a Sunday, some of the crew heated water over an open fire, washed their clothes, and did other personal chores like shaving and taking a bath in one of the washtubs in the rear end of the bunkhouse during the forenoon.

We had dinner, nothing special, and afterward it was lonesome. Someone said lets go to work and we did. It was better than sitting around, so my dad and the two lumberjacks who were working on the chute with us went to our chute job and put in the rest of the day. Sure didn't seem like Christmas, sure was better than sitting around thinking though.

I believe I explained how logging chutes were built and how they worked earlier in this text. In the hewing process, the logs are marked with a chalk line for the depth of the cut and scored with a sharp ax. Scoring means cutting in to the wood with an ax about every six inches to the line snapped on the log and this makes it easier to then hue a flat face on the chute log as the chips break upwards as you hue.

I worked best left handed with both hands, although I am right handed when using only one hand. I scored for my dad on one side of the chute and he did the hewing. The two lumberjacks worked the other side. I couldn't quite keep up; so Dad would stop hewing once in awhile and help me. He was an expert axe-man and could work either right or left handed so he took the left hand side and between us we could make chute just as fast as the other two.

The weather, being cold, we had to wear canvas gloves and my hands would get so cramped around the axe handle that I would have to slide them off over the end of the handle sometimes to get loose from it.

One day it was particularly cold and I stepped out of sight to relieve myself and when I was ready to fasten my pants (I had on two pair of jeans and there were no zippers at that time), my fingers were so cold I couldn't button up. I had a heck of a time getting fastened up again. I can clearly remember the incident and I said to myself, if I ever get on my own I am going to leave this miserable country and go someplace where it is warm in the wintertime. It took me a long time to do it, but I have finally spent a few winters where it isn't so cold.

A couple of weeks after Christmas we got word from St. Joe that there was a package at the post office for us. One of the men that was hewing chute with us, Johnny Johnson, was going to St. Joe city on Sunday to see his little boy who was staying with some older folks who were taking care of him, as Johnny's wife, the boy's mother had previously died.

I told Johnny I would walk in with him, so Sunday morning we took off right after breakfast for town. It was nine miles, three was the trail but it had been pretty well packed down by the pack string so wasn't bad. The railroad track was harder because there had been no one walking it for some time.

Well, we got there after awhile. The post office was in the store so I collected my package, then we went to see Johnny's little boy, had dinner with those old folks, and after visiting a short while started back. The days were short so we walked most of the trail in the dark, which was no problem as the snow reflects what light there is, and there was plenty of snow; but going up hill in snow is a lot harder than going down.

I had taken along a pack-sack to carry the package and when we got to camp I sure had a good sweat up. Johnny wasn't a big fellow but he sure could walk. We missed our supper, as we were too late but the package Mother had sent from Spokane more than made up for it.

I can't remember what was in it except that there was a dollar pocket watch for me and a small box of candy for Dad and me. The things were all wrapped in white tissue paper with nice little Christmas stickers on them. The first sign of Christmas I had seen, the first Christmas away from home, the first one without a tree and a present under it for everyone. It was, to say the least, an emotional experience to see that little sign of Christmas, for me at least. But I managed in a manly manner.

There was the usual crew there watching Dad and me open our little gifts. I doubt he felt any different than I did, it was almost a tearjerker. Dad would never let on; he never talked about anything like that nor did you talk to him about sentimental things. I guess I learned some early lessons in suppressing personal sentiments from him.

One day when we were still working on the dam, we came in for dinner. We came in, washed up, and waited for the cook to ring the dinner gong. No gong. So after about twenty minutes someone walked the short distance to the cookhouse to see what the trouble was. The cook had prepared dinner, dished it up, set it on the table, but when he went to ring the gong he was so drunk he fell out the door and fell down the two steps. He was so drunk he couldn't get up but he was happy. The food was cold of course, as it had been on the table for a few minutes.

It turned out the cook had saved fruit juice for some time and had concocted some kind of brew. Evidently he sampled it this day and was so pleased with the results he couldn't resist the temptation to satisfy his thirst. That was of course the end of that cook. We ate and afterward Dad and Lew Howard talked it over and Dad told me to stay in camp, as he would cook till a new cook could be hired in Spokane. I was to help him. This we did for a few days when a new cook came, then we went back to the dam job.

My dad could do almost anything, cook, blacksmith, make things out of wood or iron or a combination. Build houses, dams, was an expert with an axe, could hew a log so smooth it appeared it had been planed. He could and did whittle things out of wood, such as wooden chains and little cages with balls in them all out of one piece of wood. They were marvelous. He was a good fisherman, a hunter, knew everything there was to know about the outdoors and could even make biscuits on a campfire. He could write poetry and loved to read Shakespeare. He could do a jig or give a speech.

One thing he could not do though was sing. He thought he could but no one else did. That is where I inherited my inability to carry a tune I guess, not from mother as Mother was a music teacher as well as a regular teacher and loved good music. I did inherit some appreciation for music from her.

A Bear Chasing a Man up a Tree

I will tell the story that Len and Bob McCrey told us one evening in camp as the men all sat around trading stories about experiences they had been through. This incident took place when they were younger and were gold prospecting in British Columbia.

Bob was working in a creek bed, panning gold and Len was some little distance away, out of sight, doing the same thing. Len heard Bob yelling that a bear was after him and he needed help. Len didn't have a gun. The only thing he had in the line of a weapon was a double bitted axe.

He grabbed the axe and ran down to help his brother. When Len got where he could see, his brother was up in a small tree as far as he could get and a big bear was standing on its hind legs clawing at Bob's legs.

Len sized the situation up and without hesitation waded right in with the axe. He was finally able to kill the bear, as his brother watched from the tree. Bob said if Len hadn't been within yelling distance, and not been brave enough to attempt to kill the bear with only an axe, the bear would have done him in and maybe Len too, as he was losing his grip and also quite a bit of blood. Bob showed us his legs and they were all grooved with long white ugly scars; he proved the story.

It wasn't too long after, that we got the chute job done. The snow was about three feet deep and it snowed almost every night; if you didn't put your tools on a stump at night you couldn't find them in the morning. It was no use trying to do anything so Dad decided we would go back to the ranch for the rest of the winter.

We walked to St. Joe city on a Saturday, waited for the evening train, rode to St. Maries, got a hotel room for the night and in the morning took a steamboat to Harrison. We were lucky to catch a ride out home with a neighbor, getting home about noon. The house was as we had left it some four months before. Old Queen the horse was there, glad to see us and get a good feed of hay. The chickens were gone; I guess the coyotes had gotten them.

The house was cold and damp and lonesome feeling but we soon had things warmed up and it became comfortable. It was home, although it was never the same again. Mother was never to come back and neither was Don, to live, that is. It was lonesome and there was nothing to do, working had been better.

By that time, it had begun to dawn on me that work was to be a life long occupation. I also figured that I might just as well enjoy it if I could, as it appeared to have all the elements of permanency. We didn't have much to do and would go to town quite often just to have someone to talk to.

One Sunday a neighbor fellow about my age by the name of Levi Leeman came over with a team and wagon for a load of baled hay that his step dad had bought. Levi and I loaded the hay out of the barn – I don't know why Dad didn't help but he didn't - and when we got it all loaded Levi said to me "How about riding out to the county road with me so we can continue our visit for a little while longer?"

The snow was off and it was the season of mud. This sounded good to me so I took him up on it and climbed up on top with him. When we got nearly to the county road there was a big mud hole and down went the wagon wheels clear to the axels. After trying to pull it out with the load on and couldn't, we very reluctantly decided the only thing to do was to unload the whole load, get the wagon out on the other side of the mud hole and then reload the whole thing.

This was a job, working in the mud, and the hay had to be hand carried through the muddy place about sixty feet long, laid on dry ground, then the wagon pulled out to the dry place and reloaded. What a job! We worked all the rest of the afternoon at it, finally finishing just before dark. What a way to spend Sunday afternoon.

Speaking of mud, the month of March was mud usually and as there were no gravel roads then where we lived, it was something. That spring Dad and I carried a shovel in the car just so we could shovel a place to get out of the ruts when we came from town and it was time to turn into our place. I would get out and shovel a little trail for each front wheel to follow to get out of the main ruts. If we didn't do that we just kept going on down the road.

One day when we came back from town, we got stuck right in our own lane leading up to the house, as there was a low place there and sometimes it was muddy. Dad said, "You see if you can get the car out and I will go on up to the house and get supper." This was fine with me so I got some straw left over from an old stack that had been near there several years previously and managed to get some under the rear wheels and got the car up on dry ground.

I knew all the controls and how they worked but had never had much of a chance to practice. When I got out of the mud, I was in the hay field, which was nice and dry, and as Dad hadn't called that supper was ready, I just thought this was a good time to practice my driving skills.

I got the hang of it right away and had a good time. I kept watching the house and finally I saw Dad standing in the kitchen doorway and knew it was time to eat. I drove up to the house and much to my delight Dad stood in the doorway with a big smile on his face. He approved heartily and, believe me, that made my day. From then on, I got to drive quite a bit more all the time and soon he would trust me to go to town by myself and that was the start of my driving career. There was no such a thing as drivers licenses at that time; if you could drive just go ahead, you were on your own.

A man by the name of Dick (last name doesn't matter) wanted to rent the ranch and Dad decided to let him have it. We were getting ready to go back up to Fitzgerald Creek then and didn't have a team to work the place with, and besides that Dad had a vested interest in the logging job as he was to share in the profits from the sale of the logs when they reached the mill instead of getting paid regular wages.

He had received no pay for the time he had put in and my wages went to support Mother and Don at Stimpson's in Spokane. Dad had explained to me that it just about had to be that way as he was out of money. This was fine with me as I was willing and anxious to help out if I could; in fact, I was proud to be able to do so. It took all the money I made to keep things going. At the time, we got fifty cents an hour for an eight-hour day and one dollar and twenty-five cents was held out for board and room, leaving two dollars and seventy-five cents for you.

It might be of interest to the reader that a horse earned half as much as a man, a team got the same as a man, the board for a horse was seventy five cents and a team one dollar and a half per day.

Well, we took off for the logging camp in our Model T and we were glad to go. When we got there, we parked it beside the road down by the flume and just left it there. The snow was melting and the water was running. The dams were full and it was time to flume logs.

I was given the job of running the splash dam, down the main creek about a half mile above where the logs went in to the river. This meant I had to get going right after breakfast, and as soon as I got down there, which was about two and a half miles which I mostly ran, I would call my dad on a private phone for that purpose. He was going to take care of the dam at camp. He would open the dam gate some and poke logs through into the flume and away they would go.

It was surprising how fast they would go. After a few minutes, he would call me on the phone to tell me they were flooding. I would get down next to the flume and put my ear on the boards to listen. I would be able to hear the logs and water coming quite a ways before they came into view. The logs would be bumping in to each other and the sides of the flume.

When I heard them, I would run to the dam gate and open it up some so the flume would be full of water when the flood got there. The logs would go churning by my station and disappear around a curve. When they ran out of water at the upper dam Dad would call and when the last logs went by me and no more came for a while I would close my dam gate, to gather water for the next flood, run up on the side of the mountain where I could see the river and the end of the flume, to be sure that every thing had gone into the river.

After this I would call Dad, tell him all was clear then I had nothing to do but wait for the next flood. I could pretty well tell when it would be, by the way my dam filled. Sometimes it would be short, about forty minutes, sometimes longer; it just depended on how fast the snow melted up above.

It was a lonesome job, but it was easy. After the last flood of the day, Dad would call, and when I was clear I would walk back to camp. I would hike right along, as I was anxious to get there before supper was over with.

The flume had a walk built on the framework of the flume that ran alongside of the flume, which was two planks wide so I had good walking all the time.

Chapter 17

One nice spring morning I was on my way down to the dam and there were some logs on rollways along the flume that were cut and ready to be flumed but no one was working in the area at the time. I walked past them every morning and this particular morning temptation got the best of me and as there was a peavey there handy, I got all ready and rolled a nice round log in. There was plenty of water as the dam had filled during the night and the water was running over the gate.

There was a flat run of flume for about a hundred yards below this and I jumped on the log for a little free ride. Immediately the log started to turn and bob up and down and sway from one side to the other. It didn't take too long to figure out I had made a serious mistake.

The caulks in my boots were nice and sharp so I was able to stay on top of it, but I was busy dancing like a whirling dervish and I was fast approaching a place where the run got steep. The trouble was that by this time, the flume was about fifteen feet off the ground where it crossed a low place in the land and we were picking up speed at an alarming rate.

I had failed to take all of these things into my calculations. I was able to glance up long enough to see where we were and see that the flume cut through a dirt bank on the left hand side (the getting off side, where the walk was) and after that, it broke over a point of land so to speak and went down a real steep grade to the creek again.

I knew that I had made a grave blunder and it was about to cost me my life, if I didn't make some different arrangements with utmost haste, as if I ever fell I would never come out alive. I would go clear to the river and by then I would be ground into fish bait. What to do and no time to dawdle over a decision; it had to be right and it had to be a mighty good one as the stakes were high.

I realized it was a little late to be thinking about how dumb I had been to ever attempt such a stunt; however, thoughts of regret could be entertained later if I lived and if I didn't, well I had more immediate concerns to take care of at the moment.

The business at hand was to concentrate on getting off that rolling, Twisting, bouncing log. The answer was rather obvious, the only salvation was to jump over the side of the flume, land on my feet on a dead run to match the speed I was traveling, then stop in short order when we shot by this little patch of escape.

I managed to keep my balance and at the proper instant be squarely on the top of that squirming log. I gave it all I had and succeeded in making a perfect leap, over the edge of the flume, cleared the walk, landing on my feet in the dirt running a few steps and stopping just short of running out into the air over the edge of some small rock cliffs.

What an experience! I was so scared I could hardly walk, and was glad I didn't have to talk to my dad for a while till I got to the dam and had a chance to get the fright out of my voice. That was one of the most foolhardy experiments I have ever undertaken in a long life of many experimental adventures some good and some not so good, some fun and some not so much fun.

One day for some reason that I can't recall we were not able to flume logs. Lou Howard took a team of horses and a teamster with several other men, me included, up a side creek where there were some logs left over from the year before that the company wanted to get out.

It was a frosty morning and when we got up there, there was the log chute all covered with frost in this steep little draw.

The Logs had to be skidded a short way and then rolled into the chute. We rassled them around and got quite a string of them in the chute. When we were ready, we were all out of wind from exertion, and paused to get our breath. Someone said, "She looks like a bird," meaning everything was ship shape. About this time they hooked the team to them to give them a start and Old Lew Howard said, "Yes she does, and I think she is going to fly too."

The logs were all frost and so was the chute; they were a little hard to start but soon they took off and away they went down the chute and around a bend out of sight. In just seconds, we could hear timber crashing and all kinds of booming sounds coming up from below.

We were scared to go look but when we did, there was total chaos. The draw was full of logs, some on end, some cross ways, every way that they could possibly be. The worst part was no sign of any logging chute. It was gone, completely ripped out for a long way, just a mess. We were able to salvage some of the logs, the rest were left there among the rocks forever I guess.

The chute wasn't designed for frosty logs and a frosty chute on a frosty morning all combined. It was poor judgment on old Lou's part; he should have waited till the frost was melted before giving those logs a start down that slippery slide.

Shortly after this, one morning I was on my dam job again when Walt Russell came by on his way to camp. As the trail went right by the dam he stopped to chat with me for a few minutes, and to catch his wind. I enjoyed his company as I was just waiting for a call from Dad. My dam was about full and I knew we would be flooding soon. I had great respect for Mr. Russell, as he was a fine man; he and my dad had been good friends for many years.

Several hours later Dad called me on the phone and said to come up to camp. It was about time to flood again, but I took off and went up there to see what was wrong, I thought there had been a break in the flume, the gate on his dam wouldn't open or something. I knew something bad had happened. Everything looked fine as I walked back up, but when I got to the dam where Dad should have been, no sign of him. So I went up to the office.

Dad was there and he said, "Pack your things we are leaving." No Explanation, no nothing. We left and I never did know what happened. I could only assume Dad and Walt had a severe disagreement over something. Dad wasn't one to discuss things like that. He never said and I never asked. He and Walt Russell were never friends after that. I always felt bad about it because I think they secretly missed one another. They always had deep respect and admiration for each other before this took place.

When Dad died many years later, I sent word to Mr. Russell, requesting that he be a pallbearer at Dad's funeral, which he was. Dad never got a dime for all that work up there the fall before or that spring. It was a good thing that I got paid wages, because that was all the money there was to keep things going, mainly Mother and my brother Don staying at Stimpson's in Spokane.

We took off before dinner and went down to the road where the car was. It was fine, no one had bothered it so we left for home. Well, Dick and his outfit had moved in while we were gone. We had no place to batch. Our home wasn't our home anymore. Dick's wife, who we had never seen before, was a mentally retarded person, about nineteen years old I would guess – big, fat, dirty and lazy; boy was she dirty and lazy. Dad and I had kept a bedroom reserved for ourselves before we left. We had put a special lock on the door and had put some prized possessions there for safekeeping.

We also had two beds so we had a place to sleep. They had the rest of the house. They had a little boy and a baby. I can't remember what her name was but Dad called her Tubby, which was fitting. I guess she was about five feet four and probably weighed about two twenty. We had some meals with them because there was no choice; I could hardly stand to eat there.

She would change the kid's diaper and never wash her hands, and then handle food. I would just about throw up. She couldn't cook and she didn't care. She wasn't worth a damn except to have kids and I am not sure they were all right; I never did know how they turned out. About all they ever ate was boiled potatoes. We furnished the food when we were there; I don't know what they ate after we left. Sometimes she would go to the neighbors and stay all day, then when her husband came in from the field there would be no supper ready. What an outfit.

Dick, it turned out, was a very disagreeable and sullen type of person, not pleasant to be around. I couldn't say as I could blame him too much. But on the other hand he got himself into that mess, and a mess it was. Dad would have been much better off to have let the place just set empty. Too late this was realized; I am sure he regretted letting Dick have the place as he never did get anything from this venture either.

Chapter 18

We were home for a short while and mostly spent our time in town. If Dick had been any kind of a guy I would have helped him with the Field work for nothing, but I could hardly stand him either. It was not a happy situation and a real loser as far as we were concerned.

One day we were in town when we met a lady and her daughter on the street that Dad knew from Rose Lake. The lady, Mrs. Hurd, had run a boarding house in Rose Lake where Dad had stayed sometimes when he had been working in the area. He introduced me to them and we had a short conversation.

Shortly after this Dad decided to go to Spokane to see Mother, and see how things were going. He left me a few dollars and the car, so I would go to town every day and stay all day. I came home to sleep and sometimes I would have supper there but no more than I could help. I had to be careful though as I didn't have much money and I didn't know how long it was going to have to last.

One day while I was in town the Hurd girl, whose name was Ellen, came down the street and stopped to say hello, which was flattering to me. She was very good looking, a blonde with pretty gray green eyes. After this, I made it a point to be visible whenever I thought she would be downtown and I think she found excuses to be downtown if it could be called that.

The center of town had businesses on one side of the street for a block and the rest of the town was scattered around the hillside from the lakeshore where the boats landed, and the train station was quite a ways up on the hill. The town from the air must have looked as though it had been dumped out of a huge bucket and the pieces just stayed where they fell.

Ellen's mother was staying in a rented house taking in borders. Going to the post office was a good ploy for the girls to come downtown and it was a good place for the guys to hang out because there was a long pipe railing along the open side of the walk where it ran alongside of the building to get to the entrance to the post office. This was a good roosting place for the boys. The girls had to go this way so it worked pretty well for everyone to get a look at the opposite sex without being too obvious. It worked quite well for everyone.

Well, I got better acquainted with Ellen and the more I saw of her the better I liked her. Sometimes she would come over and sit in the car with me and we would visit. I couldn't take her to the local eatery for lunch, as I was on a cookie diet because of economic circumstances. There was no cuddling for three reasons. First was I didn't know anything about that business yet, second was the old car didn't have a top on it and therefore no privacy. I guess the third reason was that I didn't know how and I sure didn't want to offend her, as I was afraid she would never speak to me again, which would have been heart breaking the way I felt about her at the time.

There wasn't much to do in town except go down to meet the trains and the boats when they came in. There would be a morning and an afternoon train from Spokane and two trains going the other way each day also. Passenger boats met all trains and sometimes passengers and light freight would be transferred one way or the other. This then was something to do, furnishing a little activity. It wasn't very exciting but better than nothing, where there was so little going on.

The mail always came on the morning train. A man by the name of Brown Sugar Smith was the local drayman in town, who hauled everything from the trains and boats up town with a team and a dray wagon. He would pick up the mail and incoming freight, delivering it to the post office and so forth.

After this had all taken place, it would soon be time to wait for the mail to be put up then time to go to the rail roosting place. Sometimes there would be something going on at the local blacksmith shop or the garage. I never hung around the pool hall; there was nothing there for me.

One morning I was down on the waterfront and a new Ford car came in from Coeur d'Alene on a steamboat. The garage man, Harry Hanner, who later became the sheriff of Kootenai County, drove it off the boat and looked over the crowd (crowd of about ten people, which was a crowd for there) to get someone to drive it up town to his garage for him as he had driven a car down. I was standing there trying to look intelligent (that is what I did when I didn't know what else to do) when much to my astonishment he said, "Would you do me a favor and drive this new car up for me?"

Boy, was I ever surprised. My mouth didn't flap shut because it was already shut. (That is what you do when you try to look intelligent, keep your mouth shut. Sometimes if you really are, you keep it shut most of the time; that can keep you out of a lot of trouble sometimes.)

I drove that new car with great care hoping everyone in town would notice. That was the first car I ever drove with an accelerator on it. This was a model T of course. For those of you who are not familiar with those times the gas pedal on a model T, wasn't a pedal at all but a little lever mounted on the steering wheel column right under the wheel on the right hand side.

This was adjusted with the right hand to go faster or slower, when you had the time. If you didn't you had to settle for what you had till you could get to it, which sometimes became extremely urgent because it stayed where you put it. This was good at times but could be exceedingly inconvenient when both hands were needed on the steering wheel, which was most of the time on those roads in those times. Well, anyway I got it there in fine style, only wishing it had been about six miles instead of six blocks. This was the last year of this style of Ford car and there were some little improvements, the floor gas pedal was one, as the old style was a very dangerous device.

A traveling show was advertised to be held at the movie house one Saturday night. I got up my courage (and believe me it was hard) and asked Ellen if she would go to it with me. She accepted the invitation (probably secretly hoping I would ask) then I had a new set of troubles. I had a suit I had bought the year before with my radio money, that had only been worn once, but no clean shirt.

I was able to get rid of Tubby by encouraging her to visit some of the neighbors so I could use our own washtubs, our washboard, heat some water on our stove and do a washing. I washed everything I owned while I could, using our own stuff.

Boy, this arrangement griped me no end. Not only these things but I missed Dad's cooking. He was an excellent cook and a baker. When he had time, we ate good things, well prepared, not half-boiled spuds and half done tough old boiled meat.

When it came time to iron my shirts I couldn't find my mother's flat irons, (I suppose Tubby had thrown them away.) I had to iron the shirts that were ironed the hard way, on the stovepipe of the stove, which is not a good way, but a way. What you did was wipe the stovepipe off very thoroughly. You sprinkled the items to be ironed, let them set for a period of time, then pressed the part to be flattened against the stovepipe with your hands and held it there for a little while till it got too hot to hold and that's about right.

Well, came the big evening I got all decked out the best I could, had a hell of a time tying a tie, didn't know how and when I was done I felt very uncomfortable as being dressed up for me was a rarity. It was a nice spring evening, very warm for that time of year. I picked her up and with pride and dignity (remembered to hold the door for her) drove up to the theater with some of the local guys looking on.

I felt like a real man about town. My first date, and with a very good-looking, very attractive girl, and a car to drive. I don't remember what kind of show it was. Three things I do recall, however, with vivid clarity. It was hot in there. I had my suit coat on and a tie around my neck, neither of which I was used to. It was really hot (no air-conditioning). She let me hold her hand as we sat there sweltering but finally I felt her slowly and gently withdrawing her little hot sweaty hand from my hot sweaty hand, which was disappointing.

I watched out of the corner of my eye to see what she was going to do with that hand; maybe she didn't want me to hold it. She got a handkerchief from somewhere, wiped it carefully, and much to my delight replaced it in mine ever so gently. Boy how lucky could you get; what a thrill.

The other recollection of this evening that stands out in my memory was that there were two men on stage. They were bantering back and forth, cracking jokes and so forth. One fellow said to the other, "Did you ever see a duck, duck a duck," and the other fellow replied, "No but I saw a goose, goose a goose."

I thought it was quite humorous but under the circumstances I was greatly humiliated. I stole a glance at Ellen, afraid she would be insulted. I didn't know much about the opposite sex, only what I had learned from my mother. She would have been highly insulted at such an exchange.

Well, I wanted to laugh but I was trying to be a gentleman. But out of the corner of my eye, I saw her suppressing a giggle and I thought it best to do the same, not to let her know how coarse I really was. We went directly home when the show was over. I didn't even try to kiss her, not that I didn't think it would be nice but I didn't know anything about that sort of business, and if she did she didn't let on.

I was a true country boy and a decent one too. There was no place to buy an ice cream cone or anything else that time of the evening. Hamburgers had not yet been invented, even if I could have financed it, which I doubt I could have. Dad had been gone about ten days by now and the financial situation was getting kind of strained.

One day a short time later she told me she had some bad news for me. My first thought was that I must have offended her in some way and I really couldn't think what I had done. Then I thought maybe she had another guy. Well she said, "My mother is going to move to Roseburg, Oregon."

This was bad news and good news, whichever way you looked at it. I hadn't done anything wrong and she didn't have someone else, which was good. She would be leaving, which was bad. It made me feel sick; I was very fond of her and enjoyed being with her so much. Just as I thought I had found something nice it too was going to slip from my grasp.

It was crushing – she was so nice, she treated me as though I was Somebody, and she cared about me. At this time in my life I think I sort of needed a little boost for my morale. It didn't seem like things were going too good. It kind of seemed everything I had known to be solidly anchored in my life was slowly crumbling.

Dad came back from Spokane and it wasn't good either. Mother was obsessed with delusions that she was mentally unbalanced. She insisted that she be given a sanity hearing, which required a formal judicial hearing with doctor's testimony. When they were done the judge said, "I do not find you fit to be committed unless you request it." Mother replied, "I don't think I am incapable now but I feel that I am going to be at any time." With this statement on her part, the judge had little choice but to issue an order for her commitment to the State insane asylum at Medical Lake.

Poor Dad wasn't in very good sprits either when he got back. That was why he had been gone so long. There went our last hope of ever again having a home. He was very honest with me, told me all about the whole proceedings and said it was pretty final. I felt sorry for Dad and I felt sorry for Don. I felt sorry for Mother, and last I felt sorry for me I guess.

One of the low points of my life, and his too. He said he would leave Don at Mrs. Stimpson's till we got something figured out. We didn't have any income and no home. Things had taken a dramatic turn and it wasn't for the better.

There was another big lumber company in town called the Export Lumber Co. owned by a man named Fred Herrick. This company was sort of a rival of Russell and Pugh's, who Dad had never worked for. It was beneath Dad's dignity to ask them for a job but something had to be done.

We were fortunate. One day we were on the street when we chanced to meet a man by the name of Fred Bell, who was a superintendent for Herrick. He asked Dad "What are you doing Charlie"? Dad said, "Nothing right now, just kind of looking around." Fred said, "How would you like to go to work for us, building a logging road up Evans creek. It's a truck chance. We are going to start logging up there next year and we would like to get the road built this summer so it can settle through the winter to be ready for use next spring." Dad said, "When would you want to start?" Fred said, "Right away if you can." He and Dad worked out the details and Fred said, "Can you go with me tomorrow to look it over?" "Sure," Dad said. So with that Dad had a job and didn't have to ask.

The next day Dad, Fred and I went up and looked the job over and Fred told Dad that evening when we got back, "When you are ready to go, hire a crew and whatever else you will need and start." There was an Export Co. logging camp about two miles from where we were to start on the road. Fred made arrangements for us to board there and they had room for us in their bunkhouse so it was time to get to work. That night when we were alone Dad said to me, "Do you think you can handle the team on that job?" "Yes," I replied, "I am sure I can and if I need any pointers you will be there to give me a hand." "Fine," Dad said, "you are the first man I will hire. From now on you will be on the Export payroll."

Well, that helped. The next morning we went to see my friend, Levi Leaman, and his stepfather to see if they had a team of horses that could be rented for the summer. They had a nice team that they would be mighty glad to rent for the summer, the same team we had gotten stuck in the mud with. We went to town, made arrangements to have the blacksmith shoe them, and Dad looked around town for a crew.

Things were not too good in the line of work, and as he knew everyone, he had little trouble finding men. I went to say goodbye to Ellen; I was going to leave before she was as it turned out. It was a very sad parting. When we parted, she kissed me; she knew more about it than I did I guess. I left with tears in my eyes, never to see her again. I didn't even feel like washing my face that night because I didn't want to wash that kiss off. I never saw her again; they moved in a few days. We wrote for awhile and then her letters became farther apart and finally quit coming altogether. I guess she got interested in someone else. She was very pretty and I knew I wouldn't be remembered for long. So ended my first experience in romantic affairs.

We lost no time in getting things going. Dad felt pretty bad and was anxious to get to work, and so was I. The next day I went over, got the team and harness, went to town with them got them shod and took them to the ranch for the night. The next morning bright and early I started for Evans creek and the job, glad to get away from there; it wasn't the same.

It took me all day to get there, as it was about twenty miles up there at least. Sometimes I would walk, and when I got tired I would ride for a ways. I just got the horses watered, unharnessed, and fed when it was supper time. I was looking forward to that as neither the team nor I had any lunch.

Dad got there about the same time and the next morning we went down to the job. It was too far to take the team back and forth so we put a big canvas tarp over some poles for a barn and made a pole corral for the horses. Rigged up a manger, and from then on I left the horses there for the night.

We rode back and forth in a Model T truck the company had at the camp. We got started on our road and things got better, didn't have so much time to think. I liked the team; they were a good team and I got along fine. My cousin from Spokane got in touch with Dad and asked if he could work for the summer for Dad. His name was Justin Maloney, Uncle John's son. He was a college law student at Gonzaga, about twenty years old, nice fellow.

He came up and Dad put him to work with an old friend of Dad's by the name of Al Barns, who had graduated from law school in his young days but for some reason became a lumber jack. Justin was a typical city kid and knew nothing about what we were trying to do; he was good though, in that he would do what he was told.

Sometimes he would work with me and I would have to tell him what to do which seemed strange to me as he was older but he just didn't know. He thought the work was awfully hard and at times had a hard time keeping up. This made me feel pretty good; I was used to it and began to realize I was quite a man after all. The road went quite well as we were building mainly up the creek bottom and there wasn't too much grading to do yet.

One day I was complaining about the mosquito bites around my wrists and Ankles, they itched so bad. One of those old timers said, "Those are not mosquito bites they are bed bug bites." Boy, I had heard of them but never before had I encountered any. They really bothered me, so that night I started to see what I could do about that problem.

The bunkhouse in camp was an old log building and was infested with bed bugs, no way to get rid of them short of burning it down. I told Dad I had to move, I couldn't take them. They didn't seem to bother him so I didn't' get too much sympathy. There was a tent over a wooden frame with a wood floor in it called a tent bottom that wasn't being used so I asked the camp boss if I could sleep there because of the bed bugs.

He was a nice fellow and he said, "Sure if you like, the bugs are bad I know but there isn't much I can do about it." He told me to take the blankets off my bed and wash them in hot water then hang them on the clothesline for a day to dry, then move to the tent. I couldn't wait for Sunday to come till I could do it.

I got some hay from the camp barn and made myself a bug free bed; what a relief. I noticed it wasn't long till Dad ordered some steel cots from town and he joined me in my tent. Of course, it wasn't the bugs it was because some of the guys snored too loud. Then I didn't have to sleep in the hay on the floor any more.

One evening the son of the camp boss, who was going with one of the girl cookees, invited Justin (my cousin) and me to go with some of them down to Medicine Lake for a swim. They were taking the company truck that we used to go to work. We were glad to join them. There was a problem, however; neither Justin nor I had a swimming suit.

There were two girls in the group so we couldn't go in the water with them. They let us out near a big fresh water slough along the railroad track where we could get down the bank to the water. We got undressed and laid our clothes on the rails, carefully picking our way down the rocky bank to a four strand barbed wire railroad fence. While doing a balancing act on those sharp rocks we negotiated the fence and got in the water. No one could see us from the road as we were over the bank out of sight.

The water was warm, we were really enjoying ourselves after a hot hard day's work when we heard the evening passenger train whistle around the bend. Well, we hadn't thought about that.

We had laid our clothes carefully, pockets up on the rails to keep something from falling out of them. The clothes had to be moved at all cost. It had to be done fast too; the train was making good time. We made for the fence, which was about half way up the bank over those sharp rocks, in our bare feet and in our nakedness.

Boy, what a scramble that was. We made it up and back in considerably less time than it had taken us to navigate the one-way trip in the first place. There was a great sense of urgency. We didn't take time to reposition our feet when we happened to step on the edge of a sharp rock, and I think every other one was laying with a sharp edge up. We had to be back in the water before the train came, as there was nowhere to hide.

When the train went by, we were well submerged and waved to them in an unconcerned manner. Little did they know how much inconvenience and pain they caused us because they had to run that train just when we were skinny-dipping. That was a torturous trip. My feet were sore for several days and I had a good many places where I had been hooked by the wire fence and some places where the skin was missing from my backside, because of the fence. I was sore for several days from that little forced sprint over the rocks and through that four-strand barbed wire fence.

We would have to drive down the mountain from the camp every morning and back at night. The crew at the camp was hauling logs on four-wheel, hard-rubber tired trucks with only two wheel-brakes and they were not air brakes either.

This was only a one-lane road with turnouts for passing another vehicle coming in the opposite direction. Going down in the morning was no problem but in the evening, coming back up, if a loaded truck was met coming down you had to get into a turnout before he got to you. The trucks had only those two wheel-brakes and low gear to hold them. They would be heavily loaded; they could go slow but at times they could not stop. One never knew if they could stop or not, so it was imperative to get into a turnout or run the risk of getting pushed off the road or get squashed if you didn't.

The trucks then were slow and not too reliable; some of the names were Diamond T, Mogul, White, Republic, G M CIs and the famous Bull Dog Macks. Breakdowns were frequent but the tires never went flat; occasionally tires had to be replaced, though at great cost, however.

The Fourth of July was coming and Dad decided we would take off a couple of extra days to go to Spokane. He left one of the older men in charge to look after the horses and to tell the small crew what to do while we were gone. We went to Spokane and to the Stimpson place where Don was.

The next day we took the streetcar to town then took an electric train to Medical Lake. Dad rented a couple of hotel rooms and we got Mother. I had not seen her since the fall before and she appeared perfectly normal to me. It was good to see her again, but not so good under those circumstances. She was normal except she was obsessed with this delusion that some day she would go off the deep end. We had a little family reunion, which was good but short.

The morning we left Spokane we were just getting ready to board the train when Justin came rushing up (he was to go back with us) all out of breath and said he would not be going back with us. It turned out later that his mother had thought he looked tired when he had come home and she didn't want him to work so hard. Yes, I guess we all looked tired but that is the way it was.

We brought Don back to the road job with us. By this time our road had advanced up the creek quite a way. There was a good log homesteader's cabin on a fork of the creek where the horses were kept and we could drive the car up there by this time.

Dad got in touch with the man who owned the cabin and made arrangements with him for us to rent it for the rest of the summer. He went to the ranch got some of our cooking utensils and bedding and we moved the tent from the camp up there. This then became our headquarters. From then on, we batched and some of the crew stayed with us. The others lived close enough that they could go home at night.

This was a bad year for yellow jackets. They were a real problem. When you drive a team of horses, necessarily the teamster walks behind. The horses would be dragging a set of double trees and maybe a logging chain or a pair of skidding tongs or both, when the team would walk through a yellow jacket nest in the ground and then the double trees would come along and stir things up. I would come along then, just right to get the whole swarm.

They would come boiling out of the ground and I would get stung, some times severely. I couldn't run as I had to stay with the team and of course, they would get stung too. It made them hard to control, for which you couldn't blame them.

Then too we had to go back and forth and would get stung every trip. I complained to Dad and he said. "We will fix that." From then on we would get a stick of dynamite, fasten it to a long pole with a short fuse and apply it to the problem area. The resulting explosion sure settled that business. What a relief that was, from then on. If I was lucky, we would see a nest before we drove over it saving ourselves an unpleasant, painful surprise.

I have a short story to tell here. One of the fellows Dad hired was Al Barnes who I mentioned earlier as having a degree in law. Justin worked with him and a year or so later, I saw Justin in Spokane. He said, "I will never forget that fellow, Al Barnes, who I sawed with. I would be on one end of the cross cut saw and Al, with a lawsuit, would be on the other." It made me laugh and reminded me of a time when Al Barnes went into the store at Springston. One of the owners, J.J. Pugh, came out of the office and on seeing Al said in a loud voice, to be sure everyone heard, "Well, if it isn't Al G. Barnes of circus fame; are you looking for something?" It was said by those who heard it, Al replied without hesitation, "No I just came down to take a look at the menagerie."

Old Al was a good guy and could match wits with anyone, and loved it. One day before we moved our headquarters, we were carrying our lunch in a big box. It seemed I could always eat. One noon, after everyone else had finished, there was some apricot pie left over. Someone said to me, "Why don't you eat that piece of pie?" I thought I would be impolite, so I asked several guys if they wanted it and when I asked Al, his reply was, "No it looks too much like a nursery by-product for me!" Then I didn't want it either.

The road advanced up the creek to where there was going to be some heavy rock work to be done, which we had no equipment for. It was time for Don to go back to school and for some reason unknown to me to this very day, Dad decided I should take Don back to Stimpson's in Spokane and get him started back in school.

Don and I took the train to Spokane and got a street car out to Stimpson's house where Don and Mother had stayed. I told Mrs. Stimpson Don would be staying with her again for the school year. This had been the arrangement agreed on when Don left to go to camp with Dad and I. I also told her I would like to stay for a day or so if this was all right with her.

This was fine with her. I also told her that Dad would appreciate it if she would keep an eye on Don, as he was pretty young to be on his own. This too was agreeable with her. Don had a room up on the third floor where he had stayed the spring before, after Mother had left. Kind of an attic room but it was finished and had a nice window where you could look out on the street. There was a double bed a nice table, a dresser and a big closet.

I went up the street to see my Uncle Johnnie and Aunt May about the second evening we were there to explain to them what was going on. After we had talked over the arrangements for Don, as Dad had instructed me to do, Uncle Johnnie said he would kind of look out for Don. Uncle Johnnie then said, "What are you going to do?" I said, "I am going back to the ranch, and Dad and I will probably tie the road job up till spring. I am hoping the company will have work for us this winter." He said, "Aren't you going to go to school?" I said, "No, I am through school; you know I have been working in the woods for over a year now." Uncle Johnnie said, "I am going to call your dad," and with that he got out of his chair and went to the phone. He did call and was fortunate enough to get Dad at the ranch. They had a long conversation that I could not hear, after which Uncle Johnnie called me to the phone and said, "Your dad wants to talk to you."

I got on the phone with Dad and he said, "Your uncle wants you to go to Gonzaga High School so you go down and register yourself tomorrow, I think it is a good idea."

Boy, I was flabbergasted. I was struck dumb. I tried to protest but he wouldn't listen. I tried to tell him he needed my wages to keep things going, that I didn't want to go to school, that I wanted to be a lumberjack and everything else I could come up with but all to no avail.

I was just sick about this turn of events. I had just a very few clothes. Dad promised to send me some but the truth of the matter was that I had very few that were suitable to wear to school. Unfortunately, in those days, you could not wear jeans. They were lumberjack clothes, and that is what I owned.

I didn't know how to register in school. I knew where it was, as it had been pointed out to me, but I didn't even know where the door was. What a shock and a disappointment to me. Here went my little world upside down again. It seemed to be coming apart about as fast as I could handle it. Just when I thought I had things kind of figured out for myself something seemed to happen and change everything. I didn't sleep much that night, wondering how I was going to be able to cope with this dilemma I now found myself in. I was a country kid and the only time I had ever been in a formal school was when I took the seventh and eighth grade examinations. Two days in my whole life. I had been working with men and was accustomed to being with men, not kids.

The next morning I told Mrs. Stimpson what had transpired the previous evening. She was sympathetic and that was all. I asked her about staying there with Don; she said that would be all right. No help with my dilemma there.

I went to Gonzaga, found the office, and told them my story. They directed me to the proper desk and after telling this man my story, he said, "Where are your grades?" I said, "I don't have any; I don't have anything."

He said, "What are you doing here?" I said, "My dad told me to come here." "Where is your dad?" "He is in Idaho." I thought things are going so badly perhaps they won't take me and I hoped they wouldn't. I didn't know what I was doing and I wished I was somewhere else, any place would be better than here.

Dad had instructed me to find out how much it would cost and to let him know so he could send me a check. I told them that, which was acceptable. Everything totaled up to just about one hundred dollars. They assigned me to a room and I finally located it. This was the day before school started so the next day I was in high school.

To show you how green I was, there was a big gym on the first floor and after a day or so, I got brave enough to take a peek in the door to see what was in this place. They were playing basketball. I had never seen anything like this before and watched with some fascination.

The players ran around chasing the guy with the ball and about the time they would catch up with him they would jump in front of him and wave at him. Didn't make sense to me. Then he would get all excited and toss the ball to someone else or run bouncing it on the floor, instead of taking it under his arm and going where ever it was he wanted to go in the first place.

Well, they ran around there for awhile hollering at each other and someone finally threw it in a hoop-like thing up on a frame work that stuck out from the wall with a sort of fishnet hanging down from it.

I thought: Fine, they finally got it where they want it; that will end the struggle. No, the fishnet had a hole in the bottom of it and the ball came right on through. When I saw the net had a hole in it I wondered if they knew it before they started to play their game. Well they kind of relaxed for a moment and I thought it was over but no. The two tallest guys stood in the middle of the floor and another guy that didn't appear to have much to do took the ball and tossed it up in the air between them, one guy jumped up in the air higher than the other one and knocked it down where another fellow grabbed it and they all went crazy again.

Boy, I thought to myself, what a waste of time and energy. I had worked long enough with men trying to imitate them not wasting effort needlessly, that I couldn't feature all this wasted energy. I was a pretty serious young man about that time I guess.

School was close enough so I could go home for lunch. About the second Day, when I came back from lunch, there was a welcoming committee waiting for some of us new fellows (Gonzaga was a boys' school only then). When we tried to enter the building, I found out I was a freshman, whatever that was, and that a freshman was the enemy and was to be scorned. A couple of these guys grabbed me, hustled me down stairs, and were going to make me sing.

Well, I didn't sing then and I don't sing now – for them or anybody else. The truth is I can't, I don't and I won't, and I said I wouldn't. They got hold of me and started to manhandle me, which was not in my scheme of things. I managed to get in two good swings before I was subdued by as many guys as could get their hands on me and was then thrown over a thing that stood about four feet high and was covered with smooth leather, called a horse. They placed me face down and held me in this very undignified position while people with heavy wooden paddles took their turns whacking me on the rump real hard.

I didn't count how many but it seemed like the whole school and then some took two turns at it. I kind of got the message and from then on, I didn't swing on anyone. This was very unsuitable treatment to subject a young lumberjack to. Oh, by the way, I didn't sing!

I didn't know anyone, I hadn't been around, it was all so new – I had a hard time for awhile. I was so lonesome for Idaho and my former way of life I could hardly stand it. I finally made some friends but I didn't fit in very well for awhile. I didn't have very good clothes and not a dime to spend. I was just plain uncomfortable. I never was a very good student and having been out for a year it was tough. I had no one to help me or that I could really talk to. I didn't know how to talk to the kids, boys or girls, in the neighborhood and I found out they laughed at me because of my clothes and the way I acted and talked. It took awhile and I developed a sort of suspicious attitude because I thought I was being made fun of, which probably made it harder.

Chapter 19

Things gradually got better as time went on. We had cousins in Spokane by the name of Skeffington, Gertrude and Ray. Gertrude was the daughter of one of my mother's sisters, our Aunt Maggie, a wonderful lady. They were nice people, older than we, with three boys, the oldest, Jim, being Don's age.

One day that fall the Skeffington family came by Stimpson's with their car and invited Don and me to go to the airport to see Charles Lindbergh, the first person to fly over the Atlantic Ocean solo. He was a hero of the time, as he had just accomplished this feat shortly before and was making a tour of the country with his little mono plane.

We went out to Felts Field with them and after a short wait here came the famous Sprit of St. Louis (the name of the plane now hanging in the Smithsonian Institute museum; I know because I saw it there myself), gliding down like a silver bird, with the famous man piloting it. That was an event to be remembered.

I chanced to make friends with two guys who were friends, by the names of Don Gorman and his good friend Bill Conley. Bill's father was a partner in a plant that produced stull, which were at that time timbers used in the mines for holding up rocks in the mining tunnels.

This plant, where they got the logs ready, was located on the lake at Harrison. Both of them had spent some time in Harrison during summer vacation so we had a little in common. They were nice fellows and we became good friends. Don Gorman had been an alter boy and knew some of the priests quite well. I got acquainted with some of the young fellows in the neighborhood and began to feel more comfortable.

One of those had a paper route and I helped him sometimes for a pittance. Many people burned firewood in their houses then, some in heating stoves and others in furnaces. They would buy the wood in four foot lengths called cord wood then hire someone with a gas powered saw called a buzz saw to cut it into sixteen inch lengths to be burned. Others bought mill ends from the sawmills and sometimes slab wood.

I soon learned that these new piles of wood were potential jobs, throwing the wood in the basement or a wood shed or whatever. Sometimes work could be had raking leaves, later shoveling snow. In the spring raking yards, spading gardens – anything to make a little spending money. We had to buy socks, shirts, some school supplies, and other things. It was fun to get to go to a show once in awhile too. It was a constant scramble to keep up, as money was tight.

Shows then were cheap, some ten cents, the kind we went to see. Some fifteen and up to fifty and once in awhile up to sixty five cents and that usually included vaudeville. I got pretty good at rustling jobs but the competition was keen and the pay was low. It was kind of demeaning after having been associated with men and their way of operating. I could hardly wait to get back to the woods.

Dad had taken a job as a timber and lumber assessor for Kootenai County, which takes in Coeur d'Alene and the area around Harrison up to Cataldo and also Spirit Lake and Hauser Lake. When we got out of school, Dad came to Spokane to visit Mother for a couple of days and we took the train to Harrison.

Our old Ford was in the woodshed on the ranch where Dad had left it the fall before. Thank the Lord, Dick, the fellow on the ranch, couldn't drive a car or he would have had that too. We knew the tires were bad on the car, so before leaving Spokane Dad went to the Western Auto store and bought four new ones and had them shipped to Harrison for us. When we got to Harrison Dad told me to go out and get the car, and Don went along. When we got to the ranch, the tires were all flat. The only thing to do was pump them up with a hand pump, which was quite a workout.

I got the car started and we took off for town, but didn't get far before we got a flat tire. The wheels had what were called clincher rims – the rim was part of the wheel. The tire had to be taken off the wheel. No spare, and you didn't take the wheel off either. So you jacked up the car, took two tire irons, pried the tire from the wheel, found the leak in the tube, cleaned the tube around the hole, and put on some cement and a tire patch.

You then mounted the tire back on the wheel hoping that the patch held, and pumped it up. (Some fun!) The reader will find this unbelievable but we had seven flat tires before we got to town. It took us all afternoon. Was I ever glad to get there! We got the new tires from the depot and mounted them. Four more pump jobs that afternoon. What a relief and what a workout on that tire pump.

We got the camping supplies from the ranch that we had used the summer before, and headed for the woods for the whole summer. I think the first place we went was to the Little North Fork of the Coeur d'Alene River. There was no road in there at the time so Dad hired a horse and a pack saddle from a man who lived near Cataldo. We parked our car and loaded our camping equipment and grub (food) on the horse. We each took a pack sack and packed our supplies over the mountain to the Little North Fork.

We were going to camp out but when we got there, Dad knew an old fellow by the name of Jack Brandon who had a homestead there and made his living by trapping. The trail ended at his place and when he found what we were going to do, he invited us to stay there with him. This we did, and worked out of his place. We furnished the food and he furnished Dad a bed, and Don and I slept in his haymow.

When we got there, about four or five miles up and over a mountain, we took the halter off the horse's head, tied it to the saddle and turned the horse loose to go home on his own, which he did. This had been agreed on when we got the horse.

Dad taught me how to run compass for him as he cruised timber for assessment purposes. This was, at that time, virgin timber as it had never been logged and was beautiful country to see. The compass man and the cruiser first find a section corner that was established by the original land survey. This then tells where you are and is used for a point of reference. To find one on your own in the timber sometimes is quite a job but Jack Brandon knew where the corners of his land were so he showed us a corner and we could work from there.

When the land to be cruised is located, the cruiser will size the situation up and make his plan. He will instruct the compass man as to what he is to do. One method that is used, or was at that time, was to run strips through the land and this is done by the compass man by sighting with a compass and going in a straight line, and at the same time pacing, which is counting your steps as you walk, and in this manner keeping track of how far you have walked.

The cruiser then goes along behind, counting trees in a given width of the strip and estimating how many thousand feet of lumber can be expected from the land in its entirety. The compass man doesn't pay any attention to the cruiser but is extremely careful to go in a straight line and to tell the cruiser at all times where he is, if asked.

Sometimes when the terrain was real steep or the area very brushy the cruiser could sort of pick his way when the compass man had no choice but to go straight, not deviating from his line of sight taken with the compass, as the linear distance was just as much a part of the land measurement as was the line of sight. So the pacing had to be as accurate as possible.

Sometimes we saw some beautiful country before it had ever been logged or disturbed by man. We cruised a lot of timber up there, the ground was steep and the mountains were high, there were no trails and we walked every step of the way. Sometimes, when we didn't expect a hard day, Don would go with us; at other times he would stay in camp. We had to finish that location for that year and leave, as the county assessor wanted some timber land cruised in the Twin Lakes area.

There was some timber on a mountain side that Dad wanted to finish before we left for the season that was a long walk from camp. We talked it over and decided rather than walk back and forth we would take some grub with us and a couple of blankets and just stay up in the vicinity for a couple of days to finish. This we did. The weather was good so we slept wherever we happened to be each night when we called it quits for the day, providing there was water.

Well, it worked fine but, as usual, it took longer than we had anticipated and we ran low on food. In fact, we ran out of everything except some rice. Rather than taking time to go back for supplies, we decided to make do with the rice. We had rice for three days and that was it. Boy was I ever glad to get something else to eat when we did get back.

We got Jack Brandon to pack our outfit out for us, as he had a couple of horses. It happened to be the day before the Fourth of July. We went to some people's place by the name of Herskin who Dad had known for a long time, and stayed with them for the Fourth. They had a son, Bill, about a year older than I, and two girls, one, Ruth, about my age and a younger one. Ruth later became quite famous for her skills as a lumber jill (a lady lumberjack), putting on exhibitions at the Sportsman's Fair in Spokane. After this, she traveled quite extensively putting on exhibitions and finally was crowned the lady champion lumberjack of the world.

Chapter 20

One evening Bill said to Don and me, "Do you guys have any firecrackers for tomorrow"? We said, "No we just came out of the woods, we don't have anything." He said, "I will think of something, we have to celebrate a little." Don and I were sleeping in the hay in the barn. He said, "I will come up and get you guys in the morning and we will set off some dynamite."

Well, that sounded good to us. The next morning here comes Bill at five o'clock sharp and he already had three sticks of powder, a cap and fuse. There was a big, flat stump out in the field a short distance from the buildings so we took our paraphernalia out there, placed it carefully on the flat surface of the stump and when we got everything ready we lit the fuse and ran for the barn.

It was a nice clear morning with the sun not yet high, the dew glistening on the grass, and a scene of tranquility if ever there was one. The serenity of the whole Coeur d'Alene River Valley was shattered by a deafening roar, an explosion that rattled the mountains for miles around. It even scared us and we were expecting it.

It echoed back and forth, reverberating from one mountain to another for several seconds, finally fading out in the distance. We were glad when it died out and everything got back to a peaceful, quiet morning.

We waited for some little time before we approached the house. When we did, Bill's mother was in the kitchen frying bacon for breakfast and not in a very conversational mood. Everyone was up for the day. In fact, I think everyone in that part of North Idaho was awake and up for the day. Bill's Dad wanted to know what went on and Bill told him. His Dad didn't say much as I remember it, except to say we shouldn't have used so much dynamite. This we knew, but it was after the fact, as is often the case; we learn by experience and that was one to remember.

We finished the summer cruising timber near Hauser Lake and Twin Lakes. I recall an episode that took place that summer that might be worth recounting here.

The yellow jackets were very bad and we frequently ran afoul of the nests. One otherwise nice morning, we were on a south slope covered with big pine trees. I stopped to take a sight with my compass and as I was standing next to a dead tree I stuck my little hand axe in the tree trunk, while I took a sight. About the time I had made my sight, I became aware of the fact that there were a lot of yellow jackets buzzing around me. I went to take the axe out of the tree and here was a hole in the tree and they were just boiling out right next to my shoulder.

About this time, I got their message with a sting. I grabbed my little axe and ran to a patch of thimble berries that were about belt high and were real thick, I ducked down under the big broad leaves to get away from them as they were following me, and kind of pulled the leaves over my head to hide. I just got settled there and thought I was safe when there seemed to be a lot of them there too. I was crouched over a ground nest and got stung again. Would you believe I got in seven yellow jacket nests before I could get away from that hillside, getting stung once in each of the seven? There must have been something about that hillside that particularly appealed to them. I got stung so many times that summer that they didn't even swell up much after having been stung thirty five or forty times; but they would get your attention and still smarted for a while.

When it was time to go to school, Don and I went back to Mrs. Stimpson's and to school – Gonzaga for me, St. Aloysius for Don. I didn't mind it so bad this time. In fact I was kind of glad to get back, to see my friends and the city.

I got a job delivering handbills on Saturday mornings for a dollar. It took all morning but it was steady and it was a dollar that could be counted on.

Ice Skating

It got cold early that year and some of the fellows were going ice skating at Manito Park. I had no skates and had never even seen anyone skate but had heard of it. One of my friends, Bob Grieve, had some old clamp-on skates clamped on some old dress shoes of his Dad's which he offered to loan me if I wanted to go. One fellow had an old Ford car and took a bunch of us for my first skating venture, to Manito Park Pond.

It was fascinating to see the people (mostly kids) flying around on the ice, and of course when I tried it I couldn't do it but it had great appeal to me. I resolved to learn as quickly as I could, which I did. From then on when there was ice and I had time I spent it skating. Sometimes I would even walk from the north side of town all the way up to Manito (south side of town), skate all evening and walk home again. I rustled around and saved enough money to buy a pair of modern skates, which was a major investment, six dollars as I recall, and I had them for many years. Sometimes we skated on the river back of Gonzaga when it got real cold and stayed that way for awhile. However, it was pretty dangerous as there was quite a current underneath.

During these times, milk was delivered by a man with a horse and light wagon or a team and a heavier wagon early in the morning. When there was snow, they used sleighs. The mail men downtown collected mail from the sidewalk collection boxes with a horse and cart. It may seem rather primitive now but at the time was an accepted fact. Street cars were the common means of getting around town if you had a dime, which I seldom did and if I did, I saved it for something I needed more than a ride to someplace I could walk to for nothing.

Once in awhile some of us would gather under the arc light on the street corner in the evening and try to think of something for entertainment.

The Street Car Caper

One thing we did once in awhile was a very complicated prank, but if carefully executed always paid off rather well with a little excitement and devilish satisfaction for us and quite a bit more (I mean excitement), for some other people. It is a good thing it was so much trouble as had it not been we would have done it more often and would have gotten in trouble.

The first thing was for someone to get a short piece of thin lumber, such as a piece of lath or part of the side from an apple box, then go to the intersection of Baldwin and Hamilton streets where two street car lines intersected. The track maintenance people greased the rail joints to make them easier for the conductor to shift the switch when necessary with his long rod that he used after carefully stopping the street car over the joint in the track so he could set the track for the direction he wanted to go. Some grease would be dug out of the rail joint (called a frog) on the stick, and taken to the site where the plot was to be carried out, the intersection of Indiana and Dakota which was about two blocks away.

The street car had to go around that corner and up a slight incline, when coming from town. This was a sharp curve and had to be negotiated rather slowly so the car didn't jump the track. The grease was applied to both rails of the track just as it started up this little grade. This of course had to be done when there were no cars or street cars in sight. The next thing was to wait for a street car to come along from town. Timing was critical. At just the right moment as the car approached the corner someone of the group would pretend to be crippled and would start walking across the street right in front of the street car with a bad limp, looking up with a frantic look on his face (being sure the conductor saw him for safety's sake), trying to hurry but pretending to be so lame he couldn't get out of the way.

The conductor would be forced to slow down to the point of almost stopping. He wouldn't have the heart to blow his whistle at some poor cripple trying to cross the street right in front of him, even if it was poor judgment on the part of the walker. At this time an accomplice would race from a hiding place behind a convenient hedge and run unnoticed to the back of the streetcar, pull the rope (that was used to pull the trolley off the power line when it was necessary to disconnect it) up out of the reel on the back of the car and give the rope a turn around the case which would put it in a bind, thus preventing it from giving out more rope when needed, but not interfering with it at the moment.

The trolley would maintain contact till the car started up the little hill and then there would not be enough slack in the rope for it to follow the overhead power line. The car would go around the corner hit the grease and would stop. The conductor would not know what had happened yet but the only thing for him to do was back up and take another run at the hill. Because of the sharp curve he couldn't get much of a go at it, and sometimes this little game went on for several tries till he could get the grease worn off the track, all the time wondering what had gone wrong with his street car as it wouldn't pull the hill, and got all the old women on board very concerned.

They would look out the windows into the dark, not able to see anything but anxious to help the conductor find an explanation for the strange behavior of their conveyance, offering advice, logical or not, but nevertheless offering their ideas on what he should do which he did not need and which was not welcome because he already had enough trouble.

They would be getting mighty fidgety too, as we would be able to observe from our previously arranged, well-concealed lookout positions. When he would finally get going he would get near the top of the little hill and there would not be enough rope for the trolley to keep in contact with the overhead power line so the connection would be broken under a full load.

Well, if you have ever been close to lightning when it strikes you will have some idea of what it is like when the power is disconnected under a full, heavy load such as is being used to move a loaded street car up hill. There is a flash of light with blue flame similar to lightning striking, accompanied by a deafening roar and a shower of big blue and white sparks, being kind of awesome to say the least, a real attention-getter, believe me.

The lights would go out immediately and the old women would shriek and carry on because they were already excited since the street car had been stuck and the conductor hadn't seemed to be in complete control, as he was puzzled in that he didn't understand what was wrong.

Well, there would be great excitement and about this time the poor old (everyone over thirty five was old at that time to us) conductor would begin to get the message as to what this was all about and it would begin to dawn on him that he had been had, and by this time would be furious.

He would open the door, get out and look all around, wave his fist in the Air, and yell at the top of his voice at the empty air (empty of kids, that is) that he would call the police. There wouldn't be a soul in sight but the doors of the residences would be opening, people coming out to peer in the dark from their porches to see what the bright flash of lightning with the sound of an explosion and then the shouting, was all about.

Needless to say, we were well out of sight but in such positions as to be able to view the complete payoff with hard-to-conceal glee, and the satisfaction of having pulled off a humdinger of a prank.

I became a good friend of Don Gorman's and he in turn was a good friend of the Pastor of St. Aloysius church and parish at the time, Father O'Malley.

The sexton of the church, an old brother (the male equivalent of a sister in the Catholic church) who had been there for years died, and as Father had no one to replace him, temporarily had Don Gorman perform part of the duties as a part-time job.

Sometimes Don was supposed to ring the angelus (the church bells) at 6:00 AM, 12:00 Noon and 6:00 PM. Sometimes Don would forget and would hear a noon or evening whistle that would remind him and away he would go on a dead run. That didn't last too long till Father found a permanent replacement for the faithful old brother, I don't think Don was reliable enough.

It was at this time that the parish bought the Heath place estate on East Mission where the St. Aloysius grade school is at the present time. This estate was complete with all its treasures. I was there many times helping Don Gorman help Father and we had full run of the place.

There was an electricity-driven car there that Mrs. Heath drove around town for years. The barn was there with several first-class buggies in place, the three story house with a full basement was full of treasures and antiques. There was fine china, silverware, paintings, fine furniture, things that the Indians had given to the Heaths in the early days, as they were good friends for years. (I believe I mentioned this earlier). The treasures at today's prices would be worth many thousands of dollars, probably millions. I don't recall how it was all disposed of at this time but I recall helping get ready for several sales. I think they were several auctions but unfortunately when they were held I was in school studying Latin, and I wouldn't have had any money anyway.

Don Gorman and I had the privilege of viewing it all I before anyone else touched it. We never took anything but several times it was tempting, I will have to admit. I think that had we asked Father he would have given us some little trinkets but it never occurred to me to ask.

Father was a grand old fellow. Sometimes Don Gorman was an altar boy on special occasions like Easter and Christmas. He was always involved in some church function and was good at trying to get me involved. He was a good influence on me. I have been all over St. Aloysius church, from the steeples to the basement. I have been in the background or behind the altar at some big events – Don saw to that. He was a fine young man.

His mother died about this time and he, his dad and his brother, Chuck, about the same age as my brother Don, were left alone. They had a house but due to the mother's long sickness, it was lost and they had to get a small apartment, where they batched.

I didn't know much about our faith but Don Gorman taught me a lot by his good example and insisted that I be confirmed. I was, and in fact, his father was my sponsor.

Times were tough; his father was a house painter and didn't always have work but did the best he could. I recall one Sunday when my brother and I came out of church we met the Gormans and visited a short while. I asked what they were going to do that day and his dad said, "I bought a beef roast to cook today for dinner but I don't know how, do you?" I said, "Yes I do, if you will include my brother, Don, I will come and get the dinner for you guys and you do the dishes."

Mr. Gorman said, "Can you really cook a roast?" I said, "You bet I can." He was delighted and accepted. I fixed a pot roast, mashed potatoes, brown gravy, and I think we had asparagus. I even made a pie if I recall rightly and I am sure I do as I remember working all forenoon on that dinner; I wasn't very fast. They all paid me compliments on my dinner. They said it was the best meal they had eaten since their mother and wife had died, which was a real compliment but kind of sad.

Don Gorman later became a very skilled pipe organ technician and, in fact, built the existing pipe organ in Our Lady of Lourdes Catholic church in downtown Spokane – the one in use today. I was there as an honored guest when it was dedicated. I have been told he traveled all over the northwest as a consultant for pipe organ problems as a side line; his occupation was with the telephone company.

Speaking of Latin, that sure was a hard subject for me but it was required at Gonzaga. I put in a lot of time and effort on it and was successful in mastering some of it at least. When it was time to take the final Latin exam at the end of my second year at Gonzaga, the teacher said, "The names I call out will not be required to take the exam." He read a few names of which mine was not one (which didn't surprise me) and then passed out exam papers for the rest of the class.

I didn't get one and I was just sick. Here I had worked so hard and even had some people copying some of my work through the year and I didn't even rank high enough to get to take the exam.

Thoughts of dismay raced through my head. My dad was making a great sacrifice for me to be in school and I already felt guilty that I wasn't working and helping him, and here I wasn't even going to get enough credits to pass. Boy, I will never forget how upset and disappointed I was. I felt sick to my stomach. I thought I might as well go up to the teacher's desk and see how far I had missed the mark, anyway. At this point I didn't feel there was much to lose.

He was a nice fellow and I had liked him up to this point but I approached his desk with trepidation and asked him as politely as I knew, how bad my efforts had been. He seemed surprised and said, "Why do you ask?" I said, "Well, you didn't read my name and you didn't even give me an exam paper so I could try to pass." He looked at me with a puzzled expression on his face and said, "Didn't I read your name?" I said, "No sir, you didn't." He said, "You are exempt, you don't need to take the test. You have had very good grades and have worked hard; you are a very good student. I am sorry; I must have overlooked your name."

With this, he stood up and said, "I wish to make an announcement to the class." He then told them he had overlooked my name and that I too was exempt, which was quite an honor. Boy, was that ever a relief! Soon I didn't feel sick anymore. When the grades were all in for the year, I was surprised to find that I had made the honor roll and I really felt that I hadn't let my dad down after all.

We cruised timber that summer, spending most of the time up on Latour Creek, a tributary of the Coeur d'Alene river, and some time near Twin Lakes where Dad made arrangements for us to board and stay in a logging camp. This camp was in a location where we could drive the Model T back and forth most of the time to our work, camping out only a few days.

I had another encounter with the bed bugs that summer. We moved into the bunk house of this camp and in a day or so I found I had itchy bites again and they were not mosquito bites; this time I knew what they were. I looked around for some other place to sleep. The only place I could find was under a wagon in an old shed so I got some of our blankets from our gear some hay from the barn and moved under the wagon for the rest of the time we were there. It wasn't much of a bed but at least I didn't have to share it with the bugs, and scratch all the next day. The mosquitoes were enough.

It wasn't long till here came Dad and Don to share my quarters. The food was good there in the camp and there was always plenty so it was a good place anyway. We finished the summer on Latour Creek as I remember it and went back to Spokane to school.

Dad came this time and thought perhaps he could get me in the public school system, and Don as well, as the tuition at Gonzaga was so expensive. We really had no residence in Idaho any more; at least Don and I didn't. Don had graduated from the eighth grade the spring before. Dad went with us to North Central High School and succeeded in getting us enrolled there.

It was hard to start over again after just beginning to feel comfortable where I was. Well, this was different; there were girls and that put a new slant on things. I felt I had to be dressed better and the discipline was better, which appealed to me. I soon liked it better than Gonzaga but I couldn't take part in anything because there was no money. I soon fit in, however, and got along fine in spite of the girls.

Mrs. Stimpson had poor health and had to give up boarders. She served notice on us that we would all have to make different arrangements for a place to stay. There was a lady and her daughter living in the same block as we were in, who had a fairly large old house, and they rented out part of the house as apartments. I went to see them and they agreed to rent us a small apartment with kitchen privileges. I got Dad on the phone (he was working in Sprit Lake at the time) and told him if he would give me the same amount of money he was sending Mrs. Stimpson I thought I could manage to pay rent and feed Don and myself. He agreed readily and from then on we batched and got along quite well.

I had been promoted on my Saturday morning bill peddling job and was the overseer, which required a bicycle so I could ride around over the route providing any supervision and assistance if any was needed. I didn't have money for a bike but knew quite a few guys by this time so I went scrounging around getting parts from different ones and finally put a bike together to fill my needs. I had this for several years and got a lot of use from it; it served me well and was better than walking.

The lady where we moved was elderly, her name being Mrs. Hammill. She was a widow and had a daughter, Hattie, who was in her late fifties and single. I was lucky enough to have one of mother's cookbooks and when I got stuck I would refer to it and we did fine. There were extra rooms so when Dad came there was always a room for him to use and they were glad to get the extra income, as they had very little to live on. He didn't come only once in awhile but it was a treat for me because he did the cooking for us.

The Red Plague

I got sick during spring vacation and didn't know what the matter with me was but I was extremely sick. I had a very high fever and was delirious. After three or four days I began to feel better but on the Sunday morning before we were to go back to school I got up and when I looked in the mirror I was broken out with little red bumps all over my face and then I discovered my whole body was covered with these red bumps.

After breakfast, I went to a doctor's house in the next block to ask him what was the matter with me. He took one look at me and said, "Turn your hands over, palms up, so I can see them." When I did, he took one more look and said, "You have the small pox and I will call the health authorities."

After several hours, a man came to the door and informed us that he was from the Health Department and he would take me to the isolation hospital (called the pest house at the time). When he found out that my brother shared the same bed he said he would have to go too, even though he had not been sick.

He took us to the hospital where we were kept for two weeks. We were in strict isolation as the small pox was considered a very contagious and serious disease. All the people who had the same thing were on one floor of this building – all of us in rooms of our own but eating our meals together in a large day and dinning room combined.

The food was prepared in the basement and sent up on a dumb waiter. We would get the food, set our own table, and do our own dishes when we were through. There was a nurse that was a kind of monitor but we were not sick and were pretty much on our own.

They kept Don there with the rest of us, about a dozen in all, and of all Ages. It was highly boring for the two weeks till I was all healed up and then they let us go. Don never did get it even though he was sure exposed to it.

When we got home we found out that Hammills had to fumigate the whole house and get vaccinated after we had gone. I found out later that the small pox is a serious disease; many people used to die from it and it was known as the Red Plague.

During this year I made some friends, two brothers buy the name of Long. One three years older than I, whose name was Adrian, and his brother Sylvan, about a year older than I. They were college students at Gonzaga and they were introduced to me by my friend, Bill Conlee. Bill thought because I was going to a co-ed institution, North Central High School, I would know a lot of girls. Well, that was fine and I did but I had no money to take anyone out so to know a lot of girls was one thing but to date them required money which was a mighty scarce commodity as far as I was concerned. The money I had was to be used only for emergencies when they arose, if I happened to have any. The girls were to be admired from afar as far as I was concerned, not that I didn't like them but they were expensive creatures.

The Beginning of a Change in My Life

One evening along toward spring and after the two brothers and I had become well acquainted and were good friends, they came by my place and said "We are going to the public library to look up some information for class tomorrow, would you like to go along?" I replied, "Yes, I don't have anything very pressing to do, I would." Adrian had a car and was able to support it as he had a job working part time at the Railway Express Company.

We went to the main library, which was downtown, really on the outskirts of the main business district. After I stayed inside for some time I got kind of bored; so I went out to the car, which was parked right in front of the main entrance.

It was raining hard as I sat there waiting for my friends to finish and come out. Two girls came down the street in the rain and as they approached me I took note of them, thinking they were not very well prepared for the way it was raining. They looked sort of bedraggled, to be truthful.

They were not very impressive; their hair was wet and hanging in kind of strings. They didn't look very attractive as they turned into the library. I gave them no more thought till my friends came out later with the girls in tow, and it was obvious that the girls were going to get in the car.

I was sitting in the front seat and of course got out and my friend Adrian escorted one of them to the front passenger seat. I opened the back door and helped the other one into the back seat on the curb side and got in beside her. Sylvan went around, getting in on the other side. They were both dripping wet and looked so small and young I felt sorry for them; I wondered what was going on.

It seems the guys were studying and the girls came in, got some books and sat at a table right next to them. When Adrian and Sylvan got ready to go the two girls were getting ready to leave too and they all happened to meet in the exit. Adrian said to the girls "Can we take you home, it is still raining real hard and you already look wet."

The girls had noticed that the guys had Gonzaga book covers on the books they were carrying and thought they must be Catholic, they must be respectable and as it was raining very hard by then, they talked it over a little and decided they would accept, something they had never done before.

They were surprised when they were escorted to the car where the fellow was sitting when they had come down the street. In fact, they said afterward they had made some comment to each other about me as they passed by. Probably that I was so handsome, although they later denied that was so.

We took the girls straight home, but did sit out in front of one house and visit a short while. The one who sat in front was Mary, and the one who rode in the back was Agnes. It was starting to get dark and they thought they should get in, as they didn't know us very well. We did get the phone number of the one in the front seat, who was Mary; the other girl, Agnes, didn't have a phone at the time.

Little did I realize then, that the events of this brief evening were going to impact the rest of my life. We said we would give them a call some time later.

We went on to our respective homes and did discuss the girls briefly as I recall it now; I think we thought they were quite young.

We did call Mary's house on Saturday and it so happened that Agnes was there. They seemed friendly and so we asked them if they would like to go for a ride on Sunday afternoon, which they agreed to. I can't remember what happened to Sylvan but I took Agnes and Adrian took Mary and thus started a long and lasting romance for both couples. This was May 19, 1930.

I didn't have any money for entertainment. Adrian had the car, a four door Whippet sedan, and some money for gas. We went out to Minnehaha Park along Upriver Drive.

We strolled around, looked at the water going over the dam, and picked some wild flowers. Mary had a little camera and took some pictures. It was a nice, warm, spring afternoon and we got to know each other a little better.

We found out the girls were students at Marycliff, an all girls Catholic High School. I also

Agnes Rohner (later Custer)

found out that Agnes was just seventeen years old and didn't have a dad. Her mother and father had divorced years before, and her mother worked to support her and her four sisters, of which she was the oldest, and a brother a year or so older.

We brought them home before dark as we had promised and that was the first date of many that later turned out to be a very lasting relationship. School was going to be out soon. We saw the girls quite a few times and got better acquainted. I guess we were able to take them to a show or two and then school was out for the season.

Chapter 21

Dad was working for the Panhandle Lumber Co. out of Spirit Lake now, as he had worked himself out of a job with the county. The timber that needed to be cruised was all done, no more timber to cruise. He had told me there would be work for me at Twin Lakes piling brush that was left from the logging operations.

Well, when we got up there something had happened; the arrangements he had made had fallen through and there was no job. I never did find out what had happened. It was disappointing and there was nothing to do but go back to Hammill's.

I was at loose ends, and getting a job in town was out of the question unless you had some connections, and I was about as unconnected as you could get. Dad was paying for our apartment rent yet so we had a place to go at least. He gave me some money to get by on but I didn't feel right about it and wanted to work and help as much as I could.

My brother, Don, and I stayed there batching. I was able to peddle some bills and take my new girl, Agnes, to a show occasionally, getting to know her better.

My friend Sylvan didn't have work either but was figuring on going to Dayton, Washington to work in the wheat harvest as he had done the previous year. He had written to a man he had worked for and had a promise of a job putting up hay until the regular harvest started and then the promise of a job for the regular harvest itself from another man.

I thought this sounded good, so wrote to Dad telling him that I was going to go harvesting the day after the Fourth of July. He came to Spokane, stayed for several days and took Don back with him when he left.

The Wheat Harvest

I bid my new girl, Agnes, goodbye and the morning after the Fourth of July Sylvan and I took a bus to Dayton. I was able to go to work for Sylvan's friend, a man by the name of Barney Acher, making hay.

We worked for him about three weeks till the hay was all put up. It was hot and I was soft but I was able to cope. I worked hard, I remember another fellow and I field-pitched twenty three loads of hay into wagons in one day, all for two dollars a day and your board.

This feat was talked about among the crew and was considered by everyone to be quite a deed, a mighty big day's work. (I felt like it too that night as I remember).

One of the built-in fringe benefits of working in the fields there at that time was the fact that there were rattlesnakes in the area. When one approached a shock of hay (which was a pile of hay that was gathered up and piled in a small mound like a miniature haystack), it was with some caution. The hay shock was a good place for the snakes to get in the shade and they frequently did, I was told. When we pitched hay on the wagon two of us would put our backs to the wagon, stab the pitch forks into the top of the shock and lift as much hay as we could up over our heads and place it on the load where the man loading the wagon would spread it around, distributing it in such a way as to build a load that would stay on till it got to its destination.

When I first started out, I had visions of a rattlesnake slithering out of the hay and right down my neck as we lifted the hay high over our heads. It never happened, to me at least, but I heard plenty of stories of it taking place. I never did see a rattler but I came along right after they had been killed several times.

Barney liked me and asked a farmer friend of his if he would have a harvest job for a good man (me). The man, Mr. Prater, said he would. Well, this was great so I worked till the wheat was about ripe enough to start cutting – nearly time to go to Prater's for the new job – when Mr. Prater called up and told Barney he was sorry but he already had a man working for him putting up hay and he was going to use him and wouldn't need me after all.

Boy this was bad news, as it was getting late to get a harvest job. Times were tough and competition was keen. Besides, I didn't know anyone, no connections. Saturday night came and it was the custom for everyone to go to town. The farmers always provided for the hired help to go too. We would take our dirty clothes to the laundry, pick up the clean ones, and get a bath at the barber shop where they had facilities, and get whatever else we needed, like tobacco. The once a week bath sure felt good, believe me, after working all week in the heat with sweat and wheat chaff down your neck. Man, oh man, it would be hot and we would sweat, believe me.

When I went to town the next Saturday night I got cleaned up and then I kept asking around to see if anyone had seen Mr. Prater. He was a real old timer, well known and happened to be one of the county commissioners so everyone knew him.

Finally, someone pointed him out to me. I felt I had nothing to lose so I gathered up my courage and approached him, introducing myself. I was polite but to the point. I told him he had promised me a job that I had been counting on. I had been recommended, that I was a good worker, that I needed the work and too, that I didn't think it was quite fair of him to go back on his word.

Much to my surprise he heard me out – he listened patiently and intently. When I had run out of reasons to justify my case, he said, "It wasn't right on my part, I am sorry. After I had promised Barney I would give you a job I realized I had a good man working for me haying, and not knowing you I just thought I would keep him." He talked to me for a little while longer.

I was pleasant, sincere, and as persuasive as I knew how to be. Mr. Prater was polite, listening to me when I talked and said, "I will hire you. I like your approach, you seem to be honest and you sure are straightforward. Do you know how to tend header on a combine? That will be your job, and taking care of horses too." "Yes," I replied, "I can handle that just fine."

When I said that I wasn't lying. I didn't say I had experience, I just said I could handle it, at the same time wondering what a header looked like and feeling little pangs of fear in my belly, as though I had swallowed a little something that didn't particularly agree with me, like a small handful of glass marbles or something that was going to give me trouble later on. I knew horses but I sure didn't know headers.

That was a good evening for me though. This was the first time I had ever been out completely on my own and I didn't think my dad completely concurred with me going in the first place but he didn't interfere. I was determined to make good and I desperately needed a job to attain my goal.

The time was arranged for me to come to work for him, the beginning of the week after the following week. He asked me if it would be possible for me to bring a string of horses down to his place when I came as he was borrowing six horses from Barney for the combine team.

This was fine, as I thought this was a good way to cinch the deal and, too, I would be able to show that I at least knew how to handle horses. I did have a problem, however, that made me kind of uncomfortable: I didn't even know what a header looked like, as I had never even been up close to a combine. Well, I would just have to learn some things real fast.

Barney, bless his heart, kept me busy fixing things and doing odd jobs around the place that week. He told me what the header on a combine looked like and how they worked and what generally would be expected of me. Unfortunately, he didn't own one so there was none to even look at till I got to Prater's. I spent the week worrying about that header business and what I didn't know.

Sunday morning I started out with six horses Barney picked out to be suitable for working as a team. He told me where to go and which roads to take to get there – it was about nine miles.

When I got there, Mr. Prater showed me what to do with the horses, where to water them and where to hang the harness. The Praters were fine old folks and the first thing Mr. Prater told me was to "call me Dick".

They insisted I sleep in the house; the rest of the crew had to sleep in the barn. This made me feel a little more comfortable but I was still worried about the next morning. I was scared about the header business but I knew how to hook up horses and that was part of the job.

Each one of the crew except the combine man had six horses to take care of. There were twenty four horses required to pull the machine. That meant the first thing in the morning, before anything else was done, you would catch your string of six horses as they milled around in the corral (I don't know who felt more stiff and sore, the horses or the crew) and tie them up in their proper places in the barn. They were let loose at night in a big corral so that they could roll and be more comfortable and could eat hay from feed racks.

The next thing was to feed them some hay and a small bucket of rolled oats. Then curry and brush them off, paying particular attention to their shoulders where the collar was pressed against them all day as they pulled their heavy load. It might be of interest to those of you who do not know, that horses sweat like men do and are subject to sore shoulders when working in hot weather. Then put the harnesses on, each one having their own as they were all fitted to a particular horse. Horses are like people. They come in all sizes and shapes so harnesses are adjusted to the individual horse and were carefully kept track of.

After this little exercise was accomplished, it was go to the house. We washed up outside with cold water from the well, and if you were not awake by this time you were when you finished washing. Breakfast would be ready, the food would be on the table and there would be plenty.

It would consist of hot baking powder biscuits, fried bacon or ham, and eggs, hot cereal, hash brown potatoes, and if we didn't have biscuits, we would have pancakes. There would be syrup, homemade jelly, and sometimes homemade marmalade or preserves. This would be about five thirty or a quarter to six in the morning. If it was any later, we hustled, as we were behind schedule.

After this it was get your string of six out of the barn and keep them from getting all tangled up, as they were not in a mood to be too cooperative; they knew a hard day's work was ahead of them. Then it was tie one behind the other so they could be led and go to the watering trough for a drink, enough to last till noon in that heat, then head for the combine, wherever we had left it when we had shut down the night before.

When you got to the combine there was a long chain out in front of the machine that the horses were hooked to. Four rows of six abreast, three on each side of the chain. Someone always stayed out in front till everything was hooked up and the driver was in his seat with the lines fastened to the leaders firmly in his grip. If you were able to get this all done without someone getting horses all tangled up the day was off to a good start.

The driver sat up high and way out in front of the machine on an extension that was at least eight feet in front of the front wheel and about eight feet above the ground. The framework for this device looked something like a wooden ladder stuck up out of the front of the combine on an angle so it placed the driver's seat over the wheel horses. The seat had sides on it so the driver wouldn't get thrown out when we hit a ditch, (he should have had a seat belt) and a foot rest to brace his feet on with a brake pedal that was hooked to the one front wheel so he could control one wheel, at least to some extent.

The seat had a box on the back of it for rocks and was replenished frequently. The rocks were for throwing at some of the horses, who were lazy and didn't want to pull their share of the load. The brake on the single front wheel was used to stop that front wheel or to help slow the machine down when we were on a steep hill so it would not run away with everything, and was always applied to slide the wheel to cave in the bank of the ditch when we would drop into a ditch which was quite frequent.

After dinner, I asked where the machine was and was told they had pulled it out into the field and it was all ready to go in the morning. I said, as casually as I could, I guessed I would go up and take a look at it. This I did, and looked it over quite carefully; it was out of sight of the house so I had a good chance. I got a pretty good idea of how my part of it worked and kind of checked out the levers and controls.

After looking things over, I felt better. I could see how to operate the device for lowering and raising the header. I found out where the controls were for operating the engine, which was also my responsibility. I felt much better and was looking forward to the next day with confidence. That evening the rest of the crew came and I was introduced to them and was all set for morning.

Mrs. Prater woke me when it was just getting daylight. Everything went fine; I could handle my horses as well as anyone else. Mrs. Prater was an excellent cook and had a hired girl to help her, so we had a good breakfast and went to the machine. Dick was semi-retired and went along with us to help get started. He showed me how to hook up my horses to the chain and helped get everything organized. When it was time, he helped me start the gas engine on the combine that was the power for the sickle and the thresher.

This had to be hand cranked and was about shoulder high so was not easy, and sometimes would kick back so hard it would knock the hat off your head. When everything was ready, he got on the machine with me and said, "I will just give you a little instruction on how high I think we should cut the stubble and help you get started."

That was great and after I watched him for a few minutes, he turned it over to me and went to the house. I got along just fine and by noon, I felt perfectly capable, having gotten rid of the feeling that I had when we came out in the morning that I had swallowed a big handful of cold marbles and they were in my belly.

The combines of those times were pulled with the horses around the steep hills. The main machine had to be kept level or it wouldn't separate the grain from the straw and chaff, in which case grain would go out with the straw and be wasted. The machine was leveled by an apparatus which, when activated by the combine man, would raise or lower one side or the other or raise one side and lower the other at the same time, whatever the needs were. This would then keep the machine level on a steep hillside.

The header was where the grain was cut with a sickle and where it fell on to a canvas apron, which was a big endless belt that elevated the grains, stalks into the machine to be threshed (separating the grain from the straw and chaff). The straw and other unwanted material came out the back and was dumped on the ground as the machine moved along.

The grain came out of a spout and was caught in burlap bags called gunny sacks. This was tended to by a man called the sack jig. It was the job of this man to fill the sacks and set them in front of the sack sewer who sat on a seat provided for this purpose, where they would be sewed by him and then released down a chute to be left on the ground to be picked up later. This function took place on a platform on the side of the machine called a doghouse, where the supply of extra sacks was also kept.

The sacks were sewed shut with a special needle, called appropriately enough, a sack needle, and heavy twine. This was a semi-skilled job and if you were a good sack sewer, there was usually no trouble finding a job. A sack sewer, when available for work in a farming area during harvest time, wore several needles in his hat band and this then was sort of a badge to be worn with some little pride, (or at least some so thought).

These sacks were supposed to be closed with thirteen stitches, no more, no less, and were not supposed to leak when they hit the ground. The header was carried on a wheel out on the end of it and in our case, this was about twenty feet away from the main machine. It was attached to the opposite side of the machine from the dog house on a sort of hinging arrangement so the machine could be tipped back and forth from side to side to be kept level without affecting the header, which had to be constantly adjusted as the terrain changed. This was my job then, to see that it was in proper alignment, and to compensate also for the different adjustments of the machine as the combine man tilted it from one side to the other as the needs arose.

I also looked after the engine if it needed attention, throwing it out of gear if need be or shutting it down completely when we were done with it, such as quitting time. I was also responsible for filling it with gasoline and checking the oil every morning and noon.

I stood on top of the machine right up in front and signaled the driver with a little rope tied to his belt if we wanted him to stop or needed his attention for some reason or other. The machine made a lot of noise when it was running and he could not hear us from way up in the air and out in front where he was, so he had little idea of what was going on back where the action was. This rope was our signal system.

The driver had his hands full taking care of where we were going. He had to see that we were cutting wheat and if the ground was steep as it was when we went around a hillside he sometimes had to put the lead horses up in the uncut grain to keep the header up in the grain as the machine would slide down hill as we went forward which was a very uncomfortable feeling, to put it mildly. Sometimes we crawled along on steep ground kind of corner wise as we slid and went forward at the same time, hoping we wouldn't tip over. When we went forward down a steep place, the driver would lock his front wheel and let it slide while the combine man leaned on his big brake and really controlled the speed of descent, which was kind of scary.

The combine man was the boss and everyone answered to him. He stood on top near the back and looked after everything, seeing that the threshing was done properly (not wasting grain) besides keeping the machine level and braking when necessary.

It was quite an operation, we drug this huge contraption around over those steep hills with a chain and twenty four horses hooked to it, and it worked. There were some accidents; machines tipped over and there were team runaways, but we were lucky.

We did have some excitement one morning. Fortunately, we were up on a flat piece of ground when the driver stopped suddenly and hollered back to me that there was a porcupine out in front of the horses. I shut the engine off and asked the combine man what we should do. He said for the driver to stay in his seat and keep the horses under control, and for one of us to run out to the lead horses and grab the two center horses by the bits in their mouths to help the driver control them. Then he said, "The rest of you go out and herd the porcupine out away from the horses."

We all jumped down and ran out in front of the horses. One of the men grabbed hold of the horses and the other fellow and I chased the animal away out in the field we had already cut. The horses were prancing and dancing and were very nervous but they calmed down when we got the porcupine away from the vicinity. The combine man came out with a piece of iron pipe that was carried on the machine for some kind of a tool and we were able to dispatch the animal with that. I then found out horses are terrified of porcupines and we would have had some real trouble if the driver had not seen it in time and the horses had walked up on it.

I sometimes look back on those experiences and wonder that it all worked, but work it did.

Work was the name for it and after a full day at it and after you had taken care of your string of horses, had your supper, looked at your horses, watered them again, turned them loose for the night and saw to it that they had hay in the feed rack, you knew some way that you had put in a day. In other words, no further entertainment was desired and as it would be getting dark by this time, you completed your day by going straight to bed.

When we finished cutting the grain on this farm, we moved to another place Dick had rented. It was quite a job; the header had to be removed from the machine so we could get it through the gates. There was a whole wagon load of hitches and so forth. There was no one living in the house on this next place so a lot of equipment as well as some household items were moved.

We were strung out like a circus. I took a bunch of horses and went ahead opening gates for them and someone else closed them so I didn't see anyone on the way. They told me in the morning where to go and that there would be a well in a field below the house where I could water the horses.

I got there and tied some of the horses to the fence so they would not get tangled up and took the rest of them to the well where there was a big watering trough. I took the lid off the top of the well and pulled up water for the trough with a bucket and rope that was there.

When I got enough water for the horses, I took a big long drink without stopping to get air, as I was real dry. I hadn't had a drink all morning and it was noon by this time, about ninety degrees in the shade and no shade. The water was cool and felt good in my parched throat, but when I did come up for air what a terrible taste. It was awful, it was ghastly, nauseating to say the least. The worst thing I had ever tasted up to that point in time. I thought for sure I was going to get sick and throw up but I didn't.

When the rest of the outfit got there Mrs. Prater got out a big lunch she and the girl had prepared to bring along because they knew there would not be time to prepare a meal by time we should eat. I told her how bad the water from the well down in the field tasted; in fact, I still had a bad taste in my mouth. She was dismayed and said, "Oh, don't drink that water down there; we have spring water here at the house for drinking. The well in the field has dead rats in it. We just use it for the horses." Boy, I felt like a horse and then I didn't have much appetite for lunch. I never did get sick, though I should have.

When we finished harvest, Dick asked me if I wanted to stay on working around the place till school started – a matter of a couple of weeks. I was glad to do this, as times were tough. It only paid a dollar a day but a dollar was a dollar and so I stayed.

Another fellow by the name of Don something stayed also. He had us going over the fields that were cultivated and ready to be planted for next year's crop. The fields were free of weeds but there were occasional Russian thistles in them and as they were green and had not yet gone to seed, he wanted them cut.

He gave us each a hoe and a file to sharpen it with and we would go from one plant to another chopping them off with the hoe, by putting one foot on top of those big round weeds bending them over and then whacking the main stem off with our sharp hoe. It was hot and this fellow, Don, and I were the only ones working there.

One evening when we came from the field, I asked Don, "Why do you wear those long hot leather puttees on your legs?" They were made of heavy leather and fit around the calf of your legs from the top of your shoes to your knees and had leather straps to fasten them together with. They were World War One cavalry officer surplus attire. He replied, "The rattlesnakes like to get under those big weeds we are cutting to get out of the hot sun. I wear them for protection from being bitten by a rattler."

This was a revelation to me and it made an impression. The next morning when we started out I was putting my foot on the top of those big round weeds very gingerly and didn't push them over any farther than I had to in order to get to the stem to whack them with the hoe. The sun got higher and it got hotter and I got less vigilant when along about eleven o'clock I stepped up to a big weed, put my foot on the top of it, bent it over and gave it a good, vigorous whack – and out from the other side came a big jack rabbit.

That woke me up in a flash. Before I could realize I had not been bitten by a rattlesnake I let out a yell, threw my hoe over my shoulder, and started to run all at the same time. I must have run twenty five or thirty feet before I was able to get control of myself. My fellow worker, Don, who happened to be near at the time, sure got a good laugh out of that. We were fortunate – we never did encounter any snakes. But from then on, I was more alert.

Chapter 22

When summer was over I came back to Hammill's house where I had left my things. They were glad to see me and made me feel welcome. They had proposed to Dad that in the fall when Don and I came back for the school year they would board and room us for the same amount of money he was sending me, sixty dollars a month. This suited me fine, as they were better cooks than I was; besides, cooking wasn't one of my favorite sports.

They even did our laundry and it worked out fine. About the only thing I didn't like was the tapioca pudding they had every Friday night. It could be counted on every Friday night without fail, never a miss, and it was awful. It wasn't good like our mother had made. Both Don and I hated it the way they made it but we didn't want to hurt their feelings so we ate it like good soldiers, though thoughts of what was coming for dessert sometimes kind of spoiled the whole meal.

They were good old ladies though and were very thoughtful. Hattie, the daughter, seemed about as old as her mother, who was about seventy three at the time. Hattie was in her mid fifties I would guess. She was one of those people who was old at an early age. We were kind of handy to have around as we split the wood, got the coal and wood in from the wood shed and carried out the ashes. The house was heated with a stove and the cooking was done on a wood stove. We mowed the lawn during lawn time when we were there, helping out when and where we could. We soon became a family is the best way to put it. Don and I went back to North Central, my senior year.

I had been writing to my girl Agnes all summer and had been looking forward very much to getting back to see her. It seemed she wasn't as glad to see me as I was to see her for some reason, which was a let down. I called on her a few times but it wasn't the same, so I didn't go back. I was very disappointed, as I had become very fond of her to say the least. There were lots of girls at school but I just didn't have much interest in anyone else for the time being at least. I took several girls out to shows but it wasn't the same. I did hear about her though, as her friend Mary was going steady with my friend Adrian, and in that way I learned she was not going steady with someone else.

Things went along this way for awhile; I was trying to forget all about her, not having much luck, when one evening I got a telephone call from her. After we had exchanged pleasantries she said the purpose of her call was to see if I would accompany her to a house party one of her high school girl friends was having.

Well, this was indeed interesting and as my social calendar was not that crowded, I accepted. I didn't know anyone else that was going to be there, not even the hostess, so wasn't looking forward to the event very much. But I determined to go and do my best to show Agnes that she was overlooking a good bet when she wasn't interested in me.

I resolved not to be retiring, as I usually was when I was not very well acquainted. We went – she introduced me around. They were all strangers to me, which made it a little hard. I had made up my mind though that I would enter into the spirit of things and have a good time and be a good sport, in spite of the fact I felt about as uncomfortable as a long tailed cat in a room full of old ladies in rocking chairs.

They played games. One of the girls was an accomplished pianist who played for us and everyone sang songs but me. This is where I drew the line! I can't sing, but no one noticed. If they did, no one bugged me about it. Later there was a delicious sit down supper served.

As the guests were called to be seated, I escorted Agnes to the table pulling her chair out for her and helping her get seated. She needed help about as much as I needed a pair of corked shoes about then, but I figured it was the proper thing to do. I had heard somewhere along the line this was what you were supposed to do. I was trying to be a gentleman of the first order as I felt I was on trial in front of her and all her friends.

Everyone had a good time – it was an excellent party. I felt fortunate to have been invited. It was the first time I had enjoyed myself in quite awhile. A long time afterward I found out that the mother of the hostess asked her daughter later, "Who was the one gentleman in the crowd that was so courteous as to seat his girl friend?" The truth was, I was too busy minding my manners to be aware of how others were handling the etiquette situation.

I must have done something right as things started to become more friendly after that evening. We saw more of each other, I was encouraged to come around more often – we had a lot of fun. I taught her to ice skate and we went on hikes. Sometimes we would take in a show when I could finance it.

The Show

One time I went to see Agnes on a Sunday afternoon and as I was in possession of a dollar, I asked her if she would like to see a show. She said she sure would, as there was one at one of the theaters she particularly wanted to see. Well I hadn't taken this into consideration when I inadvertently gave her the option to choose. This posed a dilemma for me, as one dollar was all I had.

Some of the shows charged more at times, when there was an especially popular picture showing, like sixty cents. Boy, how do I get myself out of what may turn out to be a rather embarrassing situation if this show costs more than I have? I said sure that's fine, that's where we will go. I had to think of something fast.

As we walked along I was working on it and fortunately I was able to come up with a plan. In those times there were at least a dozen theaters in town and they all had big marquees out in front and big a-frame signs out on the sidewalk near the curb with pictures on them of the current offering, to attract attention and lure you in. The current prices were always posted above the cashier on the top of the box office where they could be seen from out in front if one didn't get too close to the ticket window.

I figured if I worked it right I could get her interested in looking at the pictures near the curb as we approached the box office, and engage her in a discussion of whether or not we should go to this particular movie or not. This then would give me time to glance up above the window where the cashier sat to see if the price was more than fifty cents each. I figured if it was, I would start pointing out reasons that made me think it wouldn't be a good show to see, not, of course, mentioning the one uppermost thought in my mind. I

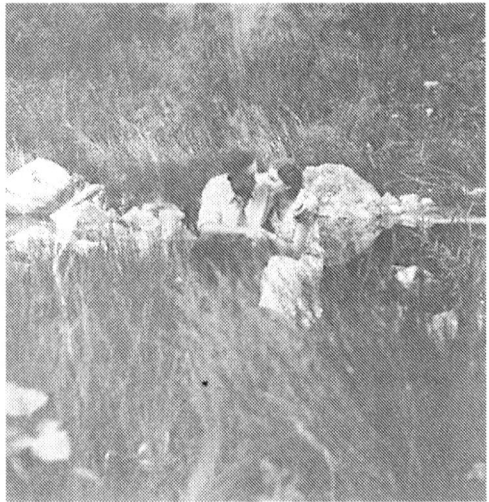

Agnes and I early in our relationship

figured too I would suggest that we should shop around for something that I hoped I would be able to convince her would be more to our liking, and more within my monetary capabilities.

We approached the theater and I was able to maneuver her over near the curb on the pretext that I wanted to study the pictures a little bit to see if it looked like a good show, meantime fingering my lonely dollar in my pocket knowing it was going to be the deciding factor in our choice.

I glanced up casually and much to my relief the price was fifty cents. I strode up laid down my dollar and asked for two tickets with as much confidence as though I had a whole pocket full of them. She had little idea of the thoughts that had been going through my mind, or the consternation she had caused me.

Uncle Ed's Car

Sometime during this year, I received a letter from my Uncle Ed who was an insurance man, sometimes working in Canada. He had been in the states and bought a new Model A Ford car. When he went to drive into Canada, they wanted so much duty on it he decided to store it at the border and left it there. In his letter, he requested that I go up to the border, get the car and bring it to Spokane to keep till he came down the next summer.

He enclosed a note for the release of the car as well as money for fare, gas, and to pay the storage fee. The car was at Eastport, Idaho on the Canadian border, which happened to be on the Spokane International Railroad.

I called, found out there was a train leaving about seven in the morning, arriving at the border about one in the afternoon, so that would give plenty of time to get most of the way home before dark.

I took the train, things worked out fine, it was a pleasant trip and I got home in good time, shortly after dark. The roads then were not like they are today. The next morning I wrote out an excuse for having been absent from school the previous day, signed it Mr. Custer as I always did when Don or I needed excuses, and that took care of that.

There was no place to put the car at Hammill's house so it had to be left in the street. The widow lady next door had a garage with nothing in it so I made a deal with her to use the garage for cutting her lawn and getting ice for her ice box when she needed it and anything else she needed done for rent of her building.

I might explain here that the ice was procured from little ice houses in the neighborhood on main streets. There would be an attendant there and you could buy a chunk of ice from him on a cash and carry basis. There were no electric refrigerators in homes then. If you wanted to have refrigeration, you did it with an ice box and a chunk of ice in it. This ice box had a compartment for the ice and then another with shelves for the storage of food. It also had a drip pan underneath to catch the melting water to be emptied frequently. If you didn't, there would be water on the floor and then it would be remembered.

These boxes were insulated and some were quite elaborate. A piece of ice of about ten or fifteen pounds would last for several days as I recall, and sold for about two cents a pound.

My uncle had stipulated I could use the car to get our mother for a day whenever I wanted. I used it to get my girl Agnes once in a while for a ride, but didn't abuse the privilege, and too, gasoline was a prohibitive factor, even if it did only cost nineteen cents a gallon.

One time I had taken my uncle's car to take my girl Agnes for a little ride. It was a nice, warm evening and when we came back, she invited me to come up to the house and sit on their front porch for awhile. They lived on a street that went up a steep hill and their house was kind of down below street level. The closest place to park was a little road that ran along the level parallel to the street a little way, came near their house and then turned and went between some more houses and out to the next street. I had parked the car in this little curve out of the way.

It was a nice evening. It was dark and we were sitting on a couch on their porch enjoying the evening and each other's company when I happened to look down where I had parked the car. There, in the faint light of the street lamp, I saw what appeared to be two men trying to get into the back of my car. The car was a coupe with only a single seat and what was called a turtle back (somewhat similar to a trunk nowadays). This was locked and it appeared they were trying to gain entry.

I had no weapon but I couldn't just sit there and let them break in without some form of resistance I didn't think, but I really didn't quite know what to do. I didn't hesitate long. I told Agnes to stay there, not to come down to the car at any cost. I jumped off the porch, only a couple of feet, and ran over to a rock wall that ran alongside the house. There were some loose rocks along the base of the wall. I hunted around till I found two of about the same size that I could hold comfortably, one in each hand, and I was loaded.

I crept down the path and sneaked up behind these two guys who were busily engaged in trying to get into the back of my car and didn't hear me. I got right up close behind them, raised my hands with a good rock in each one all ready to crash them down on one head, then the other, and said in a loud voice that I desperately hoped didn't convey the real fear I felt, "Turn around with your hands up."

Well, it worked really well. They both turned around with their hands high in the air and started to stammer weee- wee arr-arr are deputy sheriffs. I didn't offer to put my rocks down and they didn't take their hands down either.

I said, "Well what are you doing monkeying around my car?" They said, "We are looking for liquor; we are from the dry squad (as it was known then)." I said, "Ok, you can take your hands down now but I was ready to bean you both." They said, "You sure had a good approach you scared the hell out of us." Well, I kind of laughed and said I wasn't feeling too comfortable myself but I wasn't about to stand by while you guys took over. They said they didn't blame me. They showed me their badges.

It turned out they had raided the house on the corner for selling moonshine and seeing this car parked kind of behind it, thought it might be involved in the moonshine operation (as it was called in those times when prohibition was in force).

Well, came the fifth of June and I graduated from North Central High School, this was 1931. Thanks to my uncle I was able to get my mother and she was the only one that attended the event, to support me.

I was proud of this accomplishment; it had been quite a struggle for me without much guidance and it had been a great sacrifice for my dad also.

There was no work. The great depression was on, things were tough. It was hard to get a start. No one knew it but things were to get worse. Dad had gotten a job cruising timber for the Northern Pacific Land Company, a subsidiary of the Northern Pacific Railroad, and had gone to western Montana to work. If school had been out about two weeks earlier, I could have had a job running compass for him for the summer.

He had to leave in somewhat of a hurry. He told me to look after things and take care of Don. He gave me money to pay our board and room for a while and said he didn't know when he would be back. There was a whole crew of timber cruisers. They had thousands of acres to cruise as there was some kind of settlement to be made with the Federal Government and it was necessary to have a complete timber inventory.

My high school graduation, 1931

There was no work to be had unless you had connections, and again I was not connected. I couldn't find a job but I still was peddling hand bills for the furniture company so I was able to do this on a near full time basis. It sure didn't pay very much, better than nothing though. It was quite frustrating, here I was out of school, ready to take on the world and it seemed to be spinning in front of me and nowhere to grab a hold so to speak.

My friend Sylvan and I were close and he had no work either. I was able to get him and Don on, peddling bills with me. Sylvan and I decided we would go harvesting again after the Fourth of July, as we were sure we could get jobs there, as we did have some connections.

My time wasn't all wasted, however, as I had time to see my little girl friend, Agnes. This had grown into a steady relationship by now and was taking on an air of permanence by this time. Adrian was still going steady with Mary and had a day or so of work once in awhile at the American Railway Express Co.

Mary's stepfather, Louie, was herding a big band of sheep back in a wilderness area of central Idaho. As he was all alone and needed help, he got word out to Adrian that he could come down and work for him all the rest of the summer and into the fall if he wanted to.

Adrian decided this would be more profitable than the little work he was getting from the express company. He notified Louie he would accept the job so Louie sent him directions how to get there, which was no little feat in itself, believe me.

About the time Adrian was figuring on going, a huge forest fire had broken out and was burning out of control some distance north of where Adrian would be leaving the end of the road but still in central Idaho. We talked it over and it was decided to take an old Model T touring car belonging to a friend of Adrian's and Sylvan's, who was gone for the summer working some place. This fellow had told them to use it any time they wanted to.

We three devised a plan to take Adrian to where he had to go, then go to the fire and see if Sylvan and I could get a job fighting fire. We got some gear together and took off one morning bright and early. We took Adrian to the junction of the Selway and the Lochsa rivers where they come together to form the Clearwater River. At that time, this was the end of the road. There was a suspension pack horse bridge across the river and a cabin where a bachelor lived and that was Lowell, Idaho.

We went to the cabin and the man knew where Louie was, about fifteen miles from there by pack trail. He said he would give Adrian instructions in the morning as to how to get there, and would rent him a horse to take his duffel, and food that Louie had ordered. He had an extra bed and Adrian was to stay there with him till morning. It looked pretty wild and it was.

We wished Adrian luck, and did have some misgivings about leaving him in such desolate circumstances. It was kind of hard but you had to do what you had to do.

We had heard the fire was near Nez Perce. When we got there, we got gas and they told us it was near Orofino. We drove there, getting there about eleven thirty that night. We went to a little restaurant, had something to eat and asked if there was some place we could roll out a bed for the rest of the night. The lady said there was a little city park nearby, which we were able to find in the dark. We couldn't get the car very close to a good place to sleep, so we just parked it, took our bed rolls to a nice grassy place and hit the sack. We were tired – it had been a long day.

We wanted to get up early; so I located the North Star and lay down with my face to the east so the rising sun would wake me up, which it did. When I woke up I heard voices and lo and behold right next to us was a Family, all up and dressed. The lady was getting breakfast over a campfire. Where they carne from I will never know but I presumed they came about the time it was getting daylight. We sure hadn't seen anyone around the night before.

Well, the problem was we had left our clothes in the car so they wouldn't get damp from the nighttime dew. All we had on was BVDs. I woke Sylvan up and tried to talk him into going for the clothes but I couldn't get him to do it. I finally said I was going to make a run for it, which I did (the first streaker).

I got on the other side of the car from the people and got dressed, then I went to get my bedroll. Sylvan was still in bed and begged like a good fellow for me to bring him his clothes but I wouldn't do it. He finally had to make a break for it.

The lady next to us had been taking in everything as well as preparing breakfast. Did she ever laugh at Sylvan when he did his streaking! She even clapped her hands, much to his embarrassment. His face was so red that when we washed up in that cold creek water I doubt he even felt how cold the water was.

We got some breakfast and new directions to the fire and left. It was a poor dirt road and some places were steep. We came to a hill that was quite long and very steep. When we got near the top, we ran out of gas. The gas tank on a Model T was under the front seat and sometimes, if the road was too long and steep, the gas, which depended on a gravity feed to the carburetor, wouldn't flow. The solution to this then was to turn around and point the car down hill for awhile till the carburetor filled, then turn around again. Or, if you could, you could just turn sideways or you could cup your hands around the filler hole in the top of the gas tank and blow real hard and hold some air pressure in the tank, forcing the gas to the carburetor, and then resume your journey.

Fortunately, the road was wide where this happened and we managed to get turned sideways enough so we got the tank higher than the carburetor and got going. We finally got to the fire headquarters and hunted up the boss who asked us if we had been hired in Lewiston.

We explained we had not but had gone to a lot of trouble to get there and were anxious to work. He said, "We need all the men we can get; I will put you on. Park your car over there. It will be all right and I will keep an eye on it while you are gone. The trail is right there and just keep walking; it is nine or ten miles to the fire where they are working. Do you fellows have caulked boots"? We said we did.

He took our names and gave us a slip to give the fire boss when we got to where camp was. He said, "It will be a hard walk." We assured him we were tough and up to it. It was all mountains, either up or down, and hot. No place to get a drink. We got there about six in the evening, just about the time the crews came in from the fire lines. We were tired, dirty and hungry. No food since about five in the morning and then not much as we had very little money and were on a skimpy diet.

They had plenty of food, such as it was, so we were able to get filled up. The boss gave us each a new sleeping bag (the first one I had ever seen) and a tool called a pulaski, which was assigned to each man as his personal tool. It is a forest fire fighting tool similar to an axe with an axe blade on one side of the head and a heavy hoe on the other.

He said, "Go up on the hillside and dig yourself a level place to sleep and in the morning bring your sleeping bags down to the camp here so the packer can move them for you tomorrow." He gave us a pencil to put our names on the tag on the end of our bag.

We found a little fairly flat place on the side of the mountain, dug out enough dirt to make room for our two sleeping bags and called it a day. It wasn't quite dark yet but it was close enough for us. It seemed like I had just gotten to sleep when I heard someone yelling, "Daylight in the Swamp!" Like hell it was! It was pitch dark, it wasn't light yet, and they were hollering to come and get it.

We put our pack sacks in our sleeping bags and stumbled down to the camp, which consisted of a tarp over a pole where the fire boss had his tools and time book. We threw our sleeping bags on a huge pile of them, hoping we would see them again sometime. The cook had a little flat place near the little trickle of water that came down the draw. They had dug a shallow pit for a cooking fire, and put some iron pipes across it and that was the kitchen. He had boxes and buckets and cans scattered all around and a gas lantern hanging from a tree for light. Talk about working under adverse conditions, and here he and some helpers were trying to cook breakfast for two hundred men, in the dark.

The cook had some great big frying pans and a big kettle of coffee on the fire. There was very little water up on the side of that mountain and the cook had that all corralled. That made one thing simple – you didn't have to wash up before breakfast. No water so you didn't wash.

We lined up and as the line moved up near the fire, a guy gave each of us a tin plate, a tin cup, a knife, a fork and a spoon. When we got to the business end of the line, we got some soggy pancakes that were cold, some half cooked bacon, a piece of bread and a little can of fruit, with a cup of coffee.

We found a place to sit and by this time, it started to get light enough to see what you were eating. There wasn't much so it didn't take long to eat. We soon hit the trail to the fire line. It was four o'clock in the morning.

The fire line was a cleared path, so to speak, cleared of anything that could burn. The fire had usually burned up to the line on the fire side and been stopped by removing anything that would burn or by shoveling dirt on it or some other means. Sometimes when there was timber that was on fire and there was danger of the trees falling across the line, they had to be cut and fallen back into the fire. It was hard, hot, dirty work, but it was work.

The foreman we were assigned to took us about three miles up and down along the line dropping off some men as we went to put out hot spots and taking the rest of us to the main fire where we worked grubbing out brush or chopping out trees that were near the line. When the trees were big and had to be cut, we had crosscut saws. Sometimes it would be real hot from the fire and extremely smoky. When these conditions prevailed, the boss would gather up eight or ten men and we would take turns in pairs running into the tree and sawing as long as we could and then another team would take a turn while the rest of us rested and caught our breath. Sometimes it was so hot about a minute or so was all you could stay there.

After I had worked quite awhile and was about to choke for a drink of water, a fellow came along with a big five-gallon water bag on his back. For those of you who do not know what a water bag is I will explain.

It is a bag made from canvas-like material with a hole and metal spout in one corner of the top to fill it with, and to pour from. This hole is plugged with a cork. They usually hold about a gallon and a half and have a rope handle fastened to the top to carry them with. When they are filled with water they get wet on the outside but do not leak, they just sort of stay moist on the outside and that cools the contents slightly. They don't seem to leak, not much at any rate.

Well, the Forest Service had some like I never had seen before. They were five or six gallon size and they fit on your back, held there by a couple of back straps as backpacks are held in place. They also had a little spigot or faucet, if you will, that water could be drawn from. This bag then was carried from the nearest source of water fit to drink by one of the men assigned to this job.

If one was lucky, this fellow would come along every three or four hours and stop for you to get a drink of water. He would stop and there was a tin cup hanging from a snap on the corner of the water bag on his back. One would unhook the cup, open the little spout, get what water you wanted, and drink all of it. There was no rinsing the cup or rinsing your mouth or wasting any water in any manner as the fellow may have had to carry that water a long way in the heat. The farther it was to water the less often you got a drink. Too, the water always was at the bottom of any terrain so any way was up, no matter where you went. That meant the water was carried up hill. Everyone drank from the same cup, which was common in those times.

When it was noon time or whenever the guys got around, they brought us sandwiches all wrapped up with waxed paper. They were very dry but they were edible, and a small can of fruit. That was it; I don't know where they made the lunches. They were having a hard time getting food to us, as I understood later there were nine hundred men on that fire in different places.

It was a huge one. One evening when we came in, they had stew to eat. The cook had just about run out of stuff to cook so the boss had sent several men with pack horses to a sheep camp farther back in the mountains where there was a big band of sheep being grazed for the summer. They bought several sheep and butchered them on the spot. The weather was ninety or a hundred and they probably didn't know what they were doing. Well anyway, they packed that hot meat on the horses, as there was no time to cool it as should have been done. As I said before, the weather was hot and by the time it got to camp, it wasn't in very good shape.

The cook didn't have much choice; he had to feed us something so he made a big stew. When Sylvan and I got to the dish up place, we each got a big plate of this stew, some dry bread, a can of fruit and a cup of coffee. We found an old downed tree to sit on and tasted the stew, which we were both looking forward to as we were running on pretty skimpy rations. Boy, it was awful! The meat had a tainted, spoiled taste. It was so bad you could smell it before it got to your mouth. It gave the impression it was something that should have been buried several days before. We were left with little choice. We had to eat to survive. We kind of held our breath and got some of it down.

I was getting along, but just barely when I heard Sylvan sitting beside me making some sickening sounds kind of gagging and gurgling, when he suddenly turned around on the log and started disgorging his stew in a very disgusting unappetizing manner on the other side of the log.

This was extremely distasteful to me, as I was struggling to keep my own food down as it was, without such a distressing performance going on beside me. I sat there chewing on something and couldn't seem to get it to a condition I felt comfortable with swallowing. I felt if I couldn't chew it I sure couldn't digest it, and besides I seemed to be getting something stuck between my teeth. I reached into my mouth, removing what felt like a piece of an old felt hat, some of which was stuck between my teeth. I felt compelled to check it out visually and when I looked to see what could be so damned tough it turned out to be some sheep wool. Much to my distress, I suddenly lost my appetite and joined Sylvan in his misery. We both lost our supper and had no more appetite for stew. I don't remember for sure now, but I guess we had our little can of fruit and dry bread and that was it that night for supper. Not much after having put in fourteen hours of hard work.

The next morning we went over for breakfast and the cook had prepared omelet with powdered eggs, and some soggy pancakes that he must have cooked sometime during the night along with dry bread, and the small can of fruit. We each got a helping of the omelet. When we started to eat, some of the egg powder had not been stirred enough to even get wet; as a result there were dry lumps of egg powder in the stuff and when you bit into one of those lumps believe me it had all the taste of the smell of rotten eggs when they are broken. If you have never experienced that you have no idea what a disgusting experience it is.

Sometimes I now wonder at the crude ways of some things during those times. I don't know what they did if someone got hurt, get a pack horse and if he couldn't sit in a saddle I guess they would have lashed him on some way and hoped for the best. Going back a few years I guess the same thing would have had to have been done when I worked on Fitzgerald Creek.

Camp was usually away from the fire on a pack trail, or someplace where the horses could be brought with the supplies. This was good because we didn't have to breathe smoke all night unless the breeze shifted. It was a good thing as sometimes when we got to camp in the evening one could only see a short distance, like a hundred yards or so, from having been in the heavy smoke all day. But by morning, one could see again.

That day they put Sylvan on the side of a mountain where the fire had been stopped with a fire trail running from the top to the creek in the bottom of the canyon. They took me to the opposite side of the same mountain and assigned it to me. Our job was to go over the trail and where fire was burning along the fire line, put it out.

This was done with a shovel and dirt or by squirting water on it from a five gallon water bag with water carried up from the creek at the bottom of the canyon on one's back. The squirting was done with a little hand-operated pump and a small hose that was inserted in the top of your water bag. This worked quite well except that it was a long way down to the bottom and then back up that steep mountain side in the hot sun with that heavy bag on your back. I might add that the water was used mighty judiciously after one of those torturous trips to the creek.

I met Sylvan at the creek a couple of times during the day and we agreed we would work as hard as we could that day and then the next day or so we could take it easy because we would have our territory in such good shape. When the boss came along that night and we headed for camp he complimented both of us on the good job we had done.

Chapter 23

The camp had not been moved and everything was in place that evening when we got in. I don't remember now what we had for supper that night but I know it wasn't mutton stew for sure. It's a wonder they didn't poison us all with that stuff.

The next day the boss took us out on the fire line to the same area, scattering men along the way as we went, assigning them to spots along the way, giving each man as much fire trail as he thought they could patrol, without the fire getting away from them. When we came to the territory Sylvan had worked on the day before he put some other guy on that side of the mountain. When we got to my side, he put another fellow on my side, which was kind of disturbing to both of us.

He took us to some new ground where the fire wasn't as well under control as we had left ours the night before; in fact, it was real hot, with a lot of fire close to the line, requiring much work to get it so it would be safe. He said, "You two are good men. I can trust you. I don't trust those other fellows with these hot spots!" Big deal, we thought! He went on to say that every time his back was turned they sat in the shade and didn't do anything. We were disappointed, disgusted and mad but we didn't say anything. This was the reward we got for working so faithfully the day before.

Well, we had the same situation as we had the day before. We had to work hard to keep the line under control all day long, carrying water and burying anything we could that was burning on the ground, with the shovel and dirt.

We were about all in that night when we got to camp. After supper, the main foreman went around picking out men that were being laid off. Sylvan and I were in the bunch they were going to keep, but we told the foreman we would quit as we thought we had other jobs to go to.

The next morning, after our cold, soggy, miserable pancakes and can of fruit, we took off for the headquarters where we had left the car. The distance was about eighteen miles by now, as we had worked back along the fire, away from the end of the road. We were some of the last of the men going out to leave camp for some reason or other, but before long, we began catching up with some of those who had left earlier. I will always remember one fellow sitting beside the trail on a big rock, resting, with his shoes off, rubbing his feet, who we overtook.

When we went by him, he said, "How much farther out is it?" We said, we didn't really know but the last trail sign we had seen said it was still eleven miles, and that was probably a mile back; so we guessed it must be about nine or ten miles yet. The poor fellow said, "They told me it was around eighteen from camp, where we left, out to the road. I have already walked twenty miles and now you guys say it is still nine or ten miles. I don't know what in hell everybody in this country wants to lie about it for." We left him sitting there with his shoes off rubbing his feet and talking to himself. We surmised that he must have been one of those whose work we had been doing, as well as our own.

We got to where the car was, along in the afternoon. Everything was as we had left it, but no place to eat. We left for Orofino and the river, no steep hill to go up on the way out. We were in need of some bathing about then. I don't know which I wanted most; I was so hungry and so dirty. It was a hard decision. If we ate first, we couldn't enjoy the meal because we were so dirty. If we bathed first, we couldn't enjoy the bath because we were so hungry. We finally decided the best course of action would be to clean up first. We thought, and probably rightly so, that we might be thrown out of a restaurant if we opted to eat first.

We found a place where we could get to the river, and went skinny dipping. We got to wash our faces and take a bath, which hadn't been done for almost a week. Boy did that ever feel good. After that we went to a restaurant, had a square meal for a change, went to the little park, rolled out our blankets, and went to bed for the night.

The next day we drove over to Dayton, then out to the ranch where Sylvan had worked the year before, and got the promise of a harvest job for him. Then we went out to a ranch where the man was going to use a Cat (Caterpillar tractor) to pull the combine, the first in the country to try this. I located him and asked for a job tending header for the upcoming harvest. This time I could say I was experienced with some degree of honesty and confidence. He promised me a job starting the next Monday morning. Our timing was perfect, as harvest was to start the next week.

We came back to Spokane. It was Friday night and we swung around by Agnes's place. We were in luck, as she was there. I arranged to take her to a show the next night, and went to Hammill's house.

Don was there but he was not happy. He wanted to go live with our cousin Gertrude and her husband, Ray, and their three boys. Their oldest boy, Jim, was Don's age. Don was running around with this Jim, who in my estimation was not a good influence on Don, but there wasn't much I could do about that, especially if I was going to be gone. I went to see Gertrude and after talking it over with her, I was able to make arrangements with her for Don to board and room there with them for the same fee that Hammills were charging, till either Dad or I got back.

Saturday night I took Agnes to a show, and bid her goodbye again. Sunday we took off in Adrian's car, heading back to Dayton for the harvest. Sylvan took me out to the farm where I would be working and then went to his place about ten miles away. This year was to be different.

I have already mentioned this man had a Caterpillar tractor to pull the combine with. This was a first in the country. It was a lot better because there were no horses to contend with each morning, noon, and night. There were other advantages also. There was better control of the combine where the ground was steep, and also where we had to cross ditches made by heavy rains. The speed could be slowed to a creep when we would slide, where the ground was steep, which was most of the time. This cat was the biggest one that was made at this time. It was a number sixty.

The starting mechanism was rather crude. If the engine was cold, as it would be in the morning, some little priming cups on the side of each cylinder had to be opened. A little gasoline had to be put in each one (about a thimble full) so it could go directly into the cylinder, then the cups were closed again. When this was accomplished, a big iron bar, about an inch in diameter and four feet long was stuck into one of several holes that were spaced evenly in the rim of the fly wheel. The flywheel was exposed on top and was on the rear part of the engine itself. This bar after being inserted in one of the holes was given a downward thrust in the direction of the engine's rotation, with as much force, vigor and speed as the person starting the engine could muster. The holes in the flywheel were straight on the forward side and sloped on the reverse side, so that when the engine did start the bar would automatically come loose. Electric starters for big engines had not yet been invented.

Sometimes the engine would backfire and when it did, the starting bar would not come out because the engine would run backward part of a revolution. This could be extremely dangerous to the holder of the bar. If he was not able to release the bar from his grip immediately, the operator of the bar could be thrown up in the air, to come down on his head on top of the cat or the ground, either being a poor option. If you were lucky, it would start after a thrust or two. If not, the whole procedure had to be repeated. Sometimes it was hard to start but once running it performed faithfully.

There was still another advantage; it did not have to stop to rest no matter how hot the day. It would just keep on chugging away, hour after hour.

The days were hot and long. We ate breakfast at five and got to the field as soon afterward as we could. The greasing of the machine and gassing of the engines was all done the evening before when we quit for the day. The sun would be going down when we came in. One nice thing though was that there were no horses to feed and curry. I don't remember for sure but I think I got four dollars a day and board, and the season lasted till about the middle of August.

When we finished harvest, I was anxious to get home to see my girlfriend, Agnes. Sylvan had a few days work yet so I went home on a bus. I went back to Hammill's, which was headquarters, or home, if you will. I had not heard from Dad all that time and neither had they. I thought I would go to see how Don was getting along, hoping the arrangement I had made with Gertrude would meet with Dad's approval.

Much to my dismay, I found out Jim and Don had run away and were now in South Dakota. Jim Skeffington had relatives there. They had taken freight trains back there and had been gone for some time. There wasn't much I could do about that except worry. I knew our dad was going to be angry. First of all he would be angry at me, and then Don.

He was going to be upset with me because I didn't take better care of Don. I once again found myself in the somewhat unenviable position of being responsible for conditions over which I had very little or no control, and no real authority.

I couldn't find any work – I looked every day. The depression was very, very serious by this time. You couldn't buy a job. The streets, Main and Trent (now Spokane Falls Boulevard), were lined with men out of work, yet wanting to work in the worst way. I didn't quite know what to do; for once, I kind of wished I could go back to school.

After about a month Dad showed up. I had to tell him where Don was. I was surprised and relieved he didn't say too much, to me at least. We went to see Gertrude. She was sorry but there wasn't much she could do about it either. Dad paid her the money she was entitled to as per the agreement I had made with her.

My mother, of course, knew that I was looking for work. She, bless her heart, took it on herself to write to one of her brothers, my Uncle Tom, who had an apple orchard near Wapato, which is near Yakima, asking him if he would have work for me picking apples. She received a reply from him that I could pick apples for him while it lasted, and that he was just about ready to start picking.

About this time, Don showed up. I guess Gertrude told him his dad was looking for him, because he came home to Hammill's house. I never did know what Dad had to say to him, but I am sure he said something. I was glad I wasn't in on it.

I was running out of money to pay my board and room, and beginning to wonder what to do. Dad had made no commitments as to what he was going to do and I was getting kind of uneasy.

Chapter 24

The day after Don came back Dad, out of the blue, said to me, "What are you going to do now?" This was sort of overwhelming. I knew instantly what he meant. I was on my own from here on. Fair enough! He had seen me through high school, which had required sacrifice, and now it was up to me.

I was surprised I guess, more than anything. I had never given it much thought. I had been on my own to a certain extent, more or less, I suppose; yet he had always been there somewhere in the background and most of the time supporting me. When I look back on it now I guess I thought we would sort of stay together Dad, Don and I.

The Custer Men
Dad and I on the left; Dad and Don on the right

The ranch had been sold several years before to help pay expenses. It was, as I say, a surprise to me, but I got the message. Without hesitation, I said, "I guess I will go to Wapato to pick apples for Uncle Tom." He replied, "When are you going?" I said, "Well, I think I might as well go tonight." I seemed to think that freight trains ran mostly at night I guess. Dad didn't say anything much. It wasn't what I had expected.

Now, looking back, I sort of thought we would have a talk and he might give me some idea of what he was going to do. It could have been that way, but it wasn't. He didn't know what to do himself, I guess. Times were tough. There were no jobs.

He didn't have one, and no prospects of one that I know of. He seemed kind of troubled but if indeed he was I never did know what about. He never mentioned anything. He wasn't a man to talk or to tell me much. I had never given him or my mother any trouble in all my life. I always was responsible, even as a little kid, and they always gave me responsibility and held me accountable. I tried to do the right thing and always did my best. I had worked hard when there was work to do. I never drug my feet, so to speak. I never let anybody down. In retrospect, I was kind of surprised that the three of us were not going to stick together and batch somewhere, maybe at Hammill's house. I guess it was sort of in the back of my mind that some day we might have some kind of home again. I don't know what I had expected. It seemed kind of final, and it was. We were never very close after that day. In fact, when I think back, I guess we were never very close. He was not the kind of dad to talk things over much, with me at least.

When we next met, which was some months later, it was as though we were sort of strangers. I talked to Don, as he knew about riding freight trains. Matter of fact, he knew quite a lot about it. He said that the Northern Pacific freight trains going west stopped behind the Sperry flour mill as they came from the freight yards before pulling out of town.

I gathered up some work clothes and packed my packsack. In the afternoon, I went to see my girl, Agnes, when she got out of school, to tell her where I was going and say goodbye. I went back to Hammill's and after supper I bid them all goodbye and took off for the freight yards. Dad did seem to have some concern when I left and told me to be careful.

The First Freight Train Ride

When I left, it was dark of course, and when I got to the freight yards, it seemed even darker, and spooky. The weather was clear and frosty feeling, but there was no moon. There were shadowy figures around. I suspected they were bums. I kind of comforted myself with the thought that I too, was one. I figured I had better fit in the best way I could. I talked to someone and he confirmed the information Don had given me: that everything going west would stop there for orders before pulling out onto the main line.

I stood around waiting and sure enough, in a couple of hours a freight train came along and stopped. It looked to me like it was going west and this looked good enough for me. This was my first taste of getting used to the fact that the trains ran when they wanted to, not when I was ready to go. Patience was compulsory if you were to use that mode of transportation, I would soon learn. What I didn't realize at the time was that this was, in reality, pretty good service. It was quite common to wait many, many hours for trains. In fact, this was par for the course, so to speak.

I didn't like the looks of these guys that came out of the shadows to look for a place on the train to ride. I didn't like the thoughts of getting in the same box car with any of them. I did notice, however, that not many seemed interested in this train and made no move to get aboard, but thought nothing of it at the time. I kind of held back, and after they all seemed to sort of disappear into open cars or someplace, I started looking for a place for myself.

I went toward the back of the train and found a box car door open and spoke out. No one answered so I presumed it to be empty. I threw my pack in and jumped in. The door on the opposite side was closed, which was good. There were some kind of used steel plates on the floor. They had slight bends in them, but aside from that, it appeared to me to be a good place to ride. They didn't lay flat on the floor, or flat against each other. They were sort of springy when walked on but no real problem, not yet anyway.

After about fifteen or twenty minutes I heard two short whistle blasts, I heard the air being released from the brakes on the car I was in and the same thing on down the string of cars, and soon we took off. I was on my way, everything was fine.

As we went through town, I looked out the door at the city lights. It was fun, and then we were out in the country, nothing to see. We picked up speed. No more fun. As we picked up speed it got cold. I got out of the doorway. It got colder. I was able to get the door nearly closed to shut out most of the wind but it got colder still. The car I was riding in had a wheel that was a little flat on one side. This is caused from having had the brakes on and this wheel sliding on the rail without turning for a distance, at some time or other. Every time it made a full revolution, it would hit that flat spot and give a little jump. Every time it jumped the steel would bounce up and then down, as though there were spring between the sheets. Boy this was a problem.

I hunted around in the dark for a place where it seemed to bounce the least. I sat down and wrapped my arms around me to hold my sides because I got a severe side ache. It was dark, cold and lonesome.

After several hours we stopped, then did a little switching and then stopped for good. I waited for awhile and, hearing nothing, I got out to see what was going on. Nothing, absolutely nothing. No one in sight and everything quiet. I decided they must have all gone to bed somewhere.

The train I was on had gone on a side track, and there it sat. Boy, I was cold. Everything was covered with white frost. I looked around that big engine. No one in sight. I could feel heat corning down from up on the side of it, but it didn't do me any good way down on the ground. There was what was called a running board around the side of the boiler way up high. I crawled up the front of the engine and along the side on this running board and laid down with my back against that nice warm engine. That felt good for awhile, but the front of me got colder, so I had to turn over. I kept this up the rest of the night.

Along about daylight, I heard stirring around and I got down and went back to my box car. Soon the train started switching back and forth. It was what was called a local and they had many carloads of sheep to unload, at unloading pens. I later learned local trains stopped frequently and did local switching, and because it had no white flags on the front, it was not a through train. They had waited till daylight to unload the sheep so they could see what they were doing.

Well, I took this all in but I was still cold. I saw some of these sheep men going into the caboose and as there was smoke coming out the stovepipe, I knew there was a stove in there. I kind of watched and when I thought they were all out, I went up the steps and walked right in. Sure enough, a nice warm atmosphere and a glowing stove, and no one around. Boy, did that ever feel good.

I got warmed up pretty well before a train guy came in. I let on as though I was one of the sheep men and made a remark about how it got cold out there handling those cold irons on the gates. He said, "Sure, might as well warm up, it is cold." After I was nice and warm and I could see they were finishing the unloading process I scurried out of there before someone decided I wasn't one of the crew.

By this time, it had warmed up some outside, and the sun was shining. I hunted around the train and found a different box car to ride in the rest of the way to Pasco. When we got into the yards and stopped, I got out of the yards as soon as I could and took the road to town, which was at least a mile or more. There were several men doing the same thing and, as they acted as though they knew what they were doing and where they were going, I followed them. I got talking to one of them as we walked along, and fortunately, he was full of information and was willing to share it with me. He told me that the trains going west and south had to cross the main street in town and they always stopped just before they crossed the street. He said that was the place to catch a west bound train. He said that the flagman at the crossing, (no automatic signals in those days) was very friendly and that he would give out information, as to where the trains were going, and about what time they would be leaving. He also informed me to be sure to check to make sure I didn't get on a south bound train, as I would wind up somewhere in Oregon before I could get off. This guy was very helpful in furthering my education in the ways of free train riding. There were so many men on the move I think the town and the railroad people were glad to get them on the road and out of town.

I looked around, found a greasy spoon place to eat and had some hotcakes and coffee. Usually, near the railroad tracks, meals were cheap. For example, hotcakes and coffee would be twenty cents. You could get a small patty of hamburger, some hash brown potatoes, a slice of bread and a cup of coffee for thirty cents. This sounds great now, but the trouble then was to get the twenty or thirty cents.

After getting fed, I went to the tracks and found out the next train west that would be carrying the two white flags and was called a Manifest (meaning through train), wouldn't be leaving till late afternoon. Nothing to do except find some place in the scarce shade and swat flies for amusement.

Well, in due course it came into sight and sure enough it stopped short of the crossing, and up on each side of the front of the engine was a white flag. (I should say they had been white at some distant time in the past. Nevertheless they were close enough for my purposes.)

I found an empty box car along with some other guys and climbed in. By this time I felt more comfortable. It was daylight and it seemed to me they were just about like I was. In fact, we were all poor and all going someplace else. This was a way to get there; maybe not a good way, but a way, and so it sort of seemed we all had a kind of common goal.

This train meant business and we soon took off going right along. Once in awhile we would go on a side track and stop for awhile and a passenger train or another freight train would go by. I knew about where Wapato, my destination, was and only hoped they would stop there when we came to it. All I could do was hope that they would, as there is no way one can get out of a moving box car unless it is moving very slowly.

Along in the night sometime we passed through a town and I could see the name on the depot as we passed by. It was Toppenish, never heard of it before. I asked some fellow who was looking out the door with me where Wapato was and he said, "The next station." Boy, I was standing on one foot then the other, hoping that train would stop. I was in luck, as after awhile we started to slow down, and looking out I could see we were entering a small town. The train stopped and I jumped out. I walked up the track a short way and there was the depot and the name on it, Wapato.

I had clothing enough for the temperature; it wasn't very cold that night so I found a place near some kind of big building near the tracks under some big bushes next to it, and spent the rest of the night there. The next morning I found a nice little irrigation ditch with clean water in it and washed up. I bought some breakfast and looked the town over, which didn't take very long.

I knew my uncle lived several miles out of town but I didn't know which way or how far. I made several inquiries at the two pool halls, but no one seemed to know him. I finally thought of the post office.

When it opened, I went there and asked the clerk at the window if he knew Mr. Maloney. He said, "I don't know him personally but I know the name, just a moment." He called out to a man sorting mail in the rear somewhere to see if he had Maloney on his rural route. It turned out that the rural carrier did and he came to the window. I told him that I wanted to go to Maloney's place but didn't know where it was, and asked him if he could direct me. He was a real nice fellow and we later became friends. He said, "Yes, Mr. Maloney is on my route and I will be delivering mail to him in about an hour or so and if you are not in a hurry I will let you ride out there with me if you want to." I said I would be more than glad to wait, as I had no means of getting there other than walking.

I waited till he was ready and we were soon out in the country delivering mail as we went along visiting. He was a real swell fellow and we enjoyed each other's company.

After a few miles he said, "That big white house down the road there is your uncle's house" As we approached it a man came out the driveway and crossed the road waiting for the mailman to stop. My newfound friend said, "That is Mr. Maloney." He gave him his mail, stuck out his hand and wished me well. I shook hands with him, thanked him for his help and the ride, and promised to see him later.

Chapter 25

I jumped out and caught up with my uncle, who I had never seen before, and who was crossing the road to his house. I introduced myself to him and said that my mother, his sister, had said he might have some work for me. He seemed glad to see me, welcomed me, and said, "Yes, we are already picking apples and you can go right to work." He took me to the house and introduced me to his wife, who was my Aunt Eunice. They had two boys and a little girl all under the age of ten. This was his second marriage, as his first wife, my Aunt Tess, had died of the flu in 1918, leaving him with three girls and a boy.

His son Jim, who was a senior in high-school, was staying at home. The other children from his first marriage were all gone. Uncle Tom showed me around the place, which was a forty acre apple orchard, at that time considered large. He also said I could sleep with his son Jim and told me to put my things in Jim's room.

He had a small crew picking, just getting started, so after dinner (which we now know as lunch) he took me out where they were working and got me started. He explained that the stems had to be left on the apples, that they must not be bruised or shaken from the trees or dropped. He also explained how to set a fruit ladder and how a picking bag worked and a whole bunch of things. How to set the ladder so that when you went up the ladder with your empty picking bag you were able to gather a full bag before you came down so as not to be wasting time running up and down the ladder. Boy, I didn't realize there was so much to it. I had picked a few apples when we were at home, but we just pulled them off any old way and dropped them in a bucket. I am afraid I didn't pay my way that first afternoon, as there were too many things to remember.

When Jim came home from school that afternoon Uncle Tom brought him out in the orchard where I was working and introduced us. Jim was a year or so younger than I was, but we got along great. He gave me some pointers and picked along with me till quitting time.

Jim and I had a good time visiting after supper and he was delighted to have me for a roommate. The only real problem was that his stepmother wasn't much of a cook and we were usually hungry. One of Jim's older sisters, Mary, was teaching school in Wapato and would come home for the weekends. She was a good cook and would take over the cooking while she was there. Jim and

I looked forward to that, believe me, and we took full advantage of the opportunity to stuff ourselves. I soon mastered the art of picking apples but it was a way of making a living that had no particular appeal to me.

It was about the first of November, the nights were frosty, and in the morning about daylight those apples were mighty cold. In the evening, when we quit, it would be so dark that one would have to feel around to find the fruit. We finished all the picking late one afternoon and I was anxious to go. I had had enough of apple picking. Uncle Tom paid me and after supper I thanked them all, told them goodbye, and Jim took me to Wapato with his dad's car and I was on my own again.

I went to the train depot hoping an east bound train would stop to pick up some freight cars. Along about midnight a train west bound came to a stop. I stood looking at it and had a sudden inspiration. It had white flags; it was a manifest, but it was west bound. I saw an empty box car with an open door and that was an invitation to go for a little ride. I had the sudden desire to go west. What the heck, I had never seen any of this country. It would be a good time to go to Seattle, see the ocean; it was an exciting thought.

The idea was entrancing, why not? I soon convinced myself that I should go for a little trip as a reward to myself. There were no yard bulls, (railroad detectives) in Wapato. I jumped in and soon was on the way to Seattle, or somewhere. The ride the rest of the night was uneventful but the next day I had a rather interesting experience.

It was in the afternoon and I was sitting in the doorway of a box car with another fellow. The train was making its way slowly up the east side of Stampede Pass over the Cascade Mountains. The scenery was beautiful, all in fall color, the sun was shining and we were sitting with our feet hanging out the open doorway, just riding along enjoying ourselves, when we heard some yelling behind us.

There were about a dozen men in that car I would guess; some fellows were sitting in the opposite doorway doing the same thing we were doing. Others were back farther in the ends of the car sleeping or just sitting around.

The yelling was coming from a scruffy looking character, if such he could be called. He had a dirty, long, black coat on and was a dirty, wretched-looking individual of medium size standing between the two open doors in his sock feet with his dirty toes sticking out holes in the ends of his socks, yelling at the fellows sitting in the other open doorway. He told them to get up as he was going to close the door – his feet were cold.

They protested and when they did, he became violent, screaming at the top of his voice, "You move or I will cut your hearts out." Well, the fellows sitting in that door got up. He did close the door and laid down right there.

Pretty soon he jumped up and said to the man and I sitting in our door, "My feet are cold I want that door shut." The fellow sitting beside me was a nice fellow. We had been visiting and I was enjoying his company. He looked like a big, good-natured lumberjack to me. My kind of guy. I hated to get up; as I say, I was enjoying the day and the company.

I put my hands behind me to raise when my companion said, "Sit still, I will take care of him." Well, I didn't want any of that heart cutting out business but my friend seemed very confidant. He said, "Put your shoes on if your feet are cold, they are laying right there." This derelict said at the top of his voice, "Get out of the way, I am closing the door. If you don't move I cut your heart out." The lumberjack said to me, "Well that so and so #%*@@#, we will see about that, don't move."

As the door was going to hit him first if the derelict closed it I just thought I would wait to see what was going to happen before I moved. My new friend never even got up. He turned around and looking up at this miserable creep said, "Why you #*%#@ so and so, you take your shoes and get back in the back of this car right now quick, because if I get up I will throw you right out the door on your head. And furthermore you stay in the back there till this train stops and when it does you better be the first one out the door, because if you are not I will throw you out head first."

Well, that was the end of that. When the train did stop, the guy was real anxious to get out. Believe me, he had his shoes on and he was gone. I guess he didn't want any part of that landing on his head in the cinders business. Needless to say, I was quite delighted by the outcome of that episode. It did make me realize that not all these guys riding the trains were after all buddies, just because we had a common bond of riding the same train.

I got to Seattle the next night riding in a refrigerator car (called a reefer for short), designed for shipping perishable goods. The cars were well insulated so tended to be a little warmer when the weather was real cold. They had compartments in each end of the car for ice if need be, or heaters in the winter time, to keep the contents being shipped from freezing. The ice compartment had vents from the ice compartment to the cargo compartment of the car but they were screened off with heavy screen so the area where the merchandise was stored could not be entered from the ice compartment. The end ice compartments were entered from the top of the car, and there was a place that could be ridden in if they were not sealed or if there was no ice in them, or heaters. There were vents in the bottom where the melting ice could drip out and the cold air could come up from below. The floors had rough slats or grating – not at all comfortable.

These compartments were not designed to encourage occupancy by people. There were some other disadvantages also. To name a few, they were drafty, you couldn't see out once you got down in them, and last but not least, you had to be sure to secure the hatch latching mechanism so the hatch or door

188

could not be locked down, unless the door or hatch itself was completely opened first. This then gave you a chance to get out or at least to call out first. This was rather important, as if you were locked in, you might be locked in forever, or at least forever for you. Again, this was a way, not perhaps a good way, but a way.

There were some advantages to them though sometimes. You were out of the wind for one thing. You could call out down into the dark void if it was dark and ask if anyone was in there before you clambered down in with some unknown, which was kind of nice. You didn't run the risk of getting your heart cut out in case you didn't happen to be in the company of a big good natured lumberjack. You could only hope they would be truthful enough to say so if there was someone in there already.

If I was there first I devised a way that seemed to work quite well to keep someone from joining me. It always worked, for me at least. I would holler out in as gruff a voice as I could muster, "Get the hell out of here, I am using this place, there isn't room for you." It always seemed to discourage them, as I was never bothered.

Well, back to Seattle. When the train got there, I was asleep in a reefer. It was raining, and the first thing I knew I heard someone rattling the locking bar on the hatch above. I let out a yell and got out of there as fast as I could. It turned out a car inspector was on top and wanted that cover closed tight. He waited for me to get out and said, "You sure scared me."

Well, he scared me too. Little did I know what was in store for me. I hadn't seen anything yet. Was I ever glad someone had told me about always leaving that bar out so the whole cover had to be lifted to get that bar back into position so the lid could be locked. I got down off the top of the car to the ground and was just kind of sizing things up, figuring out what to do next. I didn't have long to ponder.

A man appeared out of nowhere it seemed, stepped right in front of me and said, "Stick up your hands." What impressed me strongly was that he had a gun in his hand, pointed right at my chest. What an introduction to Seattle!

Well, I didn't even have to think about what he said, my hands just went up automatically and I didn't have any trouble keeping them there either. The first thing he did was frisk me. I remember I had thirty five cents in my pants pocket, which he took. He felt of my shirt pocket and fortunately, I had a small bag of Bull Durham tobacco with cigarette papers on the side of it in that pocket.

He said, "What is that?" I replied, "Bull Durham." He left it. What he didn't know was that pinned inside of my long-john underwear was all the money I had. A twenty dollar bill and a few ones, in one of those little tobacco sacks. It was fortunately exactly under the shirt pocket with the little sack of tobacco and cigarette papers.

He dumped my pack-sack out on the ground, scattered the contents around, and seeing nothing of value, only some well worn work clothes, he must have decided to look for more lucrative victims. He left without a word, which was all right with me. I didn't think he had anything more to say that I wanted to hear. He left me standing in the rain, contemplating life, to gather up my meager belongings and get my act together.

This I soon did, as I had already taken a dislike to this particular place. I soon got out from among the freight cars so I could see around and take stock of my surroundings. At this time I didn't even know where I was, not even what town, if indeed it was a town.

I could see in the distance many lights. Yes, it was a town. I presumed it was Seattle which, after I had walked two or three miles, it turned out to be. It was about four in the morning as I remember so I walked uptown and just looked around. I hid my packsack under a stairway when no one was looking, so I wouldn't have to carry it, and got something to eat where there was a washroom so I could clean up a little.

Later that day I found a rather clean looking hotel with rooms for fifty cents a night. I retrieved my packsack and got a room for the night. It was plain but seemed to be respectable, to me at least.

There were bathrooms at the end of the hall and a big china pitcher of water with a china wash bowl and a container to dump the water in when you were through washing.

I had hardly got my packsack off my back when there was a knock on my door. I opened it and there was a woman standing there, kind of a plain Jane looking type. She said, "Did you call?" I said, "No, I didn't." She said, "Is everything all right?" I said, "Yes, I guess so, I haven't had a chance to check yet."

I took a quick glance around; there was a chair and a bed with an extra blanket folded neatly at the foot of it. There was a small table with the water pitcher and the basin. There was a dresser in the corner with a looking glass. What more could one want?

She said, "Well, are you sure there is nothing else you want?" I said, "No, I don't see anything else I will need." She said, "If you do, my room is at the end of the hall." I said, "Thank you very much," and with that, she left. I thought to myself, gosh, for a cheap establishment they sure go to a lot of trouble to see that a person is satisfied. It was much later that I figured that one out for myself.

I walked all over the downtown area. The waterfront was what had the greatest appeal to me. I saw the salt water, saw big ships unloading cargo, and saw rats down underneath the wharfs on the rocks when the tide was out, as big as small rabbits. I saw boats that would take you for a harbor tour for fifty cents. I longed to go but was afraid to spend the money. I saw fire boats (new to me). I walked and looked all day and all evening. It was the most fascinating place I had ever encountered.

The next day I decided to spend another fifty cents for a night's lodging so I could look around some more. I found the most interesting place. It was a store called YE OLDE CURIOSITY SHOP.

It was located right on a wharf and I saw things there that were almost beyond my comprehension, such as a genuine mummified human being. A genuine shrunken mummified human head. A common pin with the Lords prayer inscribed on the head of it, with a magnifying glass arranged so that the inscription could be read. All kinds of things to fascinate a country boy.

I browsed around there for several hours, finally ending up buying a wooden post card for my girl, Agnes, who was seldom out of my mind for very long. I also bought her a little back scratcher with a genuine ivory hand on it (she has this little souvenir even to this very day, 62 years later).

I saw many strange stores. I saw cable cars and many things new to me. The cable cars were interesting. They ran up and down those unbelievably steep hills in the rain. They had a device that hooked onto an endless moving cable down in a trough or a big crack in the pavement in the middle of the street. When they wanted to go, they just gripped this cable, which was traveling all the time, and when they wanted to stop, they unhooked from it and put the brakes on. Fascinating indeed.

There were more foreigners than I had ever seen in my whole life. After the second day I was satisfied, I had had enough, I was lonesome, I wanted to head toward home. What home? I knew I didn't have a home and that made me more lonesome. I longed to see my girl.

Someone had told me how to get a cheap meal in a working man type of restaurant. You waited till after the meal was over and they were about ready to close, or it was just about time for the next meal. You went in, sat at the counter and laid down ten cents or fifteen cents. When someone came to wait on you, you would say, "This is all the money I have to spend for a meal. I am hungry and I will eat whatever you will give me for this money. I am not particular. If you might have something left over from the previous meal I will be grateful."

It most always worked and sometimes they were glad to give you a big plate of food and a cup or two of stale coffee. I was hanging onto my money the best way I could, as I was afraid it wasn't going to be a familiar item to me, for the foreseeable future at least.

I found out that to get a freight train out of Seattle proper was pretty hard to do. That the trains were all made up in a place called Auburn. This was a little town about fifteen miles from Seattle and there was a trolley car that ran from town out there. I took this trolley the next morning, found the Northern Pacific yards and scouted around till I was able to find some guys waiting for an east bound train. They said there wouldn't be one till late afternoon. We found an empty box car and got in out of the rain.

After awhile I got bored waiting and went looking around. I found some heavy waterproof paper in an empty car. In another empty car, I found some real strong twine. I took some of the paper and some of the twine and after looking around I was able to find a stick that I could whittle down to make an awl to poke holes in the paper with. I took my accumulated material back to the original box car where the other fellows were and sewed up a great big bag that I could slide into and pull my pack-sack into also.

When some of the other fellows saw what I was doing, they thought it was a good idea and did the same thing. This was real strong paper and tough as well, yet it folded quite flat and took up little room. The train was finally made up and a brakeman told us when it would leave. There were no yard bulls around; we were able to get a good car to ride in. It was still raining but we were dry and it was nice and warm in my paper sack.

Chapter 26

It took a couple of days to get to Spokane as I remember it now. When I did get there the first place I went was to see my Agnes. Then to Hammill's house. Dad and Don were gone; the Hammills said they had gone to Coeur d'Alene.

I went to the relief department of the county assistance program, to see if I could get some form of assistance. They would give me some food but no form of housing. I talked to Mrs. Hammill and Hattie, telling them the situation. They said I could stay there as they had rooms that they could not rent anyway.

I was required to work several days a week for the assistance I would be getting, which was fine with me except I had developed a hernia and wasn't in very good shape for working.

The county had a doctor who did surgery so I applied for an operation. This was granted and a date for me to enter the hospital was set.

The Hospital

I went to the hospital on a Sunday afternoon for surgery the next morning. Everything was all right that night but the next morning the trouble started. A student nurse came in who I knew a little bit; she was the sister of a friend of mine, Denny Berry. Her name was Pat, a real nice Irish, fun-loving person about my age. I found out soon she liked to pull pranks too.

She said to me, "When did you have a bath last?" I replied, "Yesterday just before I came up here." "You will have to have a bath this morning; I will go to the bathroom and draw the water for you."

Soon she was back and said, "Come with me." "Where are we going?" I wanted to know. "Oh! Just down the hall a few doors," was her reply. "No way," I said, "I don't have a bathrobe and I am not going to go anyplace with this miserable little excuse of a nightgown on." This little garment was open in the back and only came down to just below my belt. This was not enough cover up for me to go parading around in front of a bunch of girls.

This was Sacred Heart Hospital, and at the time was also a training center for nurses. Most of the nurses were students in different stages of training. There were lots of them, they were buzzing up and down the halls, sometimes looking for something to do. They were nearly all young girls, which I had no objection to, except I had no desire to have them poking fun at me.

Pat said, "I will get you a bathrobe," and disappeared. She was soon back without any robe, but had a pair of slippers about three sizes too big for me without any backs in them above the heels. She said, "This is the best I could do but I have cleared the hall for you; no nurses around. It is only a little way."

She conned me into it. When I stood up there wasn't enough gown. It didn't cover up my anatomy sufficiently to satisfy me. She insisted I go with her. There was no one around. I slipped my feet into those slippers; they fit me like a small pair of skis. I bent my knees and skied those horrendous slippers along trying to keep them on my feet and keep covered up at the same time. She was right, no one in the hall. But to get to the bathroom a good sized room had to be gone through first.

This was a room with many slop sinks in it, where the nurses washed out bed pans, etc. When she opened the door to this room she had all the girls gathered there quietly waiting for me to make my entrance. I came in, innocently skiing along in a half crouch with the sides of this gown grasped firmly in each hand on each side of me trying desperately to stretch it to do a job that it just wasn't big enough to do.

When I got in the door, I received a big cheer and a gleeful clapping of hands as they were all gathered awaiting Pat's prize. Boy, I never was so mortified in my whole life.

This was 1931 and when I think back, it is hard to believe how crude things were. They wheeled me into a room with bright lights in a big wash tub sort of arrangement on the ceiling.

I asked if I could see the doctor before they did anything to me. He came in all wrapped up in a white gown; I suppose he thought I was going to back out the last minute. Far from it. I said to him, "Could you take out my appendix while you are at it? It has bothered me from time to time." He replied, "We will take out everything but the kitchen sink." I said, "Fine, thanks," and with that he was gone.

The next thing I knew a man slapped a rag on my face covering my mouth and nose and poured ether on it from a can. The next thing I knew I was in a great deal of pain. I felt as though they had taken out the kitchen sink too. This went on for several days then it subsided gradually and I was able to take an interest in things.

I was in a six bed ward with five other young fellows. We had fun with the nurses as they came to our room and shared their goodies with us. Someone with some money would buy them a box of candy for a treat and they would give us some. They were nice girls and we used to enjoy joking with them when we were not miserable. They kept me seventeen days. When I got out I was pretty weak but being young and tough I was soon better than before and fully recuperated.

I couldn't find any way to earn a living. The depression was raging then, if such a term could be used.

Men out of work, families desperate. Lights being turned off because people could not pay the bills. The city shut off some people's water because the water bill was not paid.

Spokane County set up a food supply depot near the court house in an empty store building, where some food was dispensed. The food being given out was not consistent. I don't know where it came from, but it would be different things at different times. The main items were flour, beans, rice, potatoes, some fresh vegetables such as cabbage, carrots and turnips. Sometimes apples or dried prunes, maybe a little chunk of salt pork. Oh yes, they gave out brown soap that came in wooden boxes. This was used for dishes, clothes and for face soap.

Some, who had their lights turned off, could get a couple of gallons of kerosene for lamps. There were families pulling food on hand sleds from near the courthouse on Broadway, where the county dispensed the food and kerosene, clear to Hillyard because they didn't have the seven cents to ride the street car.

These supplies had to be obtained each week and you settled for what was dished out to you. The amount was proportional to the number in the family.

The county gave wood to those who could qualify for it. Sometimes it would be wet or green, sometimes mixed. If it was too wet to burn, you scrounged around in it till you could get enough that was dry to build a fire and then you dried wood so it would burn. This was done by putting it in the oven if it was a cook stove, or if it was a heater, it was piled behind the stove or around the sides. It was pitiful. In some instances good, responsible people were reduced to extreme poverty.

I got a meager measure of food, which I carried home to Hammill's house in a packsack, where I shared it with them and they shared what they had with me. I had promised them I would pay them back some day when I could, but I couldn't see any end to it and I kept going farther behind.

In the meantime, there had been a shelter set up by the county for single men. It was on Trent Avenue near the river in an abandoned brewery. This was a big, old building with different levels of balconies and floors in it. They boarded up the windows and the open places to keep the wind and birds out. They set up a couple of giant sized heating stoves for some heat and made a kitchen and a dining room in the basement. There were nine hundred men staying there – it was a big outfit.

I felt frustrated to say the least, at not being at least self sustaining, but I didn't know how to go about it. All kinds of men who had experience in trades, railroad men with years of seniority, skilled men of all kinds out of work, looking for work with something to offer. I really didn't have anything to offer much except just plain labor. It was very discouraging to a young fellow just trying to get started, without any particular skills. I went along this way for a while but decided I would be so far in debt to Hammill's I never would be able to pay them off.

The Hotel DeGink

I decided to go to this shelter on Trent, as I would get my lodging and my food, and I would not be obligated to anyone for it. I left my stuff at Hammill's house, as that was the nearest thing I had to a home, and went down to the facility. I registered in the office and, as I had received assistance and was a local resident, I qualified and was accepted.

They gave me a tick (explained below) for straw, two blankets and a card to have punched every time I worked, which was three days a week, and two small bags of tobacco with cigarette papers attached. This card was very important. It had to be presented every meal to be punched; without it, you didn't eat. It also had a place on it to be punched once a week when you had a shower or bath. It also had a place to be punched for your two little bags of tobacco each week.

This card was a pass. Any time you were challenged by someone with authority it had to be presented and be up to date on the work punches. Believe it or not, if you were not a local resident you could not qualify for a card. If you didn't have a card, you could only stay for a day and you had to move on.

After receiving instructions, I took my tick and blankets, went to a straw pile under a shed out in the back and filled it with what I thought would be the right amount of straw. (A tick is a cotton bag the size of a single bed to be filled with straw and fastened shut on the end to keep the straw in. This, then, is placed on the boards or what ever you sleep on, in place of a mattress and springs.)

I then came in and started to look for a place to sleep. I first went up some stairs and sitting there at the top of the stairs was a man about fifty years old (kind of an old fellow), a nice looking man who said, "Looking for a place to sleep?" I said, "Yes, I am. I would like a lower bunk if I can find one." He said, "I don't think you will find one." I replied, "I think I will look around for one anyway."

This was the first place I had looked and there were many places on different levels and I hadn't had a chance to look the place over yet. He said, "I think you had better stay here with me." I left my packsack and bag of straw and my two blankets with him and did look around. I soon found out he was a dorm monitor for that particular level, the one who kept strangers out and watched after your possessions if you had any.

I didn't find any place I liked the looks of better and none of the monitors I liked the looks of either, except him. I came back and he assigned me an upper bunk, which was three beds up, but right on the aisle where he could see it at all times. He was a nice fellow and we became friends. His name was Mr. Brown and I always called him Mr. out of respect for his age. Seems funny now but that is the way I was raised.

These beds (called bunks) were built out of lumber, and were assembled in units. Each unit was stacked three beds high, two wide and three long. Each bed was separated by a one inch thick by twelve inches wide board. That meant I had a one inch board at my head one on the side and one at the foot separating me from someone else. I put my straw tick in my place, spread it around nice and even, made my bed with the two blankets, got my packsack, and I was home.

In order to get up to my bed, I had to step up on the edge of the lower bunk and then on the next one. At night, I could put my boots under the lower bunk but all dressing and undressing and all clothes had to be in your bunk. There was no outside light coming in the building but the lights were kept on day and night, so there was always light.

There was a big wash room in the basement of our building, which was entirely separate from the basement where the dining room was. There were at least thirty toilets along one side of the room without any stalls or partitions – right out in the open. There was a trough hanging on part of a wall about fifty feet long for a urinal. There was a row of wash basins; there must have been fifty or sixty, along another part of a wall. There was a big shallow depression built into the floor along part of a wall with several drains in it. There were pipes over head with shower nozzles hanging down from them, there must have been room for at least forty men to shower at the same time. There were stationary wash tubs to wash your cloths in and some lines to dry them on.

When this chore was undertaken, time had to be allowed for drying because you had to sit right there and watch them or you wouldn't have any left when you came back. You brought your own soap too if you could afford it, otherwise you washed with just plain water. Life was interesting, so was the food.

As I believe I said before, the kitchen and dining rooms were down on a lower level but on the back side of the complex it was ground level. In order to eat, one had to go out and around in the back about a block and then get in line out in the weather, whatever it was – cold, rain, snow, or darkness, sometimes below zero, and wait for them to open the door to the dining room. I am using the term dining room loosely.

There were three servings at each meal. If one was working, you had better make the first session. If you didn't you would miss the street car that took you to the job site to work. It was about five miles out there but you wouldn't get credit for working unless you got the card punched when you got off the street car at the end of the line. When you got to the dining room door you presented your card, and if it didn't pass inspection – that is, if your work punches were not up to date – you were not admitted; so no work, no eat.

You were given a bowl, a spoon and a cup at breakfast time. The other two meals you got a bowl and two pieces of bread, a cup and a spoon. You stayed in line and were directed to one of many big, long empty tables. When one side was filled then to the other side. When it was filled, the next table was filled and so on. Both sides of this big room at the same time. There was no looking around for a particular place to sit, you were in line and you stayed in line. You took what you got as the line filled the places.

When a table was filled, a man came along with a water bucket. If it was breakfast, it contained pancakes, wet soggy, cold pancakes, cooked sometime before. He would reach in with one hand (you always kind of hoped he had washed some time before he came on the job), feel around till he had hold of three pancakes and throw them in your plate, which you held out. Another man came along right behind him with applesauce in a bucket. He gave you a dipper full of applesauce on top of your hotcakes. Another man came by with a bucket of coffee and filled your cup as you held it out back of yourself. If you were lucky, he didn't spill any of that scalding brew on your hand.

Again, I use the term coffee, loosely. This stuff was black and bitter, but it was hot. It tasted rather strange as though they had thrown in some old dirty socks during the brewing process. If you were not awake when you got there, you were after you drank your tin cup of that witches brew.

That was it for breakfast; it never changed not even on Christmas day, always the same, except one thing. The difference being in the applesauce. Some times, it wouldn't have as many lumps in it as other times. The difference being that a lump was where a worm hole was (some times complete with the inhabitant). You could kind of sort them out if you were careful. It could be counted on though that the pancakes were cold and soggy and the applesauce would have some worm holes in it. That was it, take it, or leave it.

For dinner (as we then called it) and supper, we had the same procedure. We got two pieces of bread and stew made with potatoes, onions, turnips, rutabagas and carrots. Once in a while, you would luck out and get a little piece of meat. Sometimes if you felt brave or lucky, you could take a chance and say to the server, "Hey Mack! How about a piece of meat?"

Sometimes he would fish around in his bucket with the dipper and see if he could find a piece for you. Most of the time it didn't work. There was precious little meat in the concoction. These two meals never varied either, except sometimes the bread was drier than others. Again, that was it, take it or leave it.

Chapter 27

The street cars would come to pick up the crews. They were special cars that didn't stop for anyone else. They took us straight to the end of the line and then we walked to the job site about a mile or so to the main part of the golf course we were going to build. That is known today as Indian Canyon Golf Course. The ground was all timbered. We cut trees, cut brush, and burned all that was not suitable for wood. That which was, we made into wood. It was then hauled to our quarters to be used for heat. There was no waste, and all things considered, the whole operation was reasonably efficient.

Everything was done by hand. There was machinery that could have been used but it must be remembered that these projects were to make work, so everything was done the hard way. No tractors, no power drills for drilling rock that had to be removed. No power shovels, no power saws (they had not yet been invented), just hand work (we used to call it brute force and main strength) was used for everything. Some dynamite was used but the holes were all drilled by hand.

I happened to fall in with a couple of older guys that were sensible fellows and knew their way around. They were partners and worked in the woods together. They were also a good example of good men who were out of work. These two guys were drilling rock outcroppings that had to be removed. It was solid basalt rock, some of the hardest there is. These holes had to be about eight feet deep, which was hard work. The holes would later be filled with powder and blasted to shatter the rock so it could be removed.

One of the bosses sent me up on the hillside to work with them. They took a liking to me and taught me how to drill, called double jacking. One man, usually sitting, holds the drill, called the steel. This is a six sided heavy steel bar with one end kind of flattened out with the edge coming to a point like a chisel, which is what cuts the rock. This steel has to be held still and the top of it, which is about an inch in diameter, always has to be held exactly in the same place. This is important; as the other two men of the team are standing on opposite sides of the steel swinging heavy sledge hammers by raising them over their shoulder and bringing them down on the top of the steel with great force. They are called strikers and work with a rhythm, first one, then the other hitting the top of this steel bar with great force. The holder of the steel turns the steel one quarter turn every time there is a strike, hoping the strikers don't miss the steel and hit the holder's hand.

This does happen sometimes. There is no protection. Because of that danger it keeps your mind on your business whichever job you are doing. This requires team work, cooperation and concentration on everyone's part.

These guys taught me to be very proficient at whichever job I was doing. We would trade off, taking turns at both jobs. I worked with these two men each work day for a quite a while. Because we worked, the boss never bothered us and we were left to ourselves, which we enjoyed.

I remember one bitterly cold morning, way below zero, we came out to the job. Snow on the ground, everything frozen solid. These fellows (the ones I worked with) said, "We had better warm the steel before we start." I thought they were kidding but no, they meant it.

We started a fire and sure enough, they warmed the steel before we started to pound on it. Some other fellows working a short distance away didn't bother and sure enough, they started breaking their steel. One of the disadvantages of breaking it was that it would break, down in the hole, and with no way to get it out you lost all the work you had done on that hole. You just moved a little way over and started over again. It was discouraging because it might have taken several hours of hard work, and it would be lost. It was a good deal to warm the steel some, for the comfort of the guy turning the steel because the steel got almighty cold on a cold day.

Christmas came and went, time passed, I survived. I didn't have much to look forward to, though. Sometimes it was kind of discouraging. One thing for sure was that the meals were nothing to look forward to – they were depressing. About the only comfort to be taken from that food was the fact that it kept your back bone from rubbing on the back side of your navel.

I had one bright star in my sky, however, that shone for me without waver, my little girlfriend, Agnes. She never, ever, wavered. She was true, never putting me down because I wasn't doing better or making fun of me. She always offered me encouragement, never complained because I couldn't take her to a show. She supported me when it looked kind of bleak.

I would go to Hammill's house every time it snowed and I wasn't working. I would shovel the snow from their walks and get the firewood and coal in for them. I kept wood split and stacked on the back porch, and anything else I could do to help them. If there was much snow I would borrow their snow shovel and go up and down the streets asking for jobs shoveling snow. Sometimes, I could make a little money that way.

Along toward spring a fellow who slept with his head at the foot of my bunk and one space over to my left got some kind of a cold or pneumonia or something. I didn't know him but I secretly called him Russian Joe, because he could speak very little English and it sounded to me what I thought Russian must sound like. He developed a terrible cough and kept me awake at night. This went on for several days and nights, but I paid little attention to him as I had tried to talk to him a couple of times and he was not a bit sociable. The coughing did bother me though, as it was noisy and he would shake the whole unit of beds when he had a spell.

One night I didn't hear him and I thought he is better. The next morning I noticed just the top of his head sticking out of the covers and thought to myself, Poor Joe must be better and is getting some rest.

That night I didn't pay any attention to him but I did notice he wasn't coughing. The next morning I did notice he seemed to be lying in the same position and just the top of his head was sticking out of the covers, which seemed strange. When I got around to it, I told Mr. Brown about him. He said, "Let's check him out, he must be pretty sick." He said, "Come with me."

Russian Joe was still in the same position, just the top of his head sticking out of the covers. Mr. Brown pulled back the covers and he was dead as a door nail - and had been for several days. I guess he died when he had quit coughing. That night when I came in from the job, another fellow was in his bunk. Things were tough, the men were tough, and if you were not you didn't survive.

Along about this time I got the flu or something. I kept on working, but it was about all I could do to make it. I hadn't been to Hammill's house for a few days so when I got feeling a little better I went there to do the chores for them and to see that they were all right. I was still feeling kind of peaked and when they saw what kind of shape I was in they insisted on my coming back there to live. After some thought and persuading by Hattie and Mrs. Hammill I gave up on the Hotel de Gink and moved back in with them. They were glad to have me back even though I couldn't contribute much. I put in what I could but it was very little.

Hattie worked for some people part time as a maid. Sometimes she stayed with the elderly mother of the man of the house, when they were all going to be gone for the evening. One night about midnight when Hattie was baby sitting this elderly lady, Mrs. Hammill came to my room and said that she had been called by Hattie's employer. When these people had returned home, they found Hattie lying on the floor.

They soon came to get Mrs. Hammill to take her to the hospital, where Hattie had been taken. Needless to say, I didn't sleep much the rest of that night. In the morning, I got up, got some breakfast and waited around the house for news. About nine o'clock Mrs. Hammill came home from the hospital. Hattie had died, with a heart attack.

What a shock to us both. It was just Mrs. Hammill and I from then on. We got some welfare help as she had lost her means of support. I worked when I could find anything and worked for the county on, of all places the Indian Canyon golf course, three days a week. It was spring time and I could get a little lawn work or some gardening and other odd jobs.

Chapter 28

Entertainment was almost out of the question if it required any funding, but once in a while, I could manage to cook up something. The following is one of those experiences.

The Boxing Match

The former famous and ever popular world champion boxing star, Jack Dempsey, was coming to town to put on an exhibition boxing match at the Gonzaga football stadium. Having nothing better to do that evening, I went down there to see what I could see for free. I thought I might be able to position myself somewhere so I would be able to get a glimpse of him as he went from the buildings to the stadium.

Shortly after arriving, I ran into my old friend Denny Berry, who was looking for a little excitement also. We looked around for a while not being able to find a way to sneak in, or see anything. There were guards all over the place.

Finally, in exasperation we jumped up in the air and caught hold of the top of the outside of the solid wooden fence about eight feet high. We thought we would be able to see what was going on inside the stadium at least. We were hanging there looking over the top of the fence, sizing things up, when the fence started to sway. Denny said, "Custer, let's see if we can sway enough to topple it."

Well, some others saw what was going on and soon we had help. Sure enough, down went the fence. We were prepared for it and lit on our feet running. That was only half the battle though, as there was another fence about twenty feet away. These were erected to make a corridor for the patrons to get to their seats after they had been admitted.

Well, that first endeavor had been such a success that without hesitation we were immediately up on the other fence. In no time, we had it swaying, and over it went also. There we were, right on the field where the boxing ring had been set up in front of the grandstand, with nothing between us.

By this time there were guards all over the place. They were so confused by the hoard of would-be spectators advancing on them they didn't know which way to turn. When we saw the opportunity Denny said to me,

"Let's go, Custer," and we were gone, right to the front seats. We had had some previous experience in the art of sneaking in to movies so we had some idea of what to do to be successful at this sort of venture.

We rushed up to the front as quickly as possible, right to the ringside seats, and sat down. We leaned back, folded our arms, and looked around with a look of nonchalance and amazement, as though wondering what all the excitement was about.

Well, believe me there was plenty of it. Those guards were rushing around grabbing people out of the seats and propelling them toward the exits. Denny and I looked so comfortable and disinterested they never approached us. We leaned back and enjoyed the excitement immensely. We had ringside seats, the best. We felt we might as well go first class, the price was right. Although there were a good many who sneaked in that were ejected, they didn't bother us; we looked too legitimate.

We saw the performance in grand style. Denny was quite a guy, and a good deal like his sister, the nurse – a fun-loving Irishman. If Denny and I got into something, like sneaking into a movie or something like that, and Denny said, "Let's go, Custer," it meant it was time to forget it and clear out in a hurry. We were out-numbered or out-classed. In other words it meant we didn't have a chance and to leave in a hurry, something wasn't in our favor, and to depart without delay.

This was 1932, the year of the big election, Roosevelt versus Hoover. Hoover being the incumbent and a Republican was opposed to the repeal of the Volstead act, in other words prohibition. Roosevelt was the Democratic candidate who ran on a platform of a new deal in government and in favor of the repeal of the act. Needless to say, Mr. Roosevelt was elected by an overwhelming majority.

It was legal to register a few days before you were 21, which I did, and was then able to vote in the primary election. In those times the newly elected officials didn't take office until the fourth of March the year following the election.

Mrs. Hammill was a grand old lady (the nearest I ever came to having a Grandmother). She was at the time seventy five. She seemed very old, as she was very reserved, stately in her manners, highly dignified and quite frail. We got along fine.

We shared the cooking most of the time and the other household chores. She had cataracts on both eyes and could not see to read without a big magnifying glass; even then, it was difficult for her. I read her mail to her and answered her letters for her as she dictated them to me. She washed the clothes on a washboard and I did the ironing. We got along fine and had a regular family relationship.

The Relief Department gave us wood for heat, and some food, in return for my working three days a week on the golf course. I still felt as though I was spinning my wheels. We had a pretty tough winter. The county gave us wood and some commodities. I managed to make a little money once in a while – not much – but I was able to contribute a little.

The fourth of March Roosevelt was inaugurated. I can't remember if it was the next day or not, but I think it was, that he declared what was called a bank holiday. All banks were closed and there was no money except what you had in your pocket. The reason for him doing this was the fact that banks were going broke right and left.

It didn't make any difference to me, but it sure did to most people. I was driving an older doctor of medicine, Dr. Greive, who was a neighbor, to his office each day with his car, and sometimes out on house calls. He was not very steady and his family did not want him to drive any more. His daughter, who worked downtown and lived at home, would drive him home in the evening.

In the morning I would go to their place, get his car from the garage in the alley, bring it around in front where he would get in, then we would go to the barber shop where he would get a shave. This was standard procedure every morning.

One morning, several days after the banks were ordered closed, Dr. Greive said to the barber, when we came in, "I want a shave as usual, but I don't have any money to pay you with." The barber said, "That is all right, I understand, I don't have any either." The price of a shave was at that time, if I remember right, fifteen cents.

In a few days the banks were opened, those that could, that is. Some were not solvent and opened on a limited basis. You could only get a small percent of your money. Some did eventually pay out one hundred percent of deposits with no interest during the time your money was tied up, which in some cases was years. Many people lost their entire life savings and were left destitute. It was a pitiful situation.

I frequently visited my good friends Adrian and Sylvan Long. Mr. and Mrs. Long were great people and the whole family always made me feel comfortable and welcome. I hate to think back on the times I stayed there for free meals and the times I stayed overnight. Those people were like family to me. Mr. Long had an old truck and hauled wood for a meager living. He would go out in the woods where wood cutters were making cord wood (wood cut in four foot lengths), buy two cords of wood, and load and haul it to town where he had steady customers such as small hotels and so on, and sell to them. It wasn't very profitable; a means of survival, but that was all.

Sometimes during the winter the boys would go with him, as sometimes the wood had to be carried through deep snow, to the truck. One time he got the flu and so did Sylvan. When the truck didn't run, no income. I went up to their place and they needed to haul wood, so Adrian and I hauled wood for several days. It was rough; the snow was deep, the weather cold and the days were short. We would leave before daylight and get back long after dark. We usually had to unload in the dark.

One time it was bitterly cold and we got stuck in a snow bank. We had to put chains on the truck to get out and the chains were more haywire than chain. I had two pair of old worn out canvas gloves on, one pair over the other, in hopes the holes wouldn't match which they almost always did. I was working on one wheel, Adrian on the other.

I had to wire the chain together to keep it on the wheel and when I had finished I "cut" the wire off by twisting it back and forth. It eventually broke but I was unable to get one end disengaged from my glove. I kept pulling and twisting but could not get it loose. Finally, I looked down to see what was holding the wire, and through one of the holes I could see the trouble. My finger was frozen and the wire was caught in the flesh and I could not even feel it. That finger gave me trouble for many years after that when it got cold.

One trip up on Signal Point Ridge Adrian and I got our load of wood without much trouble and started to pull out when the gear shift lever broke off right in the transmission case. He couldn't shift gears.

We stopped, removed the top of the transmission, and could see what was wrong. We held a consultation and decided if we could figure out the proper sequence of positions of the two shafts in the transmission that were required for certain gear speeds we maybe could get back to town.

Luckily, there was a long-handled screwdriver in the truck. We started up and I sat there with the screwdriver in my hand. When he wanted to shift, he would depress the clutch and I would slide one of those shafts forward or back and then position the other one where it belonged and he would let the clutch out and we would be in business. By the time we got to Spokane I got pretty good at it and we had very little trouble getting around to get our load of wood delivered. The next morning we had the part welded and life was simple again.

One other time I went with Mr. Long and both boys for a load of wood. The weather was warm and we had a long mountain grade to ascend to get to the load. The truck radiator had a small leak and we ran out of water before we got to the top. There was a small trickle of water down a steep dirt embankment about thirty feet from the road. That was fine but we had no container to transfer the water from the creek to the radiator. What to do? After some brain wracking, we came up with a plan.

We had several tobacco cans between us, so we took the little paper packages of tobacco out of the cans. We stationed ourselves from the creek to the edge of the road and handed those cans of water to each other. We were there a long time. I'll bet it took a hundred cans of water to fill that old truck. A way, not a good way, but a way.

206

Chapter 29

One night on the way home to Hammill's house from visiting Agnes, I had an experience that kind of got my attention for awhile. I used to cut through the fuel yards at the north end of the Division Street Bridge, follow some railroad tracks for a short way, and then cut up the hill behind St. Aloysius church and come out at Boone Avenue and Astor Street. It was a spooky place to go but it cut off quite a little distance and at that time in my life there wasn't too much I was afraid of.

This particular night there was about a foot of snow on the ground and it was cold. I walked on a path that was tramped down that went the way I wanted to go. There was another well traveled path that crossed the one I was using about half way through the fuel yards. It was near midnight but because of the snow, I could see quite well. I observed a man coming along this other path and it appeared we would just about meet.

This did not appeal to me much, so I slowed down so he could cross in front of me. When I did, he slowed down so we were still going to meet. I then speeded up a little and he did the same. By this time, we were getting quite close to each other. I didn't want to meet him, as it seemed to be his intention to do so. I thought it over rather quickly and figured I had two options. I could try to bluff him, or I could take off running from him.

The latter didn't appeal to me, but neither did the bluffing business. I didn't have too much time to mull this over, but I thought I would try bluffing. If it doesn't work, I will run and he won't be as scared as I will be so that ought to work to my advantage, because I will have a greater incentive to go than he will. I should be able to outrun him.

With this in mind I waited till we were about a hundred feet apart and I could see he was watching me. I made a run for him, right straight at him. Apparently that was not the kind of reception he had expected, as he took off back the way he had come. I saw him drop something. He left in what you might call a high lope. I was kind of glad I didn't have to outrun him when I saw the speed he attained getting away from there.

I walked calmly over to where he had been to see what it was he had dropped. It was a piece of three quarter inch iron water pipe about thirty inches long. Boy was I glad I didn't have an encounter with him as I think he had every intention of doing me in with that pipe.

One morning I got a call from someone, I don't remember who now, that a man who was a piano tuner needed a driver to drive him around in his car. The man was in a hotel downtown and needed someone right away.

I told Mrs. Hammill where I was going and rushed down to the hotel. The man was looking for a driver and hired me. I thought he would be working around town. We got his luggage together and went down to the street where his car was parked. It turned out to be an old car. He asked if I was a careful driver and then informed me we would be going up toward Colville.

We took off and the old car ran fine, but he didn't have a very clear-cut idea of where he wanted to go. I, of course, couldn't help; I just went where he told me to go. We had no lunch and it got late in the afternoon when he told me of a side road leading off to the west. I took the road when we came to it and it was getting dark by this time. I sure was wishing I was some place else by this time. The road kept getting poorer and it did get dark.

The weather was quite cold and the road kept getting higher up in the hills and more muddy, with patches of snow, and it started to rain. No houses, nothing, but he said to keep on going, that we would get to a school and a house. We finally did come to a school and house but no one at the house. He knew where he was going all right. He said he tuned this school piano every year.

By this time it is about seven o'clock and the road is narrow, slippery and muddy. I finally told him we would get stuck in the mud if we kept going. He said to keep going and soon I did get stuck in a mud hole. Right in the middle of this one track road. Dark, raining, no shovel, nothing I could do.

Fortunately, I could see a dim light. By this time, it was about eight in the evening. I said I could see a light up on a hill so he said, "We will go up there and see if they will put us up for the night."

This didn't appeal to me much, but there was little else to do. When we got out of the car, he said, "Take hold of my arm to guide me." It was pitch dark and I couldn't see any way to get to the house, no road or path, nothing but black. Now if you don't think that is something, trying to guide a blind man down into a roadside ditch with water in it, up a steep, muddy, slippery bank, through a barbed wire fence, in the dark and rain when you can't even see where you are going yourself, I'll put in with you.

I walked him into a mud puddle and he was provoked at me for not seeing it. We struggled up a steep hill through a hay field to a small ranch house with a light on inside.

He told me to yell hello to the house when we got close. I did and a man came to the door with a kerosene lamp in his hand. I said, "We are lost, can we come in?" The fellow said, "Yes do come in, where did you come from?" My friend explained to him who we were, the circumstances and our predicament. It wasn't a very pretentious place, but it was warm, dry and cozy.

A middle-aged man and his wife lived there on a small farm. After they heard our story, they were all sympathy for our plight. When the lady found out we hadn't had anything to eat she got busy, started a fire in the kitchen stove, fried some eggs and bacon, warmed up some other food and made us some coffee. She hovered over us as a mother would. They said we could stay there for the night, and in the morning we would take his team of horses and pull the car out of the mud.

There was a sort of loft above the front room with a bed up there, where we were to sleep. When we got ready to go to bed, the lady gave me a kerosene lamp to take up there to see where we were going. I got undressed and was through with the light, so I said to my companion without thinking, "Are you through with the light?" He made me feel very embarrassed and at the same time sympathetic when he replied, "Son, the lights have been out for me for over forty years." I felt badly about the remark, and apologized. He was good about it and said not to worry.

In the morning, the piano tuner struck a deal with the people to clean and adjust a pump organ they had, for our board and lodging. The old fellow told me how to take some of the parts off the organ, and he went to work on it.

He knew what he was doing and started to whistle a little tune – he was happy. The farmer and I took his team of horses down to the car and pulled it out of the mud. When we got back to the house the piano tuner had everything put back together, and it worked just fine.

I told the piano tuner I wanted to give up the job, as no one knew where I was. I just had to get back, as everyone would be worried sick. The people where we stayed said they knew of a neighbor, a young fellow who was out of work, who might like the job of driving someone around the country. He would have an advantage of knowing the area also. They had a phone and were so ready to help us.

They called this young fellow, explaining the situation, and fortunately for me he agreed to give it a try. Boy, was I ever glad. I couldn't just walk out on the old fellow, and I was beginning to wonder how I was going to get out of this situation.

It was agreed we would meet this new man at the school we had passed the night before in the dark. The people also got the school principal on the phone and it was agreed the piano needed tuning, and the principal would also meet us at the school as it so happened it was Saturday.

I drove the car down there, we met the young man, a nice-appearing, likeable farm kid about my age, who was going to take over from me. The principal came and all the arrangements were made and I was gone. I got out of there before someone changed their mind.

I was on my way, about two o'clock in the afternoon. I walked for several miles before finally getting a ride to the highway. Luckily, after walking a short distance there, I picked up a ride clear to Spokane. I sure was glad to get out of that deal.

When I did get back that evening Mrs. Hammill was worried, as she was all alone and had no idea of what had happened to me. I often wondered how the old fellow made out. I felt very sorry for him and I wondered how he could keep getting people to drive him around. I think he said he was from Lewistown and I just don't know how he could make a living. Times were tough, believe me. He had to be admired for his fortitude. I guess he had no alternative to what he was doing, except to go to the poor farm.

Yes, there were poor farms or poor houses in those times, where old people could go to live out their time, if they had no way to make it on their own. The one for Spokane County was located at Spangle.

Chapter 30

These are some of the experiences I had when I was trying to get going during the 1932-1933 era.

One time during the summer of 1932 I had gone to Dayton to try to get a harvest job, but I was a little early, and before I found a job I got word from the Hammills that friends of the people who Hattie worked for and who lived in the valley had a job for me if I would come home immediately. I didn't know what kind of job but I figured I couldn't waste time finding out so I figured I had better get back as fast as I could.

Dayton was a poor place to get out of by freight train because it was on the end of a branch rail line. I had been hanging around town looking for some farmer who needed help, but the harvest hadn't started yet and I wasn't having much luck and wasn't working. I was sleeping in the city park and having a hard time to get enough to eat.

I went to the little depot and talked to the station master about when a train would be coming to town. He said there would be a train in that evening to pick up some cars of grain. I waited and sure enough, an engine with several box cars showed up and pulled some loaded grain cars out. I climbed up on top of one of them, and as it was summer time and the evening was nice, I just rode on top till we got to Walla Walla. There they did some switching and picked up a small circus train of cars.

It was early in the morning when they got ready to go and no place to get in out of the wind. I got on top of a car and they took off for Wallula. They must have been on short time and as the train was short, they had lots of power and a full head of steam. They made good time. In fact they made such good time I thought the train would jump the track, but it didn't. Riding on top that way you got the full benefit of the pitching and swaying from side to side – scary is an understatement.

We got there, which wasn't far, for which I was grateful. There was quite a big railroad yard there, as it was on the main line from Portland to Spokane, but nothing else. I hung around till morning and when it got daylight I found where there were several guys hanging around, waiting for a train to Spokane.

They said there wouldn't be one till the middle of the afternoon. It was a dinky little place and now I don't remember whether I didn't have any money or there was no place to buy anything or what, but I had no way to get anything to eat. The weather was hot and I was hungry, I can remember that part very well.

About two o'clock in the afternoon a train pulled in and switched some cars around and we could see that a train was ready to go. There were about twenty of us wanting to get away from this miserable, dumpy little wide place in the tracks in the worst way. We walked up along the train and found an empty box car. We got in, shut the door and were real quiet. Some of the fellows had tried to catch the one-train-a-day out, the day before, but the yard bulls had caught them and run them out of the yard before they could get on the train. They then missed the only train that day.

The train took off real fast, stopped after a brief interval, backed up, unhooked from us and then every thing got strangely quiet. Someone opened the door and peeked out. It was discovered they had cut the train right behind our car, pulled us up, switched us to another track, shoved us way back down the line about a mile, cut us off, and left us there.

Well, we could see what they were doing; they were going to leave us there. We all jumped out and ran as fast as we could back up the track toward the yard where the engine was coupling up to the rest of the train to pull out for the main line. They had every intention of leaving us high and dry, so to speak.

What a miserable turn of events, after we had been waiting so patiently all day for a ride. There were yard bulls up there so we couldn't go in the train yard. Fortunately, there was a big ditch of some kind that ran alongside the track. It couldn't have been a drainage ditch as there was nothing in that country to drain; you couldn't even get a drink of water there. We ran up that for a long way. I guess we ran a mile or better. I never knew. I never looked back; I didn't have time, I was too busy running.

Some of us got up to where the train came out of the yard. We waited till a few cars went by and made a run for it. It meant we would have to catch it on the fly if we were to get it, (meaning we would have to swing up on a ladder on the side of a car as it went by). It was hot also (meaning it was traveling fast).

Those of us who were younger and were able to get there in time made a dash for it. I was young, tough, and brave. I caught a car as it went by, being particular to get the front end of the car.

This was important, as when you grabbed a car on the fly, if it was hot, you were usually flung violently around against the side of the car, which could be tolerated but wasn't particularly pleasant. It was extremely important, however, to hang on for dear life. If you were on the end of the car, following the direction of travel, you were usually flung around the corner of the car, as was sometimes the case. This could break both your arms. When this happened the person could not hang on, of course, and fell off. This was very bad for several reasons, but the worst could be you fell in front of the wheels and that was when you gave up riding freight trains permanently.

Many of the men were not able to cope with the situation and were left behind. Those were the most ornery train men I ever encountered. We had to ride on top till the train stopped at a place called Ayers Junction. When it did I along with some other fellows, found an empty box car, got in and closed the door.

After a short while, the train crew pulled the same trick on us: shoved our car way back down the tracks, cut us off and left. This time we were watching and as soon as they left, we ran back to the train, which was on the main line, and made it.

Some time early in the morning we got into Spokane. Believe me, we unloaded as soon as that miserable train slowed down enough to get off, and walked into town. We knew they would have marched us off to jail if they could have rounded us up. By this time there were only about six of us left. I often wondered what ever happened to the fellows we left behind who were not able to keep up with the foot racing or agile enough to grab onto a fast moving train.

The job wasn't much of a job; it was out in the valley. I went out and worked for a few days but it only paid fifteen dollars a month, and board. It would have been all right in the winter time but I thought I could do better than that in the harvest. I was picking apples and I didn't care much for the people, as they wanted me to get up before anyone else and milk two cows and have this all done before breakfast, then I could get in a full day's work and do it again after supper.

I stayed with it a few days, when one morning they served me some cooked cereal for breakfast. Everyone else was eating pancakes and eggs and bacon. I kind of wondered what was going on. I got looking at this mush and seeing something in it, I sorted out a worm. I laid it on the edge of my bowl, and found seven more, eating the rest of the cereal. This left a sort of bad taste in my mouth, so to speak.

I went out to work and the more I thought about it the more I didn't like that job, so I went to the house, told the lady I was leaving, got my clothes and took off down the road.

I went back to Dayton, but when I got there all the harvest jobs were gone. Chalk up another adventure to experience. Things were tough. I knocked around awhile but couldn't stay away from my Agnes for very long.

I couldn't find any work so I decided to go to Wapato. There was usually some kind of short time jobs there if a person was willing to do them, till apple picking started. I took a freight train and left.

The Corn Feed Caper

I had an interesting experience on that trip. A bunch of us were riding on a flat car, along late in the afternoon of a nice warm day, when the train stopped out in the country, right on the main line. There appeared to be no reason for it, but the train men had a habit of doing things like that without an explanation.

There was a nice field of corn planted right alongside the track. Someone on the train got off, got through the fence, and sampled the corn. It was just ready to pick. A whole bunch of men followed suit when he came back and we saw what he had, me among them. I got about ten ears and climbed back on the train. When we went through Wapato, the train didn't stop, so I had to ride on to Yakima. I got talking to a fellow and it was agreed we would get off together and cook up a corn feed when the train stopped.

We did, and he said, "If you will get a clean can from the jungle and get some water I will gather some wood and start a fire." (The jungle was a place along the tracks where men would gather to cook and sleep and sort of hang out. Jungles were located near water and trees, if there were any, or a bridge or some little form of protection. There were usually clean cans to cook in, and sometimes wash pans, and sometimes wood for a fire. There was an unwritten rule that if you used anything you left it clean, and hung it upside down for the next guy.

I left my pack sack with him, got a couple of clean cans, and looked for water. I walked up the track quite a ways and found a nice little creek running out of a grassy field. It was nice and clean-looking, with grass growing along the bank. In fact, it looked as though it might have had fish in it. I dipped up a couple of cans of water and went back. The fellow had a nice little fire going so we husked a batch of corn and cooked it. I had a little salt and some coffee. We had a great feed of fresh corn with coffee to drink. Only a one course meal but at that time people like us, under those circumstances, were not choosy. The sun was down, it was not yet dark. It was a beautiful, warm, summer evening. Our stomachs were full, we were just sitting back picking our teeth, relaxing, and congratulating ourselves on how good life was at times.

A fellow came walking along and stopped to talk. As we had corn and coffee left over, we invited him to have some. He said, "Where did you guys get it?" We told him. He said, "Where did you get the water to cook with"? I thought, Boy this guy sure is particular, but told him willingly. I said "There is a nice little creek right up the track about three hundred yards. That's where I got our water for the corn and coffee, have some." He said, "No thanks, that little creek comes from an overflow of the sewer works over across that big field about a mile away." That declaration was an unwelcome revelation to say the least.

Well, what to do? We looked at each other and immediately lost our feeling of euphoria of a few moments before. There was nothing to do. We talked it over. We had boiled the water and we felt good so far, except we had sort of lost our appetite for any more coffee or corn about then. We cleaned up our cans and took off in different directions. I suffered no ill effects from this little caper and I hope my friend didn't either.

I went to Wapato the next day and hung around there for quite awhile. I found a place behind some old buildings near a side track, with some little trees and high bushes to crawl under. I made this my headquarters. I kept my packsack hidden there and slept there. I would get a day's work once in awhile for a dollar and that kept me in food, along with what I could rustle. Sometimes I would buy a quart of milk for seven cents and a loaf of bread for eight cents. I would take it to my headquarters, tear the loaf of bread in half (it was not sliced then) and break it up in one of my cans. I would pour exactly half of the milk in with it and that was supper. The other half I would have for breakfast. If I didn't do it this way I would get carried away and eat everything at the first setting.

This was kind of slim pickings. In those times I had no problem with keeping my weight down. It has been said, it was a way, not a good way maybe, but a way.

I had a frying pan, and a knife, fork and spoon. Sometimes I would walk out in the country a short distance and find a potato field. I would dig some of the dirt away with my hands and take several spuds. Sometimes I would get a few green apples and make sauce, but without sugar it wasn't too good.

Chapter 31

One time I got right down to nothing. It was early morning and I was hungry. I walked up the one main street, not knowing just what I was going to do. I had to eat some way or other, that was a given. There was a little bakery facing the street so I went around to the back door, and as it was open, I stuck my head in. Boy, there were good smells.

Soon an old woman about fifty years old came from somewhere and said, "What do you want?" in a real cranky tone of voice. I said "I am hungry and I am willing to work for anything you are willing to give me for my labor." She said, "All right, if you want to work split some of that apple wood." I took a look at it – it was all knots. They had used all the straight grained stuff. These pieces were too big to go in their wood-fired oven. There was an old, dull axe there and a good chopping block. Well, I was no stranger to splitting wood, so I started in. I got quite a pile done when she came to the door and said "That is enough." She said, "Come on in, what do you want?" I replied, "I will be grateful for whatever you can spare." She told me to wash up in their bathroom and sit down at a little table. She gave me a nice dish of hot oatmeal with milk and sugar, (no worms). Before that was gone, she showed up with some day-old cinnamon rolls and some day-old doughnuts and coffee. Boy, that was good.

The next morning I was right back to split wood. When she saw me, she said, "Do you want to work again?" I assured her I was willing, and when she determined I had done enough she told me that was enough. I had the same thing again for breakfast. The next day I did the same thing. Boy that wood was tough to split but I would hang in there and wear it down. The fourth day I finished it all and had a big pile for their use. When I left that morning she got friendly and confided in me a little. She said, "I have had a lot of bums come for food but when I showed them those knots they were gone. You are the only man who has ever come that was willing to work. You surprised me and I commend you for the good job you have done. Now I will be able to burn all that wood. If you are hungry and have no money you just come back, don't worry about the work." I thanked her but I didn't have to, after that.

The season got later and it got easier to find food. The apples were riper and sweeter. There was more work. The peaches ripened and were plentiful, and too I got some work picking them, I mean besides the ones I liberated from the trees for my own consumption. Then there were pears and prunes to pick and eat. I prospered a little. I got so I could buy some lard to fry things with, and sometimes ten cents worth of hamburger. I would buy a little sugar for my fruit sauce. Life got easier.

Sometimes I would go to the produce houses where the farm trucks would be unloading melons. Sometimes they would drop one when they were throwing them to each other during the unloading of the trucks. If they were not broken up too badly sometimes quite a bit could be salvaged. Sometimes a guy would look at me and say, "Stick around I think I am going to drop one pretty quick." When no one was looking he would drop one just enough to crack it and say, "Oh-oh, that one slipped through my hands," and give it to me.

I stayed around till about apple picking time and then was lonesome for Agnes. I got the promise of an apple-picking job coming up soon so decided to go to Spokane to see my girl.

The Ride in the Engine

I caught a freight train which was getting to be commonplace for me by now, but I had to catch it on the fly, which meant I had to ride on top till the train stopped.

Well, it was going to get dark soon, and as it was cloudy and cool I was getting cold. I didn't have my big paper bag with me. There were two huge, brand-new steam locomotives in the train, being transported to someplace from Auburn, where they had been built. They were just going along for the ride. They were both ahead of me in the train, but I was separated from them by several cars. I thought, boy, if I could get in one of them I would have it made. I would be out of the wind and would be warmer.

I walked over the top of the cars, finally getting to the back of the tender, which was the special car that was always hooked to the engine to supply coal and water, for the engine to make steam for power. I crawled down over the coal to the apron between the two monstrous machines. The engine had a curtain on it for cold weather use. This was a big canvas curtain that hung behind the engine cab and covered the opening between the cab and the tender, where the coal was stored. This curtain was to keep out cold air if need be.

When I got to the engine, it was getting dark. I saw no light on the other side of the canvas, indicating there was probably no one riding there in charge of the engine, which was usually the case.

I hollered anyway, so as not to frighten a railroad man or a bum when I pulled the curtain aside to enter if either one was there. No reply, so in I went. No one there, a brand new engine, all painted nice and clean. No wind, with the engineer's window to look out of, and a seat to ride on. What luck!

I had just made myself comfortable when I became aware of a hot grease or oil smell. This was strange, as there was no fire in the firebox. I looked all around but could see nothing burning or feel anything hot. I opened the engineer's window and could smell the smell much stronger. I leaned way out and looked down where the wheels were. I could see smoke and soon saw where the trouble was. There was hot iron down there, hot enough to glow in the dark. One of the big axles on one of those huge wheels was out of lubrication. Boy, this was serious.

I contemplated my position in this situation. If someone caught me there they might say I did something to cause the trouble; I could go to jail. This would not be good. If I got out again I would be out in the cold. This would not be good. If I didn't do anything and there was a train wreck because of an overheated axle and bearing, which was very probable and in all likelihood would happen soon, I was on the same train and this was not good.

I soon figured the best option open to me was to hustle up to the front of the two new engines to see if there was a man riding in it. If not, make my way all the way to the engine pulling the train to inform someone of the situation. It was very serious and time was extremely important.

It was pitch dark by this time. I left my packsack in the cab, as I sure didn't need anything to encumber my agility on my trip over the top of those wildly-pitching, swaying boxcars in the dark. I got out the little door on the side of the engine, made it along the side of the boiler, down on the coupling above the cowcatcher (as the big guard on the front of the engine was called), stepped over to the coupling on the next car ahead, and climbed up the ladder on the end of the car to the top.

There were walkways on top of the cars then. I made my way to the rear end of the tender hooked to the back of the other new engine and clambered down over the coal, all in total darkness.

I could see a dim light shining behind the curtain and knew there was a train man riding in the cab of that engine. I got right to the curtain, hating to enter, as I wasn't sure what kind of reception I would receive. I was scared he might have a gun and would shoot me before I could explain to him that I was on a mission of good will and my intentions were honorable.

I yelled out, "Corning in." I pulled the canvas back and faced a man in the dim light of a kerosene lantern, who was startled, surprised, and frightened all at the same time, by the expression on his face. It was very obvious he was not happy to see me emerge from the shadows. He didn't shoot me, that was a good start.

Before he had a chance to say anything, I said, "I know I am not wanted here but you must listen to me. I think I have some bad news for you." This got his attention. He said, "What do you want?" I said, "I got in that rear engine and smelled hot grease or oil. I didn't touch anything or move any levers. I didn't cause it, but there is something mighty hot on that engine." I told him I couldn't find it for awhile, but after opening the window, I was able to see the location of the problem, and that there was some iron glowing in the dark. When I had finished I had his full attention, believe me.

He looked scared and said, "Are you sure you know what you are talking about?" I assured him I was. He got out a big pot-like lantern, the likes of which I had never seen before or since. He got it lit and said, "Get up on top of the cab of this engine and start swinging this lantern back and forth cross-wise of the direction of travel. Keep doing it till you get one long whistle from the engine pulling the train. One whistle means stop."

I got up there and started waving my big light. It wasn't long before I got one long, wailing whistle and I could feel the engineer put the air brakes on. I got down in the cab and this fellow's attitude had completely changed.

He said, "You stay right with me from now on. When the train stops I am going back to that engine and I want you to go with me, to show me where the trouble is, and too, you can help me carry some oil." It took about a mile to get stopped. This was a manifest, a long heavy train.

In those times, on the Northern Pacific, a heavy train like this had a man called the front brakeman who rode up in front in a little cubical of a house-like arrangement on the back of the tender, and looked backward to watch the train in case of trouble. No radios at that time. This was the man who saw my light and got word down to the engineer to stop. We got a five-gallon can of oil, some tools and rags and walked back to the engine. When we got there, he had no trouble seeing what I meant.

The bearing that the wheel axle turned in was glowing in the dark. He poured some oil in it and put some rags on top of it to hold oil, and poured fresh, cool oil on them to help cool it down. Soon some of the train crew showed up. Everyone got quite excited about how close we had come to having had a serious accident. My new-found friend was very honest about the fact that I had discovered the trouble and notified him. He was a nice guy and very grateful for the fact I had reported to him.

He told me to stay right with him. He said, when we stopped the train, "They cannot move again till I give them permission." He also explained that he had checked the bearings in Yakima and at that time they were ok, but something had happened in the meantime.

When the bearing cooled down and he was satisfied he gave the conductor permission to go to Pasco. We had the main line tied up. There was a flag man out a mile or more ahead, and another behind the train. They got ready, whistled the flag men in, gave the high-ball (two short blasts on the whistle), and we were under way again. It turned out to be a big deal. He said, "You ride with me in my engine to Pasco, where I will have these two engines set out on a side track till I have a chance to inspect them in the daylight. When we get there and get them parked someplace on a side track so I know where I am, I am going to take you up town and buy you the biggest steak in the restaurant."

Sure enough, when we got parked on a side track we went up town for supper and he did buy me a steak. I refused the most expensive one, which he offered, but he insisted I have a good one. He said, "If I was going on to Spokane you would be welcome to ride with me, but it may be several days before I am ready to go after this trouble." He also went on to tell me that had it not been for me reporting this in time we probably would have had a bad wreck. If we hadn't, and the train had made it to Pasco, the axle on that set of wheels would have been ruined, and in all probability it would have cost him his job. This was quite an interesting experience.

Chapter 32

I visited Agnes for a couple of days. Her brother Lawrence wasn't working and decided he would like to try some apple-picking. He had an Indian make motorcycle with a side car. He gathered up some bedding and I got some more cooking utensils. I borrowed a small tent from some friends and we took off for Wapato, on the motorcycle. The weather was warm and we went to the orchard where I had the promise of a job. We set up camp out in the orchard under an apple tree and were ready to go to work. The apples were not quite ready for picking yet so we scouted around and found some day-work doing other things for a few days. Enough work to subsist by eating off the land as much as we could.

We soon got steady picking for a couple of weeks or so. There was going to be a delay of three or four days before some of the later apples would be ready so I told Lawrence I wanted to go to Spokane to see his sister, which he thought wasn't necessary, but I did. I took to the rails, got to Spokane, visited for a couple of days, and decided to take a passenger train back to Wapato, as it would be quicker.

I had little trouble getting aboard the tender in Spokane, as it was about ten o'clock in the evening and I was able to conceal myself in the shadows opposite the depot side of the train. When I did board I laid down as flat as I could so as not to be seen. No one saw me and everything went fine till we got to the town of Sprague, where the train took on water.

The engine stopped, with the tender under the huge water tank that stood beside the tracks. I didn't bother to get off, as I was confident there were no yard bulls around there. The fireman came back over the coal, opened the door on top of the water tank, pulled down the big water spout, stuck it in the opening, stepped on a little platform on the spout, pulled a rope with a handle on the end of it, and water poured into the tender.

It only took a couple of minutes to take on hundreds of gallons. I don't know if he resented me being there or not. I stayed aboard but was careful to stay out of his way. He over-filled the tank so that it ran over. There was a steel rim around the top edge of the tender, which kept the water from draining away. When he was finished I had to step in the water to get back to my riding place, where I was kind of out of the wind but my feet were sopping wet and it was cold.

When we pulled into Pasco I figured I had better get off, as we were right under some very bright lights. I stood back in the shadows and when I heard the engineer let the air brakes off the train I stepped out to get aboard. Out of nowhere was a big yard bull right in front of me. Boy, was I surprised. He had appeared as if by magic from thin air. He said, "Where do you think you are going?" I said, "I was going to Yakima but I just changed my mind." He said, "You sure did; now you get the hell out of here, and if I catch you around here again you will be going to jail." I took him at his word and left there as rapidly as I could. He caused me great inconvenience but I didn't try to explain it to him as he seemed to be in a very uncompromising frame of mind, and I didn't think he would understand anyway. I was forced to continue the rest of my journey by freight train, which I caught on the fly as it crossed the street leaving town the next afternoon.

We stayed till the apple-picking was over, coming home with a few dollars, which I gave to Hammills to apply on what I owed them for back board and room.

Shoveling Snow for the County

I particularly remember one bitterly cold morning during the winter when I was working three days a week for the county on the golf course. When I got off the streetcar that took me downtown – where I would transfer to another streetcar that took us to the end of the line where we would get off and walk the rest of the way to the job site – there was an old bus parked there. One of the bosses from the golf course job was standing there in the freezing wind. He told me the crew would be going out in the country to shovel some snow. Well, that didn't sound too bad to me as I was dreading that long walk in the wind. The old bus was nice and warm and we were all joking about getting a nice ride out in the country some place.

When we finally got there it was down near Spangle on a county road. There was a cut through a big hill and the road was full of wind-driven, hard-packed snow. No road, it just ended at the beginning of the road cut through a hill. We pulled up and got out of our nice, warm nest into that biting wind, and our enthusiasm was rapidly replaced with disenchantment. The contour of the hill was the same as it had been before the road was dug through the hill.

The man in charge had a plan and it worked quite well. We were each given a scoop shovel and we were assigned a spot to start digging. Some up on top, others down where the pavement disappeared. You could throw that hard-packed snow up in the air, and when the wind caught it, I don't think it settled down till it got to the next county. When a man had dug in to where he couldn't throw the snow out of the cut another man would dig a shelf in the bank above the first fellow and the snow would be passed up to the fellow above. It worked very well and soon most were dug in to where we were out of the wind and we soon warmed up. When someone up on top wanted to get out of the wind for a while, we would trade off.

We got back in the bus to eat lunch but the bus wasn't running, and so cold none wanted to tarry. We went right back to work to keep warm. It wasn't so bad after all and we put in the day there. We were about half-way through the cut, which was about thirty feet deep, when we stopped for the day. We were told we would be back the next day to finish the job.

The next day the wind was down when we got there but that cut was full of fresh snow, drifted in from the surrounding hills. The whole previous day's work was wiped out; we started over again. Soon another bus-load of men showed up from somewhere and then it went faster. Along about noon the boss climbed up where I was working with some other fellows and said, "Be careful now, there is a school bus down in there." We thought he was kidding, of course, but we were on the lookout and it wasn't long before we did come down on a yellow roof. The school bus had tried to get through the drift several days before, when the drifting first started, and had become stuck. Everyone got out and the bus was abandoned.

We got the road opened that afternoon with the help of the other bus-load of men. The wind had gone down so it went faster. When I think back, I remember that the county gave us tickets to ride to and from work. It cost seven cents a fare on the street car, but most of us didn't have seven cents.

Chapter 33

In the spring of 1933, after President Roosevelt had been able to get his feet on the ground, he was able to get Congress to enact some new legislation to help people out. Many make-work projects were started, such as the Civil Works Administration, called CWA, the Works Progress Administration, called the WPA, and many more such as the Civilian Conservation Corp, called the three C's or the CCC.

This was a program for mostly young males to give them something to do to make a little money, and perform work that would benefit the country in general. One who joined up was required to sign up for an enlistment period of six months and go wherever you were sent to work. An enlistee would be paid the handsome sum of thirty dollars a month plus board, room and clothes. Twenty five dollars of this money had to be sent home to parents. The army was going to feed and house the workers and the work was to be performed on public projects of a non-competitive nature, such as National Parks, Forest Service improvements etc. The work was to be supervised by the department that was getting the work done such as the Forest Service.

Well, I wanted to get on with my life if I was to have one, which I was confident I would if I could just get started. I was young, strong, healthy, and full of ambition, but didn't or couldn't – like thousands of my peers – seem to get a start. I did some inquiring and determined I would be eligible as a candidate for the CCC's. I talked it over with my Agnes, who was kind of waiting in the wings to marry me I felt, if I asked her, when I was able to make a living and offer some security. I talked it over with Mrs. Hammill, explaining how I felt, and she understood.

It meant a big change for her, as I was about the only one she had, outside of a niece who lived in Colville. The niece came down and we talked it over. They were in agreement that I should go for it. It wasn't much but it was something. I had hopes it would lead into something later. I suggested I send my twenty five dollars a month to Mrs. Hammill for six months to repay her for the times when I was unable to pay my way when I lived there.

I made application and was given a date to appear for a physical and to be sworn in, if I was accepted. This was kind of sad. Mrs. Hammill and I were very close and had a high regard for each other. She was a fine, old lady and I truly thought a lot of her. I knew it would never be the same again. I hated to leave her all alone. She was quite frail but also very brave. I didn't know what would become of her, or me either, for that matter.

The CCC's

I appeared at the appointed time and place, joining about a hundred other guys in a big room. We were told we would be given physical exams, and if we passed we would be accepted, sworn in, and from then on we would be considered the same as enlisted men in the regular army and would be told what to do and when to do it.

They had us line up along one wall and told us to strip all of our clothes off, everything, and leave everything we had in a pile on the floor. No dignity, no privacy, no formality.

We were then told to form a line. This, it turned out, was going to be a very familiar command: form a line. Every time we did anything we formed lines – when we ate, when we went to do any work, and when we came back form work: form a line. I guess those sergeants could only operate with their men lined up, like we were going to have a parade.

When we were all lined up, feeling very uncomfortable in our nudity, we were passed from one inspection station to another around the room. Each had a little table and a clerk and when you advanced to his station you gave him your score sheet. There was a specialist there (to use the term loosely) who looked over your eyes – next station, ears, etc., down the line – checking your throat, counting your teeth, and poking you wherever they figured you would be most vulnerable. We were made to squat, stoop, bend over, twist, jump, and do pushups. We were subjected to some other procedures that would have been embarrassing in a private doctor's office let alone in a public place which had a cold stone floor that sort of made one hump up to begin with.

They checked our knee joints and our ankles as though they wondered if we could walk. It made me wonder how the heck they ever thought we got there in the first place. The results called out by the examiner were all duly recorded on your score sheet by the clerk and carried along with you as you progressed. Before we were through I was wishing I was someplace else. When they couldn't think of any other indignities to subject us to they said we could retrieve our belongings.

When we were all dressed again we were lined up about three deep and sworn in. We were told that if we deserted before our six-month term was up, without having proof of having a self-sustaining job, we would be given a dishonorable discharge and would never be able to work for the Federal Government in our entire life time. This was all very scary; there were some sober-looking faces in the crowd by this time, believe me. I was a little older than most of them and was a little less intimidated by the formality and stern tone of the voices. I had been on my own for quite awhile so to speak. I figured if it got too tough I would leave and they could do whatever they wanted to.

We were marched down to the street and lined up. After a little while a special streetcar came along, just for us, and after boarding we were taken to Fort George Wright. (Editor's note: Fort George Wright is now the site of Mukogawa Fort Wright Institute in Spokane.) We got off and lined up, and then were marched over to a small village of tents all lined up in neat rows. We were lined up in a row and counted off into units of eight, and were told that from then on we would be in a group of eight.

We were marched to the tents and down the rows. Each group of eight was assigned to a tent. We left our baggage on a cot in the tent, which we claimed for our own, then we lined up and marched over to a supply building where we formed a line and passed by a counter where we were issued brand new clothes, 1918 GI clothes left over from World War One.

That was funny. The little guys were out of luck, there were no little sizes. Some of them could just about turn around in their new clothes without unbuttoning them. They had their pant legs and their sleeves rolled up three or four turns. Some of them had pants with the crotch hanging so far it was just about dragging out their tracks in the dust. I was lucky; most of my clothes fit reasonably well, even the shoes. We were told we had to wear these outfits all the time and to send our civilian clothes home. When we all got decked out, we were a comical looking group of recruits. The regular Army soldiers called us the ragged-butted recruits and made fun of us.

We were the first company of two hundred men to be formed at Fort Wright, which was an infantry and light cavalry post of the regular Army at that time. This was something new for them and they enjoyed marching us around and trying to put us through different drills. We were rather indifferent to their games and cooperated just enough to stay out of trouble. We sort of put up with them and they put up with us.

We were there for a week when they told us we were to be leaving the next day. This was early in May – the weather was getting nice and the whole company was jubilant. Fort Wright wasn't our favorite place. That evening I went to see Agnes to tell her I was leaving the next day. We were going to a place called Sullivan Lake up near the Canadian border. Everyone felt that as soon as we got up there the Army would let up on us, as we would be working for the Forest Service, which turned out to be true.

Sullivan Lake

Early the next morning we boarded Army trucks and went to Sullivan Lake, which was about a hundred and twenty miles. It was about six miles from a little town called Metaline Falls on the Pend d'Oreille river. It was a beautiful setting and all virgin forest. I was delighted with the prospects of this country. The only drawback being that it was so far from Spokane. Not many cars on the road then and rides were hard to get. No one in camp had a car, and with only five dollars a month for spending money there was no money for gas if you did have one.

The first thing after we got there was to line up. The Army sergeants and some corporals who came along with us picked out men for crews and showed us how to set up the big tents – one for a field kitchen and more to sleep in. We had our blankets in our duffel bags and were issued new Army cots to sleep on. By the time we had a camp pretty well set up the Army cooks had supper ready to eat. All we had had to eat since early morning breakfast were some dry sandwiches – we were ready. This was our introduction to mess kits. These were to be our eating utensils from then on. Line up to get one.

We were each given a mess kit. These were ours to take care of from then on. It was a very necessary piece of our equipment if we wanted to eat, we were to find out. Without it you didn't eat. Not eating regularly was not something to look forward to; I had learned the hard way earlier.

These mess kits were made of heavy aluminum in an oval about eight inches long and five inches wide. They were about an inch and a quarter deep with a removable shallow lid. The lid had a little ring on one end of it. The lid fit on top of the main dish part, with the flatware inside, which consisted of a knife, a fork and a spoon, all with short handles but a generous working end on them. The lid was then held in place

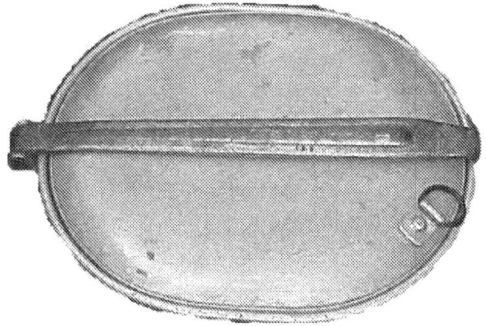

World War One Army Mess Kit

when the utensil was not in use with a bar, which hinged to the main dish on one end. It was folded over the lid and snapped down in place. They were practical, and kept the inside clean when not in use, at least if you could get it clean when you finished eating from it.

The routine was this: Line up again, pass by the food, hold out your mess kit – not a simple procedure – with the open side up. Be sure to have the little bar sticking out toward you with this little shallow tray lid with a little ring on it, with the ring slid over the end of the little bar. You had to hold every thing in a certain order, fingers holding the mess kit, bar sticking out toward you, thumb holding the lid balanced on the bar with the opposite end with the ring slid over the bar to hold the lid in place on that end. Yes, this thumb was busy, keeping everything in balance. Not a simple feat to accomplish, requiring practice and some little skill.

Your flatware went in your pocket for later use. The right hand held the cup, a big cup holding about two ordinary cups, or a pint. It too was made of aluminum, having a handle that folded out on one side to hold when picking it up. There was a little locking device on the handle that had to be locked very securely every time the handle was used. Many a fellow, who got careless and didn't attend to this little detail with care, lost his fresh, hot coffee right in his shoe, as this is where it usually went when the cup suddenly turned upside down. When you were in the food line, it was not uncommon to hear a howl of anguish from someone ahead of you. You knew instinctively some poor fellow had been careless and was in extreme discomfort with a shoe full of hot coffee.

The food was set up on tables and as you passed by with your mess kit held out, someone back of the table dished up whatever they had at their station to eat. You took what they gave you, there were no seconds but they usually gave out plenty. The bad thing was, though, you got it all in the same dish, the mess kit. Sometimes you would have different food all mixed up or piled on top of something else.

When you got to a place to eat it, frequently it wasn't too appetizing. When you got hungry enough one never noticed. In the lid you got your pudding and sometimes it was hot and thin. Sometimes it would be canned fruit. In either case, it would be thin and runny. If you were not careful, or skilled at balancing, it would burn your thumb or you would tip the tray a little and it too would be in your shoe, or you would lose it on the ground. Either way it was gone. Tough luck, that was it till the next meal. If you wanted bread, it would be sliced and piled up near the coffee. The butter would be there also, but where to put it? Last was the hot coffee. A fellow would be there to ladle up your cup full, as your hands were all used up by this time.

When we got the buildings built we went through this procedure in the building but then we had tables to eat on and benches to sit on. When you were finished eating you went outside and passed by a wash tub of hot soapy water, with a fire under it to keep it hot. You hung your cup by the handle on your belt, slid the little ring on the lid over the bar-like handle on the mess kit, dipped them in the water and scrubbed them with one of several long handled brushes sticking out of the water to scrub them with. Then you rinsed your cup and tools, moved to another tub of hot water and hoped it was reasonably clean for rinsing everything. There was no way to dry them; you folded everything up wet and that was it.

Sometimes the water got cool and greasy. It was somewhat less than appealing to think about eating your next meal from that greasy dish, but by the next meal, you usually had forgotten about it. If you hadn't you would wish you had.

228

The next morning after arriving at Sullivan Lake we were all lined up once more, had roll call and then were asked to volunteer for various assignments as they were called out. Plumbers, carpenters, cooks, general labor etc. I chose carpenter and was soon glad I had. I didn't know much about it, but a little. Before noon I was working with an older fellow on building a bunkhouse. I had to laugh about some of the fellows though. The cooks were washing pots and pans and peeling potatoes. The plumbers were digging ditches. The foreman in charge of building the buildings was an older man who knew what he was doing and I was soon given some responsibility, and kind of left to do whatever needed doing.

We got the buildings built and I was given the job of camp carpenter. I was pretty much my own boss, which was neat. I kept busy fixing things, building shelves, cupboards, and other things that needed to be done.

Chapter 34

One forenoon the young fellow, Anderson, who was in charge of the infirmary came to me and said, "I have a problem and I wonder if I could get you to come over to the infirmary shack and help me for a while?" Bob McDaniel, a friend of mine, had cut his foot the night before. Anderson said, "The doctor is gone, would you come over with me and look at Bob's foot?" When we looked at the foot, Anderson said "I think it needs stitches in it, what do you think?" I agreed it sure did.

Bob had been taking a shower the night before when his foot had slipped down in a space between the wooden slats on the floor, designed to let the water run through but keep the feet out. When he went to pull his foot out it had hooked on a piece of sheet metal under the slats and cut the top of his foot. He had a bad cut, bone deep and three inches long. Anderson said, "I have all the equipment here to put stitches in it with, but I have never done anything like this before, have you?" I said, "No, but I think it had better be taken care of as, the swelling looks bad and it is going to get worse." Bob agreed and said, "If you two guys will do it, go ahead." Anderson got out the doctor's supplies, lit a fire in the wood stove, heated some water in a pan, and picked out a needle and some cat gut. That is what they used at the time, for suturing. He put the cat gut suturing thread in the hot water to soften it and sterilize it at the same time. He gave the needle the same treatment so they would be sterile. We got poor old Bob's foot up on a chair and carefully bathed it.

We had a little discussion over who was going to do the sewing job, but I told Anderson, you are supposed to be the doctor. He finally threaded a needle and pushed it in one side of the wound, but when it came to the thread it didn't want to come on through. I held the foot and Anderson finally pulled it on through, then the other side of the wound the same thing. Poor Bob sat there saying, owah! owah! He pulled the flesh together and tied a knot. We let poor Bob rest a little and then did another. Well we managed to get three stitches done, when the doctor came walking in.

Boy, was I scared. I was afraid we were going to really get it for doing what we had no business doing. Not to worry, the doc looked over what we had done and said, "You boys are doing fine, but it is a little hard on the patient." This was no surprise to us, particularly Bob, but we were doing the best we knew how. We hated hurting our friend so bad but didn't know what else to do.

Anderson and I certainly were not enjoying ourselves either. We were only hoping there was a better way. Bob had not complained, he was tough.

The doc said, "You are using the wrong-shaped needle, here, let me show you how." He selected a slender needle with little sharp blades on each side that cut a little slit in the skin and flesh for the thread to come through. When he got all ready to put the needle in, he got right to the skin or flesh and gave the needle a little quick jab and the needle and thread went right through. Needless to say, this worked much better and was much easier on the poor patient and the two attendants.

The doctor was stationed at our camp but took care of another camp up the river from ours, also. He had received an emergency call from the other camp the evening before and after taking care of the patient, it being rather late, just stayed there for the night and then checked on his patient again before returning to our camp the next day. He hadn't bothered to call Anderson to explain when he would be back.

The Guy Who Was Slow On the Draw

The emergency was that a fellow had had his finger cut off. The way that this came about was that it was Sunday afternoon. Two fellows became bored and, for excitement, they were playing dare you. They had a chopping block and a sharp hatchet. They were taking turns putting their finger on the block while the other guy would take a whack at it with the hatchet. Well, as you might guess one fellow wasn't quite fast enough on the draw and didn't get his forefinger off the block in time. That was the end of that. No more fun, no more game, no more finger.

Getting to Spokane once in awhile was a problem as there was very little traffic in those times on that road. We could usually get a week end pass but transportation was difficult.

One Friday afternoon after work, I got all ready and as soon as supper was over with I took off hitch hiking. I got down the road about twenty miles and wasn't having very good luck. It was getting dark and I was getting discouraged when a car came along. It stopped for me and was I lucky, it was an Army officer from one of the other CCC camps and he was going to Spokane.

Boy, I was happy till I found out how drunk he was. The road was crooked, Narrow, with no guard rails, and was along the west bank of the Pend d'Oreille river. Some places it was quite high above the water and frequently someone drove off into the river. This man was all over the road; I was scared but at the same time, rides were hard to get.

We hadn't gone far; it was dark by this time, when a buck deer jumped into the road right in front of us. He ran down the road staying about thirty feet in front of us and I thought sure this guy would run right over it. Soon I couldn't stand it any longer and said, "Look out for the deer."

About this time, the deer changed lanes and got over in the oncoming traffic lane. I was greatly relieved, but only for the moment. The driver finally saw the deer, where it had been, and said, "Oh, there is a deer in the road." He switched lanes. Now we are behind the deer again, both of us in the wrong lane, and gaining on the deer. We went along this way for about fifty yards or so with the deer about ten feet in front of us, when it changed lanes again. This was a relief to me except we were on the wrong side of the road.

Finally, he saw the deer, where it had been, and said, "That darn deer is in front of us, I had better change lanes," which he did. Now we are on the right side of the road again but back behind the deer and really close, about five feet behind now. I could almost feel us hitting the deer and winding up in that cold, dark river. I guess the deer finally got tired and jumped in the ditch. We just missed its rump as we went by.

I guess it finally dawned on the car driver that his reflexes were a little slow. He said to me, "Can you drive?" I gave him great assurance, not only that I could, but that I was a good driver and that I certainly would be more than glad to do so. Little did he know how glad I would be to get my hands on that steering wheel. He pulled over and we changed seats. When we came to the little town of Cusick, he looked out and saw a beer parlor sign shining out the window. He had to have a beer and offered to buy me one. At this time, I had no desire for anything to drink. In fact, after the demonstration I had just had on reflex impairment I didn't think I would ever have another drink as long as I lived. I was ready to take the pledge. I was still sort of cherishing the fact of still being alive.

We went to the beer parlor. He must have decided, by this time, I was all right because after he had quaffed a couple of bottles of beer I said I thought it was time to go and he agreed.

He told me the address in Spokane where he lived, up on the north side. He then slouched down and went to sleep. I found the place, a nice house in a nice neighborhood, and pulled up in the driveway. I woke him up and helped him out of the car and up to the front door. It was about midnight and there were no lights on. But he insisted his wife would be there. He rang the door bell and I held him up so he wouldn't fall off of the porch. After awhile a lady came to the door. He greeted her warmly, but it appeared to me that he was much happier to see her than she was to see him. I kind of got the impression this was not the first time he had come home in this shape. I handed him over to her, gave her the car keys, and got out of there before she had time to accuse me of getting him drunk. I figure he could straighten that part out with her later, and if he didn't it wouldn't make any difference to me anyway.

After awhile I had kind of worked myself out of a job, everything was in good shape around camp. There were four or five teams of horses working on the little Forest Service airport that was being built there. One of the teamsters was leaving the three C's for a regular job. I heard about it so I went to see the ranger in charge of all the work, to see if I could get the job driving that team. After he talked to me a little he said, "Sure that will be fine."

It was the best team on the job. I was very fortunate to get them. They were big, strong horses, mild-natured and not lazy. They weighed about sixteen hundred pounds each and were well-matched. The names, I still remember, Spec and Dan.

In this day when draft horses are not in common usage, and of course little understood by the average person, it might be of some little interest to explain a few things.

Horses can be very intelligent, and they can, like some people, be real Dumb. They have personalities. Some are high-strung, some learn quickly, others are slow to catch on. Some are foxy and tricky. Some ambitious, some lazy. Some are faithful and loyal, others flighty, sometimes treacherous, and mean. Some are kind and will do anything to please you, if they understand. There are others that are strong-willed, mean, and ornery, and never seem to get over it. In other words, they cannot be trusted. Most horses, after they have matured – that is, after they have been around for awhile – can sense, as soon as you speak to them and when you pick up the reins or lines (whichever term you choose to use) what kind of teamster you are. If you hold a tight line, they know immediately you are in command.

Teamsters, too, are different. Some are business-like and mean what they say. They hold a tight line and know what to expect of a team, yet at the same time they are kind and don't ask more of a horse than it can do. They will rest a horse when they are out of breath and will see that they are well-fed and watered and properly taken care of. They will pet them and let the animal know it is liked. However, when they say, "Get up!" (which means go) and tighten up on the lines they mean go now, not when the mood happens to strike the horse.

When they say, "Whoa!" (which means stop) they mean stop now, not some time later. If they say, "Get over, gee!" (right) or "Get over, haw!" (left) that is what is meant and they don't figure on saying it again. If the commands are not complied with immediately steps are taken to call it to the offender's attention, in a manner that won't be forgotten. This kind of driver does not put up with any foolishness but at the same time uses good judgment, is kind and, above all, is consistent. A good horse soon learns what is expected of it, feels secure and comfortable, and will respond accordingly and with willingness.

There are two other kinds of teamsters. One kind, when picking up the lines, never tightens up on them. He holds a slack line and the horse is never quite sure if the teamster means what he says or not. When this kind of driver gives a command, he doesn't have a very positive tone of voice, and sort of coaxes the horses to move. At the same time he jiggles the lines and tells them, "Get up!" several times. The horses soon sense this lack of confidence and are quick to take advantage of it. They soon are not necessarily mean, but kind of pokey.

The other kind of teamster is mean to the animals and abuses them, sometimes asking more than a horse can do, and are not consistent. They shout at the horses, jerk on the lines and don't show consideration for them. As a result, those horses are nervous, scared and jumpy. It is easy to see why. I was good to my team and they were a joy to work with.

The airport got along pretty well and it was decided to send three teams to a place called Hughes Meadows, to work on making a landing strip there for small planes. This was to be used to fly in men and supplies if they were needed in case of fires. This place was quite remote and could only be reached by a seven-mile pack trail from near the end of the new road being built by our crews up Sullivan Creek at the time.

They were establishing a camp up there and had hand-picked twenty five men and three teams to go. I was chosen to go, and we were to be there for about six or seven weeks. I was delighted, as I knew it would be in a wild part of the country and would be nice and peaceful.

I made it to town to tell my girl, Agnes, I would not be in for awhile and the mail would be slow. Bright and early on a Monday morning another fellow and I (his name happened to be Anderson, also) took off with our two teams, with harnesses on them and our blankets and clothes tied to the harness, for the long trek up the road to near the end, then by trail over the mountain and down the other side to Jackson Creek, and down the creek to the meadow, about twenty miles all together.

Chapter 35

It was beautiful country, virgin timber, and never had had a road in it before. We got to our destination just in time for supper. The crew had been there for a few days and had everything set up. All we had to do was unharness our horses, and water, feed, and curry them. There was a pole framework there with a big canvas tarp over it for a barn. There were three pole mangers and stalls under the tarp, and posts to hang the harness on.

The crew had prepared everything for us. There were two tents set up to sleep in. Everyone was sleeping on the ground on some straw, with their Army blankets. They had reserved a nice flat place for Anderson and me on one end of one of the tents, where we could get out without disturbing the other fellows, early in the morning. We had to get up earlier than the rest of the crew to feed, curry and harness our horses, to be ready to go as soon as breakfast was over with.

We settled in, and when we went to eat, no mess kits; there were white, enamel plates like they used in logging camps, with regular cups and conventional flatware. It about broke my heart not to see that damned mess kit. We had tables, we could dish up our own food, and we had the best cook from the main camp, a fellow by the name of Charlie Hall. It was completely different. Good food, they even had pie sometimes. When we finished eating we walked out, no dishes to do. All we had to do was pick our teeth.

We worked six days a week and were promised time off for the Saturdays we worked later on. We had a good outfit and a young Forest Service guy for a boss who knew what he was doing. He ran it like a logging camp, and since the men had been picked, we had a good bunch and life was peaceful.

Everything was fine except Anderson. He was an older fellow (about fifty), a real nice guy. We got along fine and we liked each other, except he was no teamster, which didn't bother me much, and he snored. The only time the former bothered me was when we had to both hook onto the same thing at the same time, like a stump or some long heavy poles we had to drag clear across the meadow, something that one team couldn't pull alone.

We would get ready to pull and he would speak to his horses and jiggle the lines, then sort of cluck to them. They would wiggle their ears, switch their tails, shuffle their feet a little, and then he would sort of coax them. Finally, they would start to move and slowly take up the slack out of the rigging and then finally go.

I would be hard put to gauge when they were going to be available to do their share of the task. If I wasn't careful, we would run over them. That was very annoying but it didn't happen very often; I could put up with that.

The snoring was something else, though. I had to live with it every night, as we slept side by side. He was a very nice guy. I didn't want to hurt his feelings but something had to be done. I couldn't get any sound, uninterrupted sleep. He would get in his blankets and go to sleep, just like that. About the time I would get relaxed and was dropping off to sleep, he would start in. He would snore, he would snort like a buck deer, then groan as though he was in pain. After a little while of that he would sort of strangle, cough, and start over again.

At first, I would lay there and be concerned that he was having some kind of fit or something. After awhile I would hope he would. When I couldn't stand it any longer, I would bump him with my elbow. It didn't do any good; he would make a little barking grunt sound, maybe change an octave, and start over again. Something had to be done. I looked around for some place else to sleep, just big enough for one guy. I found a little pup tent just big enough for two men but not big enough for three.

I didn't say anything but I had heard another team was coming in. I picked out a nice little flat area and talked to the boss. He was a good guy and I told him of my problem and asked him if I could use that little extra tent. He said, "Sure, but how are you going to keep Anderson from moving with you?" I said, "I have a plan, I am going to wait till that new teamster comes to camp and I will ask him if he wants to move in with me, but I won't tell Anderson." The boss said, "I hope it works for you; I won't say anything. Good luck," and laughed.

The new teamster came in, and as it so happened the two sleeping tents were full, so he was an extra. I got to him when he got in that evening, told him I was going to set up a little tent and asked him if he would like to move in with me. I told him of my problem and he said he wouldn't say anything to anyone.

I got busy and set up our little tent over near our makeshift barn (listening to the horses all night would be better than putting up with Anderson), got some straw, and got everything fixed before Anderson even knew what was going on. He said, "Gee! I wish I had known you were going to do that I would like to have moved with you." I don't think he ever found out, I hope not.

One Saturday, Anderson said to me, "Tomorrow lets go up on Jackson Creek, you know the one we came down on our way in here, and pick some huckleberries to send home. I saw them when we came in and I think they should be just about ripe now." I said, "I don't have a home and I wouldn't know how to get them there if I did have." Well, he relied, "You are always talking about your girl aren't you? And some day you are going to get married aren't you?" Well, I had to say, "Yes." He said, "I will show you how to do it."

The next morning, after we had taken care of our horses, we took a couple of gallon fruit cans each and struck out. We went up the trail a couple of miles and, sure enough, there were berries on both sides of the trail. I had never picked any before but he showed me how. It was indeed quite simple but very tedious, just pick them one at a time. We missed our lunch but we got our pails full.

When we got back to camp we each got a substantial wooden box (everything came in wooden boxes then) and picked a whole bunch of big thimbleberry leaves. We lined the boxes with a heavy layer of leaves, put in half our berries, then more leaves, another layer of berries, and topped it off with leaves again, and nailed the lid on. We found some timber crayon and wrote the addresses on the boxes.

I sent mine to Agnes at her mother's house in Spokane. I put a note inside on top of the berries, telling her what they were and to get her mother to help her can them. I also told her they were for pie only. I had very little faith in her ever seeing them, and if she did, I didn't think they would be fit to eat, but Anderson said it would work.

The next morning the packer loaded them on a pack horse in his string and took off over the mountain to the end of the road, where they were turned over to the truck driver, who then hauled them to camp. They stayed there till Tuesday morning when a different truck took them to Metaline Falls to the Post Office. On Wednesday noon, they were put on the train to Spokane. I later found out she got them in perfect shape on Friday. She and her mother canned them and we were later to enjoy them in wild huckleberry pies.

One evening some of the fellows went up the creek a little way and killed a couple of good-sized porcupines, bringing them back to camp to eat. I helped dress them out and the next day Bob, the cook, and his helper, roasted them for dinner. It was very good, tasting rather like fresh pork.

The Lookout in the Storm

One Sunday I asked the boss if another fellow and I could take my team of horses to ride bareback up to the top of the nearest fire tower lookout on Hughes Ridge. He gave me permission and we did this.

It was about five or six miles, as I remember it, by good Forest Service trail, up hill of course. The lookout towers, as they were called, were placed on the highest peaks or ridges with the best view of the surrounding areas. It was a nice afternoon when we started out but as we neared the top of the ridge, it got more overcast. We thought nothing of it, but if we had only known, we would have turned around and gone back.

We got up there and tied the horses to a tree at the edge of the clearing, which was circular, and about one hundred and fifty feet in diameter. Right in the center of this clearing was a rock out-cropping and the highest spot on this ridge. Sitting right over these rocks was the tower itself, mounted about thirty feet above the ground on four good, sturdy log legs.

These legs were set at an angle, being much wider at the bottom than at the top, giving the whole structure good stability. On top of these legs was a deck about twenty feet square. There was a steep stairway going up to the deck. The building itself was about twelve feet square and was in the middle of the deck, leaving a walkway all around about three feet wide, with a railing. The building had windows on all sides so the lookout had a three hundred and sixty degree unobstructed view of the surrounding country for miles. The building and deck was anchored down to the ground with steel cables on all four corners so the wind could not dislodge it.

On the very top of the little house was a copper lighting rod sticking up in the air about eight feet tall. At the base of this rod were four more copper rods firmly attached, with one running down each corner of the building to the ground. This was to drain off (so to speak) the lightning when it struck the tower.

In the exact center of the room was an iron pipe fastened to the floor with a round metal table on the top of it, about shirt pocket high. This little table was about three feet in diameter with a map of the whole area glued to it. The center of the map was the exact spot where the lookout was located on the map. There was a pivoting device mounted on a pivot in the center of the table that could be turned in any direction and sighted on any part of the area that could be seen. On the very edge of the map all the way around were marked the degrees of the compass, three hundred and sixty in all.

This arrangement enabled the lookout to sight in on smoke, or something Suspicious, and be able to tell headquarters over the telephone at just what angle he saw it from where he was, and over how many ridges or canyons. They in turn would draw a line on their map from his location to the site he gave them, and when another lookout called in from another place with a sighting on the same evidence, they were able to zero it in, having a rather precise location of whatever it was. The people at headquarters then would make a decision on what to do about it. There were few roads and sometimes no trails near a new lightning strike that would have started a fire.

Sometimes, though very rarely, the lookout himself would be ordered to go to the fire if it appeared to be small and reasonably close, say within three or four miles from his location. He kept a pack made up with emergency rations for two days, a couple of pair of clean socks, a compass, a collapsible canvas bucket, a shovel and an axe, ready to go at a moment's notice if told to do so.

The rest of the furnishings consisted of a small, wood-burning, flat-topped cook stove, a single bed with a couple of mouse-proof wooden storage boxes underneath, a couple of mouse-proof cupboards, a shelf with a water bucket, a dipper, and a washbasin. There was a wooden table with a wooden chair, and a gasoline lantern – that was about it.

The lookout man was there for the season and stayed in his station day and night. If for any reason he had to leave for a bucket of water, for wood, or for any other reason, he had to call in and tell the office at headquarters where he was going. When he returned he called to tell them he was back again. It was a lonesome job and the only time he had a chance to talk to anyone was if someone came to visit him or when the packer came, usually once a week, with supplies. There was no visiting on the phone. It was only to headquarters and was for business only.

When there was a lightning storm, he had to count the strikes in all directions and mark them down. When it was all over he called them in and told where they were, and then for several days afterward he kept careful check on these particular spots.

When we got to the lookout, the man there was tickled to see us and to find out what the news was. Well, all the news we had was almost a week old, but it was news to him. We visited a little while when the clouds rolled in and it got darker. The lookout said it is going to storm and soon too. He pulled the lightning arrester out on the phone (a device that disconnects the phone line and sends the lightning surge of current to the ground).

I said, "I had better move the horses down in the timber a short ways where they won't be apt to get hit by lightning. Does it strike up here?" "Does it strike here? It strikes here every time we have a big storm like I think we are going to have right now," he said. He went on to say, "It is too late to move the horses now, they will just have to make the best of it. I hope they don't get hit. Stay where you are here inside, where you are safe, or you may get killed. You two fellows sit on the bed, it is made of wood, and I will sit on the wooden chair. Don't touch any iron, the map table, stove or phone. Just sit still, you are in for a show."

About that time, a bolt of lighting hit with a blinding flash, and at the same time came a crash of thunder with a roar like the world had caved in. It was terrifying. It was so loud it made the earth tremble, and the tower too. The phone rang, and a ball of blue-colored lightning about the size of a small grapefruit, came out of the phone and jumped across the room to the stove. Bigger balls of fire, red and blue, rolled down the corners of the building on the lightning rods and disappeared to the ground. I thought for sure we had had it. I never saw anything like that before, and I thought I had seen lightning. It was a real attention getter, believe me.

It wasn't long before we had another one and then another, none of which were as severe as the first one. For those who have never been close to a lightning strike I might just mention that it makes the hair on your body stand out. This is not from fright, although that would be a good, valid reason, but from magnetism in the current as far as I know. After awhile things kind of calmed down. I got up, being careful not to get near any metal, to look out the window. The poor horses were standing there in the drenching rain that had started to come down when the thunder and lightning subsided somewhat. They were so scared they were standing there trembling.

I felt bad, as though I had abandoned them when they needed me. We didn't stay long after that. We both had had enough of that business to last us for quite awhile. The lookout told us when everything was over he would call headquarters. If he didn't call in or respond to their calls after a reasonable length of time they would send someone out to see if he was still alive, or if he had been struck by lightning, a comforting thought.

We told our new friend goodbye and good luck. We climbed on our wet horses and as soon as we got into the timber, we felt better. It was a nice, wet ride back to camp. It didn't take nearly as long to get back as it had taken to get up there. The horses were in a hurry and so were the riders. I gave the horses an extra ration of rolled oats and a good rub down and no one was the worse for wear. In fact, we all had a bath, whether we needed it or not. I was sure grateful no one was struck by lightning, man or beast.

The last job we did in that camp was to skid some long, heavy logs across the meadow for building purposes the next year. This was kind of interesting. It was a long, hard pull. I would pull them out of the woods and get them ready. Then I would unhook and go back near the rear end of the log. With a horse on either side of the log, we would hook a pair of logging tongs onto the log and in this way we were able to push it. In the meantime, another team would hook up to the front end and they were to pull. The trouble was in getting started.

I would have to wait for the other team to make up their minds as to when they were going to go. If I wasn't careful, we would start when they were supposed to and we would push the double trees right up on their heels.

When this job was done, we took our horses and personal stuff out to the main camp. I delivered my team to the Forest Service barn, never to see them again, as all the team work was done for that year on the airport.

Chapter 36

I had several days of leave coming so I got permission to go to town, as I was anxious to see my girl. The camp was shutting down and the personnel were to be transferred somewhere, we didn't know where yet.

I had been thinking how to buy Agnes an engagement ring without any money. I had a good Savage 30-30 rifle I had bought from a fellow one year when I was harvesting at Dayton. That was the only thing I had of any value. I decided to sell it and see if I could get a ring for her with the proceeds. I thought I could begin to see a little light at the end of the tunnel as far as my life was concerned, not much, but a little.

I still owed Mrs. Hammill some money but I was getting close to the time when I would have that obligation taken care of. I sure couldn't make Agnes any promises as far as when I would be able to support her, but I felt she was entitled to a commitment from me as to hopes for the future. I knew I would be transferred someplace, I had no idea where. It might be that I would not be back for awhile. She had been waiting patiently, never complaining about my slow progress in the world. It was about par for the course at the time, for a young fellow without any skills or much education and no home for support. Times were extremely tough; it was very difficult to get a start.

Getting Engaged

I was able to get a pretty, little engagement ring, with my rifle money. It was fashioned in two colors of gold, with a genuine diamond set in it. The stone wasn't very big, but it was genuine, as was the intention it was to be presented with. She knew I didn't have any money. She didn't expect to get one then, although she was longing for one in the worst way. Things were looking rather bleak as far as romance was concerned. I was going to be transferred and when she would see me again was an unknown. Things were looking rather hopeless to her. She knew there was no hope for us at the time.

I arranged for a date with her and when no one was around, I made my little presentation. She was overwhelmed; I can't find words to express her joy. She was so happy. I didn't know how much it would mean to her. It was worth the sacrifice I had made to get it. It meant so much to her, and because it did, it meant a lot to me.

From then on, we felt we had a bond that hadn't been there before. We had something to share, some hopes to look forward to, and we were confident we would have a future together. I am proud to say, at the time of this writing, she still wears the little ring, well over sixty-one years later.

Agnes and I

I went back to camp and worked around camp for a few days when I was chosen as one of a crew of fifty men to be transferred to the St. Joe River country to build a set of camps before winter. That was good news to me, right down my alley, so to speak. This was familiar country to me, and again, wild and pretty. We loaded all the camp equipment we would need, along with food and tools, in baggage railroad cars in Metaline Falls, which was on the Milwaukee Railroad at the time. That night a good friend of mine and I were chosen to go down there and act as night watchmen. The next morning a truck came down and we rode back to camp, got some food and our duffel bags, and that evening we were on the train bound for the St. Joe.

We got to where we were going in the dark of the night. They stopped the train right on the main line and we started to unload everything. Most things were handed out to fellows who set them down beside the track. Others carried the stuff down a steep embankment and scattered it around in a field. It finally got daylight so we could see what we were doing.

We got everything off the train and it left. What a mess, stuff all over the place. The fellows in charge got us organized and we went to work, setting up tents, sorting things out.

After awhile things began to take shape. The kitchen tent was set up First, with its big wood burning stoves. When we had everything set up, the cooks had a meal ready for us. This was about eleven in the forenoon. We hadn't had anything to eat since the sandwiches we had the noon before.

We ate and then they told us to take time for a rest. Everyone was pooped, we were ready for that, and as we had everything set up, we all lay down on our cots. We had the rest of the day off and the next morning we could see where we were and what had to be done.

We were to build a set of buildings for crews to live in that would be building a road up the river. There was no road there at the time. Soon a freight train stopped and we unloaded lumber from a flatcar. We just threw it down the hill in no order, the idea was to get it off the railroad car and let the train get on its way.

I worked as a carpenter, building buildings. The weather was good and we again worked six days a week so that we could get done before the winter set in. It was a pleasant place on the St. Joe river, in a homesteader's little field of about four acres. The old fellow, whose name was Faniff, had leased some ground to the Forest Service for camps to be built, to house the road crews. Just before the camps were completed I saw a note on the bulletin board asking if anyone in camp had any knowledge about locating land boundaries.

This turned out to be rather interesting for me. I went to the headquarters tent and saw the lieutenant, the man in charge. I had never talked to him before but he seemed to be a nice fellow, and reasonable.

I explained to him that I had worked with my dad and knew how to run lines and establish boundaries. He explained to me that he had to submit a report to the Army telling where his camp was being built and the exact land boundaries and complete legal description of the land being leased. He was very honest with me and admitted he had no knowledge of this sort of thing. He asked me if I thought I was capable of doing this.

I told him if old Joe Faniff would show me the legal description of his place so I could get a start, and I had a compass, I would be able to do it without question. He produced a compass, which was a hand held one, but good enough for my purpose. He confided in me that the Army and the Forest Service didn't get on very well with each other and he hated to ask the Forest Service for anything if he didn't have to. He told me to tell whoever I was working for in the morning, that I was on special assignment, and to report directly to him from then on.

The next morning I went down to old Joe Faniff's cabin. I approached with caution, as he was not on very friendly terms with some of the crew. From what I had heard around camp, he had some moonshine (whiskey) and sold some to some of the crew. There had been some trouble over the payment. One night, about eight in the evening, he got mad and ran some guys away from his place. And to hasten their departure, he shot some holes in our stovepipe, above the roof line, with a 30-30 rifle. That got everyone's attention pretty well. After that, there was a sign on the bulletin board to stay away from Old Joe's place if you didn't want to get shot.

As I said, I was a little wary, but I knocked on his door and when he opened it, he knew I was not the enemy and invited me in. I explained to him what I needed and he was friendly enough. He got out some papers and showed me where, on the map, his property was located. I asked him where the section line was and he showed me on the map and told me about where it crossed the river. That looked reasonable. I asked him where the first section corner was and he told me about where I could find it.

I went back up to camp, got a good sharp axe and went to the river. The only way to get across was to wade. The water was cold and about belt deep, a poor way to start your day. I hunted around in the trees and brush, finally finding an old blaze on a tree, and then another, and then with the compass I was able to follow it.

After working my way through the brush for nearly a quarter mile, I found the place where Joe told me it would be. I was able to locate the original post and it was still legible. It turned out to not be a section corner but what was called a quarter post, meaning it was a half a mile to the corner post either way. This didn't jibe with what Joe had told, by half a mile. I located a witness tree and was able to chop it out and it bore out the evidence on the quarter post. This meant trouble for me. Life is never simple.

I checked my line going back, cutting some brush out of the line of sight as I went. That evening I went to see the lieutenant and explained that everything was off by a half a mile. He said, "Are you sure?" I said I wanted to go back the next day with a man and sight my line with a compass to the river, and also at the same time pace off the distance, and that by the next evening I would be able to tell him quite close as to where we were.

He was a little dubious when I told him Old Joe's description appeared to be off a half mile. I told him I needed a man to help me for a day so we could cut some brush so I could sight better with the compass and pace the distance more accurately.

The next morning I took a man with me and we ran the line back to the river and I was able to get a good sight across the river and had my man drive a stake there on our side for reference. I also knew by that time that it wasn't too far to the section corner on our side of the river. We ran a compass line up on the side of the mountain and when I figured where it should be, we found it after hunting around a little.

This verified what I had discovered the previous day. I was happy and I knew I was right on. That evening I reported to the lieutenant. He was impressed but a little skeptical. I suggested he call the Forest Service telling them what I said. I told him to tell them they had a problem with the land description on the Faniff land. I kept my man and we went ahead laying out the ground and making a map of the buildings and water line etc.

One afternoon I got a call to come to headquarters and when I got there, the lieutenant introduced me to a man who was from the Forest Service. The lieutenant kind of reviewed what I had told him and said he had filled the man in on it.

The Forest Service man then asked me a few questions and then proceeded to tell us both that, "I didn't know what I was talking about and that Joe Faniff had been paying taxes on that property for forty years and if it was wrong the Forest Service would have known it and would have corrected it years before."

The lieutenant looked mighty uncomfortable. I was smart enough to listen patiently. When he had finished I told him the lieutenant had asked me if I could do this little project, and I had assured him that I could. I had done it and was very confident that I was right but if he didn't want to believe me I really didn't care, but I knew I was right.

He kind of choked on that for a little bit and then said, "You will have to prove it to me." We agreed he would go with me the next morning to look at the section corner that I claimed was not a corner. I didn't say anything about wading the river but I thought, "I bet before you get back you will believe me."

The next morning I went to the headquarters tent and he was all ready. I could have taken him up on the mountainside where it was nice and dry to show him a section corner, and proved my point. But I thought, "I will just save that for an ace in the hole (so to speak), if I need it later." I had done a little thinking, too, about how smart he had been the night before and I figured, "I will just cool you off a little for starters and let you walk around with your shoes full of water all day. Maybe we will get along better when you find out how the real world is."

We went down to the river and he said, as we approached the bank, "How do we get across?" I never even broke my stride. I just walked right in, right up to my hips. I didn't want to give him a chance to back out. He wanted proof and that was the way to get it. I kept right on going just as though we were on dry land saying over my shoulder, "Just like this."

The water was clear, cold, and swift. I never looked back to see if he was coming. I was afraid if I did, he would start to protest and maybe back out on me. I sure wanted to get him in that cold river. He didn't have much choice. When I got to the other side, I looked around. He was still in the middle, picking his way across very carefully. I didn't blame him for that; the current was running about five or six miles an hour. The bottom was smooth, slippery rocks and required close attention to stay right side up, which was utmost desirable if you didn't want to take a good swim down the river aways.

I waited for him. He said nothing and neither did I. I took him to the section line marker and showed him the post with the inscriptions on it, as well as the two witness trees I had uncovered before. He agreed with me that it was a quarter post, not a corner post. We paced back along the line the best we could, crawling through the brush. When we got to the river, I showed him my stake on the opposite shore. He agreed it looked just about right. When we got back through the river, all the smart stuff was gone out of him. It was the middle of the afternoon, and not having had any lunch might have had something to do with it too.

We went to the tent, got out the map and he could readily see how right I was. He told the lieutenant that he had to admit I was right, but he could not see how the Forest Service could have been wrong all this time. Sometimes victory is sure sweet, even if you have to just about drown a guy to prove a point.

Chapter 37

We soon got the word that we were going to be transferred to western Washington. I wrote to Agnes, telling her to get my brother Don to walk her down to The Union Depot to meet me at nine in the evening of the appointed day, as we would change trains there and be on our way. They told us we would not be able to leave the depot, but we would be there for a few minutes.

The depot was in a rough part of town at that time and there was no money for a taxi. Our time for arrival was nine in the evening. We packed our duffel bags on the appointed day; the train was right on time. (You could almost set your watch by train arrivals and departures in those days.)

It stopped right at our camp on the main line. We got aboard and pulled into Spokane right on time. I got off as soon as I could and sure enough, there stood Don and Agnes. It was kind of sad, I didn't know when I would see her again. I was sure it would not be before the next spring. This was the middle of October. There was no way I could get home on a weekend, from way over someplace on the west coast. I was sure glad she was wearing that little ring she was so proud of. I felt sure she would wait for me. All too soon, they called all aboard, we kissed goodbye and I got aboard.

It was a special train and much to my surprise on board was the rest of our camp personnel from Sullivan Lake. We arrived at Ft. Lewis the next afternoon – no breakfast, no lunch. We got aboard trucks with covers on them in the pouring rain. What a dismal place!

They took us to a tent city; there must have been a couple of hundred tents set up. We were assigned tents, six to a tent again. It was cold and wet but there was a wooden floor in the tent and it was dry. A little stove sat right in the middle of the tent in a shallow box of dirt. We got a fire going and it wasn't long before it got dark, but we were fairly comfortable sitting around the stove on our cots.

A bugle blew and someone said that meant to go to eat. Stand in line in the rain with your good old mess kit in one hand and your cup in the other, with the rain dripping off your nose. Finally, we got to the door of a building. It was the mess hall and was not bad, with tables and benches to sit on. The food wasn't bad either, but by that time we wouldn't have noticed the quality. We were traveling on an empty gut, so to speak.

We were there a few days, and the weekend came. We all had from Saturday morning till Sunday night off. I had a friend who said, "Let's go to town." The rain had let up a little by this time and we agreed we would go out on the road and see if we could hitch-hike a ride to town, being Tacoma.

We soon got a ride in the back of a pickup with a man and woman. When we got to where the street turned to go downtown, the man stopped and said "We are going to Seattle, if you want to you can go on into Seattle with us, we will be going right downtown." I said to Eddie, "I don't have enough money to get something to eat and get back to camp if we go that far." He said, "I have five dollars. Can we do it on that much? If we can, I will loan you your half of the expenses and you can pay me back on payday. I have never been to Seattle and I would like to see what it looks like." I said, "Sure, we can make it fine on less than that, I will show you how."

We told the man we would go, and we huddled a little closer to the back of that truck cab to keep out of the rain as much as we could, and rode on into Seattle with him and his wife.

They let us off right down near the Totem Pole as I remember it, in the rain. We agreed to skip dinner to save our resources and just have supper. We took in the waterfront and Ye Old Curiosity Shop and the ferry docks, where it was nice and warm inside. I told Eddie "I will show you how to eat cheap and then we will go to an all-night show where we will spend the night for free."

We waited till about seven O'clock and went looking along skid row for a restaurant that looked empty, from the street, and went in. It was run by a Chinese man. We had our C.C.C. uniforms on and everyone knew who we were and that we didn't have much money. I told him, "We have only fifteen cents apiece for supper. If you have something already cooked, leftover from supper, we would eat whatever it is that you can give us for fifteen cents."

With that, we each laid our fifteen cents on the counter so he would know we had it, and too, so there would be no misunderstanding. He said "liver and onions", and with that, he dished us each a heaping platter of fried liver and onions with fried potatoes, along with a couple of slices of day old bread, and each a cup of not-too-fresh coffee, and said, "How is that?" I said, "Fifteen cents is all we have." He said, "I know, that is OK, enjoy your food," and rang up the fifteen cents. Boy, we came out of there feeling better.

We walked around till about ten o'clock and then went to a fifteen cent show. That was the last show, and after three movies and a news reel in between, they started over again for the rest of the night and you didn't have to leave. At seven in the morning they turned off the movies, turned on the lights, and announced everyone had to leave. Still raining, we got a stack of hot cakes and some coffee for breakfast, which could be had for twenty cents if you were not too choosy about where you ate.

248

We had every intention of getting the most out of our little vacation so we walked around the rest of the day, looking at anything we could see for nothing – ships, and big ferries coming and leaving, all very interesting to a couple of land lubbers We had ten-cent hamburger for lunch.

In the late afternoon we went to the ferry dock and got a ferry for Tacoma; it was cheaper than the bus. I can't remember now but probably the fare was thirty five cents. We took a streetcar from Tacoma to Ft. Lewis for another dime, and we were back in time. It was a nice, cheap trip, and we both enjoyed it.

We were there for about ten days and it rained nine of them. We were told we were going to Twin Rivers. Wherever that was, no one knew. We went by truck down around Hood Canal to the Olympic Peninsula and then thirty five miles west of Port Angeles. The camp had already been built by someone else, like the one we had built and left on the St. Joe.

What a miserable place. It was located about half a mile from the shore of the Strait of Juan de Fuca, between two little rivers known as the Twin Rivers. This is located in the vicinity of the famous rain forest. The camp itself was located on a flat place up on the ridge between the two rivers, in the brush at the end of an old logging road. It might have been a pretty place in the sunshine, but I never saw it shine during the time I was there. You couldn't see out, all that could be seen was brush.

The day after we got there, when it came time to fall out after breakfast, it was pouring rain. I thought, they won't go to work in this kind of weather, surely. Well, little did I realize that if you didn't work in the rain you wouldn't work all winter. We traveled in open, stake-rack trucks, standing up, and were pretty well wet before we got to the job site. We were put to work cutting brush out of an old road to get it ready for improvement, to be used as a forest fire protection road. It was miserable but there was an incentive to work and that was to keep warm. At noon, we were taken back to camp for our dinner and then back we went in the rain. After a few days we got used to it and then it wasn't so bad. We had that old, woolen G.I. underwear and when it got wet, it was warm if you kept moving.

After a few days, I couldn't take any more brush cutting and digging in the mud with a pick and shovel. I had to figure out something else; I felt this was beneath my level of competence. I knew a fellow from Colville, a married man who was a little older than I, a real nice fellow by the name of Sterling Onstot. I asked him where he was working and what he was doing. He and about four or five other fellows were cutting wood along the main road for camp use. They were also falling old snags that were left over from the logging days that were a hazard because they might fall across the main road.

If any of these snags were not rotten, they were cut up for wood too. He said he would be glad to have me for a partner for falling if he could get me on that gang. He gave the lead man a story about me being a former lumberjack. He in turn told his boss that he needed another man because the wood they were getting at the time was farther from the road and he couldn't keep up with the demand of the camp. The wood all had to be hand-carried out to the road.

It worked; they looked me up and told me to report to the falling gang one morning. This was better. Sterling was a great guy and we got along fine when we worked together. We would fall a big tree and then we would each take what was called a bucking saw, and saw off big blocks of wood and carry them out to the road for the truck to pick up. This was better, no one telling us what to do, working at our own gait. We produced our share of the work and no one bothered us.

The Big Tree

One morning when the truck stopped to let us off the foreman said, "I have a special job for you two fellows tomorrow. Bring your falling axes and your falling saw in with you tonight. I want to take you to a special tree that I want cut out along the highway. I don't want to put just anybody on it; you two are the best fallers in the gang. I want you two on this job."

Well, we talked about it during the day, wondering what was so special about this particular job, we just couldn't imagine. The next morning we could hardly wait to see what was in store for us. Before we left camp, the foreman said, "Get that nine-foot falling saw from the tool house, some wedges and a maul. Take your regular falling saw and your axes. Put them in this truck along with four springboards. We will go in this truck with the road crew that is working on the west side this morning."

Then we knew what it was all about. I had never seen a nine foot cross cut saw before. In fact, I didn't even know they made them that long, neither did Sterling.

About ten miles from camp, the truck pulled over on the shoulder of the road. Standing there a little way from the road in the brush was one of biggest dead snags I had ever seen. (A snag is a tree with the top broken off.) Some of the road crew unloaded our tools while the foreman, Sterling and I looked over the situation.

The tree leaned slightly toward the road. We sized it up and we all agreed which direction we should try to fall it, which was directly opposite from the road. The foreman said, "This is your day's work. If you finish before we come back with the truck this evening just stand around and wait for us, this will be a good day's work." With that, he left with the truck.

These big Douglas Fir trees have bark on them at least a foot thick. They are always larger in diameter at the base than they are up a few feet. In order not to saw farther than necessary the cut for falling them was made up on the side of the tree above this swelling, if possible, to save work. Or sometimes the saw would not be long enough to reach all the way through at the very base. Getting higher on the trunk to cut was accomplished by working on what was called a springboard.

Sterling said, "The thing we are going to do is swamp out a good running trail for ourselves just in case this thing decides to go somewhere besides where we want it to. We are not going to have time to fight the brush trying to get out of the way of it."

When we had that done we set our springboards. A springboard is a two by six board with a piece of iron fastened on one end, shaped in a manner so that when a proper style notch is cut in the side of a tree the board can be set in it and it will support a man. This way one can get up in the air to cut a tree where it is not so big around. You stand on the ground and, reaching up as high as you will be able to clamber up, you make a notch. You stick a springboard it, then standing on this one, you do it again farther up the tree. I don't think I have ever seen cuts more than three notches high, which would be at least ten feet up.

We cut two notches and started our undercut. When we got through the bark that tree was dry and hard, with quite a lot of pitch. We got a good bottom cut and then we had to chop down to the cut with our axes. This undercut was so big that a man could sit in it without having to bend over. Boy, what a job.

Sterling was a better axe man than I was, so finished his side a little before me. He said, "I will jump down and get a fire going with some of these dry chips, for the coffee, while you finish your side." Well, we had plenty of chips. There was no shortage of fuel, that was for sure.

He had the coffee just about done when I finished and we stood around eating our sandwiches in the rain. We agreed we had better get going as soon as we could, as it was past noon then and we had a lot of sawing to do yet, and we were both tired. We had put in a hard morning, never even stopping once for a smoke. We chopped a couple of notches for our springboards and started in on the back side of that tree. When we got through the bark the wood was rotten. Soon our six-foot saw was not long enough and we got the nine-footer.

Believe me, that was real work. The wood was rotten and tended to bind in the saw cut, making it harder to pull than if the wood had been solid. But of course, it cut somewhat faster if you could stand the pace.

We cut in quite a ways when we figured we had better wedge the cut so the tree would not lean back on the cut and we would never be able to lift it. We put in some wedges and the wood was all rotten and the wedges just mushed out, so to speak. We cut some big wooden ones out of vine maple and put them in, and we just made a hole in the side of the tree.

We tried cutting some more and the saw wasn't long enough to reach through the cut any farther. By now we were all in. We had been working as hard as we could all afternoon and now it was starting to get dark. There was nothing we could do anymore. The truck came and the foreman came over to see how things stood.

He sized it up and said, "We can't leave it like this, the wind may come up during the night and it will surely fall right over the road. Someone might get killed. You two fellows stay here and keep watch on it. We will go on into camp and when we come back we will bring some dynamite."

This was quite disappointing to Sterling and me. We were tired, wet and disgusted. About this time, we didn't care what happened to the tree. We were worn out from having struggled with it all day in the rain. We kept a fire going, and in a couple of hours the foreman and truck driver came back with a gas lantern, about fifteen sticks of dynamite, some fuse, and some detonating caps. They had their supper and didn't think to bring us anything to eat. Then we were disgusted.

This was about eight o'clock, still raining steadily. We were able to get a hole in the tree where we had done the wedging by digging around with an ax. The foreman wanted to just put in a couple of sticks of powder and see if that would bring the tree down.

We talked him into using all the powder he had brought with him. By this time, we didn't give a damn where the tree fell, just so it came down. We loaded all the powder they has brought with them, with a cap and about four feet of fuse, packed some mud in behind it so it wouldn't just blow back out the hole, and took off for the road.

After a little while, kerboom! The tree stood. We were somewhat leery to make an approach for fear it would fall at any moment. Sterling and I were tired, too tired to run very fast. Well, come to think of it, I guess we could have done a pretty good job of it if we had looked up and seen that tree toppling in our direction.

The foreman told the truck driver to go back to camp and get some more powder. Sterling spoke up and said, "Bring a whole box. We have been working on that damn tree all day and I am tired of it. I want it to come down this time." The foreman didn't say much but told the truck driver to go without him.

He stayed there with us; he could tell we were out of patience. When the man showed up with the dynamite we had a nice hole to load into, almost halfway under the tree. We unpacked the whole box, carefully packing it all in the hole, with another cap and four-foot fuse. We packed it in nice and tight with mud back of it, picked up our tools, lit the fuse and took off for the road. That time we heard a really big kerboom, one that rattled our heads.

The tree stood for a moment and then slowly kind /of /twisted on the stump and started to fall. It didn't go where we had intended, but did fall somewhat parallel to the road and out of the way. What a day!

Sterling and I didn't strain ourselves the next day. The foreman didn't stop to see how we were doing. We didn't want him to do us any more favors, at least not for awhile.

Chapter 38

Getting your clothes washed and dried was a real problem. There was a wash house with warm water, and tubs with wash boards, but no soap. That was a problem. If you had some, some friend would borrow it and then neither of you would have any. When you got them washed, there was a drying room to dry them in, which was a good deal. It had two big wood stoves and it was hot in there. But sometimes when you came back to get your clothes they would be gone, especially if you had done a good job and they were nice and clean. You might find some dirty ones and then you could start all over again. We all had the same kind of clothes so they could not be identified. When you washed you just about had to sit there and watch them till they dried.

The Mittens

I noticed that some of the men had brand new mittens and they were good ones. The pair I had were called three-fingered mittens, issued to World War One soldiers so they could shoot a rifle without taking them off. They were miserable things but better than nothing. I took mine over to the supply room to see if I could get a pair of the new ones. The fellow there looked at them and said "No!" When I asked why, he said, "Yours are still good, they have to be worn out before I can issue you new ones."

I thought to myself, so much for trying to take care of things. When Sunday came, right after dinner, I took my three-fingered mittens down to the tool shed where there was a grindstone. (This was a device having a stone wheel about three inches wide and about thirty inches in diameter, mounted in a frame with a seat on it. There were two pedals that could be pumped up and down like bicycle pedals, to make the wheel go around to sharpen tools such as axes etc.)

I put my mittens on and sat there pumping this wheel, holding my hands one on each side of the wheel, with the mittens rubbing the sides of the stone. It took quite a while but they were well worn out by the time I finished with them. The next day I traded them in without trouble for a nice new pair.

The Salmon Run

One Sunday some of the fellows came back to camp just before noon after having been down to the west Twin River, saying there were salmon swimming upstream. After dinner, several of us thought we would go have a look-see. We thought that if we could catch some maybe we would be able to get the cooks to cook some of them for us. We talked to them and they said they would, if we were able to get enough of them to make it worthwhile.

We had no way to catch them so we took an axe along to make wooden spears with, if it was practical. When we got there, about half a mile from the ocean itself, sure enough, there were lots of salmon going upriver, which was about two feet deep and about fifteen feet wide at the place where we chose to fish.

We made some spears out of alders that grew along the bank, sharpened them and jumped in the river. We were not very proficient at spearing, and the fish were fast. We finally devised a plan that worked pretty well. We gathered some good sized rocks, putting them at the head of a pool. We placed them across the waterway making a little dam that the fish had to get over to go on upstream. Then some of the fellows would go down stream about a hundred feet or so and kind of herd a bunch of fish up into our pool. When they tried to go over the rocks, we could spear them quite well. Some of them had white spots on them. They were nearly ready to spawn and were not good meat, so we passed them up, only taking the good ones.

We must have gotten thirty or more. They were about thirty inches long and weighed about six to eight pounds I would guess. They were just out of the ocean and the ones we chose were in prime shape. That next night we had a big feed of prime salmon for the whole camp.

Not too long after the tree incident, the lieutenant sent for me. He had another problem for me to take care of. He needed to locate this camp to send to his headquarters. He said he knew I could do it and for me to just go ahead and take care of it, doing whatever was necessary. I told Sterling about it and said I wouldn't be with him for a few days.

There was a small farm down near the beach so the next day I went down to talk to the fellow living there. It turned out he was the owner, and was very helpful. He knew where his boundary lines were, showed me a section corner and the section line. Every thing jibed. I had little trouble to locate the camp. It just took some pacing through the wet brush and some compass work. I ran lines around and made a map of the buildings and the grounds as best I could. I gave a land description of their location.

The lieutenant was very pleased with my work. He also needed to send in a report of what the Forest Service was doing in the field, the work that was being accomplished. He asked me if I would do this for him, as though I had a choice. I went out with one of the trucks in the morning to one of the job sites. I had to make an estimate of how much road they had built, the yards of dirt that had been moved in making cuts and fills, and a general estimate of progress. I wasn't very well qualified for this but the lieutenant thought I was his man and could handle it to his satisfaction. That was fine with me as that beat sawing wood all day. But I missed my partner Sterling.

There were several compensating advantages to this though. No one had any authority over me particularly. I was able to get into camp for a hot meal at noon if I worked it right, which I soon saw that I did. There were no crews there at noon but I got to eat in camp. By sorting some pitch out of the wood pile and splitting it for the cooks, I got to eat with them. They made pies and had steaks for themselves and plates to eat from. Boy this was a treat, believe me. I hadn't tasted pie for so long I had forgotten how good it was, and I didn't miss that mess kit one little bit for one meal a day.

Jack Frost

One day I was walking along the main road in the rain, trying to get back to camp in time for dinner, when a Forest Service pickup came along going the same way I was. He stopped and asked where I was going. I told him and he said he was going in too. I recognized him as the Forest Service boss but I had never talked to him. He asked me what I was doing out there, walking down the road. How did it happen I wasn't working? I told him and he was not very enthused about the lieutenant checking on his part of the work. I told him I just did what I was told to do. He hastened to tell me that he understood and that he didn't blame me, and in fact if I needed any help to come to him and he would help me, but he would not help the lieutenant directly.

I had to laugh to myself. I thought to myself, the last thing I want to do is get myself caught in the middle between those two guys. I will have to be very careful how I handle this. It sounded like a little deal I had had, on the St. Joe. I thanked him for his offer and we introduced ourselves.

His name, it turned out, was Jack Frost. I told him mine, and of course it meant nothing to him, but his meant something to me. There was a good chance he was my mother's first cousin. I said to him, "I know a man by the name of Will Frost, is he any relation to you?" "Will Frost? That is my brother," he said. This man then was my mother's first cousin. "Do you know Will?" he said to me. I could hardly believe it. I said to him, "I met him once is all, but I do remember him. You are going to be surprised when you find out who I am." He looked at me with a kind of questioning look on his face. I said, "Yes, my mother's maiden name was Ella Maloney, I am her oldest son."

He just about drove into the ditch, he was so surprised. He just couldn't get over it. He said, "She is my cousin." We got to camp about then and he said, "After you eat come over to my office, I want to visit with you, to find out about Ella and the rest of the Maloneys, can you tell me about them?"

After dinner, I went to his office and we had a long talk. My mother's mother's maiden name (my grandmother) was Frost. He wanted to know all about the Maloney family, what I was doing over there and about my dad and what he did, our family and everyone else I might know about. He called for me a few days later – he wanted to see me.

He said, "There isn't much I can do for you here, but I can make you a truck driver. You will make a little more money and you won't have to be sloshing around in the mud." Well, that sounded pretty good to me. He said, "As soon as there is an opening it will be yours."

Well, things had been moving in another direction at this time on the home front. Agnes had written, in one of her letters, that there was work to be had at home, which was kind of exciting. Both Adrian and Sylvan had gotten jobs at the Union Works. Some of our other friends had gotten jobs. It turned out that the other friends were working on a government make-work program called the Civil Works Administration, or the CWA. This was also started by President Roosevelt, somewhat similar to the CCCs. Some married friends of ours who were on relief now were working and getting paid money for it. It sounded like there was hope at last.

I wrote to her asking for the particulars and to find out if there was a chance for me to get on it. She asked her friends about it and they gave her assurance that I could, if I was home and if we were married. Well, of course this had great appeal to both of us. She thought that if we got married we wouldn't have any trouble and that the pay was enough for us to get by till I was able to get a real job. She wanted me to come home in the worst way.

Finally, she asked if she could talk to the priest at Our Lady of Lourdes church about us getting married. I thought it over pretty carefully and laid awake nights worrying about it. Finally, I wrote to her telling her she could. I thought it wouldn't hurt, and in the spring when I would be automatically discharged and have a little money saved up, we would get married.

The next thing I knew she wrote telling me our wedding banns were going to be announced in church, which signified our intention to be married. I wasn't ready for this yet. Things were moving faster than I had anticipated. I was scared out of my wits. I was in a near state of panic. It was too late now but I didn't have any idea what I was going to do. I could just barely make a living for myself, let alone for two of us. I was kind of terrified. This kind of got out of hand. I didn't know just how I was going to cope, being so far away I didn't have much control of things.

This is about the middle of December, 1933. A notice was posted on the bulletin board that all those men who had been on the St. Joe camp-building job were to be granted leave of ten days as a reward for having worked such hard, long hours and giving up their Saturdays to get the buildings done in record time.

I was in a quandary. To begin with, I had no money, maybe three dollars or so was all. I was on special assignment yet, I didn't want to lose that, and I was going to be up for a promotion soon. On the other hand, I wanted to go home in the worst way. This was tough to figure out.

I was talking to my good friend Bud Tanner; he had been on the St. Joe job and I asked him what he was going to do about going home. He said, "If you will go with me I kind of figured I might go home, but if you are not going to go, neither will I." Well, we talked it over and he didn't have any more money than I did. We planned and finally figured we could make it home, but we would have to bum our way on freight trains, and it was going to be tough as it was going to be cold. Another problem would be getting to Seattle.

That agreed on, we started making plans. I went to the lieutenant and talked it over with him, telling him I still had some work to do on my project. He assured me it could wait till I got back from my leave and that it would be fine with him for me to go. I was on real good terms with him by this time. I went to see my second cousin, Jack Frost, telling him I would be gone for a few days. He said, "Fine, if anything comes up while you are gone I will just wait till you get back."

I had that all taken care of, things were working out just fine. In fact, I was already kind of looking forward to getting back to camp after the trip, as things would be better for me till spring. My obligation to Mrs. Hammill was paid off and by spring I would be able to have saved a little money.

Bud knew his way around as well as I did, if not better. We had everything figured out pretty well except getting to Seattle. He said if we could just get to the ferry at Port Ludlow, we would be in good shape. We could ferry across the sound to just north of Seattle, walk to the Great Northern freight yards at Interbay, which is not far, then we would be on the main line of the Great Northern to Spokane.

I went to see my friend, the lieutenant, telling him of our problem. I explained to him there were others that would have the same problem getting to Seattle and that if he could see his way clear to send a truck to Port Ludlow it would solve our first problem. He said, "I will give it some thought."

The next day a notice was posted on the board that a truck would be leaving the next evening right after supper, for those of us who had leave coming and were going home for Christmas. The truck would take us to Port Ludlow, where we could board a ferry to Seattle.

That was splendid news to everyone who wanted to go but didn't know how to get to Seattle from where we were. There was no public transportation.

No one worried about how to get back when we returned, at least I didn't, and neither did Bud. The way it turned out, it was just as well.

Some of the men had money, as their folks would send them money from home. Bud and I were not in this category. We were strictly on a thrift trip. We were able to make some bread and butter sandwiches at the table and hid them in our shirts to get them out of the mess hall. That was all we could get our hands on in the line of food for the trip.

The day we were to leave, it was raining as usual; it had been raining continuously day and night since the first of December. I kind of got things in shape so when I got back I would know where I had left off on my lines and drawings. I was able to arrange it so I was in camp all afternoon and had all my clothes dry and was ready to go.

The Trip to Spokane

Shortly after supper, the truck pulled up in the rain. It was a regular Army truck, with a canopy over the back and seats along each side of the truck bed. It was nice and dry but of course, no heat. It was about eighty miles to Point Ludlow, I guess. We got there about ten o'clock and there was no ferry there. The truck driver wanted to get back so he left and we stood around in the rain. There was a little waiting room there, but it was closed for the night. There was a sign in the window that said the ferry would dock at eleven thirty for the night and make the first trip of the day at six in the morning.

Sure enough, after awhile we could see lights coming out of the rain, and when they had tied up they put a passenger gangplank out and we were allowed to come on board. We all paid the purser our fare, which I think was thirty five cents. He said we could just lie on the floor for the night and we would be all set for the first trip in the morning.

This was just great. They had steam heat and it was nice and warm inside. So was the floor, as it was a steam-powered ferry with the passenger deck on top and the lower deck for cars and trucks. We got warm and took our heavy woolen overcoats off, got them dry and were in good shape when they fired up in the morning. Sure enough, at six o'clock the whistle blew and we were off for the other side in the dark and rain.

We got ashore in the dark yet, but Bud knew where we were and said we just go up the tracks about a mile and we will be right in the railroad yards. He directed everyone else to walk south along the tracks and it would take them to Seattle proper. There were about fifteen of us and about six of them said, "Can we go with you?", meaning Bud and me. We didn't know them, we had seen them in camp but they were younger than we were and we didn't even know them by name.

We asked them if they had brought their overcoats, they hadn't. We asked if they had any food, they didn't. Bud looked at me and then said, "I am not going to be responsible for you fellows." I spoke up and said, "Neither am I. We have worn all of our woolen clothes, even our overshoes. We are prepared for a cold ride. It doesn't appear to me you are dressed for going with us. You have only rain coats and no boots. It is going to be cold when we get over the mountains."

They said, "Can we just go with you? We don't know how to ride a Train." We said, "We will show you how but you are on your own."

As we got to the yards, we met a switchman. He said, "Where are you guys going?" We told him, "Spokane, for Christmas." He could see we were CCC's. He was a nice fellow and instead of kicking us out of the yard, gave us the information we needed. There was a train being made up right then that would be a manifest eastbound and would be leaving as soon as it was put together. He even told us what track. He said, too, for us to get in an empty box car, out of sight, shut the door and be quiet or we might get kicked out.

We started to where the man had directed us and these kids started talking and congratulating themselves on how lucky they were to get in with us. They were walking behind us and making a lot of noise. Bud turned around and said, "Shut up if you are going with us. Shut up or we won't show you how to ride a train."

Well, they got the message. We found a car and all climbed in, almost closing the door, and were quiet. Every once in awhile we would hear some one walk by but no one bothered us.

In about an hour we felt the air come in to the brake lines, which meant the engine was hooked to the train. We could feel them test it; we heard the two-whistle highball, and we were on our way. Bud opened the door part way to be sure we were going the right direction and give us some light. He told the kids they could talk then. We got out our dry sandwiches wrapped in newspaper and shared them with these kids. It wasn't much of a breakfast, but it was all we had.

It wasn't long before we were in snow. The train labored up the mountain sides and once in awhile, it would stop for something. We would jump out to go to the can; otherwise, we just rode along watching the snow get deeper and deeper.

We finally got to the top, or where the long tunnel was (eight miles), through the top of the Cascades. Bud and I talked the food situation over. We had to come up with something. Bud knew Wenatchee. He said it was in a valley and the tracks ran parallel to the town all the way. He said the rail yards were at the lower end of town. We knew the train would stop there, for how long we had no idea, but presumed it would be for several hours.

We decided to send the kids down to the yard when the train stopped. We told them to look around when they got there and they would find the jungle (the hobo campground) off to one side of the tracks. We told them to look in the bushes and they would find clean tin cans hanging upside down on the bushes. We told them to get some and some clean drinking water and dry wood and to get a fire going.

They wanted to know what we were going to do in the meantime. We told them when the train slowed down enough for us to get off as we went through town we would get off and try to get something for us to eat, and that we would be down as soon as we could. We had already planned to get some canned heat for the night, as we knew we were in for a cold ride to Spokane. We decided we would get off the train and each of us would take a side of the main street and stop at every grocery store and every meat market, asking for a loaf of bread or a piece of bologna. Bud was going to buy a couple of cans of canned heat and I was to get a pound of coffee. This we did. We would leave our duffel bags outside in the snow and walk in empty handed, begging. By the time we got to the lower end of town we had gathered, I think, four loaves of bread and maybe a couple pounds of bologna, in chunks.

When we ran out of stores we went on down to the yards looking for a fire. There was none in sight, the snow was about a foot deep and it was about twenty five degrees. We finally found those kids standing around in the cold. No wood, no cans, no water, and of course no fire. Neither Bud nor I was in a very jovial frame of mind about this turn of events. We got after them and they scurried around getting the things they were supposed to have already done. Instead, they had stood around waiting for us to show up. I guess they were city kids and had never been around. I really don't think they thought Bud and I would show up at all, and they were probably scared. It was a desolate scene, I will admit, but we were not responsible for their plight. We were all cold and hungry.

After we gathered some wood, we got a fire going and that helped. They got some clean cans and water. I got some coffee going that smelled good, and things were looking better.

One of these kids produced a butcher knife out of his duffel bag and said we could use it to cut up the bread and baloney. Why he had it I will never know; he must have stolen it from the camp kitchen. There was a pile of railroad ties about table height right near our fire so I cleaned off some of the snow and got a place to use as a table to cut up the bologna and the bread. (Bread was not pre-sliced in those days, neither was the bologna).

When Bud started to lay out his haul, one of these kids started to reach for a chunk of the meat. I grabbed the butcher knife and waved him off, saying, "If you don't step back I will run this knife right through you. Now you guys just stand back till Bud and I get this evenly divided and then you will get your fair share." Boy, I couldn't believe how greedy one of them was. I don't know, he may have been frightened. I decided we were not going to have any of it at any rate.

Bud and I divided everything up as evenly as we could and then handed it out. We had plenty of hot coffee so everyone got all they wanted. We all got warmed up with the fire and the hot coffee. We washed out the cans for the next guys and stood around the fire till the train was about ready to leave. In the meantime, I had taken charge of the knife after the little incident.

Bud and I had it figured out that we would ride in the ice compartment of a reefer car, which would of course be empty. We told those kids how to do it, and at the same time suggested they could ride in the boxcar we had come over in.

When we were all ready to go I gave the knife back to the guy that had produced it in the first place, Bud and I climbed up on top of the train, hunted till we found a car with the ice compartment unlocked and got in. I don't know what those kids did – we never saw them again.

Chapter 39

After the train had been on its way for awhile and we were starting to get cold, Bud got out a can of the canned heat. He said, "Now I will show you how to use this."

Canned heat was a solid substance that came in a small can, similar to a little paint can, holding about half a pint. You took the lid off and lit the contents, which was about the consistency of vaseline, with a match. It contained a high amount of alcohol and burned with a very hot little blue red flame. We each had on our big, heavy, long woolen overcoats.

He sat down, pulled his overcoat down all around him putting the canned heat, with the little flame going, between his bent up knees. Pretty soon he said, "Boy does that ever feel good." After he got warm it was my turn, and indeed it did feel good. When we were both warmed up, we could sleep a little while till we got too cold. This we did as the train rolled along. Periodically we would climb up and open the trap door to have a look to find out where we were.

Finally, it started to get daylight and we could tell we were nearing Spokane. I wanted to get off in town as we went through; Bud wanted to go on to Hillyard, where the train would stop. I kept track of where we were and when we got within a mile or so I said goodbye to Bud, got out, and rode the rest of the way on top.

It was now daylight, clear and cold. I later found out it was twelve degrees above zero. The clock on the Great Northern station tower said seven o'clock. When we crossed the Howard Street crossing, they were going slow enough for me to bail off.

I was so cold I was afraid I would not be able to run when I hit the ground; fortunately I was able to make it. This was excellent time, bumming your way from the ferry dock to Spokane in twenty four hours. The first place I went was to the Coffee Inn restaurant, where you could get a cup of coffee and a doughnut for ten cents. In fact, I stayed for two helpings.

The next place I went was to see Agnes. I was dirty, smelled of smoke from the fire the night before, and of fish. The refrigerator car we had been riding in was evidently loaded with smoked herring. The compartment we rode in was partitioned off from the cargo compartment but the odor was a little strong. She was so glad to see me she didn't mind but she did say I smelled like fish.

I had left some clothes at their house with her brother Lawrence, in his closet. Sometimes I had stayed overnight with him. He had his own room with a double bed. He had a genuine feather bed, the only one I have ever had the pleasure of sleeping in. Believe me, they are soft and comfortable.

Agnes was all excited about getting married. She was sure I would be able to get on the CWA program, which paid forty dollars a month. She made a good case sure enough, telling me how little it would take for us to get by on, how she was willing to sacrifice, and what a cozy little home she could make for us if she just had a chance.

This was well and good and I was in agreement but I was scared. She had never been hungry. She didn't realize how the real world really was. We went to visit our friends who were working for the CWA. They were sure I would be able to get on if we were married. I thought it over and got the feeling it shouldn't make any difference, whether I was on one make-work project or another. This had to work though. If I resigned from the CCCs, Agnes's mother could not take us in; she had all she could do to support her family, which consisted of five girls and her son Lawrence. Times were so hard; a lot of people were so poor it was pitiful.

If we went into this venture, some way I just had to make it work. She wanted me to resign, come home, get married and start out. She had more faith in providence I guess, than I had. She had been sheltered all of her life, I had different experiences to draw on when I made a decision. Agnes finally talked me into getting out of the CCCs, getting married, and hoping that some way it would all work out.

I had a friend who ran a little Mom and Pop grocery store over near Hammill's house on Hamilton Street. We were good friends and, in fact, I used to take care of the store for him sometimes on Sunday. He worked long hours, seven days a week. Occasionally he would want to get away to take his wife to a show or something. I went to see him, asking if he would write me a letter saying that he would have a job for me if I got out of the CCCs.

My friend Adrian was still working, but his brother Sylvan had been laid off. They had an apartment rented and I spent my nights there and got most of my meals there. I am ashamed to say how many free meals I have eaten at their place and at the home of their folks during my times of struggle. They were fine people, all of them. I was always welcome. They were so generous and would have shared their last crust with me. In fact, there were some times when they almost did. I was like one of the family.

I had Mrs. Hammill paid off and I really had no place to go. I had the last check from the CCCs, which she gave to me when I went to see her, that was it.

My time was running out, but in the meantime there were some complicating factors to be dealt with. There had been an unusual amount of snow that fall and early winter. Suddenly the weather turned warm, real warm, and stayed that way. The renowned floods of 1933 occurred. The water kept on rising and everything was flooded. The rail lines between Spokane and Seattle all washed out. They washed out east of Spokane also. Everything was washed out, and it was about time for me to be going back. The plan was that I would go back, turn my papers over to the lieutenant, give him my letter, get my official discharge, tell Jack Frost I was leaving and thank him for his consideration, pick up my personal belongings, and make my way back home. I wasn't looking forward to the trip; it was going to be a hard one.

It was the middle of the winter and a tough time to be on the bum. There was no transportation through the mountains – everything was closed. I didn't want to be late getting back to camp. I had a good record and I wanted to go out that way. It kept on raining and the water got higher.

The water got so high in the river that it was running down Trent Avenue (now called Spokane Falls Boulevard). I was going to have to leave early if I was going to bum my way back and get there on time. The only conclusion I could come to that would work at all was to walk through the mountains where it was washed out. This was not a good solution but I was young and tough and I felt I could accomplish it.

The Christmas Of 1933

The day before Christmas, in the forenoon, I went to the Great Northern downtown yard to see what I could find out about train movements. There were none; however, I did learn the first work train was going to go out to the washed-out area that evening, but I could not learn just what time. I figured I would be on that train. My plan was to ride it as far as it went, walk through the washed out area or areas, and hopefully be able to grab a ride on something going down the other side, back for supplies. I figured eventually I would get to Interbay again. Not a good plan but a plan.

I went back to Agnes's house, got the clothes I would need for the trip, ate a sandwich, bid Agnes goodbye and told her I would be back in a week or ten days. I went back to the yards to wait for that train. It was raining, half rain and half snow, not very cold, about thirty degrees I would guess. I don't think Agnes had any idea of what I was going to undertake in the time I would be gone, she didn't seem to be too concerned. I guess she had wedding bells dancing in her head.

It got dark and it was wet. I managed to stay dry, but I finally got Cold – still no train. I looked around for some place to try to stay warm.

I saw a small kind of a shed-looking structure with little wisps of steam coming out of it. There was no one around so I looked in. It had a doorway opening but no door. It turned out to be a sand house where they kept sand to sprinkle around when it got slick I guess. There was some steam heat to keep the sand thawed out. I got in there and sat on the sand. I hadn't been there long when a train man came in with a lantern for something. He was greatly surprised to see me there and said, "What are you doing here?" "I am trying to keep warm," I replied.

He said, "Don't you have any place to go?" I told him I was waiting for the work train to come down from Hillyard to see if I could get a ride to Seattle.

He was a good fellow. He explained to me that no trains were running then. I explained to him my plan and then he told me the work train wouldn't be along till about eleven o'clock. Instead of kicking me out he said, "Hell man, this is Christmas Eve, you come in with me into the switch-man shack where it is nice and warm." I said, "They will kick me out and maybe call the cops." He said, "The hell they will, come with me." I followed him and when we got there, he went in first and said to me in a loud voice, "Come on in."

There were six or seven men sitting around, some at a table playing cards. He announced to them in a loud voice, "I found this fellow out in the sand house trying to keep warm. This is Christmas Eve, can you imagine that. I invited him to come in and he was afraid he would get kicked out. The first guy that tries to kick him out will have to kick me out first do you hear that?" Then he laughed. They all laughed and said almost in one voice, "Come on in where it is warm."

There were steam pipes on the wall, like a radiator, they were nice and warm. They had me get my back up against them and did it ever feel good. They had a bottle of whiskey and were all feeling mighty benevolent.

After awhile I heard an engine moving around outside and said, "I had better get out there, as I don't want to miss the work train." They told me not to worry, when the train was ready to leave someone would let me know and for me to stay in where it was warm and dry.

Sure enough after awhile one of the crew came back in, saying it was time for me to come out. He even had a place for me to ride. He showed me to an old passenger coach. It didn't have any windows and no seats. On both sides of the aisle there were tools. In one end was a little room with a door on it and a little window with glass in it. It was just big enough to lie down in and the door was nice and tight. This switchman had hunted around in the dark with his lantern and found this for me. What a nice Christmas present! The only one I got. I got in and shut the door and we were soon on our way. I was nice and warm with my big coat on and had a good ride.

Along about daylight I could hear men walking through my car. After awhile I heard them coming back. I cracked the door a little way to look out as they passed by. By this time it was light enough to be able to see quite well and, lo and behold, I knew one of them. I quickly opened the door and said, "Hello Oscar." His name was Oscar Olson. I didn't know him well but we did know each other.

He just about jumped out of his skin, he was so surprised to see me there. He said, "What are you doing here?" I told him and he said "Did you ride here all night?" I assured him that I had, he felt bad. He said, "Did you have anything to eat?" I told him I had eaten yesterday noon for the last time. He said, "I'll tell you what to do. The cook car is on the other end of this car, that is where we have been, getting our breakfast. You go in there and tell the cook you overslept and you want your breakfast." I said, "They will throw me out." He said, "No they won't, they will think you are one of the crew. They wouldn't dare. Then when you get done, you come in the car on this end where the whole crew is. That is where you should have been all night." He went on to say he would be sitting on a bench just inside the door waiting for me.

I went in the door of the dining car and there were two long tables, one on each side of the car. The cook and two helpers were sitting at one of the tables eating their breakfast. I said, "The boys forgot to wake me up and I just about missed breakfast." The cook was a real crab. He said, "If you are going to eat in my dining car you had better get here on time after this or I won't let you eat. From now on, you be here with the rest of the crew. Sit down on the end there where that plate is." They had all kinds of food. I assured him I would be on time from then on and dove in. There was bacon and eggs, pancakes and syrup, fried potatoes, toast with jam, coffee, and doughnuts. Needless to say, I ate a good hearty breakfast. It had been a long time since the sandwich the day before and I didn't know when I was going to be able to enjoy this very pleasant form of self indulgence again. When I had finished I thanked the cook and left.

I picked up my packsack and went in to the car ahead of mine. Sure enough, there sat Oscar wanting to know all about me and where I was going. He worked for the Great Northern in Hillyard and was laid off. When the railroad needed any help they called in regular employees who were laid off, if they could do the work that had to be done. He had been called the day before and had boarded the train in Spokane the night before. There were about thirty men in the crew. They were going to work on some bridges that had been washed out right up near the top of the Cascades, on the west side of the mountains. Boy, this suited me, as I was sure I would be able to get from there down to Interbay, one way or another.

Oscar said to me, "Why don't you try to get on this gang and work a few days with me?" I told him, "I have to get back to the camp, resign, get the rest of my stuff and get home. I am going to get married soon after I get back. Besides, I don't know much about building bridges." I also told him, "I have never worked for the railroad a day in my life."

He was a real nice fellow. We sat there thinking for awhile when he said, "I have been thinking this over. The foreman will soon come in here with a time book. He will take all our names down and get our little green cards we picked up from the railroad employment office in downtown Spokane. You wait till he has everyone else's name and then you tell him you got a call yesterday afternoon but by the time you got downtown the office was closed so you couldn't pick up your ticket. Tell him you need work and you just took a chance that he would need all the B and B men he could get." Oscar said, "He might put you on."

He went on to say, "He will ask you if you are a B and B man and you tell him you are. I will speak up and say you are, I have worked with you before and that you are a good man. It is worth a try. His name is Tor Torson. He is the main foreman for the B and B gangs." "What does B and B mean?" I asked. "Bridge and building," he said.

It wasn't long before Mr. Torson came in and he did just as Oscar said he would. When he finished he said, "Did I get every body?" I said, "No, you didn't get me." I explained to him about not getting a ticket but figured he would need all the help he could get. He said, "I can't use you if you don't have a ticket." Oscar spoke right up saying, "He is a good man, I have worked with him before." Torson looked at me and said, "All right, what is your name?" He took it and I was in.

Oscar said, "You had better grab one of those bunks and put your packsack on it, and now make yourself at home." In the meantime we were riding along in comfort, something kind of foreign to me.

The snow was getting deeper all the time as we made our way up into the mountains. Oscar said, "I think we are going to the west end of the big tunnel (eight miles long). There are side tracks there and a little station. I understand the trouble is down the hill on the west side a short way." We went through the tunnel and pulled over on a side track. When the train stopped, the dinner bell rang and you can bet I wasn't the last one in the dining car. I didn't get left out this time. When we had finished eating at precisely twelve o'clock, this was Christmas day, the call went out – let's go!

I kind of followed Oscar, we were taken down the track a short distance where there was a low bridge that needed repair. They left about eight of us there with some tools, and the rest of the crew went on down the track. We worked till six o'clock when we stopped for the night. The engine and a car came back up, picked us up and took us back to our bunk car.

After supper I told Oscar I was going to walk up to that little railroad station by the name of Scenic, to see if I could get the telegrapher to send a message to the camp for me. I went up there and talked to the agent, who was most accommodating. He said he would send it to Port Angeles and they would place it in the mail that night. That meant the camp would get it the next day.

I made up a message to the effect that I was stranded in the mountains due to the flooding conditions and could not get back on time. I further stated I had with me a letter certifying that I had a job and wished to resign. That was the best I could do and I hoped for the best.

Oscar and I worked together on that low bridge for a couple of days, completing the repairs, then they took us down to the big bridge to work. That was ninety five feet off the ground in one place. We went to work at six in the morning and quit at six at night. It rained or snowed nearly all the time and was miserable, being cold and wet.

They brought some big generators in and strung big electric lights around because it would be dark before quitting time and again when we started in the morning.

One night I came in and found someone else had been in my bed. They put on a night crew, they slept in our beds during the daytime, and we used them nights. We left in the morning before they came in and they were gone in the evening before we got in. It didn't matter too much; I was wearing long, woolen underwear day and night. The bunk car was warm all night so one didn't pull the blankets up very far. I never saw him and he never saw me.

It was extremely dangerous because everything was wet and sometimes icy, but always slippery. Oscar and I were given the job of spiking braces across the pilings as they were driven in the ground by the pile driver. The braces were big heavy timbers that some men above us would pull up with ropes, and hold in place till we could get them secured. We would work with one hand and hang on for dear life with the other. We would cling to the pilings as best we could, one of us holding the big long spike while the other one drove it in with one hand and a big heavy hammer.

Believe me, we earned our wages. The foreman who gave us orders was a sensible man who didn't get excited and he never bothered Oscar or me, if you were doing the best you could he left you alone.

We were not quite done with our spiking job when they decided to run an engine over the new bridge. The foreman called down to Oscar and me, telling us to climb up out of where we were working. I sure was glad of that. I had no desire to be underneath that big steam locomotive when it went overhead for the first time. They brought the engine up and he went across and back very slowly several times. I sure would not have liked to be in that engine but everything seemed to be fine.

We finished up, I think it was New Year's Eve afternoon. The trains were running to beat the band. The foreman told us we were through and that a passenger train would pick us up after supper for the trip back to Spokane. I rode back in a manner that I was unaccustomed to – in style (it was called riding the cushions in those times in hobo lingo).

Chapter 40

After I sent the telegram I kept worrying about how I was going to make out with the CCCs. I wasn't going to have time to go over and back before we were to get married, not the way I had to travel, at least. I had not come up with a workable solution yet by the time I got back to town. I think I stayed in the depot when we got in, for the rest of the night, as it was late.

The next morning I went to see Agnes. After I had finished telling her about my experience, she said, "A letter came here for you while you were gone." It was from my friend, Lieutenant Felts. He had received my telegram. He said he understood the circumstances, they were beyond my control. It would not be necessary for me to return to camp. He further said to mail him the letter of resignation along with the letter of a job confirmation and he would send me an honorable discharge.

Gosh, was that ever good news, that solved one problem for me. Now all I had to worry about was getting married and making a living for two instead of one. I looked forward to the first, but was quite anxious about the prospects of the other.

Getting Married

We had only a few days till we were to be married. Agnes had made arrangements with Father Kennedy at Our Lady of Lourdes church for us to be married at the seven o'clock mass on a Saturday morning, which was the sixth day of January, 1934.

I stayed with Adrian and Sylvan when I got back, for a few days, till I could get organized, sort of get my act together. They had an apartment in the St. Elmo, at 174 South Brown Street. The apartment house owner had a two-room vacant apartment he was refurbishing at the time. Agnes and I looked at it and decided it would be just fine. The owner said he could have it ready by Saturday for us to move into.

It was furnished and rented for ten dollars a month. It had a kitchen with a gas cook stove, a table and chairs, plenty of cupboards, a sink and counter space. The front room had a double bed with sagging springs, a big chair and a divan, also with sagging springs. There was a long walk-in closet and the front had two large windows looking out on Brown Street.

I collected my wages from the railroad. I sure was lucky; I got paid second class carpenter wages, thanks to Oscar, clearing fifty nine dollars for the week's work. I never saw Oscar again after we got off the train. I hope I do in the next world; I still want to thank him one more time.

Agnes was honored with a wedding shower one evening, which was a well-kept secret and came as a complete surprise to her. She was given a generous bounty of gifts for our use in setting up housekeeping during the week before we were married. She could hardly wait to show me all the nice things that were given to her by friends and relatives.

I asked my brother Don to be my best man, she asked her sister Dorothy to be her bridesmaid. Before I knew it, it was time to get the wedding license and then came the day.

Saturday morning was clear and bright – no snow, but cold. My friend Norman DePender borrowed his father's car and drove us to the church for the ceremony. Don, Dorothy, Agnes and I rode to the church, everyone else had to walk. The four of us walked down the aisle together. It was a simple wedding with but few spectators. In due course, I slipped the little ring on her finger and I am proud to say it is still there today sixty one years later. With that, we were married. Agnes's mother had a wedding breakfast for us and a few relatives, and then we were on our own, we were a new family.

Our Wedding Day
Me, Agnes, Dorothy and Don, January 6, 1934

There was no honeymoon, it was unthinkable. We made several trips, walking, carrying our possessions to our new quarters, which were ready, all clean and fresh-smelling of new paint. We worked all the rest of the day getting everything arranged. We were so busy we didn't take any time out for lunch.

About the time it got dark, we finally had it all arranged to suit the new little bride. We decided we had better go get something to eat. We were too tired to fix anything ourselves. We walked downtown to a little restaurant we knew of and had a hamburger deluxe, which was a nice hamburger with a small helping of potato salad and a little side dish of baked beans with a cup of coffee, all for fifteen cents apiece. That was our wedding supper. We were so tired we could hardly struggle back to the apartment and up to the third floor.

When we opened the door and turned on the lights we were overwhelmed by the sight of our little place. It was so cute and so homey and so inviting. I carried her over the threshold, and we had a home of our own. Humble as it was, it was our home. To us it was a delightful sight, we could hardly believe it.

She had transformed it from a couple of empty rooms into something like this. We had been so busy all day that we had never stopped to look at it. I was so pleased, so happy to feel I had a home at last. I couldn't get over it.

Our new life was pleasant but when I went to make application to get work on the CWA work program, they would not accept me, as I had not been on relief. I tried to get on that so we could get on the work program our friends were on but no go. Because I had left the CCCs, they had nothing for me. Boy things were looking pretty serious. We had paid rent for two months in advance. We didn't spend a dime we didn't have to. I looked for work but there was none. Agnes had taken a cosmetology course and had her license to practice but she couldn't get a job either. She had a few clients that she would go to their homes and do their hair for them on Saturdays. She didn't get much for it but it was something.

We were finally able to get a little help in the line of surplus food. I got a little work shoveling snow but it didn't snow much that winter. I finally got some part-time work at W. P. Fuller, a glass company, through a friend of mine who worked for them. They paid regular wages but it was not steady, there was not much building going on, and they could only use me for extra help when needed. Spring came and my friend Bud Tanner got out of the CCCs and came to visit us. He mentioned that Jack Frost was going to be running a CCC camp on Ruby creek up near Cusick, on the Pend Oreille River. I wasn't getting much work from Fuller's; the future didn't look too promising, so I decided I would go to see Jack, to see if he could do anything for me. We were hard up but we were getting by, just barely.

People who read this, if anyone does, will not believe how hard things were for some of us during those times. Agnes and I talked it over and there was only one way for me to make the trip, and that was for nothing, which I was pretty good at by then. We got up real early one morning. The weather was good. Agnes made me three little lunches, I put them in a sack with a safety razor, a towel and some clean socks, bid her goodbye and was off, telling her I would see her in a couple of days. Luck was with me that day.

I got several good rides and was on the main street of Cusick a little before noon. I had done some walking and was kind of tired and was looking for a place to get a drink of water and then I was going to walk out to the camp, wherever it was.

I glanced up and there driving down the street was Jack Frost in a Forest Service pickup. Fortunately, he stopped and I ran up to where he was and said hello. Of course he was glad to see me and after shaking hands he said, "What are you doing up here, Do you have time to ride out to camp with me for dinner and a visit?"

Well, you bet I had time, I had lots of time. He went on to say, "After we have a visit I will be sending this truck back to town and you can ride back with the driver, how does that sound to you?" I jumped in with him and on the way out, I told him what had been going on in my life and also asked him if he could get me a job someplace up there. We got to camp just in time for dinner and of course, I ate with the elite.

When we had finished he took me to his office and said, "There isn't much I can do for you here but while we were eating I was thinking. I have a good friend in Spokane who is the head of the Forest Service aerial survey program, his name is Howard Flint. Lieutenant Felts at camp Twin Rivers spoke highly of your ability to establish meets and bounds (which means locating lines and corners of property) after you left last winter. He said you were very competent. Howard Flint might just have something for you. I will give you a letter of introduction to him."

Well, this held out little hope in my estimation but it was interesting at least. He told me to go out and look over the camp while he wrote me a letter to Mr. Flint. He soon came out of his office with an open letter for me to Mr. Flint. We visited a little longer until the truck was ready to go, he wished me luck, I thanked him, we said goodbye and we were never to see each other again. This is another guy I will thank in the next world if I get to see him, and if I get there.

The truck took me back to town, about ten miles, for which I was Grateful. I didn't have to walk. It was about mid-afternoon and I was on my way back to Spokane already. I walked a mile or so when a Washington Water Power Co. pickup truck stopped for me as I gave him the old thumb signal. When I got in the fellow asked me where I was going. I said "Spokane." He said, "Well, I am going to Spokane too."

I could hardly believe my good fortune. Here I was, all prepared to spend the night out someplace under a tree or a bridge and eat a cold sandwich for supper, with another for breakfast. I walked across town after he let me out and still got home about six o'clock.

That evening I read the letter from Jack Frost to Mr. Flint. It stated that I had had considerable experience in timber locating and would be a valuable person if he had an opening along those lines. Boy, this was a little heavy; I wasn't that experienced, I had been kind of lucky.

I took my letter to Mr. Flint's office the next morning, giving it to his secretary. He soon came out to greet me and was very cordial. He spoke highly of Jack Frost and said, "I wish I had something for you but I don't at this time, but I am going to send you to Steven Wykoff, the head of the Blister Rust control program. Steve might have something." He wrote on the bottom of Jack's letter, "Dear Steve, this man comes highly recommended by a good friend; I hope you will have something for him."

I hot-footed it over to Mr. Wykoff's office and asked if I could see Mr. Wykoff. The lady at the front desk said, "No, he is busy." I said, "Would you please give him this letter from Mr. Flint?"

In about a minute out he came, introduced himself, and invited me into his office. He was most pleasant and took a genuine interest in my background. He asked me if I was willing to go out of town for the summer. He said, "I might just have something for you in a few days, leave a phone number where I can reach you."

In a couple of days, I got a call to come down to see Mr. Wykoff. This time when I went to the front desk the girl called him and I was invited right in. He said he had an opening for a Blister Rust checker (whatever that was). It was available immediately. The location was out of Noxon, Montana. He went on to say that he would like to have me on the job the following Monday morning, and that it would require an appointment from Washington D.C., which he would apply for immediately.

In the meantime, till the appointment came through starting Monday morning I would be paid at an hourly rate of the equivalent of $167.00 a month, which would be my salary when it became official. Would I accept this job at that rate of pay?

I just about fell out of my chair. I tried to act somewhat casual when I replied, "Yes, that would be satisfactory and that indeed I would make arrangements to be in Noxon Monday morning." Mr. Wykoff dictated a letter of introduction and when it was ready he signed it, gave it to me, and I was on my way.

The Blister Rust

Boy, where was Noxon, Montana? What did a Blister Rust checker do? And last, what was I going to do for money? This was about Wednesday. Agnes and I talked it over and made some fast decisions.

First, I would borrow thirty dollars from Agnes's brother, Lawrence. We would see if Agnes could pay board and room to her mother for the time I would be working. We would give up the apartment and move our belongings to her mother's house, as she had plenty of room for us to store our meager possessions there. I would have to buy a pair of caulked boots and find out where the hell Noxon was so I could get there some way, by Monday morning.

Well, everything went together fine. I was going to take the Northern Pacific passenger train to Noxon, which is a small town just east of the Idaho line on the Clark Fork River. Saturday morning I got a call from a man who said his name was Kermit Miller, the chief in charge of all the Blister Rust checkers working in Montana. His office was in Noxon. He was in town and understood I would be reporting to him Monday morning. I said, "Yes, that was my intention." He said, "I am going to be driving back to Noxon Sunday morning. How would you like to have me pick you up and you can ride up with me?"

Gosh! Things were working out so good it was scary. Sunday morning Kermit showed up at the appointed time with a brand new Forest Service pickup. I bid my little bride goodbye, threw my packsack and new caulked shoes in the back, jumped in and was off to the woods again.

We hadn't gotten out of town until he started telling me about the problem the checkers were going to have working on land that had never been surveyed. There were no section lines or anything to establish where the land was in relation to other surveyed lands. There were no reference points to work from. I had momentary reflections of, here I go again, and thoughts of maybe this had something to do with why I was hired. I thought to myself, "I don't know anything about Blister Rust and I hope I am not over my head on land survey too." Little flickers of doubting thoughts started kind of licking at my brain, kind of like little tongues of flame when you first light a bonfire.

He went on to say there would have to be a good many miles of section lines run to establish accurate boundaries and land descriptions of the work areas. They didn't have a large compass to work with that was accurate enough for these purposes. I thought of my dad's big staff compass, and mentioned it to Kermit. He was immediately impressed and obviously interested. I thought to myself "If I could borrow it from Dad I might make my position a little more secure."

I was feeling kind of outclassed about this time. I said, "If you want to swing around through Coeur d'Alene I will see if I can borrow it from him, with the understanding that I go where the compass goes. It is a good instrument; he has had it for a good many years and prizes it very highly."

Kermit jumped at the chance, so we did just that. Dad was good about loaning it to me and when Kermit saw it, he was delighted. He said, "This is exactly what we need on this job." I said, "Remember, I go with the compass." He agreed saying, "Fair enough."

When we got to Noxon, Kermit said, "There is an extra bed here in the back room of the office where I sleep. You stay here tonight with me and in the morning I will take you out to the camp where your bunch is working and I will introduce you to your supervisor. There is a local baseball game this afternoon; would you care to go to it with me?" I said, "I thank you for asking, but I think I would rather do a little brushing up on some literature if you have some around here on Blister Rust." I was scared and just about then not feeling too secure.

He had lots of literature and I concentrated on it desperately hard, absorbing all I could in the time I had, trying to get a general idea of what was being done that I would be checking on.

I found out there were several naturally-growing plants that were helping spread a disease called Blister Rust that was destroying the natural growth of the white pine trees. I had spent a lot of time in the woods but had never paid any particular attention to individual plants; they were just brush to me. There were pictures of these plants that I immediately recognized when I saw them. I got some extremely valuable information in that afternoon of intense study.

The next morning Kermit took me out to one of the camps, where my boss was. Kermit introduced me to him, a man by the name of Ralph Young. Mr. Young said, "So this is the man who has never had any experience in Blister Rust before, who is to be a checker. I got the message; I knew I had a strike against me. All of the checkers for that area, of which there were six including myself, were at that camp by this time. The other fellows were out in the brush some place doing something that particular day. They had had school there the week before and I had missed that, of course. I wasn't feeling too comfortable about this time.

Kermit told Ralph, "Chuck, here brought a good compass with him and knows how to use it. He and his compass will be a valuable assist to you when you have to run lines, and oh, by the way, that instrument is to be in Chuck's possession at all times, that is part of our agreement for the privilege of being able to use it." Good old Kermit. I knew I had one friend and in a good place.

When we started working, we began by surveying. We had to go nine miles to a government survey line, then find a corner to establish our location. We then sighted and measured a line back to where the regular crews were working. We had to establish lines around all the territory that was going to be worked that year.

This took all six of us a couple of weeks. While we were doing this, I got myself quite familiar with what the regular crews were doing and what the bushes looked like that the men were digging out and pulling by hand. There were six or seven different varieties and all classed as Ribes. However, I had to identify each separate variety by name on my reports and maps.

When we got all the lines run we were each assigned a camp, except two of us who were given a camp and a half to check. Our job was to go over the ground that had been eradicated to check to see how good a job had been done. I was given camp fifteen and half of camp thirteen, which was at the end of the road. All the camps consisted of thirty five men, including a camp boss and a checker, and of course a cook and helper.

The camp boss and I slept in the office tent. When or if the camp boss was not there I was the next in command. We were three miles up a creek from the end of the road by trail. Everything had to come in by pack horse train. It was beautiful, wild country and the highest mountains I had ever been around.

By the time we had all the lines run I was well toughened in, had my new shoes well broken in, and could keep up with any of them. I was also familiar enough with what I was supposed to do to feel confident.

My territory took in the south side of a huge mountain, a creek bottom, and part of the mountain on the opposite side. I also had half of camp thirteen to cover. I would take a sandwich and a small can of fruit (one is all the cook would give us) in a little cloth sack, tie it to my belt in the back where it wouldn't hook on the brush, and take off all by myself. I would run a compass line and pace all the way (counting my steps) just as I had done when working for my dad when he was cruising timber. There was one difference; I was looking within a fifteen foot boundary on either side of my imaginary line, for missed ribes. When I found a ribe, I would identify it and estimate the number of lineal feet of stem and branch length of the plant, pull it and record where I had found it and be on my way again. I would try to get to the top of that mountain by noon if I could.

Sometimes it would be tough going and it would take longer. I would be hot and so thirsty I couldn't eat that old dried out bread in the sandwich; I would take the meat out, eat it, throw the bread away, eat the little can of fruit and get going again. I would move over along the boundary line the proper distance and start back down. Sometimes it would be easy, but if it was hard I would have to hustle to make it by supper time. When I would get down to the creek or camp, whichever came first, I would be so dry I would think I would drink the creek dry. After supper I would have to work up my notes and show them on my map that I had made to scale, of the territory I was working.

Bear Country

There were a lot of bears in that country, but as a rule they didn't bother much. I had one experience that kind of got my attention for awhile one morning, though.

I stopped on the steep mountainside at the edge of a little open place to take a compass line shot. There was a big, fallen tree about sixty feet above me, lying crosswise of the hill. I stopped, pulled my compass out and took a reading. When I looked up to focus on a point, there, right where I wanted to go, standing on this log, was a big black bear, looking down at me. It had not been there a second before, but it was there then and it was a big one. This was a real big bear, about four feet at the shoulders. Having seen two or three bears a week I was a fair judge of the size of a bear and this was the biggest one by far.

Usually I would holler at them and they would run, but that didn't work this time. I hollered several times and nothing happened. That bear just looked at me as if to say, why are you hollering at me. I am right here, I hear you. It was positioned exactly where I was supposed to go with my line.

After a couple of minutes of us looking at each other, I decided it was not going to move for me and I was not going to argue with it over a little space up on the side of that mountain, where there was lots of room for everybody. Besides that, I didn't want to outwait him; I figured he had more time than I did so I thought I had better make some other kind of arrangements.

I took a ninety degree compass sight along the hillside, paced off a hundred steps, took another ninety degree turn, which put me back in the direction I wanted to go, and went another hundred steps. Then I did this again and was back on my line. The bear was still standing there, only he had turned completely around, watching me continuously. I will have to admit I was a little concerned about his interest in me. After all, I was all alone; it was just the bear and me.

I went on my way, looking back over my shoulder from time to time for awhile, but I didn't see it again. When I worked up my notes and my map I made a note, "Offset of one hundred paces for huge bear." This map and the field notes went to headquarters in Spokane to be worked up during the winter months. I often wondered what was said when they came across that in the office. The other checker that checked the other half of camp thirteen sent home for a pistol and carried it all summer, as he was scared of so many bears.

The area he and I worked that summer has since been declared a wilderness area and there never have been any roads built in the upper reaches of the east fork of the Bull River.

I had another encounter one evening that was kind of interesting for awhile. I had to walk down to camp thirteen, about three miles each way, on Wednesday evening to leave a report of what had been checked for the week.

Ralph Young would pick this up on Thursday morning for his records, to be forwarded to Spokane. I would wait till after supper, as I usually wouldn't get in early enough to go before supper. I would usually get back just about the time it would be getting good and dark, if I hurried.

On this particular occasion I was on my way back, on a trail that was on a little flat above the creek. There was a big rock with a little brush sticking up around it about five feet high that the trail made a sharp bend around. I was walking fast with my head down, and as the trail was deep with dust from the pack horses having used it I was not making any noise. I started around this little clump of brush when a fair sized bear, about as high as my belt when standing on all four feet, came around the brush from the opposite direction right in the trail, not making any noise either. We met head on with only about four feet separating us. I stopped and so did the bear. Before I could do anything at all the bear stood up on its hind legs, with its front legs extended toward me as though it was going to attack. It let out a mighty roar, turned on its two hind legs and jumped toward the creek. This was all accomplished so fast I didn't have time to figure out what I was going to do. I will admit I was startled but that bear was more scared than I was, or he had much better reflexes than I did, I am not sure which. In any event, he was gone before I could get going. The next jump the bear made he lit in the creek and then I could hear it crashing through the brush up the side of the mountain. I soon recovered and had to laugh at how scared that bear had been.

We had two little black bear cubs that hung around camp, and sometimes in the evening they would raid the garbage pit. One evening when they were there someone suggested we have a little bear roundup. Almost everyone in camp turned out except one fellow who would lie on his cot in the evening and read. He was kind of a loner and never mingled much with the other men. He was asked to join but had declined, deciding not to take part in this little experiment in bear management, that we set up mostly for our own amusement. He chose not to participate in the fun – at least not to begin with.

We all got a good strong stick and formed a big ring out in the brush around the little bears, then started to close in on them. Wherever they turned, there was someone there with a stick to hit the brush and chase them back. Soon the circle got smaller and they were frantic, rushing one way and another in a frenzy, trying to get away.

It wasn't long till the circle was not very big and one bear made a successful break for freedom. The other one was desperate then, and ran right between two fellows in spite of their best efforts to stop it. It ran right in the open flaps of the tent where the fellow was laying on his cot, reading.

When the bear came to the other end of the tent, which was staked down tight to the ground, he was going too fast to change course. He just put his nose to the ground and sort of scooped that tightly-drawn tent canvas up with his nose and kept right on going.

That tight canvas snapped with a twang, like someone hitting a lone note on a banjo. The tent peg flew like a small rock from a sling shot, and the bear was gone. I don't think he even slowed down. The guy laying on the cot reading had no warning of what was about to happen.

The first thing he knew something black went streaking right by him, and the tent shivered like a shingle in the wind. He didn't stick around to see if anything else was about to take place, but came out the open end of that tent with eyes sticking out like two big glass marbles, wearing an expression of terror on his face as though he had just shaken hands with a ghost. I don't know which sight was the funniest, that poor little terrified bear, or that panic-stricken man, clutching a book in his hand with his hair standing on end. It was hilarious – the effort was well worth the reward to that little entertainment-starved community.

I saw my supervisor only a couple of times during the summer, I think because he had to walk three miles up to my camp. This suited me just fine, as I didn't feel I needed any supervision. Once he told me I was missing ribe in a creek bottom and I was able to prove to him they were not even ribes, but small devil's club plants, which he was quite embarrassed about. The other time he told me he didn't think I was covering enough ground, which astonished me, as I was going early and late, sometimes working Saturdays and even some Sundays. When we finished the season it turned out I had covered the second highest acreage of anyone in the whole district.

Chapter 41

One time that summer I decided to come to Spokane for the weekend to see my little wife. After all, it was kind of lonesome. I had worked every Saturday and a couple of Sundays so I didn't feel guilty about quitting a little early Friday afternoon, which I did. I took my weekly shower, which was accomplished by heating a five-gallon gas can of water carried up from the ice cold creek, in a little fire pit dug in the dirt by some of the fellows out behind the tents, near a tree standing on a little dirt bank. When the water got about the right temperature I was all ready with my clothes off. I grabbed the can of water, climbed up the bank, and dumped it into another can with a bunch of small nail holes punched in the bottom of it hanging from a limb of the tree. Then I ran around and got under the nice warm shower, soaped quickly and rinsed before I ran out of water. It could be done but you didn't stand around soaking and singing.

I walked down to camp thirteen, where I could eat if I wanted to as I was also taking care of half of the checking for that camp. I had made arrangements to ride to Sandpoint on Friday afternoon after supper, with a man who lived there and was working in camp thirteen. I could catch an evening passenger train from Sandpoint right into Spokane. I was standing around the train depot waiting for the train to come, which was a little late, when a man with a packsack on his back approached me.

He said, "Have you ever stolen a ride on a passenger train?" I said, "Yes, I have, why?" He went on to say he wanted to get to Spokane that night and didn't have any money. I told him how to do it and then I had an inspiration. I said, "Well, it is a nice evening and I don't see any reason why I should pay for a ride either, I will just show you how, we will ride the tender." (The tender is the car that is attached to the rear of a steam engine locomotive to haul coal and water.)

Sandpoint had a water tower there for the engines and when they pulled in, the fireman took on water. We stood back on the opposite side of the tracks from the depot and waited. When I heard the engineer let the air out of his brakes I had the guy climb up the tender ladder and I followed him. The Northern Pacific was a coal-burning line. They had big tenders that were easy to ride on, but sometimes you got smoke and cinders in your face. The faster they went the lower the smoke trailed back over the engine and sometimes it was kind of bad, particularly if you were riding on top, where we were.

It was a nice evening and we made good time. When we went through Rathdrum we must have been going seventy five miles an hour. It was still daylight when we approached Spokane, although the sun was down. I explained to my companion that we didn't dare ride into the depot for fear we might get picked up and jailed. I took his packsack on my back, and said, "I will get off first, then when you get off they will have slowed down more and it will be easier for you to handle."

I was very careful to instruct him in detail about getting off on the fly. Which foot to land on, to light running and so forth. I got off without mishap, although they were going pretty fast but rapidly slowing down. When my friend went to get off, to my horror he put the wrong foot down first and fell. Fortunately, he didn't fall under the wheels but he did fall flat down with his hands out, so he scratched his face up pretty good. Poor fellow, he said, "I know what you told me but I got scared and forgot what you said." I gave him his packsack, told him I was sorry, and never did see him again.

When I got to Agnes's mother's place, she said, "I am so glad to see you, give me a big kiss even if your face is dirty." I had gone to great pains to get all cleaned up nice for my trip and then I had kind of shot it down by riding on the tender behind a coal burning, soot spewing steam locomotive pulling a passenger train. I didn't know it at the time but this turned out to be the last free train ride of my life. It was a good challenge, a good ride, one to remember the close of one phase of my life. I am glad I did it.

We finished our season in early August. One of the other checkers (who lived in Spokane) and I were able to get a ride to Sandpoint after our last day's work. It was late when we got into town and we wanted to get cleaned up before we came to Spokane. I didn't want to show up again with a dirty face, so we went directly to a little hotel to get a room for the night.

When we walked in, with our caulked shoes, working clothes and each with a packsack the clerk said, "Do you two fellows want to go fighting forest fires?" We answered in unison, "No we sure don't, we have just come out of the brush, we are tired and we want to get home." The clerk said, "You had better stay off the street or you will get drafted by the Forest Service. They are taking everyone in town that isn't working and they will make you go."

We inquired as to when the next train to Spokane was, which turned out to be ten o'clock the next morning. We got cleaned up and went to bed. When we got up in the morning, we stayed right in the room till train time. We were too scared to go out to get something to eat. We got to the depot just in time and were soon on our way home.

Agnes had an uncle who lived in Yakima and who had a flour mill there. He and his family had come to Spokane during the summer and had invited Agnes to return with them for a visit. They would be coming back soon and would bring her back then. She had accepted their offer and during her visit had asked her Uncle Jack about giving me a job if he had an opening sometime. He had been sort of noncommittal about it, but did tell her to get in touch with him when I was available. Agnes wrote to him and as we couldn't make any definite plans till we heard from him we had a few days to kill.

We talked things over and decided that we needed some kind of transportation besides walking. We started out Monday morning to look for a car. We looked at several used car lots and everything we saw in our price range was a pile of junk, or the tires were no good, or there was something we didn't like. We looked and looked and were discouraged and about to give up for the day when we saw a Model T Ford pickup truck sitting right out in the front row of a lot, that was for sale for the unreal price of thirty five dollars.

My first vehicle, a Model T Pickup Truck

We sure didn't need a truck but there was something about it that caught my eye. I mentioned it to Agnes. It was right in front of us so we started looking at it. The more we looked the more I saw that it appeared to be in pretty good shape. I asked her what she thought and she said, "I don't care if it is a pickup or not as long as it runs and will give us good service."

I checked it out pretty thoroughly and couldn't really see why it was priced so reasonably. We got the man who seemed to be in charge and I asked if we could take it for a short drive. He willingly agreed and off we went. I soon found out the brakes, which were in the transmission, were bad. I thought to myself, I had better check the low gear – it too was bad.

This told me something; if the reverse is bad, the truck is beyond my ability to repair. It would require a major overhaul and that would be out. If the reverse was good, I knew what the trouble was and I could fix it for five or six dollars and it would be fine. I checked the reverse and it was fine. I then felt comfortable. I knew why the price was so reasonable; it was because the car dealer didn't know much about Model T Fords. The dealer probably knew there was something wrong but didn't know just how much it would cost to have it fixed and rather than go to the expense, reduced the price.

My dad had bought one brand new in 1919 as before mentioned. I was fascinated with that machine, as I was with all machinery when I was a boy. I was quite familiar with the inner workings of a Model T. We went back to the car lot and I told the man the transmission was not working very well, but maybe I could fix it myself. I said I would take the truck if he would throw in a few tools such a screwdriver, a pair of pliers, some old end wrenches, and an adjustable wrench, if he had something like that around.

We made a deal. Our money was in the Post Office downtown so Agnes walked downtown to get the money while I stayed there to see that the truck didn't get sold to someone else while we were both gone. She was soon back and we were now the owner of a vehicle of our own.

We went to the courthouse to the Sheriff's office, they asked me a few questions, I gave them two dollars, and they gave me a driver's license. We next went to a Ford garage where I bought a set of new transmission bands. We went to Mom's house, gathered up some camping equipment, and went back to Eloika Lake, where we had been with Adrian and Mary, and prepared to camp for a few days.

The weather was great, we slept under the stars, I cooked over a fire, we washed in the lake and went swimming a couple of times a day and just relaxed.

Much to my wife's dismay and consternation, I took the transmission in the Ford apart. Agnes was quite distressed, complaining that here we were, clear out in the wilds, the car probably would never run again and what were we going to do.

I had to laugh at her but she failed to see any humor in the situation at all. I guess this was about the first time in our long life together that she registered dismay at what I was doing and didn't have faith in my ability to do something that I had never done before.

Well, anyway I got the Ford back together and it worked just fine. We stayed there for about a week. The only excitement we had occurred in the middle of a night when I was sound asleep. Agnes woke me up and whispered that there were some animals coming and she was sure they were bears. I sat up and when I could get my eyes open and get a little used to the light I saw five or six cows coming down to the lake to get a drink of water. Well, that taken care of, I laid back down and then she kept me awake till they left because she thought the cows would walk on us.

When we got back to Mom's house there was a letter from Agnes's Uncle Jack Altmeyer and in it he said to come to Yakima, he thought there would be a chance to find some work. We made immediate plans to go to Yakima and left the next day. We didn't get ready to go till late in the afternoon but that was all right with me, as the weather was warm and one of the traits of Model T Fords was for them to run hot.

We said goodbye to everyone and left about sundown. Shortly before we got to Ritzville the car started to miss and didn't run very well. We made it into town but, as it was about nine o'clock everything was closed for the night. I drove down the main street and the only thing I saw open was a pool hall. I stopped there and went in. I asked the man behind the counter if he happened to know where the Ford dealer garage owner lived. He said, "Yes, I do but if you want to talk to him he is sitting right over there playing cards," as he pointed to a table of fellows playing cards.

I went over and the man looked up as he saw me coming and asked, "What can I do for you"? I told him I was just passing through town and my Model T started to miss and that I had checked it out and it appeared I needed a new timer.

He said, "Well, it is time for me to quit anyway so I will open up and sell you a timer, but as it is late I will not install it for you. If you can fix it, fine, if not come back first thing in the morning and we will get you going,"

I bought the timer, drove down the street till I got under a street Light, got the hood up and went to work. In about a half hour, I had the new timer on with all the wires hooked up. I crossed my fingers and started it. What a relief; it ran like a watch.

We drove down the road till we were just outside Pasco, where we pulled out in the sage brush a short distance and rolled out our bed. Agnes inquired about there being bears around but I was able to assure her we were safe from any bears. I didn't bother to tell her about it being rattlesnake country, though, as I thought she might get nervous and not sleep well.

After a good sleep we had breakfast in Pasco and then went on to Yakima. Jack and his wife, Ruth, were hospitable and asked us to stay with them till we could find a place of our own. We rented a cabin for a week; this was the days before motels.

It was furnished enough to get by, with a little wood-burning cook stove to cook on. After a trip to a grocery store we were in business once again. It felt mighty good to set up house-keeping again and be on our own, even in a one-room cabin. The future was rather uncertain but we would take care of that in the future. We had to find a more permanent place to live for one thing. This was costing fifteen dollars a month and we had to do something about that pretty quick.

Housing was scarce; times were tough. I looked and looked – nothing. I kept on looking, finally finding a little vacant house set on the back of a nice, well-kept lot in a nice area. I had a hard time finding the man who owned it, but he didn't want to rent it. It had been vacant for years.

After much talking on my part he agreed to let us move in if I would clean it up, keep the lawn watered, cut the grass, and take care of things. I promised to do that and fix up around, like trim the shrubs and so forth. There was a good double bed, a good heating stove there, but not much else to set up housekeeping with.

We were not daunted however, and did move in. We needed everything, but though we had a little money we were careful about how we spent it. We had a baby coming and we knew this was going to be a big expense. We made do.

Now, when we think of it, we have to laugh at how we got by for awhile. We had no chairs or table; we sat on the floor to eat and used wooden apple boxes for a table. Although Agnes could not bend over very well at that time, she never complained about what we didn't have, she was a good camper, a good sport through it all, good times and bad.

Jack got me some part-time work in a grocery store and we got along. Then there was some part-time work for me at his mill sometimes. It was a small mill with five men working steady, and sometimes another man or two, depending on how busy they were.

I was told to come to work on a Monday morning after we had been in town a month or so. I took my lunch and told Agnes I would be home about five thirty, as I supposed it would be an eight-hour day. When it got to be a little after five and no one slowed down, I inquired when quitting time was and they explained it was six o'clock – a nine hour day. This was new to me as where I came from, everything was an eight-hour day except when harvesting, which was different.

A few years before the Industrial Workers of the World (IWW) had established that as a standard in the lumber and mining industry in our part of the country. IWW was a somewhat radical labor movement, mainly in the lumber industry. There had been some significant gains for working conditions in the Northwest but not in farming localities, I guess.

It might be interesting to digress here briefly to expand a little about the radical labor movement of the late 1910's and early 1920's. It was a socialist-oriented movement that was organizing anyone who wanted to join, to bring pressure on society in general, and particularly industry, for better working conditions and higher wages. Their ultimate goal was a more even distribution of wealth. They were prone to having wildcat strikes, disruptive labor disputes, sabotage and violence. They were a bunch of radicals and if you were a dues-paying member you carried a red membership card to prove it. Some men carried a card just to stay out of trouble if they were accosted, even though they were not in sympathy with the movement.

The lumber industry started a counter movement for the serious-minded who wanted to work and tend to business. This organizing was called the Four Ls, the Loyal Legion of Loggers and Lumbermen. It was said in slang terms that the initials IWW stood for I Won't Work while the Four Ls were called the Lazy Lousy Loggers and Lumbermen. So much for that.

I think it was the very next day they were real busy at the mill – as the apple harvest was in full swing and there were a lot of transient workers in the valley – that they rented an extra truck. It came about noon, and after dinner we started loading it. All kinds of different size sacks of flour and feed. All kinds of different brands. I wondered who was going to deliver this and then thought, it will be all ready for one of the regular drivers the next morning.

Well, we got it all loaded. It was about two o'clock and they presented me with the book of orders, saying, "It is late, you will have to hurry."

I said, "Where do I go?" I was told lower valley, Wapato, Donald, Zillah, Toppenish, Buena, Sunnyside, Mabton, and Grandview." Oh boy!

I didn't know how to drive the truck, which was way overloaded, hard to steer and hard to stop. I didn't know how many gears or where they were in the shift pattern. I didn't know where the towns were and how to get there. Adolf, the plant manager, told me what streets to take to get out of town and what road to take to get to my first stop. Then to ask there how to get to the next place.

The truck, being overloaded, was, of course, underpowered, which required a lot of shifting both up and down. Somewhere along the line I had acquired the skill of knowing how to double-clutch shift, which was good because an overloaded truck is no place to practice, believe me.

It was hot and I was a little bit nervous. I took off, and as soon as I was out of sight of the mill I pulled over to the side of the street and moved the shifting lever around till I knew the order of shifting and how to get in reverse.

I found the first stop but when I went to deliver, it was hard, as I didn't know the brands or sizes I was to unload from the orders I had been given. But I got along. I worked as hard as I could and as fast as I could. I was afraid to look at my watch to see what time it was because I knew time would run out on me. I sure didn't want to haul anything back.

When I got to the last stop the store was closed. I inquired around, got the man's name and called his home. He was not home, but his daughter was, a grown woman. I explained my predicament to her and she agreed to come to the store and let me in, which she did. It was eight forty five but I was done.

Everything came out even, so I felt good about that, I apparently had made no mistakes. That was a day to remember. It was a dirty trick to pull on a new man. I didn't realize it at the time but Adolf was against me because I was a relative of Jack's.

I got some part-time work at the mill. I worked hard, I listened and I watched. They needed an extra flour and feed packer for a while. They showed me how and let me try it a little bit and then I was brought in to pack flour and feed all by myself on a shift. You had to keep up with the output of the mill or the mill would have to shut down because there would be no room in the various bins for the flour and feed. If the mill had to be stopped that was serious, as it was a lot of trouble to get it started and adjusted again. I was keenly aware of this, and if I did cause the mill to go down I knew my name would be mud.

The flour was packed in white cotton sacks, in various sizes, by a packing machine, weighed, then sewed shut with a high-speed electric sewing machine, stacked on a hand truck and then wheeled out into the warehouse. The feed was packed into burlap bags by different machines, hand sewn with twine and a sack-sewing needle, and hand trucked to the warehouse. This job required a good amount of skill, which of course I didn't come with.

I did it. I had to work as fast and as hard as I could all day long. Some days I carried my lunch back home because I didn't have time to eat it. This job was very hard on hands, and sometimes I would have to get up in the night, start a fire in the wood-burning kitchen stove, and heat some water to soak my hands as they would be so swollen and hurt so bad I could not sleep. I got to be a good flour packer, however, and that was another job I could fill, as well as a truck driver and a warehouse man.

Chapter 42

The night of November 27, 1934, we retired as usual. About ten o'clock Agnes woke me up and quite calmly announced she thought she was going to have our baby. Being new at this sort of thing, we thought we had better go to the hospital, where they confirmed the fact that she was. By this time she also knew she was too, even if she was inexperienced.

It turned out to be a long might for us. I stayed with her until they came to take her to the delivery room, where I thought I would be excluded. Not so, the nurse said, "We want you to come, too."

They took her to a large room and made her reasonably comfortable, and instructed me to stay with her and assist her in any way that I could. That I did, helping her when she got sick to her stomach, putting cool wet cloths on her forehead, and consoling her as best I could, all the while feeling guilty about the pain she was enduring, wishing I could share it with her.

After awhile they wheeled another lady into the room and after getting her situated, everyone left. Soon that lady got sick and there was no one to help her, such as hold a pan for her, or put a cool cloth on her forehead, or console her by talking to her so I took over. I was quite busy going from one to the other when the nurse came back in the room.

It was just when I was with the other lady. I thought to myself, "Now I suppose I will get bawled out." But no, she came over, took a look at what I was doing and said, "You are doing a good job, I really appreciate your help, as I have a patient in the next room who is in critical condition that requires all my attention. If something happens that you need me for stick your head in and call me."

We three spent the night this way. About six thirty in the morning the nurse came, checked things out and said, "It is time to call the doctor." He soon came and took over and it wasn't long until our baby was born. He didn't look too good to me but the nurse and the doctor said he was a dandy boy and assured me everything was fine. Well, it didn't look fine to me. I didn't argue with them but I sure thought there sure should be a better way to introduce new people into this world.

I wondered if my poor little wife would live but they were quick to assure me that it was just business as usual. When they got the little guy all cleaned up and in a basket he looked different. He had black hair and was a dandy. I was a real proud new dad, feeling a new sense of responsibility. We named him Charles Edward.

When I wrote to my dad telling him the good news, and telling him we were going to call him Charlie here is what he wrote back:

> God bless the little stranger who bears his grandfather's name;
> May he grow up to be a man of great renown and fame.

I have often wondered if that woman I took care of that night didn't wonder who I was and where I came from. She was very responsive to me and seemed grateful for my helping her, which I am sure she was.

When Agnes and the baby came home after a ten-day stay at the hospital, which was standard in those times, the weather was cold, but I had the house nice and warm. I had a surprise for her, a brand new washing machine with a power wringer. No more scrubbing on a wash board, no more twisting the clothes by hand to wring the water out of them. It may not seem like much now, but it was a big deal for her, no more washing by hand on a wash board. This was the first new thing we ever bought.

Things were different around home when we got everyone there. The baby took a lot of care and this changed life somewhat. We had no way of heating the baby bottle during the night when the fire was out, so that meant starting a fire just to heat the bottle. We didn't even have a hot plate. I hit on an idea that sure saved a lot of trouble.

I went to a second-hand store where I was able to get a used electric percolator. This was a real time and trouble saver, believe me. In fact we had it for a good many years.

I didn't have steady work, but enough to get by on. Then in the spring things picked up. Later the truck driver for the little truck quit and I got the job. By this time I knew my way around and I knew the inventory. A new truck had been purchased and at last I had a steady job.

We needed a different kind of car, as the pickup was open and had no heater. Every time we went someplace in the pickup the baby would get cold and then would seem to get a bellyache. He would be fussy, which seemed to affect him mostly at night. Well, that was when it affected me most too, as I needed my rest; there was no napping the next day for me.

We looked around and found a four-door Chevrolet sedan at a reasonable price, and traded our pickup in on it for a little more than we had paid for it. Boy this was luxury. It had no heater but glass all around and no wind. I bought a length of stove pipe, and with the aid of an old pair of scissors and a pair of pliers I fashioned it to fit over the exhaust manifold, cut a hole in the passenger side of the floor board, made a little grill with a slide in it to close it off when not needed and we had a dandy heater.

Our "Luxury" Sedan

In fact I fashioned a holder to hold the baby bottle and if we went any distance and needed to feed the little guy Agnes could lay the bottle in this little rack, hook it to the little heater grill, and heat the bottle in short order. We had plenty of heat and a hot bottle any time we needed it. Poor man, poor ways but it worked just fine.

Things went along fine for a year or so, when one morning things changed. The first thing in the morning at the mill we two truck drivers and the two men in the warehouse would load both the big truck and the little truck. I would have some short trips and the other driver with the big truck would generally be gone all day, with a big load, anywhere from ten to fourteen tons, traveling a long distance.

This particular morning when Frank and I were loaded we both went into the office to get our invoices checked before we took off, and laid our individual order books on the counter. Jack happened to be there with the office girl, May. He picked up Frank's book while May checked mine. Jack finished first, with Frank's book, and handed it to me. I said, "No, that is Frank's book," thinking he was confused. Jack said in a loud voice, "No, you take it; Frank doesn't work here any more."

I was dumbfounded! I took the book from Jack's hand, at the same time glancing at him. He seemed to be very angry and in no mood to explain, to me, at least, what it was all about. I took the book and got out of there as fast as I could before I wasn't working there any more either.

I got my lunch bucket from my truck, climbed into the big rig and wondered how to get in first gear and where the rest of the gears were and how many there were. I had never even ridden in it before. Later I had some experiences with that truck that come to mind, when I stop to think about it, that might be worth relating to the reader, if ever there be one who takes the time to read about some of the experiences of a common, hard-working man.

To begin with, the truck was always overloaded and underpowered. The brakes were inadequate and the rear view mirrors were little – the same size as those on an automobile. There was no spare tire carrier so the spare wheel and tire had to be carried in the van and moved constantly with every loading and unloading.

Standing by my flour truck in Yakima, WA.
(Young son Charlie is on the hood)

One trip I was going after a load of wheat when I got a flat tire out in that desert-like region between the river and Connell. I got the spare out of the van and changed it but when it came time to get the flat tire back in the van I couldn't, for the life of me, lift it and hold it while I got another hold on it to tip it into the van. I struggled with it till I was worn out and no way could I make it. All along, no one came along, what to do?

I finally took the tailgate chain, hooked it to the wheel and tire and drug it down the road about a mile to a spot where I was able to back the back end of the trailer down into the ditch and up against the bank on the other side. I then rolled the tire and wheel down in the ditch, up the bank and into the van. Not a good way but a way. It worked.

Occasionally, I would go empty but most frequently I would load up in the morning, being real lucky to get away from the mill by nine or nine thirty, go to White Bluffs with a load, unload, then down the river to the ferry crossing the river, and to Connell.

I would go to a grain dealer in Connell who would give me directions to the farm where I was to pick up the load of wheat for that day. The wheat was all in sacks piled on the ground and covered with a thick layer of straw to protect it from the weather. The sacks weighed from one hundred thirty eight to one hundred forty two pounds to the sack.

They never varied. The farmer and I would put five sacks on the tailgate of the truck then I would jump up on the tailgate, stack the sacks five high on a hand truck, and wheel it to where I wanted it, and stand them up. Then I would jump down and repeat the process. I would load one hundred and eighty sacks with the last ten being put on top along with that miserable spare wheel, which meant they had to be lifted six high which was right up to my chin.

Occasionally I would be lucky to have a good farmer who would get up in the truck and help, but not often. They would stay on the ground, rest, and catch their breath, while I put the wheat where I wanted it. I weighed one hundred and fifty five pounds at the time. This was a load of right at thirteen tons. Not a big load by today's standards but it was big then, with our power and equipment.

I would get back to the mill anywhere from eight o'clock till ten o'clock in the evening. Boy, talk about a hard day. We had no phone so poor Agnes never knew when I would be home for supper. She thought she had it hard and maybe she did. Overtime was for free; the pay was the same regardless of the hours you put in.

One of those long days when I got home real late and it had been about one hundred in the shade, I dropped into a chair and said, "Boy, am I tired!" She replied, "I don't know why you are tired, all you do is sit in that old truck all day." Well, needless to say, this was a real revelation to me.

One trip I was loaded and started for home on a county road. I was going up a steep hill in first gear, about two miles an hour, when suddenly the truck stopped in its tracks. The engine started to roar and the rig started to roll backwards. Bad news; something had broken and I had nothing to hold the truck with except the foot brake and the parking brake. I pulled the parking brake on as hard as I could but it would not hold me without the foot brake too. I was unhooked somewhere between the engine and the drive wheels; what to do?

Well, I sat there hoping someone would come along to help me. No one did. I couldn't take my foot off the brake pedal. No power brakes so I had to push real hard. There was a canyon on the right hand side of the narrow, two-lane road and a steep bank on the other side. I had a curve behind me and was afraid to try to back down, as I would have had to back down about three quarters of a mile.

I was getting tired and my leg was starting to quiver by this time. There were good rocks on the bank to put behind the wheels but I couldn't get to them. Something had to be done before long, but what? I thought and my leg quivered. I looked around in the cab and all I had was a big heavy jack and a box with a meager tool supply.

An idea came to me. If I could get the base of that jack behind a rear wheel long enough to hold while I could get over to the bank and get a big rock, I would be all right. When I took my foot off the foot brake, the truck would start to creep slowly backward. I pondered my plight and came up with an idea.

I got the jack and held it in my hands studying it. I planned how I would get the driver's door open; I figured which foot would hit the ground first and about how many steps it would take to get back to the rear wheel, and how I would place the jack when I got there.

I said a little prayer, got myself all psyched up, took a deep breath and went for it. I got the jack base in place and held my breath as the truck settled back against it. It held. I raced back and forth across the road with rocks till I had all the wheels securely blocked. I then stood in the road wondering what to do next.

I heard a tractor in a field and on looking over, about a half mile away, was a man with a big caterpillar tractor plowing in a field. Just what I needed. I walked over there and as luck would have it, I knew him. I had hauled some of his wheat previously.

I told him of my predicament and asked if I could hire him to pull my rig up to the top of the hill and off to the side of the road. He said sure, that it was about quitting time anyway. He said, "I will unhook from the plows. I have a heavy chain – we will go and give you a pull." He pulled the pin on the plows, I got on the cat with him, and we just went across the fields to the road and hooked up to the truck. He pulled the truck up a little and held it while I got rid of the rocks and retrieved the jack. He pulled me to the top of the hill about a half mile to a wide place off to the side of the road, where I could leave the rig out of the way.

The farmer (his name was Middlestad) said, "What are you going to do now?" "Well, I have not figured that out yet, start walking I guess." It was ten or twelve miles to town, I would estimate.

This little caper I was not looking forward to with any great amount of glee. Mr. Middlestad said, "I'll tell you what. You get back on the cat with me and we will go back to the plows where I will leave it for the night. My pickup is just over the hill. We will get it, go to the house where my wife will have supper ready, eat and then I will take you to town. How does that sound to you?"

I said, "Mighty good, believe me, but I hate to put you or your wife out that much." He was a real nice guy and assured me that he would be glad to do it.

This we did and he was right, his wife did have a good supper ready and seemed glad to have company. He took me to town, where I got a room at the little old hotel. They had a phone in the lobby. I got on the phone with Yakima and got Al, the mill foreman, on the phone at his home to advise him of the situation.

I asked him to see if he could get a new axle that evening and get it on a Greyhound bus so it would be in Connell the next morning. I also asked him to go to our house to tell Agnes I wouldn't be home that night. I also asked him to have someone call the grain dealer first thing in the morning asking him to advance me some money when I stored in. I couldn't finance anything like I might run into. In those days if I had a fin in my pocket I was well off. (A fin was a five dollar bill.) Al asked if I needed help putting in the new axle. I told him I thought I could do it. At the time I had no idea the obstacles that lay ahead.

The next morning I got up early and, after eating, I went to a junky-looking service station. I told the proprietor my predicament and asked if he could help me for a fee. I think he was as hard up as I was by the looks of things. He was a good guy and readily agreed to help me if he could. I made arrangements with him to get a long piece of pipe out of his junk pile, and rented a grease bucket with a pump and some grease rags. I also arranged for him to take me out to my truck when I was ready.

I went to the bus stop but no axle. The people there said the bus would be in shortly. It was and the axle was there.

I went to the grain dealer and he gave me some money; and the service station man got a young fellow who just seemed to be hanging around there to watch the station for him while he took his pickup and hauled me out to my truck.

Well, I got out there and went to work. I pulled both axles out and sure enough a piece was broken off one of them about four inches long. I went to poke the piece out with the piece of pipe I had brought along just for that purpose. I could not push it out from either end. I tried everything I could think of but no way would it budge. I had to take the inspection plate off and there it was, the piece stuck in between the gears and the axle tube. There was nothing to do but to take the whole rear end gear assembly loose and drop it down a few inches to get enough room to get that little piece out of there.

I worked till about four o'clock in the afternoon to get that done. All I had to work with was an eight inch adjustable wrench, a pair of pliers and a screwdriver. If I had had the proper tools, it could have been done in an hour and a half or less.

I had no water to drink, no lunch, and it was hot. One good thing though, was when I got it all back together it worked fine. I got home, as I remember it, about eight that evening, hot, tired, hungry, dirty and covered with grease.

Another time it was cold; I was sent to the lower valley with a big load to deliver along the way to the lower valley. Then I was to pick up a load of wheat up in the rattlesnake hills above a place called, in those days, Witstrand. I finished my deliveries and was nearly up to where I thought the wheat ranch would be when I met a pickup coming toward me. It stopped right in the middle of the two lane road. There was no way I could get by. There were three men in it and one of them jumped out and came running to the truck.

I was beginning to wonder what was going on. He rushed up to the truck and said, "Are you after a load of wheat?" "I sure am," I replied. He said, "Well, where have you been? We have been waiting all afternoon for you and as it is almost dark we gave up on you for today." I told him I had been delivering flour and feed and had been hurrying as fast as I could go all day. I was sorry but this was the best I could do.

He said that they would go back and help load, as that was the reason for them being there. They were neighbors and had come to help. When we got up to the ranch there was about three inches of snow on the ground. The place where the wheat was stored was down on a steep hillside on a little narrow road about a hundred feet below the one I was on. On down below that was more steep hill and then a creek at the bottom. The only way for me to get down there was to go over the bank, straight down the hill, and turn on the lower road.

When I got there, I was too long to make the turn in the road and stay on the road. Boy! I got out of the truck, sized it up and said, "I am sorry I can't get down there. No way, it is too steep and slick. When I break over that bank, as slick as it is, I will slide right across that other road all the way to bottom and end up in the creek.

All three of the neighbors and the farmer himself were standing there watching me with kind of sheepish expressions on their faces. Well, I thought to myself, what is so damn funny. They should know better than ask me to go down there. I was tired, and after the one fellow had asked me what had taken me so long to get there after I had worked so hard all day hurrying to get there, I wasn't in too much of a mood to stand around arguing with someone about where I would take my truck.

After a few seconds, the farmer spoke up and said, "We just wanted to see what your reaction would be when we showed you where we wanted you to go with that big rig." They all burst out laughing. The farmer spoke up saying, "I have a Model Sixty cat in the shed, I will fetch it and hook on to the rear end of the trailer, that way I will be able to let you down the hill nice and slow, how does that sound to you?" They all burst out laughing again, as I guess they could see that I had been getting a little perturbed. It was a good joke on me. I had to laugh with them.

Well, he got his cat out and we hooked up to the back of the trailer, he took the slack out of the chain and I started out slowly. It was not a good feeling when I broke over the edge of the bank. He was a good operator though, and held just enough tension on the chain so that I had to pull a little bit and it worked perfectly. When it came time to load two of them jumped up in the truck and wouldn't let me do anything but run the hand truck. They sure were good fellows and said, "You have been working all day, now you just put it where you want it, we will do the rest," and they did.

I never had it so good. We were loaded in record time. It got pretty dark before we got done but we were able to finish. When we did the owner said, "You all come to the house for supper." I started to tell them goodbye when he said to me, "Where are you going?" "I am going to Yakima," I said. He said, "Well, I meant for you to come too." I protested but he would have none of it.

We all went to the house, met his wife, washed up and sat down to eat. The owner could hardly wait for his wife to sit down with us to tell her about the look on my face when they showed me where I was to go down the hill with the truck to load. Everyone, including myself, had a big laugh. We had a delicious meal – they made me feel comfortable and I really enjoyed it. It was one of the good days, even if I didn't get home till late.

Jack got the bright idea that I could haul feed to Connell when I went there for a load of wheat, and did not have a load for White Bluffs. He mentioned it to me. I told him it would not work, as the ferry was fully loaded with just the empty truck. He wanted to do it anyway, saying to take half a load, about seven tons. I worried all the way to the ferry. I didn't say anything to the operator. It was the spring of the year; the water was high and swift. When I pulled on, I thought the front of that ferry would never stop settling down in the water. The ferry man finally signaled for me to stop. (He had to tell me how far to pull ahead as I could not see the front over the hood of the truck).

I took every bit of room between the front and rear ramps. He had a hard time pulling me off of the beach, but he did and did we ever settle down into the water. He went up stream about a half a mile along the shore and then cut out into the current. We slowly made our way across as we drifted down stream rapidly.

When we finally got near the other shore we were down below the landing about a half mile. We took a long time getting back up above the landing because the current was stronger on that side of the river. There was a big rock just above the landing and also some just below. It was a feat to navigate between the two when the river was lower with not so much current, but now I could see we were going to have a problem.

He was a very good operator and got sideways to the current, drifting downstream. Just before we got to the opening between the two big rocks sticking up out of the water, he gave his engine full throttle straight ahead. We got part way to the shore but drifted sideways into the rock on the downstream side and could go no farther. We were stuck about twenty feet from shore.

The ferry man got a couple of long pike poles and we both pushed against the down stream rock as hard as we could. Slowly we were able to get the ferry about three feet off the rock. I kept pushing while he ran to the other side of the ferry where the engine was, but by the time he got fired up we had drifted against the rock again.

The current was so strong I could not hold it by myself. We did it again; this time we gained a couple of feet. We had to stop to rest a little while and then did it again. We kept this up till we finally got the front of the ferry into the sand and it would go no farther.

We had to take a rest – we were both about all in. The beach was eight or ten feet away yet, but due to the added weight of my load, we were not going to get any closer. He said, "If I could I would take you back where we came from but we won't be able to land there either."

He let the front ramp down as far as he could and the water was still about three feet deep. He had a plank on the ferry, which we used to get ashore. He had some driftwood in a pile off to one side. We started carrying wood and old fence posts and all sorts of pieces of scrap lumber to try to fill the deepest part of the gap. We gathered up all that was around there. We sized it up and it didn't look good. What were we to do?

We talked it over and made a joint decision. I would try to drive off. If I got stuck he would have to go somewhere he knew of to see if he could get a heavy tractor to pull me out of the river. This prospect didn't sound too good, as it would be expensive and would take at least half a day. Then, too, there was the trailer that might high-center. We had to do something; it was not going to get any better by itself.

We decided I would drive off as fast as I could. He would open up the throttle of the ferry engine wide open to hold the ferry up against the beach. I would rev up the truck engine as fast as I dared and let the clutch out and try to jump the truck off on that pile of wood we had between us and the shore.

He got ready and he gave me the signal. I opened my throttle almost wide open. I took a deep breath and dropped the clutch out as fast as I dared. Off the front end, I went and didn't go too far down, and about the time it hit the beach the rear wheels hit the wood. I was scared stiff but it did keep going and I felt solid ground under me. The wood and water flew in a big shower but we kept going. It was a rough ride but it sure felt good when it was over with.

I helped the ferry man pick up the mess, some of which floated down the river. He said when we were all done "Well, that was some experience wasn't it? Were you as scared as I was? Don't ever come back over here again with anything in that truck. If you do I won't take you across." "I will assure that as far as I am concerned it will not happen again, I don't want any more of that," I told him. "Neither do I", he said. It took us about three hours and it was plenty scary.

The day before Christmas in – I think it was 1935 – I was sent to Ellensburg, Cle Elum, Ronald and Easton with a full load. I was hopping to get in a little early that afternoon as it was Christmas Eve.

No way – it had been arranged for me to pick up about half a load of wheat out west of Cle Elum to bring back to the mill. I finished unloading and started out to get the wheat and it started to rain. The temperature was about twenty degrees, and when it fell, it froze into ice immediately and was getting slick. I found the place to load and by this time, it was beginning to get mighty slick. I got all the wheat they had, about half a load, and started out.

It was still raining and freezing. By now, everything was ice. I had little trouble with traction, as I kept my speed slow and as long as the road was straight things went ok. I did, however, have trouble seeing, as the rain was freezing on the windshield, and anything else it came in contact with. When I got to the main highway, where the pavement headed south, it was a disaster – a smooth sheet of ice. Everybody was going very slow.

I had no heater, no defroster. The windshield would freeze over and I would have to pull over and clean it off. When I would get out to do so it was hard to stay on my feet it was so icy.

I noticed, as I met some of the trucks coming at me, some of them had what appeared to be little short candles on the dash, heating the windshield, and they could see. When I got to Ellensburg I stopped to see if I could buy some but they were sold out. I got down the road to where the road started down the Yakima River canyon, which was crooked and had a lot of hills to go up and down. It was still raining and freezing. There was a little service station there so I stopped to see if I might find a candle – no luck here either. The proprietor and his wife lived in the back; his wife was there and overheard me. She volunteered the information that she had heard an onion slice rubbed on the windshield would help to keep ice from freezing.

She sold me a big onion and sliced it in two for me. There was a man and a woman standing around there who asked me if I was going to Yakima and if they could ride with me. They were trying to get to Grandview that night to be with relatives for Christmas. I felt bad but had to tell them I was very sorry but the truck insurance would not allow me to carry riders. Too, I told them, under the conditions I was not sure I would even get to Yakima myself.

I rubbed the onion on the windshield and started out. It did help a little but not for long. After about four or five miles I had to stop to clean the windshield. It was so slick that I would have a hard time standing up. After the second or third time I stopped I looked back and I had a string of cars and trucks back of me. When I stopped they all stopped, no one would go around me so that I might be able to follow their lights for a ways anyway... no way.

When I stopped, which was frequently, they stayed right in line. I got so I just stopped right in the road without pulling over because it was simpler than trying to guess where the edge of the road was.

We finally got to Yakima and to the mill, about seven o'clock, and backed up to the mill loading dock. The office lights were all on and when I went in, here was the crew and the boss all drinking and rolling dice. They were all in a feel-no-pain state of mind, feeling very foxy and gay. They all spoke almost in unison, "Where have you been? You have missed all the fun."

Yeah! Where had I been? Here I was, still scared half stiff, all tensed up from having driven a big rig on thirty five miles of glare ice, the other half of me about frozen stiff from the cold, and my eyes about to pop out of my head from the strain of trying to see where the road was. I was cold, tired, hungry, and sober. I wasn't in much of a mood to be made fun of by a bunch of drunks.

Just about then, the phone rang. It was Jack's wife, Ruth. At that time, on the main street of Yakima, there were gutters along the street side of the curb that were about sixteen inches deep and about a foot wide. The cars angle parked. Ruth had been downtown and when she had started to back out into traffic she had dropped a front wheel in the gutter, as it was so slick, and she was stuck. She had to leave the car and take a cab home and was waiting for Jack to show up.

When he got off the phone he said he wanted everyone to go down to help lift the front end of the car out of the gutter. He looked around and decided that I should drive, which turned out to be a wise decision. It was just about the last thing imaginable I felt like doing about then, but he was the boss. I said I would take my truck as the engine was already warm and I had a pretty good deal of weight aboard for better traction, and, too, the guys could scatter some of the sacks of wheat around to sit on.

When we got there, everyone jumped out and lifted the front end of the car up and someone straightened the front wheels out. As this was being done, the guys were making a lot of noise and laughing, when a police car came along and stopped to see what all the noise was about.

Right away, they said, "You guys are all drunk; who is driving?" I spoke up and said, "I am, we are just leaving. Everybody in the truck." The cops said to me, "Are you sober?" I assured them that I was and that I would take care of everything. I had a little trouble convincing Jack that he too should get in the truck and not to argue with me or the police. I finally got them all loaded and we went back to the mill. I had Jack riding in front with me and when we got back to the mill, he was cold.

He said. "Boy, I am cold." I took advantage of the opportunity and said, "Yes, I'll bet you are. I am too. In fact, I have been cold all day long, I can hardly wait to get home to get warm." I could hardly believe my ears as I heard him say, "You need a heater in this thing, we will get you a heater right away." I had caught him in a benevolent mood.

Sure enough, the next week he kept his word and I was given a hot water heater (which at that time was a new device) to put in , with the admonishment to put it in on Sunday and not to tell Fred, the other truck driver, as he would want one too. Well, I did a little inquiring around during the week to see how they were installed and put it in on Sunday, as that was when I had to do all the work on my truck anyway.

Home at last, Christmas Eve, and was I ever glad to get there! My little family was glad to see me too. They never knew what my day had been like, but thankfully it all turned out to be a joyous occasion. We were all together and happy.

Chapter 43

I had some other experiences that made my life interesting for me on occasion during my truck driving career, such as having to carry about two tons of flour and feed on my back for a whole city block. There was a driving storm and because the snow was so deep I couldn't get the truck up that street in the little town of Ronald, about three miles farther up the road into the mountains beyond Roslyn.

Another time I was in the trailer unloading feed at a feed store in Ellensburg when a man came around to the back where I was, all excited, saying your truck is on fire. That got my attention right away. I jumped out and rushed around to the front, and sure enough, the smoke was pouring out from under the hood.

I raised up one side and the wiring was all smoking. The man had a box of household baking soda in his hand and said to put that on the burning wires. For lack of anything better I scattered that around the flames, and it did help. I was able to get a shovel and throw dirt on the rest of it till I got it out.

When I got ready to go the truck would not start. I had to walk up town to an auto supply store, buy some new wire, and replace quite a bit of the wiring under the hood and some under the dash. When I got done, it ran. I lucked out again.

I was approached several times by other truck drivers while making Deliveries, about joining the Teamsters Union. Yakima was being organized at the time by the Teamsters, so I approached Jack about the subject. He said it was out of the question and that no one was going to tell him what wages he would pay and that was it. I knew I was going to have trouble sooner or later but he had no sympathy for me. I didn't know what to do about it so didn't do anything.

Sure enough, one morning as I was pulling out of town with a load a car with four big, burly fellows in it drove up beside me, blowing the horn and motioning for me to pullover. At first I tried to ignore them but they kept crowding me, forcing me to pull over or run into them. I pulled over and stopped. Before I could even get out there were four great big guys at the drivers door telling me to get out, they wanted to talk to me.

I got out and they surrounded me. I thought for sure they were going to work me over. They wanted to know when I was going to join the union.

They went on to say that I had been approached by warning, and that if I continued to ignore them I would be in real trouble. They gave me an ultimatum, that if I didn't make application to join the union within ten days I would suffer the consequences. I didn't bother to ask what the consequences would be. I didn't need to. A milk delivery man had been found dead in an alley in downtown Yakima early one morning and as far as I know, the murder had never been solved.

I told Jack about what had happened. I also told him I would have to join or quit the job, which I sure didn't want to do. It was decided that I would join the Teamsters but my pay would not change. I made application and was accepted, becoming a member of Teamsters Union 524. After awhile I was contacted by the union business agent and told to bring my pay check in every pay day to the office to verify the fact that I was getting union pay scale, which of course I wasn't.

Jack told me they would make out my pay check from the mill, paying the proper scale, which I could show to the Teamsters, then when I cashed the check I would refund the difference to the mill, which I did. Boy was it hard to pay back that money after payday. I had no choice, like it or not.

Well, life went on; we moved from Mr. Barret's house to a little better house with a little more room but not much. After awhile we found we were going to have an addition to our little family and would require more room than we had where we were. We got a place with two bedrooms, a nice front yard with a hedge around it where Charlie could play, and a place in the back for a garden. It was a nice-looking place after I got it cleaned up, but it was as bad as a tarpaper shack for holding heat, in the winter time. In fact, it was the coldest house we ever had the misfortune of living in during our entire married life.

This brings to mind an incident that occurred while we lived there. One Sunday during the winter we went for a little ride so Agnes could get away from the house a little. There was a glassed-in back porch on the back side, where the back door opened. Someone had an idea to have a washing machine out there and had run a water pipe up with no faucet on it, for a washer.

I had no idea there was water in it. When we came back from our little ride, upon opening the door to go in, I was met with water – water everywhere.

The water pipe had frozen and chosen this time to burst. There was water in the back porch, the kitchen, and water in the front room. There was water in the cellar, under the house, everywhere.

Well, I got the water shut off and started to sweep it out the back door and the front door. The partition between the front room and the kitchen supported the chimney, which was brick and quite heavy. It had made the floor in both rooms sag at the partition. There was a little pond there that went from the kitchen clear around through the door and behind the stove in the front room. I didn't have much luck trying to sweep the water up hill. I struggled with it for quite awhile and thought, there has to be a better way. Fortunately, I had a carpenter's brace and bit among my meager tool supply.

I took the brace and bit, bored a hole in the kitchen floor behind the stove where the low place was, and let the water drain under the house. I did the same thing in the front room. It worked fine; I stood happily by, watching my problem disappear like magic. I was soon rid of the water. Agnes said, "That is terrible, to bore two holes right in the floor, what are you going to do now?"

I had that part all figured out. I got a cork from the kitchen and put it in one hole, pushed it in good and tight, then cut it off flush with the floor and it didn't even show. I did the same with the other one, and that solved the water problem. Again, not a good way but a way.

In spite of this place being cold it was a nice place, with a screened-in front porch in the shade when it was hot, and we did enjoy our stay there.

Our baby was to be born in June, and we asked one of Agnes's sisters, Virgina (nicknamed Virgie), to come down for a visit during the summer vacation. She was in high school at that time and had no plans for the summer. When she came we asked if she would be interested in staying and working for the summer, and to be there when the new baby came, which she readily agreed to do.

This was a big load off my mind, as I was still driving truck and never knew when I would be home. This worked out well for all of us and she stayed all summer, going home when school started.

Fortunately, one night about midnight Agnes woke me up, announcing that she was going to have to go to the hospital. We went, and after a long night of pain and strain, our new baby was born. He was a dandy. Virgie was there to take care of Charlie and did a good job for us.

We named the new-comer Jack, after Agnes's Uncle Jack, and gave him the middle name of Armstrong after the famous general whose middle name was Armstrong. Jack was born June 16, 1936. I missed a day of work, so the big truck didn't go that day. I had to make up for it, though, as I had to put in longer days till I was caught up with deliveries.

The longer hours extended for several days and I had no way of getting to see Agnes, as when I got in at night the visiting hours at the hospital were over and the door would be locked. Virgie had no way to go see how things were going, and we were concerned and worried.

After about four days I thought something had to be done with regard to visiting my little wife and new baby. I worked as fast and as hard as I could one day and the best I could do to get to the hospital was about nine o'clock. Sure enough, the doors were locked. I had previously rung the door bell and when someone answered they would not let me in, telling me visiting hours were over, and that was that! Some way I was going to get in there if I could, but how? I went around to the back and looked things over. She was on the third floor and there was a fire escape that I could access.

It was dark by this time. Taking a good look around and seeing no one, up I went to the third floor. There was a window there and when I tried, it was unlocked.

I crept in as quietly as I could, and seeing no one in the hall I made my way to Agnes's room, where she was all alone. Needless to say, she was as glad to see me as I was to see her. Things were going well and the baby was just fine.

After a nice visit I started to go back to the window and was just about there when, out of a door came a Nun with a very surprised look on her face. She said, "What are you doing here and where did you come from"? I was dressed in my striped overalls and didn't have a look of a visitor I guess, and beside this it was late and the lights were turned down low for the night. I thought, "Now there is going to be hell to pay for sure."

I hoped they wouldn't send me to jail but I might as well tell it like it is and see what happens. I explained to the sister in detail, the circumstances, while she listened patiently till I had finished. She then said, "I understand your dilemma and I really feel sorry for you. From now on, if the door is locked, you have my permission to come in the way you did this evening. If you have any trouble just tell them you have my blessing. I am the Sister Superior, God bless you and your family." With this, she left and so did I. At this time, I don't remember if I had to enter this way again or not.

Lawrence, Agnes's brother, came to Yakima to work in his uncle's mill, and boarded with us for awhile, then got a place of his own for awhile, then moved back in with us. Things went along for some time without anything exciting happening. The regular warehouse man at the mill quit, leaving a vacancy in the crew.

I had had enough truck driving to take care of me for the rest of my life by this time. I was tired of the long, hard hours of overtime I had to put in, when the warehouse man got the same pay as I did. I had to work harder than anyone else too. I took care of the truck on my own time and never got an hour off to show any appreciation for all the extra effort. I told Jack I wanted the warehouseman's job, and since I had been there quite awhile I felt I was entitled to it.

This did not go over well at all, I could see. A truck driver by the name of Ballinger had just been laid off by a friend of Jack's who had a trucking business and was forced to reduce his forces because of a lack of work. This friend had called Jack to see if he knew of any work, as this was an exceptionally good employee and he needed work. This all happened at just the right time and he was hired to take my place. I took the new man to every customer I delivered to, and covered every inch of the routes I drove, even to hauling wheat from

Connell and the ferry. I could not help but think, what a difference in the way they wanted me to break him in and the way I got broken in.

Ballinger was a good man and a nice fellow, as well as a good driver, but I could see that things were going to be different when he took over. In fact he told me he would not work that hard and would not put in all the extra hours without getting some time off in return to help make up for it.

I got the warehouse job and went home at quitting time like everyone else. Life got better; in fact, I even had time to work in my garden after the change in jobs. I could see, though, that the attitude toward me had changed a little. It was costing more for the delivery and I knew I was missed. I knew my time was probably running out on me. That seemed to be the pattern there and sure enough, the boss, Jack, Agnes's uncle, and I got in to a little argument one morning and he told me I was through.

I left the mill and on my way home I stopped by the Northern Pacific Railroad depot where the division head office was in Yakima, and applied for a job. The man I talked to liked me and said he thought he could give me a job as a fireman on a steam-powered locomotive. That was before diesel power was in use. That is what I was wanting.

He had me fill out an application and we had a long talk. He wanted to know what I had done in the line of work and so forth. I told of my experience running the steam engine in the sawmill on Fitzgerald Creek. When I finished the application I handed it to him and he looked it over approvingly, saying it looked good and that he thought he could put me to work right away. Boy, my spirits went up. He took the application and kind of reviewed it and then said, "Oh-oh!"

He had looked at my age and saw that I was twenty six years old. He said, "I am so sorry, I cannot hire you, you are too old. Twenty five is our top age limit." I was stunned! I had just had a birthday a few days before, when I had turned twenty six. The man said, "I am sorry, I wanted you and I know you would be a good man for the job."

What a letdown. I went home and told Agnes about what had happened, feeling pretty dejected. We sat down to talk things over. She suggested, why not move back to Spokane as we had no ties in Yakima particularly. We had regretted having to move to Yakima in the first place just to get a job. We talked it over first and the more we talked the more we liked the idea.

Agnes was delighted at the prospect of getting back to Spokane again and was in a very cooperative mood, which helped my spirits considerably. Before noon we were making plans to move. We decided that since I had to find another job, I might as well look for a job in Spokane where the prospects would be better.

I did some inquiring and found we could ship our belongings by rail in wooden crates or boxes. This was a lot cheaper than any other transportation and they would pick up and deliver door to door. There were no rental trucks or trailers in those times. That helped us to make that decision and we got busy.

I got some cheap lumber with the car and made some crates for some of the bigger items. They were not very pretty but they worked and made the trip, and that was all we needed. We were in apple country. Apple boxes were cheap and plentiful and were made of wood. I bought some and packed a lot of stuff in them and they shaped very well. I made arrangements with a second-hand dealer to buy what we were not going to take, and in a day or so we had things shaping up.

It was August, the weather was warm and we could leave the doors open, which helped somewhat. It took some planning, but we managed to make everything come out even, got utility bills paid and had everything that was to be shipped gone. We got everything loaded in the car that we were taking in the car.

We had a nice garden and we were getting tomatoes and other produce from it. We had picked all that would keep and that we had room to take. We told the neighbors they could take what was left. Agnes had saved out food for our supper, which we ate standing up, as we had nothing left to sit on.

It was a nice evening and the sun was just about to go down. Agnes fed baby Jack; we had a nice soft place fixed for him just in front of the rear window. She tucked him in for the trip. Then we put some last-minute things between him and the top of the front seat. We got in, with Charlie sitting between us, and we were on our way. The old car was loaded to the roof.

I planned it so we would drive at night so it would be cooler because of the heavy load we had. It was about eight o'clock in the evening. We were headed into the unknown again, but this time with two more responsibilities than before. I was worried, but never let on, as my little partner had her own responsibilities to take care of. Finding a way to make a living and a place to live was my job, which weighed heavily on me at the time.

We took it easy and in a couple of hours we pulled over to the side of the road for a rest stop and to check on our baby, as we could not see him from the front. That is what you did in those days. There were no rest stops. You waited till no cars were coming and did what you had to do. We had it all figured out, how to check on little baby Jack without having to unload a bunch of stuff on the side of the road. We had a flashlight and just looked in the rear window. There he was, laying on his back sound asleep, enjoying the rumble of the car.

We got along fine and pulled up in front of Agnes's mother's house about seven in the morning, after several rest stops during the night. Everyone was tired but Jack. After a change of a diaper on him, he was ready to see what was next. I unloaded the car and went looking for a place to rent for not much money, as we sure didn't have very much. Good old Mom said we could stay with her as long as we wanted to, but I couldn't think of that. I assured her, just long enough for us to find something of our own. I was determined that would not be long.

I looked for something suitable but found nothing that we could afford. Late in the day, I stopped in to see a friend from high school, Norman de Pender, who was living with his folks. He was going to Gonzaga University, studying law, but was not home yet.

I visited with his mother till he came and we talked about me needing a place to live. His mother said to him, "What about that place on eleventh that has been vacant for awhile?" He said, "It is for sale I think." I said, "I can't buy a place, I need to rent something." Mrs. de Pender said to Norman, "Look at it and see if it would be a good investment and buy it for an investment. Frank (Norman's dad) and I will help you if you need help. And if it works out you can rent it to Chuck.

When Frank got home, he said yes, they would do that for Norman. If he wanted to be a landlord it would be a good way for him to get a start. I said it will have to happen pretty fast, as I have some freight in the railroad depot that I will have to take delivery of soon. Mrs. D, as we called her, called the depot and sure enough, they had my freight there. They said they would keep it there for a few days before they would start charging me storage. de Penders said they would get on it in the morning.

I went back to Mom's house with some hope of having a place but could not sit back and wait. I looked for a place the next day but came up with nothing, but I kept looking. In a couple of days Mrs. D called and said it was a go deal and that we would be able to look at the place and talk to Norman about renting it from him.

We went to see it and it was a nice house with plenty of room on one floor and two rooms upstairs. Norman got the house and we agreed to rent it for fifteen dollars a month. We were able to take possession right away and the railroad delivered our freight to us. We had a home again.

The place needed cleaning up, painting, and new linoleum laid in the kitchen, and some other work which I agreed to do along with the rent. Norman was to supply the necessary material.

Fear

Along in the middle of the night, after we had laid linoleum on the kitchen floor after supper and I was dead tired and sound asleep, the following events took place.

We had taken everything out of the kitchen, even the kitchen cook stove (which was called a range), and a wood and/or coal burner, which was also very heavy. It was even heavy for a strong man and one small, willing wife for a helper. We had worked hard and late cutting and fitting, trying to get it to lay flat. We finally got it down the best we could but it still had waves in it from having been rolled up. It had to relax and creep into place gradually so to speak. We hunted around and put anything we could find on it to hold it down for the night. We had worked hard, it was late, and we were tired.

We had gone to bed. I was sound asleep when I was suddenly awakened by a not too gentle poke in the ribs with a sharp little elbow, and quiet whispering in my ear announcing that there must be a burglar in the house. This was not welcome news under the circumstances and while still more asleep than awake I tried to shrug it off by saying, let him go and maybe he will leave on his own.

I was so tired that my first inclination was to ignore him and go back to sleep. There was a persistent whispering in my ear. It finally dawned on me that something was going to have to be done.

I got wide awake and started to take an interest in what was going on in the kitchen. Agnes said, "Listen." I did, and heard noises as though someone was walking very slowly across the kitchen floor.

By now, I was taking more than a casual interest in things. I got up very quietly, going into the next room, which was joined by a door, which was open. This was the boys' bedroom and they were asleep. This room was next to the bathroom and connected by a door, which also was open.

The bathroom was next to the kitchen, with a door between, and it, too, was open. I looked into the kitchen from the bathroom doorway and could see quite well by the light from the street light. I paused there for awhile and could not see nor hear anything. I came to the conclusion that the intruder must have gone into the front room from the kitchen.

I went then to the doorway from the kitchen to the front room and looked in the front room. There, in front of the big front room window and crouched down, was the outline of a person. The light was poor there because of a big tree out in front of the house, which obscured my view to a great extent, but sure enough, there was someone there.

I had no weapon of any kind and I was not going to go in there empty Handed. I didn't want to monkey around either because I was afraid the person would see me and jump up, and I would lose my advantage. I looked around frantically for something to use.

The first thing I saw that was at all suitable was a vinegar bottle, about two thirds full, with a long neck. We had put on the linoleum to help hold it down till it got straightened out. Well, not exactly what I would have chosen had there been a choice, but as that was not the case I grabbed it up and decided I would sneak up behind the culprit as quietly as possible.

When I got close enough I would bring the bottle down on the back of his skull with full force. I figured he would then be lying face down, perhaps with vinegar in his eyes, and with a severe headache, and not be in much of a fighting mood for a little while at least. I thought I had it all figured out. I would have to hit him hard, not feel sorry about it. I thought, I must be quick. I would then jump on his back, get hold of both his hands and pull them up between his shoulder blades, shove one knee up against them to help hold them there, and then would have everything pretty well under control. I figured if I hit him hard enough I wouldn't have too much trouble.

I very carefully put my plan into motion. Everything worked fine, but just as I was getting into position and had the bottle high in the air a voice came from the suspect that I recognized as that of my wife. I do not have words to express my dismay at this sudden turn of events. In another instant, I would have done her in. I thought I had been scared before but that was nothing compared to the feeling that came over me then.

I started shaking. I could not say anything. I thought my knees were going to buckle under me. Agnes said, "What is the matter with you? Are you scared? You act like it, you are shaking."

She had gotten out of bed and come into the front room, unknown to me. She had crouched down to look out the big window so as to see better and not to create a shadow if there was someone prowling around outside.

When I got over the shock and could talk again we had a talk, and an agreement was reached then and there to the effect that there would be only one burglar-chaser working at a time. From then on, she would stay in bed so I would know exactly where she was. We came to the conclusion that the noise we heard was the new linoleum straightening out.

Chapter 44

The next thing was to find a way to make a living. I knew something about flour mills so I thought I had better look there first. I went to the General Mills plant on Sprague Avenue first. The man I talked to said he might be able to put me on Monday morning if I came back then, as I said I was experienced. That was encouraging.

I next went to a large feed mill and applied. The boss there said if I could sew sacks he was sure I could go to work Monday morning, as he had a sack sewer that he thought was leaving the end of the week.

This was, I think, a Tuesday, and rather than wait around till Monday I went to the Centennial Mill on Howard Street. I needed a job and some money now. I asked for the foreman and they said he had gone over town for a little while and would soon be back. I waited around for a little while and thought I might as well look around a little.

I went up in the mill and was looking it over when I came on a sweeper who spoke to me and seemed friendly. We talked a little and I, by chance, asked him what the pay was. He said, "Sixty cents an hour, and time and a half over eight hours in a day and over forty hours in a week." I thought, "Wow, I sure would like to get on there."

I went back down to the first floor to see if the foreman was back. He was, and I struck him up for a job, telling him I was experienced in mill work and could do almost anything around a mill. It was about eleven thirty in the morning. He was a crabby-looking guy and he was true to his looks. He looked me over with a critical sort of expression and said, "You have experience?" I replied that I had. He said, "If you want to go to work, be back here at one o'clock," and that was it.

I went home, ate a quick lunch, and was back in time. Everyone in the warehouse crew lined up and the foreman (it turned out his name was Art Schute) assigned them all what they were to do that afternoon. When he had that done he turned to me and said, "Follow me. He took a hand truck and wheeled it over to a stack of five sacks that were stacked one on top of each other. He slipped the blade of the truck under the bottom sack, pulled the top one back against the handles of the truck, tipped it all back and wheeled the stack of five over to a hole in the floor.

He then took the top sack off stood it on end, cut the twine the top was sewed together with, tipped the sack over, and dumped the wheat down the hole, that was connected to a bucket elevator taking it to a bin somewhere. He never said a word but went back and repeated the whole operation over again. I followed him along like a puppy dog and said nothing either. It was kind of amusing and yet at the same time kind of irritating too. It was obvious he thought I had no experience.

He then turned to me and said, "Do you think you can do that?" I said, "Yes, I think so." I felt kind of insulted that he did not believe me when I had told him I was experienced. He said, "If you have any trouble picking up any of the sacks of wheat some of the boys will help you lift the top ones up."

I was feeling just a little bit irritated by then. I said, "If they are piled right I won't have any trouble, and if I do I won't need any help. What are you paying?" He looked at me with a sort of surprised look and Said, "Forty cents an hour." I said, "I thought you were paying sixty." He replied, "We are starting at forty." I said nothing but thought to myself, "I will work till the end of the week and if I don't like it I will quit and go to the General Mills plant."

I took the hand truck and went to pick up a dump of wheat. The floor was nice and smooth, being hardwood, and slick. I was used to old, rough planks with knots sticking up in them. This was a piece of cake. The wheat was well stacked. I sort of enjoyed it. My knife was sharp and so I went to work.

I happened to look up after awhile and got a glimpse of Art peeking around a big wooden post at me. I never let on that I had seen him, just went on about my business.

After about a half hour Art came over where I was working with a time book in his hand and said, "What is your name?" I told him and he looked at me with the first sign of friendliness I had seen and said, "We will pay you sixty cents an hour." My stock went up; I knew then that he could tell a good man when he saw one and I knew that he believed me. I felt good about it, I was very confident. I could do anything anyone else could do around there I was sure.

The next day I was helping load cars of flour and unloading wheat, and got to know a few of the men. I liked them and they seemed to like me. I fit right in. When the first night after the first full day came I didn't say anything about quitting. I didn't want to. In fact, I didn't quit for thirty seven and a half years. Art was a tough fellow to work for but I never had any trouble with him.

I will here relate an incident that took place one day after I had been there for some time. Another fellow and I were unloading a flat car of cord wood. Cord wood is wood that has been cut in four foot lengths. This had been shipped in to fire the steam boiler for heat.

We were working at it when I had the misfortune of running a big sliver into my right hand. I could not get it out as it was stuck in there, and being right handed I was rather awkward with my left hand. I asked the other fellow to dig it out for me. He was holding my hand and trying to get it out when here came Schute. He said, "Get at the wood boys." I spoke up and said, "I have a big sliver in my hand and Matt is trying to get it out." Art never even slowed down but said, "Take it out at noon." That is the way it was and if I had said more I would have been fired right on the spot.

Art Schute and I became good friends as the years went by. I used to go visit him after he retired. His wife had died and he was very lonely and was always so glad to see me. If I had only known how lonely he must have been I most certainly would have gone more often.

When I went home that first night Agnes was all ears to hear how it went and what I thought of it, and if I was going to stay there. She was so glad to be back in Spokane and she wanted everything to go well so we would stay there. Well, we were back in business and back in Spokane again with no regrets, glad to be back again, and things were looking up. The year was 1937. We had been gone three years almost to the day. We were glad to be back in Spokane.

Times were tough and jobs were hard to get. I started hearing that usually during the winter the mill work slowed down and then there would be layoffs, and I was concerned. We made a lot of export flour for China and I could see that if those orders didn't come in things would get slow at the mill.

Sure enough, I was laid off one day a week, and it was an indication of what was to come. One nice fall day when I was not working I took the seat cushion out of the back of the car. We loaded up our little family and made a trip out to the valley to buy some produce to lay in for the winter.

In those days it was entirely different than it is now. Nearly everyone in the valley farmed, and in the fall there were all kinds of excess fruit and vegetables displayed along the road for sale. We bought a couple of boxes of apples, a couple of sacks of potatoes, some carrots, squash, turnips, parsnips, and cabbage. We bought all we could haul in the car. There was a good place under the front part of the house to keep all this supply.

It was a good thing we did because before spring we were mighty glad we had done so. I would work when there was work but the China export almost faded out entirely and work was sporadic for me. I looked for work but there was none. I looked everywhere. Once in a while I would pick up a day's work doing odd jobs that didn't usually pay very much, but I wasn't proud and took anything, for whatever they wanted to pay.

There was the famous WPA (Works Progress Administration) welfare work program. I finally gave up and applied to get on till things opened up again. I had to submit my work record and when it was discovered that I had left Yakima and had worked there for three years they said I was not eligible for the program, for me to go back to Yakima, as I had not lived in Spokane County long enough. Well, that was out. We said we would get by some way.

My brother Don had been working in the woods in Idaho, but he was laid off for the winter. There was no unemployment those days; it had not been started then. Don came to town and, as he had no place to go, he came to live with us.

We told him to move in; we might as well all starve to death together. He also looked for work, there was none. We ran out of wood for the heating stove and the cook stove. There was no money. Don and I went around to the vacant lots and trimmed the dead limbs off trees, gathered them up and carried them home. They were not a good source of fuel but it did keep us going. We had a lot of meatless stew that winter.

Don finally got on the WPA program and that saved us. He got the handsome sum of forty two dollars a month, for which he worked three days a week. Don gave us part of this for board, and with what I was able to pick up we were able to get by. Spring came and things picked up. I went back to work at the mill part-time and we got along till the next winter.

I knew I had a job and that eventually it would be paramount when and if I could just hang on. We were not too satisfied with the place we were living and Agnes kept looking in the paper for something else. She came across an ad for a place for sale over near the courthouse, for seven hundred and fifty dollars, six rooms. She showed me the ad and I just laughed at it. I said, "Too cheap. It must be some house for that money!" I wouldn't even bother to look at it. She kept bugging me to look anyway and she finally wore me down. I agreed to take a look just to please her. We did, and were we surprised! It was on Bridge Avenue, across from the railroad tracks, which were in a deep cut along there and were not in sight of the house. You could hear the noise though.

The place was old, but clean as could be and in good repair. Four rooms down and two upstairs. It had a small, fenced-in front yard and a nice fenced-in back yard with a lawn and a woodshed. There was plenty of room for the kids to play, and space for me to have a little garden, all fenced in the back yard. It was close enough for me to walk to work, with the added advantage of saving gasoline, as every penny counted in those days, and believe me, we were counting them.

Well, it was love at first sight. We contacted the realtor and it was not sold yet. There was only one catch; a one hundred dollar down payment was required. A hundred dollars was a lot of money, and we didn't have any money. What to do? Don was again working in the woods; I contacted him and he agreed to loan us part of the money – all he had in fact, as he had just gone back to work.

I was able to come up with only seventy dollars cash and that was all. I went to the realtor and told him we wanted the place very much but all the money I could raise was seventy dollars. I told him I would be working steady soon. I offered to give him a note for thirty dollars and would be able to pay it off soon. I gave him several character references, which he checked out. He called the owner and told her I was a nice-appearing man and that he was sure I was trustworthy and would be dependable. She agreed to let us have the place under those conditions.

The payments were twenty dollars a month. We signed the papers, gave the realtor the seventy dollars, and received permission to take possession. We moved in on the Fourth of July, 1938.

Our House on Bridge Street

It was great, the house was all freshly painted and we were so happy. We were anxious to get the money paid that we owed on the note, and also the money we had borrowed. I got steady work and we scrimped, not spending a dime that we didn't absolutely have to. There were a lot of things we needed for our new place but we got along and made do with what we had. We were used to doing without and before too long, with steady work, we were all paid up and we could relax a little and get ready for the next winter, when I was sure to get part-time work again.

Shortly after Christmas I was laid off part of the time. About the first of February, a new law came into effect called Unemployment Insurance. This is a standard benefit, now taken for granted, but was unheard of then. I was standing in line when the office opened for the first day's registration. My picture was in the paper that evening as being one of the first registering for the benefits of the new plan.

I was qualified and started receiving regular payments weekly. At this time I am not sure what the amount was, I think fifteen dollars a week, if I remember right.

We were able to get by and make our house payments. Later that year I went back to work steady. Then later on we found out we were going to have another baby. On January 30, 1940 a son was born to us, who we named James Patrick. He seemed to fit in without much disruption. Hardly knew he was around. I guess by this time Agnes must have had this new-baby thing down pat. I guess one thing different was that we had a bigger house and room this time.

I was working part-time again. We were getting by but there was nothing to spare. Virgie (now Mrs. Wanamaker), one of Agnes's sisters, was married to a service man who was in the regular Army. There were war rumblings about then and some troops had been sent to Alaska, well, rather to the Alaska Territory, Virgie's husband Joe among them. Virgie was living in a little house with her baby and was on a very tight budget. We needed someone to take care of the boys when Agnes had our expected new baby. We made a deal with her to come and stay with us. We would pay her to help around the house and take care of the kids while Agnes was gone, and also to help afterwards for awhile till Agnes got on her feet again.

When it came time I took Agnes to the hospital about ten in the evening, and Jim was born about five the next morning. When everything was taken care of and I determined I was no longer needed, that I could do no more and everyone was in good shape, I just had about time to make it to work. I rushed home, and while I got breakfast Virgie fixed my lunch and I was off to the mill. We were so hard up I didn't have money enough to buy a box of cigars to pass out to the crew I worked with, which at that time was the custom. I never said a word to anyone.

We got paid on Friday noon and when we did I made a fast trip over town to a cigar store, got a box of cigars, and ran back to the mill in time to pass out cigars to the boys before time to go to work. I don't think I had time to eat the lunch Virgie had packed for me if I remember right.

Everything worked out just fine, and after Agnes got on her feet Virgie moved back to her own place. She sure helped us out and helped herself out also as dollars were hard for her to come by also.

Everything went along pretty well for awhile. I was working part-time when I strained myself on the job and got a hernia. As it was job-related, I thought I should have it fixed so I went to the hospital and did have it taken care of.

In the meantime Agnes went to the doctor and it was determined she needed a thyroid operation to help reduce her blood pressure. What to do, no money? We talked it over and thought if some way she could have it done while

I was recuperating I could take care of the two boys if we just had someone to take care of the new arrival.

We still owed the bill for the new baby, as I didn't have enough to pay it all when we took him home. I went to the hospital and talked to the Sister Superior, explaining the circumstances. I told her I would be able to take care of things at home while Agnes was incapacitated and that I would pay the bills just as fast as I could if she would trust me, which she agreed to do.

Next, I went to the doctor and was able to make the same kind of arrangement with him. Olga, Don's wife, who had a new baby and who was a registered nurse, agreed to take our new baby, Jim, for a couple of weeks. So we proceeded with Agnes having her operation done. I took care of the two older boys, Charlie and Jack. We got along fine and it wasn't too long before we had our family back home again.

Little Jim did just fine under Olga's care and in fact he seemed to act kind of strange toward his mother when we got him home, which kind of hurt her feelings a little. It was so nice of Olga to help us out and I wasn't able to pay her anything for her trouble. I have since tried but she would take nothing; I will always be grateful to her.

Chapter 45

Some time in 1938 Centennial Mills had announced, in big headlines and a picture on the front page of the paper, that they were going to build a new flour mill. This was to be located on East Trent Avenue. It was to have more capacity than the present mill and would be the most modern in the world. This was big news, with a picture of the proposed structure on the front page of the paper. It was to cost a million dollars– that was a lot of money then.

This was going to be built on the speculation that there would be a lot of China export flour business. The plan was that with a new, modern mill they would be able to outbid other mills and get more business. Little did anyone realize that a war was going to change the world trade situation.

This was of course good news for me as I was sure that I would have steady work sometime in the future if I just hung on.

Sure enough, it wasn't long before ground was broken and construction started. It was a big job and the new mill was not put into operation till June 20, 1940. I was put on the afternoon shift in the warehouse, and was given the responsibility of taking care of whatever needed to be finished up from the first shift and whatever work the foreman designated for me after that.

I was told on the last day of work at the old mill, which was a Friday, what I would be doing. Well, I worried all weekend about how I would know how to get it all done. When I got there Art, the foreman, had about six new men for me and then I really was scared. I didn't know sickum, about the only thing I knew was where the toilet was, and the drinking fountain. I was really worried.

Well, before Art, the foreman, got me lined out for the shift I found out that he didn't know sickum either. He knew what he wanted to have done but didn't know how things worked or where anything was. I felt better. Talk about confusion!

Well, I got along as well as could be expected, learned the men's names, made a few little changes in the way Art had told me to do things, and when the shift was done I felt I kind of had a handle on things. The next day I wasn't scared to go to work anyway.

In a couple of days, when I got to work, Art and I had a talk. He filled me in on what was going on and then told me to just use my own judgment about what to do and to keep the men busy, and if there was not enough work, to have them sweep the floors or some other cleanup work. Well, I got along fine and, believe it or not, Art and I got to be friends.

After a month or so, things settled down and were running smoothly. People knew what to do and how. Some of the machinery had been modified and it was amazing how new machinery had to be changed to fit our needs.

The union, of which I was a shop steward, had made an agreement with the company that after things settled down jobs would be classified and would be put up for bid, and seniority would prevail as to the choice of jobs. I liked my job fine except I did not like the afternoon shift; I liked to be home in the evening with my family. I had been watching and thought I would like a job that I could learn, and then I could go ahead on my own and be left alone.

The grain elevator rather appealed to me and the job of sweeper came up for bid. I bid on that and got the job. Well, here again I didn't know how to run that big machinery but I knew I could learn and I did, when I got the chance. The foreman (a fellow by the name of Nick) and I got along real well and soon the other man that worked with him transferred to the feed mill and I was then in line for a better job, and by then I was able to handle it. I got the job of blending, transferring, washing, and binning all the wheat that went to the mill to be made into flour. It was my job also to transfer the barley, oats and corn that the feed mill used every day, from the elevator to the feed mill. It was a straight day job with a lot of responsibility, which gave me a feeling of accomplishment when I went home at night.

Early in my career at Centennial Flour Mill

After I was on the job awhile and understood it, I made some changes. And in a short time I became so proficient that I was given complete freedom and got my instructions straight from the scheduling source, and required no supervision whatsoever. I was on my own.

When the local wheat harvest started the next season Nick asked me if I would take charge of the wheat pit. I did, and from then on every harvest I was in charge of the farm wheat unloading, segregating the different varieties and allocating it to the proper bins. I did a better job than had ever been done before. I ran it, and nobody monkeyed with me, not even Nick the foreman. He would ask me what I wanted to do in some cases and I would tell him, and that was the way it was, just the way I wanted it. If I was going to be held responsible I wanted some authority and I had it.

My job at the new mill turned out just as I had hoped, but it took a couple of years time. We finally got a few dollars ahead and, with some assurance I would have a steady job in the future, we decided, or rather I decided, to do some remodeling.

Our kitchen was rather small and, as Agnes had plenty to do, I felt she deserved better quarters if I could figure out some way to accomplish it. I had no experience in that sort of thing but what I lacked in knowledge I made up for in courage and determination.

I didn't tell Agnes what my ultimate goal was because I knew she would ask me if I had ever done anything like that before and I would have to tell her no, and then she was going to tell me I couldn't do it because I didn't know how.

Well, I would already know that but sometimes I needed a little encouragement too. Sometimes I had a little doubt in my own mind and some reinforcement would have been welcome.

I told her I was going to make the back porch bigger, and then I was going to make a new stairway from the new addition to the cellar, which would require mixing concrete by hand in a wooden box with a hoe, and building forms to pour the concrete into while it hardened. Then I was going to lay up a stone wall and build a small roof and a new stairway with a different angle and a landing in it.

Sure enough, she said, "I hate to see you try all that when I know you don't know how. I am afraid it will be a mess and then what will we do?" "Well," I replied, "I know I don't know how but I'll bet I will know how when I get done," and get done I always did.

I added on to the back porch, making a new entrance and stairway to the cellar. I enclosed the whole thing, putting in windows that could be opened, with screens. "Next," I said, "I am going to tear out that small pantry, and make the kitchen bigger." Her reaction was, "What am I going to do for a place to put things?" I told her I would build cabinets. She was dubious but by then I guess

320

she had a little more faith in me, and also knew that it wasn't going to do much good to argue about it.

I tore out the pantry, moved the kitchen sink, moved the window, moved the bathroom door, put a wash bowl in the bathroom, and built in cabinets in the kitchen. Of course I didn't do all of this in one day, but I worked on it every minute I could.

When I got done, and painted it, Agnes had a nice, modern kitchen. She could stand at the kitchen sink and look out the window to watch the kids playing in the fenced-in back yard when the weather was nice. She also had a nice, screened-in back porch just off the kitchen.

It took me quite awhile because I didn't know how to do a lot of it, but I learned. I have never been short of ambition; I had patience when learning new things, I was diligent, I was determined, and I did not give up in despair. Was Agnes ever happy with the way it all turned out! She just loved her new kitchen with a sink under the window and all the nice built-ins. Still, she used to say to me sometimes when I was about to start a project, "You make me so nervous when you start something and I know that you don't know how to do it. I just wonder how in the world you will ever do what ever it is. I am always afraid you will not be able to get it done right and then what will we do?" Well my reply to that would be, "Oh ye of little faith, have faith in me."

It sounds as though we didn't get along very well, but we did. We had our own way; we pulled together and it worked for us and we loved each other. If it was broke, we fixed it. If we didn't know how, we learned. If we didn't have the means, we worked around it. We made it go, one way or another.

As the years went by, I took an active part in repairs at the mill, and when we had a break down, I was the one who took the initiative and took over. I either fixed it myself or got a millwright to fix whatever was needed.

The wheat washers required a lot of maintenance work as the mill was upgraded through the years and required more wheat for flour. I was keeping up but was running them way over rated capacity and the screens wore out fast. It was a miserable job and darn hard work, changing them. I worked at it till I got a method all my own and was real good at it.

The millwrights saw that I was getting a lot of overtime and decided that it was work that they should be doing. Well, it got to be a big hassle so I said, "All right, you guys go right ahead." Well three of them worked all one day and didn't get done. Since they wanted to do it so bad, I didn't offer to help. I just watched and stayed out of the way.

When quitting time came they were not done, but went home. They hadn't finished the job. I was waiting to start the washers up, as I still had half a day's work, washing and transferring wheat to the mill, to keep the mill running all night.

I went to the superintendent, who was still in the plant, and told him of the situation, and said, "What do you want me to do?" Boy, was he ever mad. He wanted to know what I could do. I told him I could finish the repair job all by myself, then take care of the mill needs, but it would take me most of the night. He asked if I would do it. I said sure I would but I didn't want any more hassles over whose work it was to keep the machinery running. I never heard another word.

Chapter 46

There were rumblings of war and the United States had been sort of preparing, but had taken no active part in the war that was raging in Europe. December 7, 1941 was the fatal day. It was a Sunday and I was home all day but we did not have the radio on for some reason or other. About seven in the evening the neighbors from next door came over and said, "Did you hear the news?" We said, "No, what is it about?" They said, "The Japanese bombed Pearl Harbor." I said, "Where is Pearl Harbor and who owns it?" Well, they filled us in on what they knew, which wasn't much at that time. Of course, we turned our radio on and got what news was available. No official announcements had been made and everything was confusion.

The Japanese had made a secret raid on our Pacific Ocean headquarters at Pearl Harbor at Honolulu, Hawaii, and we had severe damage to our Navy forces. About six months earlier all men had to register for a military draft if or when it was ever needed. After the registration there was a drawing and my number was fifty seven. That meant I would be called the very first thing.

I was quite sure I would be deferred because of my dependants, but it was no sure thing. I didn't sleep much that night. I didn't say anything to Agnes, there was no use in both of us worrying. If I was called up for induction what would she do? What would become of my family? We had no money saved up and three little kids. What would they ever do to get along on what little military pay I would get? And I wouldn't even be there to make decisions; I would be completely helpless. Who would take care of them till I would get back? What if I didn't get back? Boy, it made me sick to my stomach to think about it.

The next morning when I went to work, there was a man with a rifle in his hand standing at each end of the Trent Avenue Bridge that crossed the river, watching all the traffic. I wondered what was going on.

When I turned off Trent to go to the mill a man with a rifle stopped me and said, "Where are you going?" "I am going to work, what are you doing on the mill property?" I replied. He said he was a city fireman and had been there all night guarding the place, that the mill was classed as a strategic industry and the authorities had a fear that it might be blown up to hinder the defense effort.

I was shocked! I didn't know what to think. That mid-morning a fellow came out to the elevator and told Nick and me to shut everything down and come to the main office to a meeting. We went, and the plant superintendent was there to talk to us.

He said, "We are all faced with a very serious situation. I have called all you foremen and key men together to tell you that you are all from now on responsible for the safety of our plant, which is our livelihood."

He went on to say, "If any of you see any strangers in the plant that you do not recognize or who are not with an escort you recognize, stop them and escort them to the office and stay with them till they are cleared by someone with Authority, or escort them from the plant." Pretty serious stuff. He went on to say the authorities had called to say that we might be sabotaged, that anything might happen.

We were a sober bunch when we came from that meeting. I didn't envy him his responsibility. Little did I think at that time that some day I would be sitting in that seat with all the responsibilities, problems and authority.

I had been called in with the foremen and was treated as such, which was a surprise to me and that had an advantage that was not to be realized until later, when it paid off.

It wasn't long till the mill was busy making flour for the military. One day the superintendent came to the elevator and told Nick and me to work every Saturday, even if the mill did not run. He said, "I want you two guys to be here every day and I want this machinery to be in good working order at all times." He went on to say not to worry about working overtime, to use our own judgment. If we thought it necessary, just go ahead and do it, without asking him for permission. Boy, was that ever a surprise to us.

Overtime was much sought after in those days, as it paid time and a half. From that day on, as long as I was an hourly employee, I never asked whether to work overtime and neither was I ever questioned about it by that superintendent or any of the many that followed him.

One year during the war I had Christmas Day off and then worked every day after that until the next Thanksgiving, without a single day off. Many of those days were 10 or 12 hour days and some even as long as 18 hours. Nearly a year of working every day – Sundays, holidays, worked every day. After awhile I got used to it and when I only worked eight hours I almost felt as though I had a day off. That was war time. Men were hard to get, and many were no good when they showed up. We old timers were the ones that kept the place going.

Nick and I did ninety five percent of our own repair work. Nick didn't keep up on new developments and I did, or at least I tried to. I was interested and always have been eager to learn. As a result, it wasn't long till I took the lead on the maintenance work and often did it all by myself, which suited Nick just fine as he was not overly anxious to get up a sweat anyway, and sometimes I was in a hurry.

I learned how to weld by watching every chance I had. I was not a first class welder but I never did have a weld break either.

Every year during the local harvest I worked twelve hours a day taking in grain from the farmers. I worked hard at it and soon was able to do it quite efficiently. It might be of some little interest to the reader as to the procedure used when a farmer brings a load of grain to an elevator.

I devised a system and made some changes in the procedure that speeded things up. I first examined the load to see what it was: wheat, barley, oats, to see what kind of condition it was in, and to see what bin I wanted it to go to.

I did this by stepping up on one rear wheel and observing it, and maybe running my hand through the grain, feeling of it to determine if it was dry. I then got down and by this time the truck driver usually was out of the truck and would get off the scale. I was ready to weigh the truck and find out who the owner of the load was, make out a ticket and punch the weight on it. I then would make sure the previous load had cleaned out of the pit. I would shut the gate to the elevator, tell the driver to open the truck tail gate, and let the grain out. I would call the man upstairs to tell him what bin I wanted.

I would then raise the front end of the truck by means of an air hoist that I controlled with a handle, then grab a "sample" envelope, write the name on it, get a sample of the grain as it ran out of the truck, put it in the envelope and file it away. If by this time the man upstairs had called to say he was ready, I would open the pit gate and start the grain up to where it would go to the proper bin. I would then grab a broom, help clean out the truck, let the truck down to the floor again, weigh the empty truck, punch the weight on the ticket and present it to the driver and he or she was on his or her way.

I learned how to grade grain and judge the quality from studying and asking questions from the state grain inspectors when they were stationed at the mill. I was responsible for all the local grain that was received. When harvest was in full swing, we were busy all day long, sometimes till eight o'clock in the evening. Long, hot days.

At night, we had to move the grain out of the receiving bins, as to get ready for the next day. Another guy and I kept the wheat out of the way at night and made it all work. No one ever questioned my time. I was trusted and I appreciated it. It paid the company good dividends as I did a lot of work that I didn't have to, without compensation.

It worked for me also, as I enjoyed my freedom and did not have someone looking down my shirt collar all the time, telling me what to do next. I got my orders directly from the quality control lab and set my own pace. No one ever bothered me and they all knew as long as I was on the job things would be taken care of.

1942

It was 1942, the war was on, many of our men were gone, restrictions were being put on civilian's food. Gasoline, shoes, and various other items were being rationed.

We were learning how to adjust to it. Shortages were common. Meat was in short supply and sometimes unavailable altogether for short periods. There were no candy bars, sugar was rationed. Nylon had just come into fashion for ladies stockings but it immediately became unavailable for such frivolous things as stockings. There was a shortage of silk right away too as it was used in the war effort.

In those days, women did not wear slacks as they later did, and they had nothing to dress their legs with. There was soon coloring that would resemble stockings, in color at least. The ladies painted their legs different shades of color and went bare legged.

Cigarettes were hard to find. Loose tobacco was available so there was a lot of rolling your own done. Liquor was rationed, so was coffee. A short time later meat was rationed as well as many other things that I don't remember at the time of this writing. New tires could not be had without a permit from the rationing board, where proof would have to be shown that they would contribute to the war effort in some manner. If they were for personal use you were out of luck. I bought an old Chevrolet car because it had a set of new tires on it. I took them off and put them on my car. I then turned around and sold the old car for the same price that I had paid for it.

We had three boys and they had all been sick with scarlet fever, measles, whooping cough and whatever else came along. I even got the measles from them and was one weak, sick guy for a week.

Having been born and raised on a farm I had a longing to be in the country. I just seemed to have an idea that if we lived in the country where we would have a cow and chickens and lots of our own vegetables the boys would be healthier. I also wanted them to have more room for outdoor activities without being in the street. I also wanted them to have some chores to do to teach them responsibility when they got a little older. I had it and it was good for me. I wasn't having much luck promoting these ideas around home. Agnes did not think the country was a good idea.

The wheat harvest was winding down. I got talking to a farmer from the valley one day who was delivering wheat, and asked him if he knew of a place that was for rent, that would have room for a garden and a place to keep a cow. He said he had a place on his farm with a good house and barn that was vacant. He said he could cut out an acre of land for me for a garden. He told me where it was located and said for me to go out and take a look at it when I had time.

Labor Day 1942 came and I did not have to work – the first day off for awhile. I told Agnes we were going to look at a place out in the country to rent. I said, "Let's just look and see what we think and if it looks feasible we can maybe rent for awhile and then if it works out and if we like it then maybe we can buy something." Agnes did not like this one little bit, but agreed it would not hurt to look, but no way was she going to move to the country.

Labor Day came and we went to look. The place was on Barker road, south of Sprague a mile or more, which seemed a long way. We looked at it, but I could see by the landscape that it could be a tough place to get out of if we got much snow. Barker was a county road and would probably not be plowed regularly. Work was always a very important element in my life, and I thought it important to be there and on time. Well, this place was out.

On our way back to town we saw a place with a home-made sign out in front –For Sale – right on Sprague in Veradale. It was a very run down old place with a bunch of unpainted buildings and some old machinery in the yard near a yard barn. The house looked habitable but just barely.

There was some vacant land there all grown up with weeds. This was right on Sprague Avenue. I drove past it and then turned around to take another look. I thought I might be able to afford it because it was such a mess, and it was right on the road. I would be able to get out, in bad weather. Sprague was a four lane state highway to the east coast. "Boy," I thought, "I had better look into this."

I pulled over, parked and went to the house, which was occupied, and inquired. The lady there said the owner was the man who owned the fruit stand across the street and west about a block. I went there and talked to a Mr. Shardlow, saying I might be interested in purchasing the place if it was within my price range.

He said, "I am very busy but I guess I can take a little time to talk to you. What did you have in mind?" I told him briefly, "A house large enough and suitable for our family, room for a large garden, a place to keep a cow, and a place for some chickens."

He pondered that for a little and said, "We might be able to work that out, let's go over and size it up and see how it looks to you." (It turned out he owned a number of acres, including the portion where the house was located.) This we did, and took a walk through the house, which was rented at the time.

The house was old and unpainted. The inside was clean but needed refurbishing, but I could see possibilities. I could see where we could make it quite comfortable. It had enough room, with a three quarter unfinished basement with a dirt floor. We looked at the barn and the other out-buildings.

The barn could be used just fine for a cow, with plenty of room to store hay. There was an assortment of other sheds and various shelters of doubtful use but one could be fixed for a chicken house. There was even an outhouse in good shape.

We looked at the land and he pointed out where the irrigation water would run down to a low place in back, and said he wanted to sell the land down to that point. It amounted to about an acre we guessed.

The property was one hundred fifty feet of frontage on Sprague. One drawback was that it had its own water system, with a one hundred foot deep well and an old worn out pump with a five hundred gallon water tank in the basement for storage.

I asked him what kind of a price he had in mind. He said he wanted twenty one hundred dollars for what we had looked at. I told Mr. Shardlow I would talk it over with my wife and would let him know before the week was out, what we thought about it.

I went back to the car and got Agnes to come to the house to look it over. She was somewhat less than enthusiastic about the prospect of leaving her newly remodeled house in town and moving way out in the country.

I wanted the place. I could see a lot of hard work for both of us but a place right on the avenue? I would never in my lifetime be able afford a place with all first-class improvements on it. I figured I could overcome the problems if I had a chance. There were many, such as the well, and getting the irrigation water on the place. Getting the land ready to cultivate, tearing down the old buildings, remodeling the house and barn, and many other things would have to be done. But I was full of ambition in those days and I was eager to try it.

I didn't bother to point out all those things to my wife, as I was afraid she would be discouraged before I even had a chance and would quash the deal, and that would be the end of it. I did, however, point out to her that the bus ran right in front of the house, that the boys would have plenty of room to play right on their own place, that they would only have a half mile to walk to school and the church was only three quarters of a mile away.

I took great pains to point out any other advantages I was able to come up with. This was the chance of a lifetime I figured. I had visions of having a nice place some day. We had two hundred dollars in the bank, and the house in town we now owned free and clear. I had my work cut out for me, two jobs: first to sell Agnes on moving out there and second to talk Mr. Shardlow into selling me the place for two hundred dollars down and the rest on contract.

First things first: I told Agnes of all my ideas, and what a wonderful place it would be for the boys to grow up. I told her of the opportunities for work when they got bigger, of jobs that would be available to them. I pointed out to her all the things we could grow. I told her about having all the milk we wanted, chickens and eggs, everything I could think of that would be good, which all turned out to be true.

I wanted her cooperation and partnership. I wanted it to be a joint venture before we made a deal. It had to work for us both. She consented to go for it and I got in touch with Mr. Shardlow. He agreed to sell us the place on the terms I proposed. We met with him, paced off the land, and agreed on the meets and bounds. We shook hands and it was a deal. We didn't even have it surveyed. We hired an agent to make out the paperwork the way we wanted it, split the cost and that was it. He gave notice to the renters to vacate and gave us a position date.

The weather was good and we could hardly wait, as it was fall and we were anxious to move before the weather turned bad, which we were able to do.

Chapter 47

We moved to the valley, 14225 E. Sprague, on October 23, 1942. All my dreams came to be a reality slowly, over a period of time. This is where we lived for the next fifty three years. It was a good move and turned out to be a good investment. It did take a lot of hard work but it was worth it. It was a way, maybe not a good way, but a way and it worked. It was a wonderful place to raise our family and if our taxes had not become almost prohibitive, we would have spent the rest of our lives there.

Our new house on Sprague
Agnes and I lived here for 53 years

The boys loved the new place. They thought they were really out in the country and had a great time exploring the eleven old buildings on the place. There was plenty of room for them to play.

This changed our lives. Charlie and Jack were enrolled in the Veradale Grade School, which gave them a half-mile walk to school. The bus ran right in front of our place and all you had to do was stand there till it came along and it would stop right in front of you.

I drove my car for a short while and then teamed up with a man who lived out beyond us and also worked at the mill. If I was lucky and only had to work a regular eight-hour shift I could ride home with him. However, if I had to work overtime I would walk over to Sprague and catch a bus home. Sometimes during the war I would stand there to catch a bus and it would be full and I would have to wait half an hour for another one.

I sure hated that in the wintertime when it was cold or wet and I would be tired. Otherwise it worked till the war was nearly over. We got some rabbits for the two oldest boys, so they had some chores to do from early on.

Before spring came I got busy and tore down some of the old buildings, making room for a big garden, which I planted. Our cow had a calf, we bought a couple of wiener pigs and feed, and we were in the farming business. We bought some baby chicks and I made a brooder to keep them warm till they got big enough to fend for themselves in the chicken house with the big chickens. We fed the weeds from the garden to the pigs, along with feed that I got from the mill.

I made a deal with the mill to clean up feed that sometimes blew out on top of the roof when the feed mill machinery plugged up. I had to sack it up on my own time, but the price was right.

In the summertime we could picket the cow on the end of a long chain fastened to an iron stake driven in the ground, which we would move to different spots morning and night so she could have fresh grass. We would take her out in the morning and bring her down in the evening to be milked and get a drink of water, then take her back, move the stake and leave her for the night.

All the land from the back of our place to Valleyway was vacant, as the man who owned it, Mr. Shardlow, was not farming it at that time and gave us permission to use it.

I was busy, I can tell you. I tore down old buildings, cleaned up rocks off the ground that we were going to use for the garden, built a new chicken house, had a three-car garage built, and hauled junk and rocks to the dump in a two wheeled trailer behind the car, among other things.

My boys, Jim, Charlie and Jack, at our new place in the Valley

As I mentioned earlier, the superintendent told Nick and me to work every Saturday from then on as we must have the equipment in good working order at all times, and if need be we were to work Sundays too. He said not to bother with permission, just use our own judgment. This gave me less time at home, but it did give me more money to use.

The mill ran all the time it could, and of course if it wasn't running they were repairing, and so was I. Then when the mill ran I had to transfer wheat for them to grind.

In the spring of 1943 I planted our first garden – a big one that had to be irrigated from a ditch that ran along one side of our property. We got two hours of water in the ditch every week. The two hours was made available any two hours out of the twenty four in the day or night. If you didn't take it when it was assigned to you by the ditch rider who notified you in person or by phone twenty four hours in advance, you lost it. If you lost it there was no more till your time came around the next week.

Irrigating the garden and the front lawn took attention because there was only so much water that would come down the ditch. We made little ditches (called rills) between the rows of plants and would only have enough water for about six rills at a time. To open a rill you used a shovel and moved a little dirt aside, so the water could run in to that particular rill. When the water had made it to the end of a row, you put the dirt back to make a little dam to shut the water off from that rill. When a rill was opened, it took some time for the water to get to the far end of a row or rill.

When it had, the water had to be diverted to another and so on. It kept a person busy all of the two hours to get everything watered. (I called it shoveling water.) We would only barely have enough time to get it all done, so one had to give it their full attention. It was quite interesting when your turn came at one o'clock in the morning and it was pitch dark. There were no batteries for a flashlight during the war. I was lucky to find an old second hand kerosene lantern to work with at night.

It took some dexterity to hold the lantern in one hand, tilted to one Side, and work the shovel at the same time. If the lantern isn't tipped you can't see the ground beneath it, as the fuel tank is on the bottom and casts a shadow usually right where you need the light. They don't give much light to begin with and when you are walking around in the middle of the night about half asleep in the mud and water the last thing one needs is a lesson in acrobatics. When the water came in the daytime Agnes had to learn how to do it, which she did, and became very good at it and did a good job.

I think I mentioned earlier that we had a well on the place when we bought it. That was where we got our water supply for the house, the cow, chickens, and all other needs except the garden. The well was ninety eight feet deep and ninety three feet to the water. It was cased with corrugated road-type culvert and was five inches inside diameter.

In earlier times there had been a windmill that pumped the water, as the place was an original homestead before any electricity was available. When, after a good many years presumably, it played out for whatever reason, a single cylinder gasoline engine was hooked to the pump jack (a device that was bolted to a push-pull rod in the pump itself).

This arrangement was used for some period of time and then was converted to an electric motor that drove the gas engine that drove the pump-jack that pumped the water into the basement under the house, into a five hundred gallon water tank. That was then pressured by a small air compressor on top of the water tank which kept the pressure up in the tank to push water into the water lines. This all required daily attention, nothing was automatic. It worked most of the time, till some part in the chain, so to speak, broke down, which was frequently.

Fortunately, I was mechanically inclined enough to keep this assortment of junk functioning most of the time , but sometimes it was a trial, and tried my patience no end.

In the spring of 1943 I got permission from the War Rationing Board to buy some pipe and a water pump. At that time, you had to try to locate what you needed or wanted then see if you could get permission to buy it.

I located what I needed then applied to the ration board. They advised me I would have to prove to them my need would justify, to their satisfaction, that it would further the war effort before they would authorize the merchant to sell the equipment I wanted. I told them the machinery I was using was so antiquated it was impossible to keep it functioning, and repair parts were unavailable. I put together a list: One cow, one big calf, two hundred chickens, two pigs, a big garden, two adults, three children, a dog and a cat. I presented this list and made my case on the premise that we were trying to be self-sustaining.

Eureka! They granted me permission and I bought the needed items. My brother Don helped me install the new pump, and I installed the controls. When I got done I knew something about water wells and water systems. It worked perfectly and we sure were pleased with the results, all automatic.

Everything was fine until just before Thanksgiving when one day when I came home from work Agnes informed me she was out of water. After checking everything out I determined the water level had dropped in the famous underlying aquifer so that my new pump valve was just about two inches above the water. It had been an exceptionally dry year and we had no fall rains to help resupply the aquifer. (An aquifer is the underground water that supplies wells, springs, etc.)

We were without water, and something had to be done, and quick. I made arrangements with the next-door neighbors to the west of us to haul water from their place for the time being. I got two surplus wooden barrels from the mill, put them in our two wheeled trailer, hooked it to the car and took it to the neighbor's house. I filled the barrels with a garden hose from their faucet and hauled them home. I would back the trailer up beside the back porch against a platform I had made so we could just walk right into the trailer to get water from the barrels.

I would try to get water in the evening when I milked the cow. Charlie's and Jack's job was to go along and fill the two barrels, then turn the water off. When I finished milking I would haul it home, back up to my platform, loosen the barrel covers and all Agnes had to do was walk out the kitchen door for water. It was somewhat inconvenient but it worked. It was not a good way but a way.

The cow and chickens were another matter. We only had about forty chickens by then and I carried water to them, and to the cow, with two five-gallon buckets at a time. After checking everything out we determined the only logical solution to our problem was to hook up to Vera Water and Power.

Our neighbor on the east side of us, who lived much closer to us than the neighbor where we got our water, had a water line running down to his place from Valley Way, the road above us, about a quarter of a mile away. That neighbor to our east never offered to help us when we were out of water. It would have been so handy. I asked him what he would charge me to hook up to his water line. He said, "Five hundred dollars!"

That was a lot of money then. This seemed to be rather high, as it was an old line that broke down at times and had to be repaired. I felt that if I gave him two hundred and shared the expense of line maintenance with him he would be lucky. I asked him if he would negotiate and he said "No", with a kind of smirk on his face. I knew right then he thought he had me over a barrel with my back side up, and he was holding the paddle. He thought there was nothing I could do about it. I had the distinct feeling he would use this to sort of hold over my head from then on.

This made me feel rather uncomfortable, to say the least. I knew he thought there was nothing I could do about it. Well there was and I did it.

We had sold our house in town and were carrying the contract on it. We sold the contract and I made a deal with a contractor to lay a pipeline up to Valley Way for me as soon as the frost was out of the ground in the spring. The contractor called when he was ready, informing me he would be prepared to start digging on a Monday morning.

I made arrangements to take my vacation for that year starting that day. When I got home that Friday from work I could hardly believe my eyes. My place looked like a big construction site.

There was a huge backhoe, a bulldozer, and a couple of trucks, one of which had a lot of pipe on it as well as other equipment. I about had a heart attack when I saw it all, to think I was going to foot the bill for all that.

Sunday morning my neighbor on the east side of me came over to see what all was going on. He said, "What is all this heavy equipment doing in your yard?" I told him, "Tomorrow morning this equipment is going to start laying a water line for me up to Valleyway." He was obviously surprised and visibly shaken by that news. After composing himself somewhat, he replied, "Why didn't you tell me, we could have worked something out." I said, "I did ask you if the price you offered me was negotiable and you said no, don't you remember that?"

He looked rather sheepish and said, "I didn't think you would do something like this." I am sure he wanted to say, "I didn't think you *could* do something like this." His wife told Agnes afterward that they had a big fight over that deal, as she had wanted him to take less and have some money rather than lose it altogether, which they did.

That ended our water worries. I am sure the water supply we put in is still being used to this day, some 57 years later, as of this writing.

Our little farm kept us busy. We had many interests and plenty to do. We got a cow, and for the first time in the boys' lives they had all the milk they could drink. We had cream and whipped cream on everything, just like I did when I was a boy, until we were tired of it.

Our Spokane Valley property
I later built our garage on this site.

I taught Agnes how to make butter, which she did very well, and we had all we could use. Those were the days when refrigerators were just that. We had one with a very small freezing compartment. A new store was built near our house on Evergreen and Sprague with a big refrigeration plant. We rented two freezer lockers. This was great. We could store butter when we had a surplus, for the times the cow would go dry.

We raised two pigs and a calf each year for some of our own meat. This was frozen. We bought a hundred baby chicks in the spring. I built a brooder to take care of them and to keep them warm until they were big enough to run with the laying hens. When they got big enough, we killed the roosters and some of the pullets (female chickens) that looked like they would not turn out to be good laying hens.

If we had more eggs than we wanted, we sold the extras. I planted raspberry bushes, which did well. When Ages had canned and frozen all she wanted, we sold the surplus. We also froze corn on the cob and sold some. Believe me, when fall came we had those two lockers full. We raised a big garden each year: rhubarb, potatoes, peas, beans, corn, carrots, beets, onions, cabbage, parsnips, and when the boys were young, a very important commodity: pumpkins (for Jack O'Lanterns).

I got two hives of bees and bought a book on raising bees. I got along fine, only getting stung occasionally but they made Agnes uncomfortable when she even saw or heard one or thought she did, so I got rid of them. We had our own honey, all

The Custer Family
Jack, Agnes, Charlie, Jim and me at our Spokane home

we could eat, and it sure was good for several years. I sure missed it when they were gone.

The Honey Bees

One Saturday in the summertime I got off work early and when I got home I determined it would be a good time to look at the bees. It was a nice, hot afternoon and I knew the bees would be easy to work with. I didn't bother to put on my bee protection equipment. I just rolled up my sleeves and went out back of the garage where the hives were. I took the lid off one hive to see if there was room to store more honey. I stood the lid on end, leaning it against the stand the hives were on.

The grass had kind of grown up around but I gave it no thought. I carefully pried a couple of frames apart in the main super (the box that the bees live in.) The frames are in the box and are where the bees store the honeycomb that holds the honey itself.

Everything was going fine, bees were buzzing around me, I had my sleeves rolled up and some would land on my bare arms, walk around and then leave. If they would start to go up my sleeve, I would just shake or brush them off gently. I was very comfortable. It was warm and the clover was in bloom, honey-gathering was good and we were all happy, so to speak.

I had on a pair of bib overalls and a pair of leather boots. I straightened up to a standing position and felt something on my bare skin in a very sensitive place, walking around inside my loosely fitting boxer shorts.

I stood still and determined that I had four different guests in a place where they had no business being. They were taking different trips in four different directions all at the same time, finding my anatomy interesting. The feeling was mutual, that was for sure.

This could be bad news if I happened to move and pinch one of them in my clothing. I was standing there trying to figure out a course of action as to what to do when Agnes peeked around the corner of the garage with one eye and said, "What are you doing, just standing there with that funny look on your face? I am wondering if we are going to go to a dance this evening."

I told her what was uppermost in my mind just then and dancing all depended on how this little drama played out. She was gone in a flash, not wanting any part in helping me solve this problem. I determined that the proper course of action would be to get into the garage, to get away from all the loose bees buzzing around in the air. I held the sides of my overalls out in front of me and took little short, slow steps, trying not to pinch anyone or make any false moves. I knew there would be no dance that night unless I played my cards just right, so to speak.

Everything went well. I got where I wanted to go. I unbuckled my shoulder straps and let the overalls fall to the floor. Then I unbuttoned my boxer shorts and shook them ever so gently, and there went a bee, and then another, and then another. There was still one more unaccounted for.

I shook again – nothing happened. I knew there had to be another somewhere. I stood there contemplating my next move, when from somewhere in the confines of my garments out came the last one. Boy, did I sigh a sigh of relief! There was a dancer that night.

When we moved to the valley, I was working five days a week but soon after we moved I stared working six and seven days, and then I was busy on both ends. I taught Agnes how to irrigate the garden if we got the water during the daytime. She tried to learn to milk the cow but after a couple of futile attempts she gave up and never would try again.

After Charlie got big enough to milk it sure helped me a lot, as sometimes I would have to come home to milk and then go back to work. He was a good milker and very dependable.

When we got real busy at the mill during the local harvest time, and we were taking in lots of local grain, I always ran the scale and truck unloading operation. I also made all the decisions as to how the different types of grain were graded.

I studied the whole operation and rearranged the controls so I could manage the procedure much more efficiently, and faster. I made a practice of remembering the names of the farmers. When I was not on the pit they always asked about me. They preferred to have me wait on them. They trusted me and respected me; my word was good.

The Mystery of the Hunting Dog

Along early in the fall of about 1943 or 1944 I guess, my neighbor who lived next door east of us hollered over to me, "Come on over I have something to show you."

We went to his garage and when he opened the door out bounded a dog. Not just a dog but a big, long-legged, skinny, gaunt hound with a long, dirty tail. It somewhat resembled a Llewellyn Setter but it was over-sized. It took a quick look around and dashed over to me like I was an old Friend. And before I could get with the program he had given one of my hands a nice, juicy, bath with an oversized tongue, and then didn't even stay long enough for me to wipe my sticky hand off on him before bounding off to relieve himself on a nearby tree. It just so happens I don't have much enthusiasm for being licked, so we didn't get off to a very good start.

My neighbor was all excited and explained to me that for once he would have a hunting dog for the upcoming bird season. He went on to say he had been so fortunate that the previous owner had just given the dog to him.

After the dog got kind of settled in, it got hanging around our place quite a bit. I would chase him home, but he seemed to have a liking for me and when he saw me outside he would come right over to be in my way. I would try to insult him, and even throw rocks at him, but that didn't seem to faze him.

Then he started to sleep at our place. We had a full length porch on the east side of our house. This porch floor had never been finished and was only one thickness of boards, so it had a rather hollow sound to it when it was walked on. The floor was about thirty inches off the ground. We had an old davenport out there that the boys played on. We used to sit on it when the weather was warm and the porch would be nice and shady.

Since the porch faced the neighbor's house the dog took to sleeping on it at night. I had no problem with that except that every once in awhile during the night he would up and let out a deep, guttural growl and jump from the davenport to the floor with a resounding thump, and take off for some place interesting only to him.

The bad part of that was that our bedroom window was right over the back of the davenport. We would get the full benefit of this performance every time it occurred, which wasn't infrequent. This was not all. We would just about get to sleep when, after his excursion to wherever, he would jump back onto the porch with a leap from the ground, land with a kerwhump, and then another kerwhump to the davenport, turn around a couple of times – enough to rattle the springs – and then flop with a resounding thud and a grunt. By this time we would be mad, and could not get back to sleep right away.

This went on for some little time and it got to be quite annoying. I saw the neighbor out one day and went over to talk to him about it. I told him just how annoying it had become and asked him to please tie the dog up at night so it could not come over to our place. Well, he thought that it was quite funny and just haw-hawed.

He said, "You'll get used to it." I said, "I don't want to get used to it." I knew right then he was not going to do anything about it, and if anything was going to be done it would be up to me to do it, but what?

Shortly after my talk with the neighbor, I was talking to one of the men at the mill, and during the course of our conversation he mentioned he sure would like to get a bird dog for the fall hunting season. He lived up in the Foothills area and went on to say there were a lot of birds around his place but he needed a hunting dog, did I know where he could get one? I said no I didn't know of any.

Then I got a thought and I said, "Come to think of it I might just know of one. If you would like me to I will check it out." He said, "Boy, I sure wish you would let me know."

I had in mind the midnight thumper, Ole Friendly, as I had nicknamed him, because he was so friendly, toward me, at least. The next morning when I went out to milk the cow, which was early, I got a short piece of rope and tied it around Ole Friendly's neck and put him in the car, which was in the garage where he would be out of sight. I left the house at or a little before 6:30 so no one was around to see him go.

When I got to the mill I tied him up to Bert's car, and as soon as I saw Bert I told him that the dog was tied to his car. Later I saw him and he had gone down to the feed mill part of the flour mill and got some dog food and a can for some water, and took it out to the dog. He was delighted with the dog and said he could not believe anyone would give away a dog that looked like a good hunting dog just before hunting season.

I told him I guessed the owner didn't want him because he didn't take care of the dog very well. Bert was so delighted that he wanted to write a note, thanking the nice man who gave up his dog. I had to explain to Bert that it would not be necessary.

A few days later the neighbor came over to ask me if I had seen his dog the last day or so, as it was gone. I said, "No, not lately, that is too bad." He was lamenting the fact that it had disappeared. I consoled him with the fact that it probably was a stray to begin with and probably wouldn't stay any one place for long, that it was just naturally a roamer.

Well, we had peace at last – what a relief! No more thumping or growling in the middle of the night. Agnes and I were pleased with the result.

About a week later, I awoke in the middle of the night to what I could hardly believe – grrrrrwoof, thump, and then kerwhump, again the turning around process and whap! I thought I must be dreaming but unfortunately I was not. Ole Friendly was back. (*?##&***) The next day I saw Bert. The first thing he said was, "That dog, Ole Friendly, is gone, and I fed him so well too." I said, "Well, did you keep him tied up?" He said, "No, I thought he would stay there." I said, "If he comes back I will see if I can get him for you again." I knew right where he was but I thought I had better let things cool off a little before I tried that little maneuver again.

A day or so later here came the neighbor and said, "You know I told you about that dog disappearing?" I said, "Yes." He said, "Well, he is back again." "Well," I said, "he is probably just a tramp and won't stay anyplace very long; you had better tie him up." The neighbor's reply was that he must have liked it there or he would not have come back. My reply was, "Maybe, you never know what goes on in a dog's head."

I knew what was going on in my head, however. I thought, "If you are not going to tie him up, then I will take matters into my own hands again to solve my problem."

Well, I let it go on for several days and then I said to myself, enough is enough and we have had enough. I loaded Ole Friendly up and took him for a ride again. I told Bert I had him again and said, "Now this time tie him up for a week and feed him real well and I think he will stay." A few days later, I saw the neighbor and he said, "That dog is gone again." I said, "Well, I'll be doggoned," and he was, for sure.

I asked the neighbor if he had tied him up. He said "No." I knew he hadn't as I got reports several times each night on Ole Friendly's whereabouts, but I wanted to rub it in a little. That was the last we ever saw of Ole Friendly. I was amazed that that dog could find its way back when it had been transported to his new home by way of the mill, in such a round-about route, so to speak.

Harvest Time

I got a very good reputation for being fair and honest and was highly respected. I had to make decisions as to whether the grain was acceptable to us. Sometimes if we got a lot of rain during harvest, the grain would be too wet to keep.

I had to make this judgment on the spot. I would bite it and got so I could come real close as to moisture content. I studied how to grade barley, oats, and wheat by reading U. S. Department of Agriculture grain grading standards manuals, and got so I knew how to grade grain, but I never did apply for a state license. During harvest time I worked a straight shift, twelve hours, no time off. My hours were seven to seven, or more when necessary, as much as eighteen in a shift sometimes. If I had to work Sunday also, it would usually be only eight hours. Gosh, that felt good, like going home in the middle of the day

Agnes worked hard too. She canned lots of fruit and vegetables, as well as processed them to be frozen. The boys worked also, pulling weeds from the garden to feed the pigs and helping their mother when she could use them.

I recall an incident that now is humorous but at the time was not, at least not to me anyway. One night during harvest time I got home about ten in the evening, after having put in a 14-hour day and being on my feet all the time. A straight shift, no time off. It had been a long, hot, hard day. I was glad to get home. I was so tired I didn't know which end was up.

I hadn't had anything to eat since eleven in the morning. I was tired, hot, and hungry. The boys were all in bed asleep. Agnes too was tired, as she had worked hard in a hot kitchen all day, canning food for the winter. She had some food on the back of the stove for me. She said, "Before you take your boots off I have something to tell you. The boys worked helping me today and I told them that if they did, they could pick the string beans that we are not going to be able to use. I said they could put them in gunny sacks and when you got home you would take them down to the cannery at Greenacres and sell them for them, and they could have the money. They worked so hard and it was so hot I felt sorry for them, but they were excited. They were so disappointed when you were late but I promised them you would take the beans to the cannery at Greenacres yet tonight. The cannery is open till midnight as they are running a double shift."

What does a man do in a case like that? He goes to the damn cannery. When I got there, I hunted up the man and his first words were, "I hope you don't have string beans. I have so many now I am afraid they are going to spoil before we can get to them." I said, "Can't you take just a few more?" He said, "No way, I am sorry."

Well, I turned the car around. I couldn't take them home. I started for home and there happened to be a rather deep ditch beside the road near Central Valley High School and I had an idea. Before I had time to change my mind I stopped and threw the three sacks of string beans in the ditch and drove home. I told Agnes the man gave me a dollar a sack for them and not to bring anymore as they had all they could handle. I reached in my pocket and was lucky there were three dollars and every one was happy, including me. Then I got something to eat.

Epilogue

Dad's manuscript ends here, which would have been around the mid to late 1940s or so when Dad would have been in his late 30s. To flesh out a bit more of his remaining life and to give some of our impressions of the life Dad and Mother lived after that, each of us three sons has written a few of our own memories, below. Jim's section does a good job of outlining many events and dates of those following years until Dad's death in 2005, just seven weeks shy of his 94th birthday.

The Custer Family – 1991.
Mother and Dad, seated. Sons Jim, Jack and Chuck (Charlie), standing

The section written by Jack was provided to us just two weeks before his untimely death on February 2, 2007 at the age of 70. Jack died from heart failure after having had a major heart attack 12 years earlier. Jim and I wish he could have read this final manuscript as we wish Dad could have seen his book published, and heard the remarks and comments from his family who read it. Obviously, that was not meant to be, and we're grateful for all the two-fingered pecking Dad did over many hours to put these words into print. It was a labor of love and pleasure for him.

Chuck (Charlie) Custer
Oldest Son
April 2007

Chuck's Memories:

This is Dad's book and I don't want to try to complete it for him. Instead, I'd like to just recount a few things that might summarize my view of his and Mother's life beyond the contents of what Dad got written.

As a son the one thing that stands out for me about both Mother and Dad was their integrity and honesty. I was extremely lucky to have parents I could count on and who taught me how to live in ways that make life so much easier. There was never any question that if either Dad or Mother said something it was true and we could count on it. Unfortunately, that also meant if we'd been threatened with discipline for misbehavior that too could be counted on when we misbehaved. Needless to say we hoped they might not keep their word at those times.

I remember, when Dad worked long summer hours at Centennial Flour Mill when I was a kid, that many days he'd start work at 7:00 in the morning and get off at 7:00 p.m. He knew we loved to go out to Liberty Lake, about 8 miles away, for a hot, summer evening swim and sometimes, probably in a moment of weakness, he'd tell us he'd take us swimming on a certain evening. No matter how tired he'd be, after a particularly hot and busy day at work though, he never backed out of his promise. We went swimming.

Dad could be pretty strict but one thing I think we all knew is that he loved us totally and he showed it in many ways. We did lots of family things together – hunting and fishing trips, camping, spring drives on a Sunday afternoon with a picnic, and other activities, many of them centered on the outdoors and nature.

I remember Dad as being pretty practical and common-sense about life. He modeled that with his own life, and his actions and words were examples I've used many times throughout the years. For instance, during a few years when we were young teenagers my two brothers and I worked spring weekends selling flowers on street corners in Spokane. A man we knew in the valley had a brother who lived near Tacoma and shipped daffodils and tulips to Spokane to be sold. This guy would gather up local kids, take us and the flowers in a truck to Spokane, and drop us off on busy arterials to sell the flowers, standing by the side of the street.

At one point I had a problem with the financial end of that arrangement, however. We never knew what we'd be paid. After standing (and you definitely had to stand) near the tipped-up boxes of flowers, arm extended with a couple of dozen flowers in hand all day long, we'd get paid whatever this guy wanted to pay us. Sometimes it was $4 or $5 and sometimes $6, and it didn't seem to matter much whether the day was long or shorter.

When I complained to Dad about this, expecting help or at least sympathy, his answer was in the form of a question: "Do you know of a better job right now?" Of course my answer was "no" and that pretty well knocked my complaint for a loop. Then he'd say (and I heard this more than once), "It looks to me like you have two choices, Son. You can either stay or you can quit." Whew! That put things squarely where they should have been – I was forced to look at reality. And I couldn't blame anyone else because it was my choice. If I didn't like it I could quit. Valuable words and a lesson I cherish to this day.

This is a book Dad wrote about his life but I want to say something about Mother too since she was the largest part of his life for nearly all his years. Dad was definitely the head of the household but he listened to her and always tried to make her comfortable in the things he fixed for her, and in practical ways to make her life easier.

He supported her too. As teenagers tend to do, as I got older I got mouthy sometimes. Dad only had to intervene once or twice and you knew he meant business. If he heard us getting smart with Mother he'd say, "Now listen, you're not going to talk to her like that. She's your mother and you're going to show respect for her. Besides that, she's my wife and you're not gonna talk to my wife that way. So that's enough of that." Whew! That brings tears to my eyes as I write that. We learned.

And Mother, though she was less than 5' tall, handled her own discipline with us as we grew up. I never heard her say, "Wait until your dad comes home," expecting him to punish us for her. No, she did her own punishing. And though it was different from Dad's it was effective. As we grew taller than she, and bigger, I remember her saying a couple of times when we were probably getting pretty smart-mouthed, "Now you listen to me. Just because you're bigger than I am you're not going to run things around here. When I tell you to do something you do it. And if you ever even think of raising a hand against me you're in serious trouble." Her words were enough to put me in my place but beyond that I don't remember ever thinking about hitting her because I respected and loved her way too much to ever even consider that. But just in case… she had the warning out there!

Manners and proper etiquette were a big thing with Dad. He'd been raised by a mother who had been a teacher, and in his high school years he and his brother lived in a boarding house in Spokane where I also think he learned manners. Wherever he got it, he wanted to make sure we handled ourselves properly and knew how to behave properly as adults, he later told us. We were to shake hands with people we met, "And none of those limp, dishrag handshakes either," he'd say. So we practiced and he'd make us shake hands with him until we knew how to use a firm grip.

Table manners were another point. As with everything in the household, we were expected to say please and thank you to have food passed. And we'd get a stern look, or his famous throat-clearing (that definitely meant, Pay attention!) if we got lax in our dining etiquette. Beyond the stern look, once in awhile the back of his fork would whack us on an elbow for a more serious infraction, for instance, eating with an elbow on the table. One hand was to be in the lap, and we sure as heck couldn't sit with our chin just above our plates and shovel in the food. When we wanted to leave the table at the end of the meal the protocol was to say, "Excuse me, please." Not just sometimes, but every time. Then wait to be excused, which didn't always follow automatically. Sometimes Mother or Dad would feel we needed to stay with the family and the discussion that was going on, so we'd be told to stay.

Our Family at Christmas
Charlie, Jack, Jim, Mother and Dad – approximately 1950

I remember learning honesty from Dad when I was about 5 years old. We lived in an old house in Spokane at that time and the toilet had a tank hanging above it with a chain we pulled to flush it. It was a noisy old thing. I had used the toilet one day when Dad was home and when I came out he asked if I had flushed it. I hadn't. At that age I didn't realize he could have heard it and I knew I was supposed to flush it, so of course I said yes. He asked again, and again I repeated my lie. Then he said something I never forgot. He said, "Son, if you lie to me you'll get punished for lying. Even if you tell me the truth about something you did, if it deserves punishment you might get punished. But the punishment will always be worse if you lie. Now, did you flush the toilet or not?" What he said made so much sense to me that of course I admitted I hadn't, and he said, "Well then go in and flush it, and do that from now on." It was another of those lessons I've used throughout life. I think I felt, even at 5, that if I could be respected for telling the truth it was worth doing. I wanted the respect of both my parents and I don't think I ever lied to either of them after that, that I can remember.

Dad's text here ends almost in mid-story. We don't know why it ended so abruptly. It would be my guess that something stopped him in the middle of his writing and he may have put off beginning again because his eyesight was getting so bad as a result of macular degeneration. Well, the story ends with him and Mother living in that house they bought in 1942 until the fall of 1995, 53 years. They then moved to an almost-new house about half a mile away as the crow flies and Mother lived there with Dad for three years until her death at 85.

Though their marriage had a few of the normal rifts, Mother and Dad were constant companions, always there for each other, always in love. Mother, being a city girl, had no history with camping or the outdoors. Yet she tent-camped with us always, even going to camp when we went deer hunting for several days at a time as we boys got older. She was always a good sport and never complained about what she had or didn't have.

And Dad was always finding ways to make life easier for her, building lower shelves in the kitchen so she could reach things more easily from her less-than-five-feet height, for instance.

In their older years Mother and Dad enjoyed spending time with their grandkids (my six, from my first marriage, Jack's four and Jim's two). They would invite my kids over in the summer from Tacoma, where my family lived then, to spend a week in the Spokane Valley with them. Many times I heard of the Indian stories Dad used to make up while they all sat on the front porch on summer evenings. During one trip he made a special effort to get a small pony from a friend and have it available for the kids to ride when we were there for a long weekend.

As they got older Dad once told me he had told Mother he hoped that she would die first. She was aghast until – he recounted to me – he told her he'd thought about it and if she died first she wouldn't have to go through the pain of losing him and being alone. It was another of his ways to say, I love you.

Dad was strict and sometimes pretty stern when we were kids. But his heart was huge. For example, I remember more than a few times when I was sick and home from school. Mother had fixed comfortable pillows and a blanket so I could lie on the couch in the living room. Dad would come home from work in the afternoon (he worked the 7 to 3 shift most of the time when it wasn't harvest season). He'd walk up to the couch, kneel down, and say something like, "I'm sorry you're sick, Son. That doesn't feel good does it?" And all the while he'd be gently stroking my forehead with one of his big hands. That felt so soothing to a little boy, and I knew I was loved.

As another example of his soft heart, on Mother and Dad's 50th anniversary my two brothers and I and our wives surprised the folks with a visit to Palm Springs, where they had thought they were meeting just Karen (my second wife, who died in 1994) and me. When they discovered all three of us boys were there with our wives both Mother and Dad were overwhelmed. Dad had tears streaming down his face, as did some of the rest of us. Mother wasn't in tears at the moment and I remember her saying to him, "Well, look at you. You're all choked up and I'm not." He replied, looking somewhat embarrassed, "Well, bully for you!" We all laughed, and then so did he.

Even near the end of his life, when his eyesight got so bad he couldn't read the paper, even with his jewelry-making magnifying headset on and holding a magnifying glass, Dad never complained. He'd sometimes say, "Boy, I wish I could see," but that's all. He always took life in stride and did the best with what he had. I think he had learned young.

Even until a year or two before his death he was making apple pies from scratch, crust and all, following a recipe he'd gotten from Mother's recipes. He'd made that pie so many times after her death that he had it memorized. He couldn't see the recipe by then but he still liked apple pies and still made two at a time every month or so.

On the morning before Dad died Jim had called me in Bellevue, where I was living, to tell me Dad was hospitalized and not expected to live long. Jim said I could talk to him by phone, which I did before I drove to Spokane, arriving that night.

For a year or so, and especially in the past few months, Dad had said he wasn't afraid of death and was ready to go. He was very matter-of-fact about it. When I reached him by phone that morning he was coherent and clear. We talked a little bit and finally he said, "You know, Son, I finally figured out what the problem is. I'm laying here trying to die and it doesn't happen. I guess I'm just too damned tough."

He was a good man and we had a wonderful family. I'm so thankful and feel so blessed for all that both Mother and Dad gave me and my two brothers. I miss them.

————

As an added note I want to thank my oldest daughter, Colleen, for all the time and effort she put into transforming Dad's words into this book he would have been so proud of. She did a wonderful job.

And, for a man who was not a writer I'm so grateful that Dad recounted his interesting life for all of us to share. I think his hours of two-finger pecking paid off handsomely.

Jack's Memories

Not a day goes by that I don't think of Dad and Mother and the wonderful memories that my brothers and I experienced growing up.

Of course, this is Dad's book, but there is no way to comment or remember without including our Mother. Just a few of the many, many memories include how adventurous in nature was our Dad, and I believe that this adventuresome nature continues with my brothers and me. I remember the hard winters of Spokane and the Spokane Valley of 1948 and 1951, when we were awakened by Dad's favorite "Daylight in the Swamps" to take a ride on Sunday morning to see the results of the storm and explore how it affected the area.

I don't recall which storm it was when we shoveled out from our property on a Sunday morning. Dad took all of us to a movie at the Dishman Theatre, having worked so hard on that "loop" of a driveway and had to shovel it again after the movie. We just hoped it would stay open for the following morning, so Dad could go to work.

Dad was the "Man of Firsts". We attended the first-night opening of the Trentwood Drive-in Theatre. We were among the first to eat at the first hamburger stand in the Valley. We were the first family in our neighborhood to have a television and if something happened in the Spokane area, be it a rodeo, fair, annual trips to Natatorium Park, ski jumping on Mt. Spokane, ice-skating – if there was an activity, particularly outdoor activities – our parents made sure we could participate.

If something new was happening, Dad made his family a part of it. I recall so well ice skating on Liberty Lake, I think it was 13 nights in a row. One particular Sunday the ice on Liberty Lake was like glass and it was cold and clear with a pretty heavy breeze. Dad rigged up a sail device from several limbs he took off the beach and a large piece of canvas and we sailed over the frozen lake. Jim was in the center, on a sled, Mother and I were on one side, Charlie and Dad on the other. We caught a big breeze and boy did we scream across the lake, until we crashed...but what fun!!! Thanks Dad for being so creative.

Another fond memory was when Brother Charlie and I milked cows out in the barn (Jim was too young) singing songs and Christmas carols to the cows. "Oh come, come, come to the church in the valley; come to the church in the dell..." We loved to harmonize together. We were so great that Dad thought we ought to have guitar lessons and we both enjoyed learning and playing with our instructor Benny Loomis. We rode the bus to his studio and back and practiced hard. If Dad was going to work on Saturdays, he would give us a ride to town.

Charlie and Jack playing their guitars

In the fall, another wonderful memory was making cider out in the garage with George and Lois Harrison. We would pick the culls from under trees – Dad would purchase some or shake them from a tree in abandoned orchards up on Mica Peak. One particular weeknight while Mother and Lois made homemade donuts, we pressed something like 33 gallons of apple cider. A lesson you soon learn is not to drink too much apple cider at one time or you'll spend a lot of time in the bathroom.

As hard as Dad worked, he took time to take us to Liberty Lake for swimming in the summer (this would be probably after at least 12 hours of hard work, for him, unloading wheat at the mill – hot, tough days at Centennial Flour Mill).

Then there were the deer hunting trips to Chewelah with George Harrison and our family where Mother would cook and prepare wonderful hunters' meals over a stove in a tent. She even made bread.

We took salmon fishing trips to the Pacific Ocean and camping and fishing trips to Sekiu. I recall so fondly staying in a motel in Seattle on our return from the coast and Mother cooking up some fresh salmon. What a thrill to stay in a motel room after so many years of camping.

I would be remiss if I did not talk about our home "lifestyle" which was *wonderful*. Dad's breakfast – oatmeal every morning – except Sunday when we would all sit down to eggs, bacon, toast or whatever, and Sunday afternoon dinners and our Sunday evening suppers with cold cereal, fruit and ice cream.

Mother had a full meal prepared and on the table every night when Dad got home. Always with a dessert.

The Custer Family on a hunting trip, 1954.
Charlie, Jack, Agnes, Chuck and Jim.

We have tried to pass on some of these qualities to our children and grandchildren.

I miss you Mother and Dad.

Jim's Memories

I share the following information for all who read this book. My name is Jim Custer. I am the youngest son of Chuck and Agnes Custer. I was born in Spokane, Washington on January 30, 1940. I met my wife Jennifer Graves, from Phoenix, Arizona in 1963 and married in 1964. Jennifer and I reside in Coeur d'Alene, Idaho. From the middle of October through the middle of May we reside in Palm Desert, California. We have two children (twins), Christopher and Cheryl, born April 9, 1969. Christopher and his wife, Amra, live in Juneau, Alaska. Cheryl and her husband, Clint Branz, live in Spokane, Washington. We currently have no grandchildren.

Dad never finished his book after Mother died at age 85 on September 20, 1998 and his eyesight continued to diminish with macular degeneration. I think he lost interest although until the day he died, June 5, 2005 at age 93, he could still tell good stories as he was very coherent.

Dad had a unique life with so many world changes occurring in his span of 93 years from August 21, 1911 to June 5, 2005. I know he enjoyed re-living memories as he wrote this book using his word processor. On occasion he would say, "Well I'm not done with it yet but someday I hope to share it with you boys, your wives, my grandchildren and great grandchildren."

On Saturday morning, June 4, 2005, the day before he died, we talked about his book. He knew his time left was short and he told me he wanted to have his second oldest grandchild, Colleen Neymeyer, edit and publish the book. He said, "I know she will do a good job and get it done for me." Our niece, Colleen, spent countless hours preparing the text for this book. Thanks, Colleen for all of your efforts and for granting one of Dad's last requests. Dad always said when the book is published he didn't want "one damn word changed." However, I know he won't mind a few corrections in spelling! Needless to say, between the time of Dad's last story – late 40's and early 50's, – there could have been another book written. I will try to bring some closure to his book by sharing some of the memorable history in Mother and Dad's life from the 1950's till the time of his death – a short version.

As a family we enjoyed Dad's enthusiasm for the outdoors, including camping, hunting, fishing, skating, etc. Dad referred to my brothers and myself as 'his boys' or 'his sons'. He taught and shared with us the values of life in so many ways and he didn't even know he was doing it.

Dad always believed in family fun. He bought a pool table that we could put a plywood top on to convert to a ping-pong table. Between pool and ping-pong, we spent many memorable evenings playing games in the basement with our friends, prior to TV.

Dad always seemed to enjoy the challenge of fixing things that were either broken or needed some adjustment to function more efficiently. He used a third of our three-car garage as his workshop, which contained a welder, steel lathe, forge (to heat and bend metal), a large anvil and numerous hand-held tools. He worked with iron, steel, aluminum, sheet metal and tin. He also enjoyed working with wood and leather and had leather punch tools for belts and straps. Dad even had a metal stand with numerous sizes of metal shoe inserts he used for repairing and replacing soles on our shoes and boots. Dad also did electrical, plumbing, tile, roofing and sheet rock work during the remodel of our home on Sprague.

Quite often relatives, neighbors and friends came to Dad to have something repaired. If Dad could not repair the item using the original part, he would make a new part or redesign the part to make it work. I don't ever remember Dad accepting money for this work. He would proudly acknowledge a "thank you" and say, "you are welcome".

My favorite memory of Dad's ingenuity involved my first pair of ice skates. Dad had skated on ponds and lakes in his youth and was a good skater. During the winters of the late 40's and early 50's, January and February were extremely cold months and when Liberty Lake froze over, the skating was excellent. He introduced our family to ice skating after coming home one day with skates for the entire family purchased from a second-hand store. Dad proceeded to lay all the skates on the floor.

I noticed that the skates were black or brown except for one small pair of skates, which were white. It was easy to figure out who was getting the white skates because at age eight, I had the smallest feet. The white skates screamed 'Girl Skates' and I was not very happy about his selection for me. These skates were too big even after using extra socks. My ankles would collapse when I tried to stand so Dad took the skates to the garage. I was hoping he would take them back to the second-hand store and buy me a smaller pair of boy's skates but no luck.

Instead, he used his creative talent and made a metal brace that attached to the back heel of the skate up to the top of the skate. He made an opening on the metal support and attached a leather strap to the top where it could be secured around my ankle. This gave me enough support to put the majority of my weight on the blade of the skate instead of on the inside of my ankle. Sure enough, this did the trick and we all spent many evenings and weekends ice skating on Liberty lake.

Our school, Vera grade school, used to flood part of the play-ground during the cold winters to make a small ice rink. My brothers and I enjoyed many hours of skating before and after school. I learned later, some of the teachers enjoyed watching the little guy with the white skates charge around the ice.

Despite the fact that the skates were white, these were my special skates that my Dad had made for me. Who would have guessed that one day the little guy wearing the white skates with metal braces would go on to become a professional ice skater. Thanks, Dad.

Ice Skating
Jack, Jim, Dad and Charlie on our private ice rink

Religion always played a major role in our family. Dad would go out of his way to make sure, even on camping trips, that we got to church on Sunday. Dad introduced us to the annual Novena of St. Francis Xavier. We would attend the Novena in the evenings for about a week every March. He was also supportive of the religious education programs offered by our local Catholic church, St. Mary's. Both Mother and Dad sent us off to catechism on Saturdays when it was offered, even during some big snowstorms.

Dad was proud to watch his sons as we enjoyed life and getting our education in the Central Valley School District, Vera Grade School, Central Valley Jr. High and graduating from Central Valley High School. The three of us all left home between 1953 to 1960 to go our separate ways.

Mother always said that she and Dad had some sad moments after we had left, myself being the last. But we knew that with Dad's enthusiasm for life that their life after we left would still be fun and the void of us all leaving would soon go away. They bought a Schnauzer dog and named him Fritz and he helped fill the void.

Mother and Dad bought a pick-up truck and camper and had countless trips with their camper, pulling the boat to go fishing in lakes in Canada, the ocean and all over the northwest. They also got interested in rock hounding. Before Dad retired he said, "I better start a hobby or I'll have nothing to do after I retire." Both Mother and Dad got into rock hounding. They started making jewelry, clocks, bookends, etc. with their precious stones. They both became quite skilled in doing rock rolling making cabochons. Dad even learned to facet and made remarkable jewelry, including rings, earrings, necklaces, etc. They also learned silver and gold-smithing as well. Dad's rock machinery was in the basement and this area of the house on Sprague soon became the most occupied part of the house for Mother and Dad in the evenings.

Mother got interested in oil painting. It wasn't long before she had her own little gallery of her work displayed in the basement. Mother was so generous in sharing so many of her paintings, always framed and ready to hang, and Dad was always very supportive of her artistic talent.

Dad retired from Centennial Flour Mill on November 22, 1974 at age 63. He had worked for Centennial for 37 years. He started work as a truck driver, retiring as the superintendent of the flour mill in charge of the entire plant. Dad worked very hard for the mill, with most of his years in the grain elevator division, buying and storing wheat from local farmers. He was highly respected among his peers, with knowledge of wheat that was unparalleled. Many ten-hour days or more were common for Dad to work during the harvest time.

Dad at his desk at Centennial Mills

Dad never served in the military. He was deferred from the draft during World War II because of the importance of his job with Centennial Flour Mill. However, Dad served his country in a very special way and on May 17th, 1945, Dad and only four other representatives from Centennial Flouring Mills Co. were awarded the "Achievement "A"" Award" from the War Food Administration for outstanding achievement. Dad received a medal and certificate at a presentation honoring him and his four fellow workers. The presentation was held in front of the mill with many dignitaries present as well as the Army Air Force band. The message attached to the medal read:

> Message from the President of the United States. Food is a decisive weapon of war. Victory depends as much on our

ability to produce food as on our ability to manufacture guns, planes, and ships. Our army of farmers and processors are fighting an important battle on the food front. Working diligently and skillfully, they are speeding this Nation and our Allies on to Victory."

It was signed, Franklin D. Roosevelt. We found this detailed information while going through Dad's things after his death. Dad never said much about this special recognition. Dad did say that after the war when he talked to local service men who had served overseas, they would tell of getting tears in their eyes when they saw the flour bags that read, "Centennial Mills, Spokane, Washington".

War Food Administration Award, 1945
(Dad is second from the left)

Mother and Dad bought a brand new Ford pick-up truck and camper shortly after Dad retired. In February of 1976 they left to spend a few months down south to shorten the winter and explore some new country. Within weeks after they left home, February 26th, they stopped at Disneyland in Anaheim, California. They had their dog, Fritz with them. They parked their camper in the main parking lot of Disneyland. They came out to check on their dog and get a bite to eat, around noon, only to discover that their camper was nowhere to be found. Someone had stolen it and all their belongings, cash, money orders, medicine, motorbike and even the dog. It was their worst nightmare and a crushing blow to them. They came back home on a Greyhound bus. It was truly gut-wrenching for the entire family. Along with the camper and dog were Dad's diaries of earlier trips, gems they had worked on, etc. Dad changed all the locks on the house when he got back and put in a sophisticated burglar system because the thieves had all the keys to the house on Sprague. This was discouraging to begin their retirement this way but it didn't stop Dad.

May 28, 1976 Mother and Dad flew back to Indiana and bought a brand new Holiday Rambler motor home and drove it back to Spokane. Dad did his renovations to make it comfortable for them and in the fall they left again for the Southwest to escape the winter. It wasn't long before they bought another Schnauzer dog and named him Snoopy. That filled the void of losing Fritz.

On February 22, 1977 they discovered a little community just east of the Salton Sea, close to Niland, California, called The Fountain of Youth. The Fountain of Youth is a retirement community made up of snowbirds and offering the enjoyment of the natural hot springs on the property. With over six pools heated with the hot springs, church and community center, Mother and Dad found it perfect for their lifestyle and fit in nicely. The park was designed for RV's but eventually rented plots to manufactured, more permanent mobile homes. After four winter seasons, November through March at the park, Mother and Dad purchased a permanent mobile home on February 3, 1981. They spent 16 years enjoying their winters at The Fountain of Youth.

In the spring of 1994 they decided the drive to the desert each fall and spring was too much for Dad's poor eyesight. His eyes were getting progressively worse with macular degeneration. Mother couldn't drive the motor home, towing the car, so they sold their home at the Fountain of Youth and on March 26, 1994 they left the desert for the last time. Dad was 83 years old. They moved back to Spokane at 14225 East Sprague, their home of over fifty years. On April 3, 1994 Dad wrote in his journal, "We had a good trip back home. It feels good to be here. I guess I'm finally old, I don't feel like traveling anymore."

The home on East Sprague was on valuable land and the taxes through the years had gotten quite high. The folks decided to sell and find something newer, smaller and more practical. Dad found the perfect home on 321 South Calvin Lane, Cherry Court, less than one-half mile from their home on Sprague. Their home was one of 18 homes on a private road with a Home Owners Association. They sold their home on Sprague in the fall of 1995 and moved to their new home. They fell in love with it. Shortly after their move, Dad had to give up his driving as his eyes were just too bad. With the help of relatives, friends and the Para-Transit system they got around quite well.

In 1997 Mother started having some heart problems and needed by-pass surgery. That was the beginning of a tough year for both Mother and Dad. She had one complication after another. Extensive bleeding from the heart catheter, falling and breaking her leg, pace maker, shingles, lost circulation of one leg, etc. It took its toll over the next year and she eventually lost the circulation of the leg. They put her in the hospital and she died within a week on September 20, 1998 at age 85. Mother and Dad had been married for 64 years.

It was naturally a blow to Dad; however, as independent as he was he continued on with his life. His best friend, George Harrison, had lost his wife, Lois, a few years earlier. Now they had something more in common. Dad and George went to a weekly Valley Senior social gathering for morning coffee and rolls. After a few weeks, Dad met a lady at the weekly socials and they found a mutual admiration for each other, as she had lost two husbands prior. They both felt lonesome without a companion. After seeing each other about a year, they agreed that it would be best to be married. Dad asked my brothers and me what we thought. It was Dad's life so I told him that I would support him in whatever he wanted to do. He was 88 years old at the time; Loretha Hitchcock was 86 years old. Dad asked me to be his best man. It was my honor, as Dad was my best man when I married Jennifer Graves on July 3, 1964 in her home town of Phoenix, Arizona during our summer vacation from the Ice Capades. Dad and Loretha were married on November 30, 1999, a little over a year after Mother's death. Dad and Loretha enjoyed over five years together before Dad's death on June 5, 2005.

About noon on Sunday, June 5th, 2005 the day Dad died, my brothers, Jack and Chuck and I walked into Dad's hospital room together. Dad was resting but opened his eyes and looked up and I said, "Dad, this is Jim. Jack and Charlie are standing beside me, we're here for you." Dad said, "That's all I could ask for." Within the hour he was leaving us. Chuck, Jack, Barbara, Jennifer and myself stayed with him during his last minutes. We held his hand and prayed for eternal life free of pain, and a reunion with Mother.

Dad told Mother and I on a couple of occasions, assuming that he would die before Mother, to put on his headstone, "I did my damnedest." Mother and I would just laugh and say ok! When Mother died, Dad thought the following would be appropriate on the head stone: Agnes Custer, Wife of Chuck, Mother of Three, Dearly Loved by All. When Dad died my brothers, Jack, Chuck and I decided that the sayings for Mother would be appropriate for Dad as well. So, we just changed the name and dates and went with it. Both Mother and Dad are buried beside each other in St. Joseph's Cemetery just off Trent Road in the Spokane Valley.

Mother and Dad often said in their later years what a great life they had. From their start during the depression years, they achieved much more than they ever imagined and they were ever so grateful.

Writing this recap of Mother and Dad's last years, I felt a spiritual presence of them. Therefore, I would like to close by saying, "Mother and Dad, thank you for my life. Dad, the trips, hunting, camping, fishing, holidays and the life you gave me, the values you taught me, the love you shared, I will cherish forever. Mother, your endless love, your everyday of caring and concern for our family, the continued support you gave me, and of course all those diaper changes, clothes washed, fabulous meals, especially your desserts, will live in my memory forever."

I was always proud to say I was a Custer, son of Chuck and Agnes. I think they were proud of me too. Your loving son, Jim

Celebrating 90 years!
Jim, Chuck, Jack and Charlie on Dad's 90th birthday – 2001

A Final Word

Editor's Note: As their sons all mentioned, this book wouldn't be complete without a mention of my Grandma, Grandpa's beloved wife, Agnes. Grandpa saved some of the cards and letters he received from Grandma over the years, then shared them with his boys after Grandma's death in 1998. Several of the letters are shared below, along with Grandpa's recollection of the circumstances under which each was written.

Letters from Agnes to Chuck

Agnes wrote the following message on a Father's Day card for Chuck in 1979.)

Thank you for being such a good Dad to our children.

Thank you for "taking such good" care of me.

Thank you for being so ambitious and being such a good provider for us.

Thanks for the good times we have had together.

Thanks for loving nature and planning fun trips

Thanks for our down South adventures.

Thanks for keeping healthy and happy.

Thanks for your good steady encouragement and steadying influence.

Thanks for being the unique person you are.

I love you. Agnes

Chuck's recollection: This message was written on the inside of a rather plain greeting card. Poor little Mother, she felt so bad because she could not go to the store yet – still had her leg in a cast recovering from her long, hard summer when she had been through so much.

August 21, 1997

My dearest Chuck – Happy Birthday – 86! I couldn't even get you a birthday card this time and I didn't want Becky or Mary to pick it out for me – so this personal card will have to do.

First, I thank you for all the good years we have had together. You are so interesting and interested in so many things and made life interesting for me, too. I have learned so much since 1930 when we met.

I thank you for three good sons and your part in raising them right – men now that we can both be proud of.

I thank you for golden years on big and little trips – South for 17 years and fun in the sun and the years we were rock hounds and more.

I thank you for your loyalty to all your family. Our sons have a good dad.

Now I thank you for the last stressful years – the patience with your hip and back problems and through my heart worries and the moving and all.

I thank you for your extra patience these last three months and your caretaking – doing all the work and loving me when I'm not very lovable.

Now I pray to get well again – care for you and be your companion and helpmate. And that you have many more happy birthdays for us to enjoy in our twilight years.

Lovingly, your wife of 63 years, Agnes

Chuck's recollection (written February 2, 1999, about 4 months after Agnes' death):

I came across a little card in Mother's things the other day as I was cleaning out some of her old belongings. I thought you would like to read it so I had copies made for each of you boys so you could see just exactly how she had written it out. I have no explanation as to why she did it when she did it. It was by sheer luck I came across it. I was going through the box containing some unanswered letters and other junk. I was sorting through this stuff when I saw this little card with what I thought were some old notes to be discarded. I took a second look when something caught my eye, and was I ever glad I took the time to read it.

As I reread this I see where there is a date in the upper right hand corner that I had forgotten about; so that does fix a time. It is done in her own typical way. Bless her true little heart. Treasure this, it is precious.

What a good family we have had and what an important part she played. I too join with her in her prayers that we will all be reunited in the next world.

With love from your Dad.

1994

Dear Dad – Sons – families and all,

I love you all for your special loving ways and thank God for all I could do and be for you. He gave me such wonderful subjects to work with. I love you all in different ways – not one the less or more. I want you all to know that.

The love for my Chuck is different, too. You are the one I am with all the time. We have grown up together. I love you very much!

You boys have grown up and gone your separate ways. I plan we'll all meet again. You will all have come back to your Catholic faith with deep devotion and love. Then we'll all be together again in heaven.

All my love to all – Mother (Agnes Custer)

Chuck's recollection (written February 3, 1999):

The enclosed is a copy of a letter Mother handed me on an otherwise nice spring day in 1998. She looked me in the eye with a strange look, saying, "This is a letter for you from me." It came out of the blue, so to speak, and I said nothing to her, as I didn't have time to say anything.

She left, going into the bedroom saying nothing more and closed the door behind her. Her manner was so serious and she seemed to be a little ill at ease. I wondered what was going on; what was wrong. I was a little concerned. I wondered if she was mad – she acted so differently – as though she was about to say something but she didn't. I guess my first thought was maybe she was going to tell me she didn't like my cooking or that she thought I had mistreated her in some way. The last thought I had as I sat down to read the letter was I did the very best I knew how. I really tried to be good to her. I tried to be patient and I thought I had.

Before I had finished the whole page, my eyes were filled with tears and I had to postpone the rest till later. She had worked so hard on what she wanted to say and how she felt and how to tell me. She was all full of anxiety and tension – in other words, was all uptight which I had mistaken for anger. Nothing could have been farther from the truth.

The poor little thing had been through so much and had been so brave through it all. She wanted to express her appreciation to let me know she was grateful for what I had done. She was feeling better and was afraid she could not get the words out the way she wanted to, so she wrote me a letter and put it in an envelope. She didn't know what to say, so she said nothing.

Mother and I had our own way of getting along. Perhaps it didn't look too good to others but it worked for us. It must have lasted rather well with love till the end.

Spring, 1998

To my dearest Chuck,

I have thought of typing something to you for a long time; but I just didn't feel up to it. Finally I can see the light in the tunnel and know that each day I am improving.

I am sorry that I have been such a worry and so much care for you. I can see that it has been a serious drag on both of us. You are hurting all the time, too, and never complain. I hope you have listened to the end of my complaints. Every day should be better now.

You must know that I love you more than anything in the world. I know I haven't expressed it much; but if I didn't care – if we didn't care; would we have been together all these years with love and tolerance and patience and understanding?

As I feel better; I think more of your heart and mind in all that has gone on. How you must have been so despondent at times when I didn't seem to improve. It has been hard for you because you couldn't make it better. You have done all the things a good husband could do. I'm sure you lost a lot of sleep over me and I'm sure you thought and prayed about what to do next.

I'm sure you sometimes are at your wits end when I break down and cry. I have sometimes gotten so weak and discouraged that I just had to let go. I think it even helps to get it out, releases the tension.

Chuck, you are my very life. I wouldn't be here but for you. I wouldn't want to be. You must know that I love you very, very much. I have never been very demonstrative; but my heart is true and I want to get well for you and to be here for you, too, when you need me.

Please forgive my lack of gratitude, I just have not been thinking good for a long time. I am not yet good at expressing myself, but I love you and care more than you know. You have taken good care of me and I have taken you for granted. I hope things will improve now and I can be a good wife again. Time heals all things, but all this has taken too much of our time, hasn't it?

With all my love,

Your Agnes

Editor's Note: Shortly after her death in 1998, Chuck wrote a tribute to Agnes, describing all she'd meant to him in their many years together. A portion of that tribute follows.

A Tribute to my Wife, Agnes

A lady all the way. A wife, a mate, a partner, a companion a helpmate and a mother. A lady of many talents. A wonderful cook and baker. A gracious hostess and entertainer. An accomplished seamstress, knitter and creator of beautiful lace and other types of fancy work. She made many beautiful crocheted afghans, giving a great number of them away. Many of these creations required considerable skill. In her waning years she took up painting, becoming very proficient in a short time. In fact this turned out to be a very enjoyable hobby for her.

We met in May of 1930 and were married January 6, 1934. We were married sixty-four years, eight months, and fourteen days before the angels came, taking her back to heaven with them where, I know, she waits patiently for me to join her, once again. She paid her way and is, I am sure, being rewarded for the way she lived and for all the wonderful things she did for others during her long life. She loved and was loved by all who knew her.

She had so many attributes, I cannot begin to enumerate them all. She was a girlfriend who as such, gave me encouragement before we were married. Sometimes I became downhearted, I thought I would never amount to anything because I could not get a start. She stuck by me then and after we were married, we saw some pretty tough times. She never complained about not having enough. She knew I was trying as hard as I could. She always took excellent care of our family. She always seemed to know what to do is someone got sick. She got scared sometimes but never panicked. She was always neat and clean and always looked nice. I was always proud of her appearance. She was a good sport about most things – once in a while it took considerable persuasion on my part that what I thought we should do was a good idea. However once we reached an agreement, she almost always then entered in to the spirit of whatever it was and gave her whole hearted support.

We had a good family life. We had many good family times and we all have good memories of those times we shared. We raised three fine sons. Mother and I did our best, but she deserves most of the credit. She was the homemaker and a wonderful one she was.

She was so brave during her final illness. We both knew the outlook was not good. She knew she might never be back. She didn't complain. She was concerned about how I would get along alone – that I would be lonesome. She was concerned about her boys. We talked everything over – she asked me to promise that if she didn't make it, I would not bury her until we would all be there as a family one last time. She said, "Don't go to any trouble for my funeral if you have one – there won't be many there – I never did much in this world to be remembered for."

On the morning of the day on which she died, she was lucid for the first time in several days. The boys and I were all there – Charlie, Jack and Jim. We all went in to see her and she was awake. We all talked to her a little – she was so very weak. I pointed out to her that all of her boys were there and made sure she knew them all as she spoke to them in turn. I asked if she was in pain and she said no. I asked if it would be alright if I kissed her. She put her finger on her lips and I gave her a last kiss. I didn't know how to tell her goodbye – I wanted to in the worst way. I didn't know what to do. I leaned down and said "Little Mother, you have a straight ticket to heaven, do you know that?"

She looked up at me with a loving look in those beautiful blue eyes and said, "I do?" She seemed to be so at peace giving me a look as if to say if you say it is alright, it must be so. She closed her eyes and drifted off to sleep, never to awaken again.

I hope on that last day, she was looking down from heaven, seeing all the flowers and all the people who paid her homage at her last rites, because of what she has done on this earth. I loved her so very much.

Our Christmas Card photo
Jim, Charlie, Chuck, Jack, Agnes

www.ingramcontent.com/pod-product-compliance
Lightning Source LLC
Chambersburg PA
CBHW031457270326
41930CB00006B/137